150 Years of the Chinese Presence in California

Honor the Past
Engage the Present
Build the Future

Sacramento Chinese Culture Foundation
and
Asian-American Studies
University of California, Davis

Published by Sacramento Chinese Culture Foundation
Copyright ©2001.

Printing by Sun Printing
1990 Fruitridge Road
Sacramento, CA 95820

Sacramento Chinese Culture Foundation
P. O. Box 160941
Sacramento, CA 95816
sccfsac@yahoo.com

ISBN 0-9716186-0-7

TABLE OF CONTENTS

History

People

Community

Special Topics

Distinguished Models

September 2001

Dear Friends:

It is my pleasure to welcome you to "150 Years of the Chinese Presence in California: Honor the Past, Pace the Present and Build the Future."

Throughout American history, Chinese Americans have contributed immeasurably to the richness of our society – shaping our culture and building our nation. The legacy and achievements of Chinese Americans touch every facet of our national life – from art and architecture to computer science and engineering to sports and government service.

America's bright beacon of hope and opportunity encouraged Chinese to come to this country 150 years ago and continues to attract immigrants today. The continuous unraveling of Chinese American history is a testament that the American Dream is alive and vibrant.

Please join me as we rediscover a history so personal to all of us -- a history which must be learned and shared with generations to come.

Sincerely,

Elaine L. Chao

Elaine L. Chao

GOVERNOR GRAY DAVIS

July 17, 2001

Welcome to "150 Years of Chinese Presence in California: Honor the Past, Pace the Present and Build the Future."

The Chinese American community in California is a vital part of the unique diversity that defines the State. Throughout California's history, the Chinese American community has made innumerable contributions and will continue to play an integral role in the decades ahead.

On behalf of the people of the State of California, I invite you to utilize this publication to learn more about California's Chinese and Chinese American community.

Sincerely,

GRAY DAVIS

STATE CAPITOL · SACRAMENTO, CALIFORNIA 95814 · (916) 445-284

PREFACE

Dr. Kevin Starr*
State Librarian of California

T he publication of *150 Years of the Chinese Presence in California (1848-2001)* by the Sacramento Chinese Culture Foundation and the Asian American Studies of the University of California at Davis, should be valued as one of the Chinese American contributions to their new homeland, California. This historical story must be viewed from six perspectives: Chinese civilization as a whole, Chinese migration in the nineteenth century, California as a rising Pacific commonwealth, local California in the nineteenth century, the personal and family experiences of the Chinese in California, and the present and future of the Golden State as a center of Chinese-American civilization.

First of all, there is the perspective of Chinese civilization itself, in all its achievement and grandeur. Considered in its vastness and complexity, the multi-millennial history and culture of China represents one of the foundational elements of the human story. A significant dimension of what is to be human -- both in terms of

---

* Dr. Kevin Starr, Chief State Librarian of California, was the Chairman of the "Commission to Celebrate the California Sesquicentennial History" appointed by Honorable Gray Davis, Governor of California, year 2000.

achievement and suffering -- has been explored over thousands of years by the Chinese people. In terms of its philosophy, literature, art, science, medicine, technology, agriculture, public works and engineering, urbanism, architecture, and statecraft, China constitutes one of the two or three highpoints of human achievement.

Throughout its long history, moreover, China has consistently maintained a non-aggressive attitude towards the outside world. In one sense, China was itself an empire: an amalgamation, that is, of more than eighty ethnic and linguistic groups across a broad spectrum of social and cultural orientations. From this perspective, China had no need to venture outside the Middle Kingdom. It was, after all, a civilization, indeed a whole world, unto itself.

In the nineteenth century, however, various forces - the intrusion of foreign powers into China and subsequent wars, population shifts caused by drought and famine, the growth of a Chinese merchant class looking toward overseas involvement, a growing population in the Cantonese-speaking regions, a depression in Guangdong Province -- coalesced to prompt a mass migration of Chinese into the regions known today as Malaysia, Indonesia, Vietnam, certain islands in the Caribbean (Trinidad especially) and California. The decidedly stay-at-home Chinese, in short order, spread themselves in a diaspora throughout Southeast Asia and North America that had transformative consequences for all the societies that were the object of Chinese immigration.

The newly established state of California was one of these societies. As early as 1848, two Chinese immigrants had reached what was then the military-governed territory of California; but it took news of the discovery of gold to motivate Chinese forty-niners to make the long voyage across the Pacific from Canton to Gold Mountain (America) where they hoped to strike it rich. By

1852, some 25,000 Chinese had arrived in California in search of the Golden Fleece. Today, the Joss House at Weaverville in Trinity County, currently part of the State Park system, testifies to the vigor and vitality of the Chinese Argonauts. Each year, from 1849 through the early 1850s, thousands of Chinese miners would gather at Weaverville for inter-tong competitions and various forms of trade and celebration. Excluded by a miner's tax and other forms of discrimination from the more prosperous and easily mined gold regions, the Chinese nevertheless managed -- through skill and hard work -- to extract from the hills, valleys, and riverbeds of the Mother Lode the precious nuggets of gold that had brought them across the vast Pacific.

Thus the Chinese became a fixed and essential component of the Gold Rush. As California developed, moreover, a further challenge awaited this skilled, industrious, and hard-working people. With the launching of the transcontinental railroad project by the Big Four in 1864, the Chinese now became crucial to the construction of the trans-Sierra portion of this heroic enterprise. At the height of the project, more than 10,000 Chinese were working to bridge and tunnel through the mighty Sierra Nevada with tracks of steel. Today, in retrospect, we can see that the achievement of these Chinese workers must be mentioned in the same breath as that of building the Great Wall of China itself. Thanks to Chinese industry and social and engineering skills, the American nation stood linked by May 1869 from east to west.

Having completed this great task, the Chinese of California did not cease their contributions to the developing state. They now turned their skills, rather, to the equally important challenge of establishing agriculture, irrigation, and flood control in the great Sacramento Valley. Here was an accomplishment equal to the transcontinental railroad itself. In ages past, a vast inland sea covered the Sacramento Valley. Each winter, with flooding, that great sea made an effort to reestablish itself. Throughout the 1860s, the 1870s, and the 1880s, the Chinese fought that vast inland sea with the creation of great levees that even today are keeping the Sacramento Valley habitable in wintertime. To California the Chinese were also bringing thousands of years of agricultural skill as they planted and harvested the lands they had preserved from flood. From this perspective, the Chinese of the mid- and late nineteenth century must be ranked among the founders of an agricultural economy that even today paces all the other industries of the state. Other Chinese, meanwhile, settled in the cities of California -- San Francisco, Sacramento, Stockton, Marysville, even Los Angeles far to the south -- or established townships of their own, such as Locke.

The 1870s, however, was an embattled time for California. The glorious economy predicted at the completion of the railroad in 1869 did not materialize. Instead, a great depression began in 1873 that had devastating effects on immigration to California and the developing California economy. During that time, many demagogues, such as Denis Kearney of San Francisco, unleashed their fury against Chinese immigrants, scapegoating them for the bad times. This hostility built upon some of the hostilities of the Gold Rush era, including the prohibition against Chinese testifying against whites in California courts, which lasted from 1854 until 1872. In 1882, Congress passed the Chinese Exclusion Act, which it reconfirmed in 1892 and 1902, prohibiting further immigration of Asians to the United States. That meant that Chinese women could not immigrate to California legally; hence normal family life was difficult to establish. An entire generation of Chinese men was doomed to live their lives in loneliness, hoping only that, after their death, their remains could be returned to the land of their ancestors.

Fortunately, such exclusionary laws were modified and in certain instances repealed in the early twentieth century, thanks in great part to the efforts of the newly organized Chinese-American Citizens Alliance. By World War I and after, Chinese-American life in California began to become more recognizably family- and children-oriented. By the 1920s, in fact, Chinese-American life in California had enhanced and stabilized itself considerably.

The Second World War constituted a watershed for the Chinese-American community. Chinese-American men and women from California served across in the world in the armed forces, many of them with great distinction. When they returned to California, their outlook had become more inclusive and cosmopolitan. From this World War II generation and its immediate offspring came the first generation of Chinese-American elected officials and notables in the larger community. California, in turn, was becoming increasingly aware of the contribution of its Chinese-American citizens.

In the mid-1960s, the federal government reformed even further its immigration laws, and this in turn allowed Chinese immigration to the United States to achieve some measure of parity with immigration from Europe. Over the next thirty-five years, the Chinese community in California grew exponentially as countless families were reunited and first-time immigrants arrived from Taiwan and the Mainland. As the new millennium dawned, there were more than one million Californians of Chinese descent. California, in fact, had become an important center of Chinese culture outside China itself. Every phase of California life, in both the public and the private sector, was witnessing the presence of talented and industrious Chinese-American Californians.

And this brings us to the final -- and perhaps most important -- dimension of the story of the Chinese in California: the dimension of family and personal experience. From time immemorial, Chinese culture has revered family ties and family values, including family ancestors. Perhaps the greatest hardship to be suffered by nineteenth-century immigrants to California was the lack of family life because of immigration restrictions. In the twentieth century, fortunately, that deficiency was rectified. Today, in California, family life and values flourish in the one million-strong Chinese-American community. From these values come the well-known Chinese-American capacity for hard work, academics, thrift, self-reliance, and contribution to the community. So, too, have individual values flourished in the Chinese-American community of California. This history, in fact, is rich in the stories of individual fulfillment and achievement: stories of people who dreamt of a better life and made their dreams come true.

So then: one hundred and fifty-three years after the first two Chinese immigrants arrived in California in 1848, California has long since come to recognize that the Chinese-American experience is at the core of the California experience. Without the industry and creativity of its Chinese immigrants, yesterday and today, California would not be what it is--a commonwealth embracing the peoples of the world and the creativity of all its citizens. Chinese civilization has left a lasting legacy on the history of California and the present flourishing of its agriculture, transportation, flood-control, business and banking, literature, art, architecture, politics, and health sciences. The Chinese-American legacy has become one of the strong foundations of the California dream itself, and an essential element of the unfolding California dream.

Therefore, at the dawn of the new millennium, all overseas Chinese in general and Californians (Chinese-Americans) in particular must answer the calling to build a more perfect world where we are part of enriching her while appreciating the "California Sesquicentennial Celebration".

Acknowledgement
Vicki Beaton

As President of the Sacramento Chinese Culture Foundation, I would like to acknowledge the individuals who have made this book possible through contributions of their knowledge, time, financial and moral support. First, of course, is Peter C. Y. Leung who, before his untimely death and while serving as Senior Lecturer of Asian American Studies at UC Davis, conceived the idea for this book. He researched the subject matter for a number of years, gathered photographic data, conducted interviews and authored many of the sections of the book. No doubt, without his devoted efforts and impressive talents, the book would not have been possible. Peter's work was strongly supported by Dr. Stanley Sue, Director of Asian American Studies, UC Davis and by Dr. Eleanor Chiang who was President of the SCCF when the idea was formulated and work began.

I would like to thank C. C. and Regina Yin and the Yin's McDonald Corporation for their continuous moral and financial support. Dr. Alex Yeh, who is retired from California Education Department, served as consultant and supervised the task of editing as well as finalizing many of the chapters after completing interviews and preparing the text. To him, we owe our heartfelt gratitude.

Since her husband's death, Eileen Leung, an administrator at University Extension, UC Davis, for more than 30 years, immediately accepted the position as Board member of SCCF to continue her late husband's work. Without her focused perseverance, it would not have been possible to complete the project.

We would be remiss in not expressing thanks for the financial support of many which made completion of the project possible. The donors are acknowledged elsewhere in the book. Readers should have their interest in the book heightened by the well-written Preface by Dr. Kevin Starr, California State Librarian and also a member of the Sesquicentennial Celebration Committee. We feel great honored by and very much appreciative of Dr. Starr's contribution.

And last but not least, I am very thankful to my husband, Ret. Col. Clifford Beaton, USAF, who continuously, tirelessly and financially supported me in whatever project I undertook in the two countries I love dearly: China and America.

THE SPONSOR'S STATEMENT

Sacramento Chinese Culture
Foundation
Dr. Alex Yeh

To commemorate "California's Sesquicentennial Celebration" under the auspices of the "Commission to Celebrate the California Sesquicentennial History", we are honored as one of the sponsors to initiate this book project. We are rejoicing over a great occasion in publishing this book. We intend to honor the past, engage the present, and build the future. And this publication is a small beginning, however, a significant contribution to California's sesquicentennial story in history. We express our sincere appreciation to those who shared their success stories, and we regret being unable to document all of Chinese American contributions to the United States in general and California in particular.

Our book highlights the "Chinese Torch Carrying Descendants" upon their deep-rooted heritage and cultural splendor, and also documents their achievements in economics, education, literature, politics, science, and trade. Despite many vicissitudes, the inherited and complex legacy of cultural patterns from the past in the traditional Chinese civilization did reach its apogee many a time. Our people, as immigrants with such valuable heritage and rich culture, have contributed and continue to contribute the growth and development of California and the USA. We advocate that thirty million Chinese from all over the world should recognize Chinese American contributions to American communities small and large because of reflection of their assiduity, diligence, endurance, frugality and industry.

This book tells of the Chinese American contributions for over 150 years including the California gold rush era in the 1840s. One should be appalled at such unfair practices carried on to the extreme degree of the humiliations and abasement that continued even after the World War II period. The undeniable achievements of the Chinese to the growth and development of California's infrastructure in general and the fishing and farming industries in particular must be reserved. The vivid history of treasures left by our people for all Californians should be source of pride.

During World War II, many Chinese-Americans proudly joined the military and royally participated in the war against the Nazism and the Axis. Their contributions have been confirmed that: the "second class citizen" mentality was reduced; windows of the opportunities were opened up for them, and the right to vote was democratically installed. Moreover, the second and third generations sought exodus from the "Chinatown world" and found new challenges and worthy rewards in this diversified society. Some of them have even been elected politically in the US Congress, in the State legislative houses, in the metropolitan office and in the Governor's mansion.

After the 1970s, there was a new immigration trend, which changed the "obedient citizen" perception toward Asians by the majority. Chinese are no longer in the class of cooks or laundrymen. The new arrivers come equipped with higher educational foundations, savvy in international relations, multiple languages, and strong financial backing. They have become powerful in political and economic arenas. The majority must work with us as an influential minority.

Though the first generation of Chinese immigrants who arrived to California was confronting various difficulties in a strange land, the old country was far away and unreachable. So the Chinese had to endure struggles any other new immigrant who must work toward the American Dream.

This book intends to urge overseas Chinese to treasure the value of their heritage and culture, and to unite as an unbreakable team for a brand new and better community. Thus, the main stream of society cannot but accept the fact that the progressive California prosperity in economics, education, politics is the result of joint efforts of the majority as well as the minority. Any residues of discrimination and abasement are contrary to and insult the great California history.

It is also a call to overseas Chinese to observe and consider carefully that all immigrants new or old are coming with the common purpose of learning from our valuable experiences, to respect the invaluable history, and to look for opportunities to open up another chapter in the epic of California prosperity. Especially, the new and old Chinese immigrants must be aware of a possible break-up into small cliques internally, which can lead to isolation by current forces externally. Chinese predecessors provided a legacy for all of us to go up to the next level of prosperity. This legacy teaches us the disciplines of how to cultivate ourselves, how to harmonize our families, how to contribute to our communities, and how to keep our world peace collectively.

THE SPONSOR'S STATEMENT

Asian American Studies, UC Davis
Dr. Stanley Sue and Eileen Leung

This book is the culmination of an ambitious project conceived by the late Professor Peter C. Y. Leung, senior lecturer at Asian American Studies, University of California, Davis. When the State of California invited its citizenry to celebrate the Sesquicentennial, he had a vision to commemorate the contributions of Chinese-Americans to the history and development of California. This publication is intended to honor the past, engage the Present, and build the future. He completed a substantial portion of the project before his death; his colleagues, friends and family have subsequently collaborated to complete this worthy project.

It documents the evolution of Chinese immigrants to California from the first wave who landed in San Francisco in 1849 to seek its fortune in the Gold Rush, to the next wave who came to build the nation's railroads, to those who cultivated and harvested fruits from this land, and to the modern day entrepreneurs seeking the American Dream. Similar to the early European immigrants to America, poverty and civil unrest in their homeland led to the Chinese immigrants' early struggles to eke out an existence in a strange land.

Asian American Studies, UC Davis, proudly supports this project because the book makes an invaluable contribution in recounting Chinese American experiences and contributions which have often gone unrecognized in society. Our cosponsor, Sacramento Chinese Culture Foundation and we jointly coordinated this project which fulfills one of the historical missions to preserve our Chinese heritage for future generations. We express our sincere appreciation to those who granted us permission to tell their stories. This book project in no way is a complete account of all the stories about Chinese-Americans in different fields and regions in California for the last 150 years. Rather, it aims to stimulate interest in preserving and sharing our stories within our communities. This book is intended to foster an appreciation of how the interrelationships among history, economics, politics and education can transform the destiny for these people and us all.

Mr. Chih-Yi Wang: Founder of the Sacramento Chinese Culture Foundation*

Dr. Alex Yeh

I n 1986 Mr. and Mrs. Chih-Yi Wang (see photo on page 18) contributed ten thousand dollars as seed money to initiate the establishment of the Sacramento Chinese Culture Foundation (SCCF). Their benevolence was completely endorsed and supported by the Asian community of Sacramento and local school districts.

These supports in this city have been served as testament to the value of the foundation in nurturing cultural principles. The foundation has been an incubator for developing minds with strong morals and Chinese cultural pride in general and advocating the Chinese Mandarin language for local school districts' students in particular.**

In the history of the world, ancient China and Egypt are known as the cradles of civilization. In this

---

*This article was derived from the data provided by and consulted with Mr. Chih-yi Wang (June 10, 2000).
**Examples of the SCCF's services to the schools: (1) seed funding for new classes related to Chinese language, history, geography, or culture; (2) funds for materials/supplies such as text books, dictionaries, reference books and other learning tools for Chinese cultural/language-related classes; (3) presentations on special topics in Chinese culture, and (4) liaison among schools in the USA, Taiwan, and China.

acclamation lies the basis for Chinese pride and the continuing support for the existence of the Sacramento Chinese Culture Foundation.

The value of the Foundation is well known, but the value of Mr. Wang's contribution to Sacramento is only beginning to be recognized in the city. Mr. Wang single-handedly conceived the organizational structure, recruited board members, and assigned tasks for recruitment of members as well as developing the foundation's by-laws. When the organization became functional, he launched the issuance of academic scholarships for talented youngsters without regard to their racial or ethnic origins. Mr. Wang instituted several cultural exchanges and educational tours involving the United States, Taiwan, and China that are still continuing to this day.

In northern California, Mr. Wang is known for coordinating many community improvement projects among various charitable, educational and social agencies. Certainly, Mr. Wang's leadership and his vision became part of the fruitful and rewarding growth of the Sacramento Chinese Culture Foundation.

Biographically Mr. Wang was appointed accountant and internal auditor for the Overseas Chinese Bank Corporation in Kunming, China, at the age of twenty-three. He further developed himself by joining the Republic of China (ROC) army. In his military service experience, he ascended from platoon leader to battalion commander of an armor division. For a period of seven years he was assigned as a high level liaison Officer in charge of personnel and administration between the Ministry of Defense, ROC and the Military Assistance Advisory Group (MAAG), USA. And through his liaison efforts, the Committee for the Armed Forces Veterans' Placement, ROC was successfully established and opened up many new career doors for the retired soldiers. His excellent service record was recognized as he was awarded quite a few "Excellent Governmental Service Orders" and "the Honorable Career Achievement Medals".

Mr. Wang ended his military tour of duty in 1966 and returned to his accounting career. To reestablish himself well in his field, he completed graduate work in State University of New York at Binghamton. After he earned an MS degree in 1969, he moved to Florida where he was employed at the Lake Butler Inmate Reception and Medical Center. Due to the limited potential for professional growth and development as well as his children's educational opportunities, he ventured with his family to northern California in 1970. When he arrived at Roseville, California, he landed a job as City Accountant. He retired from that job in 1984.

Mr. Wang had been president of the SCCF for five years and its board member for two years. In 1992, he retired from those positions and was appointed Lifetime Honorary President. Mr. Wang is an enthusiastic supporter and good counsel to the leaders who currently manage the foundation.

Mr. Wang left a legacy of cultural riches that will serve as an inspiration for generations of Chinese-Americans to come in the future of Sacramento.

INTRODUCTION

Peter C. Y. Leung and Eileen Leung

The California Sesquicentennial project of the California Council for the Humanities (CCH) commemorates the history and continuing impact of the events that led to the founding of the modern state of California, beginning with the discovery of gold until California was admitted to the Union in 1850. From 1998 to 2000, many governmental, educational and community organizations throughout California will celebrate "One Hundred Fifty Years of Gold Discovery in Coloma, 1848". The California Gold Rush also brought thousands of Chinese immigrants to California and other states. Chinese American communities will celebrate their legacy in California's history through many channels.

As one of several active Chinese community organizations in Sacramento, California, the Sacramento Chinese Culture Foundation (SCCF) has supported the preservation of Chinese culture through performing arts festivals and support of Chinese language and culture instruction in public schools, colleges and universities. Asian American Studies (AAS) at UC Davis offers courses which examines the experiences of various Asian American groups in the United States. Its courses cover history, culture, legal, political and social issues. As a board member of SCCF and faculty member of Asian American

Studies (AAS), at University of California, Davis, I approached both organizations with the idea to publish this book jointly to commemorate the contributions of Chinese and Chinese-Americans to California's development. The proposal received wholehearted support.

This book covers four main components: History, People, Community and Special Topics, plus Distinguished Models feature:

History: (1) "A Glimpse of Chinese Gold Miners in California" offers an overview of why the Chinese came to work in the gold mines and how they lived. Facing extreme harassment and discriminatory local and national laws, the early Chinese immigrants' struggle in California is a testament to their bravery and contributions to the development of California's new frontier. Their determination and perseverance have also shaped American legal systems. (2) "One Day, One Dollar" summarizes the life of Chinese farm laborers in the Sacramento River Delta with a poem that captures their bittersweet legacy. (3) "Chinese Pioneer Farming Families in Suisun Valley, California 1870-1980" is based on interviews that Tony Waters (then doctoral student in Sociology at UC Davis, now Assistant Professor of Anthropology at CSU Chico) and I conducted with descendants of three generations of Chinese farm laborers in Suisun Valley. It describes the formation of Chinese communities in a rural setting, their relationship with landowners and life on the farms.

People: (1) "Honorable March Fong Eu's Story" by Col. Cliff and Mrs. Vicki Beaton chronicles the career of a Chinese woman who conquered barriers to access and leadership in California and national politics. (2) "Frank Fat: A Legendary Restaurateur in Sacramento" is derived from a biographical article published in *California History* in 1991 based on my interviews with him. Frank Fat became famous not only because his Chinese restaurant catered to influential legislators and political leaders in the State Capitol, but because he encouraged Chinese-Americans to become active in civic and political affairs of their community. (3) "The Bel Air Story" by Dr. Alex Yeh and Ms. Romy Jue, the 4th generation of Wong's family, highlights the Horatio Alger story of the Wong family whose hard work led to the establishment of a successful grocery store chain in Sacramento. (4) "CC Yin and Their McDonald Enterprise" describes how another successful Chinese American entrepreneur family has mainstreamed through active participation in community, business and civic affairs. The Yin family generously returned what they earned to help their community. (Ms. Kathy Swett, a freelance writer, professionally edited this article).

Community: Several articles written by academicians focus on important social organizations that have enriched the community during their critical developmental stages and have fostered important social networks:

A doctoral candidate in Anthropology at UC Berkeley, Joe Chung Fong was an instructor for "Contemporary Issues of Asian American Communities at the AAS" in 1999. His first article "Mecca of Chinese America: Dai Fow, Yee Fow, Sam Fow" traces the historical development of Chinese American communities in three important California cities: San Francisco, Sacramento and Stockton. He discusses how the social structure that emerged from San Francisco Chinatown influenced the development of other Chinatowns across the nation. He also comments on the co-existence of sub-units of Chinatowns: Administrative Chinatown, Co-exist Chinatown and Indo-Chinatown.

His second article, "New Chinatown and Indo-China Association in Sacramento" describes how the Southeast Asian community's social institutions help new immigrants adjust to their new environment and the effect of such institutions on education and social networks.

"The Fountain of Chinese American Growth and Development" by Peter C. Y. Leung and revised by his wife Eileen Leung describes an evolving and emerging Sacramento Chinese community. This diversified community includes six generations of Chinese-Americans plus newcomers from China, Taiwan, Hong Kong, and ethnic Chinese of some Southeast Asian countries. It samples five outstanding community organizations to tell the story of Chinese-Americans' contributions to its communities.

Special Topics: (1) Dr. Stanley Sue, Director of the AAS and Director, National Research Center of Asian American Mental Health, UC Davis contributed the essay "Chinese American Achievements in Education". His article disputes several controversial hypotheses and explanations by social scientists on the impressive achievements made by Chinese-Americans. Chinese-Americans are not a model minority group, and there is no substantial evidence that Chinese-Americans are superior in intelligence because of their heredity. Although the track record of mobility in some areas such as sports, acting, managerial positions, is weak, education has proven to be a way for Chinese-Americans to get ahead and realize great careers. Those with limited English proficiency simply take fewer courses, study harder, and find majors that capitalize on their skills in order to succeed at universities. Moreover, Dr. Sue has exactly mapped out how the current Chinese American students and academicians alike must recognize the value of Chinese culture, the adaptation of the university environment, and the limitation and potential of each person as a unique individual to study, succeed, and achieve. As an example, his article has provided an excellent model of scholastic research of comprehensive data sources as referred and documented. (2) "New Voices in Chinese American Women's Writing: Recovering the Father-Daughter Stories" by Dr. Wendy Ho, Associate Professor in the AAS and Women's Studies at University of California, Davis, introduces many women writers who recorded the stories of women, especially mothers and daughters from the 1960s to 1980s. While many Chinese American mother-daughter stories have been written, little attention has been paid to Chinese American father-daughter relationships. As fathers, Chinese American men are crucial to the familial and community building process, considering the long legal and historical denial of access to women, families and communities during the late eighteenth and nineteenth centuries. Her article focuses on the role of Chinese American men in the family.

The Distinguished Models: (1) A tribute to Illa Collin, Supervisor in Sacramento County, long time supporter of the Chinese American community is written by Dr. Alex Yeh. (2) Dr. March Fong Eu's speech addresses the unfinished business and on-going struggle by Chinese-Americans. (3) "Honorable Jimmie R. Yee's Story" by Dr. Alex Yeh documents how a councilman became the first Chinese to become the mayor of Sacramento and established a great example of fair play in politics.

The articles only cover some stories of Chinese American communities in northern California. However, it is a beginning and should encourage us to preserve stories within our communities for posterity. Sacramento Chinese Culture Foundation and Asian American Studies, University of California, Davis, hope that readers will enjoy the stories here and continue the quest to build a better future for the generations that follow after us.

In Memory of My Husband
Eileen Leung

M y late husband was a tireless advocate of
documenting the oral history of the early Chinese
immigrants to California. An immigrant himself
from Hong Kong in the late 1960's, his interest in Chinese
American history was sparked by his first teaching job at
University of California, Davis. As an instructor of
Cantonese, he discovered that most of the students enrolled
in his classes were eager to learn not only the language, but
also their cultural heritage. His first oral history project
involved interviewing Chinese farm laborers in Locke,
California, most of whom came as young men from
southern China to find a better life in the Gold Mountain,
eventually had to remain here often as single men. His
friendships with these retired laborers were mutually
beneficial; fortunately he encountered many that were
willing to share their stories. His networks with state park
rangers were forged when he was asked to restore the Wah
Hop Store in Marshall Gold Discovery State Park, Coloma.
His students at UC Davis often shared with him the plight
of their immigrant families' struggles to make a living in
America. His photographic exhibits throughout the state
publicized the contributions of humble farm laborers to the
development of California as an agricultural powerhouse.
California State Archives sought his expertise with Chinese
artifacts. Furthermore, his work with the Iu-Mien and
Southeast Asian community was filled with passion and

inspiration. He shared his vision for community service with his family as they joined him in many volunteer activities. This book is dedicated posthumously to Peter, for his love of his community and his family.

A Glimpse of Chinese Gold Miners in California

Peter C. Y. Leung

From China to America

From 1840 to 1870, China suffered a series of natural and political disasters that impoverished the country as a whole. The natural disasters included overpopulation, periodic floods and droughts, and resultant famines. The political disasters included losing the Opium War with England in 1842 and the Arrow War with England and France in 1856. As a consequence of these two defeats, more of China was opened to Western trade. Opium smuggling became widespread. In 1851, the Taiping Rebellion against the Imperial government broke out.

The discovery of gold at John Sutter's sawmill in Coloma, California in 1848, brought thousands of gold seekers from all over the world to the Coloma Valley, seeking wealth and fortune. Coloma, was described in 1848 as a beautiful hollow...surrounded on all sides by lofty mountain. Within a period of six months, the green valley had been transformed into hundreds of tents, whitening the Plain.

Experience in Gold Mining

Among the thousands who came to Coloma were the Chinese, eager to gain a piece of fortune in California's booming gold-rush economy. The number of Chinese miners was only two in 1848, but soon blossomed into the thousands in the Mother Lode. The Chinese who began streaming into California in 1850-52 were primarily unmarried men voluntarily emigrating from the southern, coastal province of Guangdong. Most came as sojourners, hoping to stay only long enough to reap a fortune, then return to their homes in China. Their families were often very poor; there was neither sufficient farmland nor jobs enough to support all of them. In addition to the need for money, geographical, social and political elements inspired their journeys. The Sacramento Daily Union estimated that by October 10, 1855, nearly 20,000 of the 36,557 Chinese located on the pacific coast were mining in the gold fields.

The instruments used by the Chinese gold miners were quite simplistic, usually a pan and a rocker. They were cheap and easy to carry which allowed the miners to move from one site to another. Chinese gold miners often worked in small groups of two to a dozen to increase efficiency and more importantly, to protect themselves against hostile white miners. The Chinese were relegated to less promising mining sites that were often depleted by the white miners.

Like most newly arrived immigrants, the early Chinese gold miners brought over and practiced many of their traditional customs from China. The attire worn by the Chinese gold miners included their blue cotton knee-length tunics, baggy blue trousers, and broad-brimmed hats along with wooden shoes. Their hair was worn in a traditional queue.

The Chinese gold miners' diet consisted primarily of rice, dried fish and tea. Chicken and preserved pork were eaten occasionally but this was often a luxury. Chinese thought that chicken and pork were abundant abroad. They dreamed of the wealth and luxury that awaited them in California.

Working along the American River for only a few cents a day and facing racial harassment from other miners, some of the Chinese were eventually crowded out of the diggings by white prospectors. The Chinese turned to other occupations such as shopkeepers and laundry workers, and established small business to serve miners' needs.

A Vanished Chinatown in Coloma

Coloma's Chinatown became the largest Chinatown in California in the 1850s. It served as a haven for the Chinese as well as other miners. Chinatown provided goods and services, such as a hair cut by a Chinese barber, groceries from a Chinese shopkeeper, and medical treatment from a Chinese herbal doctor.

By the late 1850s, Coloma's reign as the "Queen of the Mines" was nearing an end. With its placer mines petering out and most of its mining ditches converted into irrigation ditches, Coloma declined from a Gold Rush mecca into a sleepy town. The hotels, restaurants and gambling houses that once lined its streets closed their doors as miners moved to other rivers and mountains in search of gold.

Chinatown's demise began in the 1860s. In 1861, a dispute over the right to mine under an old hotel sent forty drunken Irishmen on a rampage through Chinatown, destroying property, looting and burning buildings. In addition, several Chinese were beaten and one of them died as a large crowd of spectators watched. The end came in 1880 when most of Chinatown went up in flames and the remaining Chinese left Coloma.

Today, all that remain of Coloma's Chinatown are the Wah Hop Herb and Dry Goods Store and the Man Lee Building in Marshall Gold Discovery State Historic Park. Restored and reopened to the public in 1958 after years of neglect and disuse, these buildings were originally built around 1858 or 1859 by white settlers. The brick building was leased in 1860 to Wah Hop who opened a grocery store, housing everything from a small cooking area to shelves of herb drawers and even burial urns. The Man Lee Building was a hardware store and is currently used to house an exhibit of mining techniques.

The Wah Hop Store and Man Lee Building are reminders of the legacy of Chinese Pioneers and their Chinatown in Coloma's Gold Rush era. What was once California's largest Chinatown is now a sole memory in Marshall Gold Discovery State Historic Park.

Mining in Siskiyou Region

Chinese worked along the American River and gradually dispersed to other mines where gold might be found. The California gold mines were divided into three regions: the Southern Mines (El Dorado, Amador, Calaveras, Tuolumne, and Mariposa counties), the Northern Mines (Plumas, Butte, Sierra, Yuba, Nevada and Placer counties), and the Klamath/Trinity Mines (Del Norte, Klamath, Siskiyou, Trinity and Shasta counties).

When placer mines were depleted, American miners abandoned them. Chinese miners bought the old claims and worked the abandoned tailings. Some Chinese teamed up to have developed a "chain pump" method for larger mining operation. Later, when hydraulic mining methods were used, many Chinese laborers were brought back to mining fields. By 1870, almost one third of the miners in California were Chinese.

Although some Chinese began to form their mining operations, yet control over the newcomers (work forces) remained in the hands of San Francisco's Chinese merchants. Chinese commercial agents and storekeepers, in constant contacts between their regional offices and the company's headquarters, directed the workers to any new work sites through California, Oregon, Nevada, Colorado and into Idaho.

Abraham Thompson found gold in March 1851 on the flats near a ravine called Black Gulch in northern California. In six weeks' time, 2000 miners had arrived in Thompson's Dry Diggings and eagerly found their luck. At that time, Shasta Butte City was founded in 1851. A new county named Siskiyou was established only in March 22, 1852, then Shasta Butte City was renamed as Yreka in 1852.

Travelers from north and south were spreading the word of gold found in this area. Then the Klamath, Scott, Salmon, Trinity and Shasta Rivers began to attract thousands of miners. By 1852, the Chinese began moving into Siskiyou County because of these spectacular placer gravels. It was estimated that over 1,000 Chinese already entered Shasta County in April, 1853. A big Chinatown sprang up in Weaverville, in Trinity County, where several thousand Chinese lived and mined. In early May of 1853, 35 Chinese arrived at Yreka from Shasta County. The Shasta County newspaper commented that numerous Chinese passed through on the way north to Yreka from Weaverville. Siskiyou County was considered the second Mother Lode as distinguished as the Mother Lode in the Sierra area.

Getting to Yreka was not easy during the late nineteenth and early twentieth centuries. Most travelers to Yreka rode in mud wagons (similar to stagecoaches). Numerous records pointed out that Chinese travelers rode on these wagons frequently. They always rode on the outside stages because the fare was cheaper. In other instances, they must work on the roadway constructions to survive.

From 1854 to 1860, in Siskiyou County, Chinese miners lived either within the main camp, or a short distance down the road. Besides mining, they also engaged in other jobs as part-time cooks, washers or gardeners.

The 1860 census reveals that 34,933 Chinese lived in the United States. But according to census records from 1860's until 1900, the number of Chinese in Siskiyou Country were listed as:

1860:	515 Chinese
1870:	1,441 Chinese
1880:	1,568 Chinese
1890:	1,151 Chinese
1900:	790 Chinese

Given the extraordinary mobility of the gold rush population and the hostility and language barriers toward Chinese, the census figures only provide little information. For example, in 1885 the Central Pacific Railroad System stretched its lines in all directions from San Francisco, one line extending north to the Oregon line. During construction of the line over Siskiyou Mountains 4,000 Chinese laborers were employed. Such data did not record in the census.

Yreka's Chinatown experienced numerous fires and floods in its history. A fire in 1856 destroyed almost half of Chinatown on Miner Street. The town was flooded out in late November of 1861, and the 1890's flood resulted in heavy damage to the Chinese housing and reducing the number of buildings. Other fires that burned Chinatown ocurred in 1871, 1886 and 1923. The Depression marked the beginning of the end for Chinatown as a residence for

Chinese. Several buildings in Chinatown were completely destroyed during construction of the I-5 Freeway.

Happy Camp was the center of the mining industry of the Klamath River. By 1860 or so, there were two large stores, two hotels, two saloons, two large dance halls, butcher shop, saloon, post office and four Chinese stores. Ah Ock who also owned mines and employed miners opened the "China Store". These four mercantiles were served by a pack train operated by a Chinese merchant, named China Bow. By 1880, Happy Camp's population had increased to 597, including 250 Chinese and 97 Indians. Here the perception was held that most Chinese were employed as flume and ditch diggers. However, many also leased or owned mines such as the Classic Hill which they worked.

The richest mines on the Klamath River were near Happy Camp: The Richardson Mine, the Gordon Mine and the China Creek Mine. In the late 1880's, a Chinese miner, China Oak leased a piece of mining claim at Happy Camp paying 60% royalty, spent $500,000 to dig up the mine and hired 200 Chinese to work for him. The Richardson mine had 50 Chinese miners. They operated the mine as they thought best, sending Richardson $50,000 a month. American miners, Camp and Titus owned the Classic Hill mine. One hundred Chinese paid Camp and Titus $20,000 in cash for a 99-year lease. In the Creek under Classic Hill, more than 1,000 Chinese worked there for several years.

In 1880, Charles E. Owen who came from New York State as a pioneer miner contracted with Chinese miners to work on his mine on Indian Creek. Suited for hydraulic mining, the Chinese were paid over $4,000 for the tunnel.

Joseph Reeves owned the large mines in Happy Camp, which were worked by Chinese for many years. The

Chinese who subsequently mined $100,000 to $200,000 worth of gold purchased the mine, named China Creek.

Ah Ock bought the old Happy Camp Hydraulic Mining Company's property from Siskiyou Mining Company in 1896. He then sold the property to the Oregon Gold Mining and Water Power Company in 1899.

By 1910 the only Chinese left in Happy Camp were elderly. Quong was the last Chinese to have a store in Happy Camp on Main Street. After Chinatown burned in 1910, most of the Chinese left, and in the early 1920's only two remained. They worked for Miss Minnie Reeve at her ranch.

In 1855, there had been a great influx of miners to Salmon River mining fields. What had once been a sizable Chinese mining settlement at Petersburg on Salmon's south with a number of Chinese stores in the 1850's and 1860's, was abandoned in the 1890's, so only a few Chinese left living in the cabins.

The Montezuma Mine was sold to China Company at South Fork for $50,000. In the early days there was a tremendous influx of Chinese into South Fork and vicinity. In 1866 when A. H. Denny moved to South Fork, the mining town was quite a burg with around 50 to 100 men living in the vicinity, besides 200 to 300 Chinese. Chinese inhabited Springtown almost entirely. It was reported around 500-800 Chinese -- more than in any other town in Siskiyou County.

A fairly large Chinese population lived in Etna. This settlement was at the town's lower end and consisted mainly of former miners who were employed as ranch hands and servants. China Hill was so numed because of the Chinese settlement located at its base. At one time there were at least six houses and a store. During the mining period, many Chinese were employed on the ranches of Scott Valley as cooks because each ranch hired a number of men to carry on the farm work. When the federal government required that all Chinese in this country be registered, about a hundred Chinese came to Etna to be registered. Two of the most interesting people in Chinatown was "Chinee Mary," and her mother "Old Susie," the only women in the community. In the early part of the 20th century the Chinese left the valley. Only a few remained as cooks in the hotels, restaurants and on some neighboring ranches.

There are two large creeks in Seiad to this day: Grider Creek and Seiad Creek. Two Chinese mining companies with about 12 men each worked in these mines. The Lee Yet hydraulic mine was the largest, operated by about 25 Chinese. Chinese also operated Hoskins Bar mine.

In 1894, there were 460 Chinese miners in Siskiyou County. The number rose to 484 in 1895. But at the end of the century it is believed that the Chinese had mostly left their small camps to work for such large hydraulic operations as the Homestake Mine or the Yorget Bar, or had simply moved away to more urban Chinese settlements in other counties.

In assessing the contributions the Chinese made to the economy of Siskiyou County, mining was extraordinarily important. It provided the major trade for the vast majority of Chinese males who either individually owned a mine or shared ownership in a larger company as a partner.

Violence and Legislation against Chinese during the Gold Rush Era

The white American miners did not want to share the gold with foreigners and even with natives. As early as 1850, they asked the California State Legislature to pass a

Foreign Miner's Tax. This was directed at Mexicans and South Americans. The bill forced all foreign miners to pay a very high price for a mining license. Racial prejudice and violence against non-white and foreigners were common. Because of the high tax, many foreign miners from Europe, Mexico and South America gave up and left the mining fields.

Before 1851, attitude towards the few Chinese in California was more tolerant, but toleration faded rapidly as more Chinese migrated to the gold fields. In 1851, the number of Chinese increased from 4,000 to 25,000 in one year. The flood of Chinese upset American miners again. In 1852 the California Legislature passed the second Foreign Miners Tax law. This law required a monthly fee for "aliens ineligible for citizenship," meant for the Chinese only. This tax became a prime discriminatory measure against the Chinese. The tax remained as law until 1870. During this time, the state collected over five million dollars, which was equal to one third of the state budget.

The tax, however, did not stop many violent acts against the Chinese miners. Fake tax collectors searched out Chinese miners to steal their gold. The real tax collectors were as bad as the fake ones, killing those who refused to pay. Chinese were not protected against this violence.

The August 8, 1853, issue of the *Alta California* reported, "An American yesterday attacked a Chinaman, beating him shamefully. The assailant held the Celestial by the queue and kicked and beat him until he was tired." Scattered incidents began in the spring of 1852 in the Northern Mines to expel the Chinese. One of the first recorded organized actions took place at Foster and Atchinson's Bar in Yuba County where a meeting was held and a resolution was passed denying to Chinese the right to hold claims. It also required all Chinese to leave by May 3, 1852.

On May 8, 1852, a mass meeting was held in the Columbia Mining District in the Southern Mines where a resolution was passed to exclude Chinese from mining activities. Calaveras County restricted Chinese miner's movements by requiring them to register their claims. By 1855, expulsions were also taking place in mining camps in Shasta County. In other counties Chinese were driven from mining camps by resolutions passed by white miners and as a result of violence. The expulsions forced many Chinese to leave for other localities or to enter other occupations elsewhere.

No one knows exactly how many Chinese were maimed or murdered during the Gold Rush era. It was so bad that in many communities, Chinese miners were forced out of mining operations. In 1853, the California State Supreme Court ordered California to prohibit all colored people from giving evidence in court against whites. Also California Governor John Bigler demanded exclusion of Chinese from mines and adopted a resolution to deny mining claims to the Chinese.

Although there were no Chinese in Siskiyou County before 1852, the state actions against the Chinese also encouraged various mining camps and counties to enact anti-Chinese activities. This also happened in Yreka, the County seat. Yreka emerged in 1854 as a fairly prosperous county seat and was relatively quiet for its Chinese residents. However, on February 10, 1855, Siskiyou County passed a restrictive ordinance against Chinese. The key reasons were: "1. The Chinese have no right to benefit from the wealth of American soil. 2. The Chinese can never blend in with American society. 3. The Chinese ruin the American free labor system. 4. After the Chinese make their profits the gold is shipped back to China; 5. Support the miner's tax of 1854. 6. California has suffered from the Chinese influx. 7. Wherever Chinese crowding is found, a depressed economy may be noted."

On July 4, 1856, during Yreka's Fourth of July celebration, many miners marched down to where the Chinese lived and commenced, and started kicking down doors, smashing furniture, beating up the men, and abusing the women. The white miners' brutal action, which was directed against the Chinese, was justified in American society at that era. The Foreign Miners Tax, which climbed to six dollars per head in 1856, deterred some Chinese from the gold field. Many Chinese left Siskiyou County to avoid paying such an unfair tax and rode on the California Stage Company to Jacksonville, Oregon.

Another new tax at $2.50 a month per person was levied on Chinese who did not work on the mining in Yreka. At that time, about 400 Chinese resided in this town which added $1,000.00 per month easily. Therefore, some Chinese were forced back to mining rather than working as cooks or laundrymen.

In the 1870's *Yreka Union* editorial opinions were often very biased regarding Chinese. It supported the anti-Chinese movement through the state until the 1882; the Anti-Chinese Exclusion Act passed by the Congress.

When gold began to be less plentiful after the mid-1850's, American miners, supported by the Northern European immigrants, grew to resent the Chinese. In these two decades from 1860-1880, this resentment turned to violent hostility as California underwent a series of disturbing changes. The Civil War had adversely affected eastern industries. The depression, which hit the Eastern states in the late 1860s, reached California by the early 1870's. The Chinese were made scapegoats and held responsible for most of California's problems.

Discriminatory legislation was not enough to satisfy the anti-Chinese forces. By 1860's Chinese disembarking from the ships docked in San Francisco were pelted with rocks and jeered by white mobs. Numerous acts of violence occurred in mining camps. In small cities and towns, the local Chinatowns were torched, and their residents escorted out of town at gunpoint. In cities as far as Los Angeles, major riots resulted in many Chinese being killed by whites.

The Chinese Exclusion Laws of 1882 suspended most new Chinese immigration for a period of ten years and denied Chinese the right of naturalization. The Scott Act of 1888 further limited Chinese immigration and made it difficult for Chinese living in the United States to leave this country and then return. In 1892, the Geary Act extended the Chinese Exclusion Act for another ten years, and in 1902, the Exclusion Laws made this a permanent condition. This law was not repealed until 1943 (the same year in which Chinese regained the right of naturalization). Even after 1943, however, very few Chinese were allowed to enter the U.S.A. each year. Not until 1965 was Chinese immigration put on the same footing as immigration from the rest of the world.

Since the Chinese set foot on the American soil, they have faced enormous brutal violence against them in mining camps and urban areas. From the late nineteenth century to the early twentieth centuries, hundreds of laws were passed by local, state and even Congress against the Chinese. The Chinese who came had no rights, no voice; they only could react whatever happened to them.

Conclusion

The lives and times of the early Chinese gold miners began with optimism and a hope for wealth, which were quickly dispelled by legislative and physical obstacles. What eventually allowed the Chinese gold miners to survive was a spirit and strength developed and forged to face bitterness and adversity.

Although historians and writers have traditionally portrayed Chinese in the nineteenth century American West as victims, if we look at some of the positive aspects of their experiences, they were able to meet their basic survival needs. They followed white miners into the gold fields. They worked on those abandoned mines. They did not compete with white miners, but complemented them. They invented a special device for mining, such as the "China Pump". Predominantly they showed cultural accommodation, not confrontation, because they knew they didn't have a strong government in China that stood behind them. They earned sympathy from a few whites that were willing to protect them or continue to hire them for work. A few individuals or companies were able to accumulate a considerable amount of wealth and climb up the economic ladder. It is most important that these pioneers led thousands of our people who could claim America as their new home.

Today, when one studies the history at that time, with changing attitudes and better understanding among races and cultures, it is still bitter to learn what happened to the pioneering Chinese who had suffered so much because they were "Chinese."

References

Barth, Gunther. *Bitter Strength: A History of the Chinese in the United States 1850-1870.* Cambridge: Harvard University Press, 1964.

Beesley, David. *Our Chinese Legacy.* Sierra Heritage, 1984.

Chan, Sucheng. *This Bittersweet Soil: The Chinese in California Agriculture, 1860-1910.* Berkeley and Los Angeles: University of California Press, California, 1986.

"The Chinese in California." *California History.* California: California Historical Society, Spring 1978.

Dicker, Laverne Mau. *The Chinese in San Francisco: A Pictorial History.* New York: Dover Publications, 1979.

Dillinger, William C. *The Gold Discovery: James Marshall and the California Gold Rush.* California Department of Parks and Recreation, 1990.

Jones, Joseph Roy. *The Land of Remember.* California: Naturegraph Publishers, Inc., 1971.

Lai, James S., and Leung, Peter C. Y. "The Life of the Early Chinese Gold Miners in California", 1848-1868, Chinese American Council of Sacramento, 1991

Lee, Christopher, and Leung, Peter C. Y. A Vanished Chinatown in Coloma, California, Chinese American Council of Sacramento, 1991

Return to Gold Mountain: The Life of the Early Chinese in California. Chinese American Council of Sacramento, 1991.

The Siskiyou Pioneer and Yearbook, The Chinese in Siskiyou County, A Glimpse from Yreka. California: Siskiyou County Historical Society, Vol.6, No.3, 1990.

The Siskiyou Pioneer and Yearbook. California: The Siskiyou County Historical Society, Vol. 4, No.5, 1972.

Wacker, George E. "George E. Wacker: Yreka-Chinese," *Memories from the Land of Siskiyou: Past Lives and Time.* Ed. Gilbert W. Davis.

One Day, One Dollar—
Delta Heritage

Peter C. Y. Leung

The Chinese farm laborer is virtually extinct in today's American labor market. Yet only a century ago Chinese labor was as much in demand in California agriculture as it was in mining, railroad construction, land reclamation, fisheries, and light industry. In spite of the anti-Chinese movement and resultant exclusion laws, Chinese laborers played a crucial role in developing the Sacramento River Delta where they were employed in the construction of levees, in land reclamation, and in agriculture. These Chinese represent the last wave of Asian immigrants to arrive in the Delta, and their lives are an important segment of its history.

This article speaks to the harsh and spartan life endured by many Chinese who made the Sacramento and San Joaquin Delta a major agricultural area in the 19th and 20th century. As an example, Wong Yow toiled in the Sacramento Delta and earned only $1 a day for an average 70-hour workweek. Due to the completion of the railroad in 1869, many Chinese were forced to move to the Delta where levee construction work was very attractive. There they drained ditches and built hundreds of miles of levees and reclaimed some 88,000 acres by the year 1880. When that work was finished, many stayed on as laborers and tenant farmers.

Thousands of Chinese settled in the small communities of Courtland, Locke, Walnut Grove, Isleton and Rio Vista. They continued to endure hard labor and discriminatory laws. Over the years, fires destroyed most of the Delta's Chinatowns, but Locke remains active. Although many of Locke's buildings stand empty, it has been designated a national historic landmark to keep North America's last rural town built by those Chinese from passing unnoticed into oblivion.

Delta Heritage

A hundred miles of levee built
The tule marsh made fertile
Generations of knotted hands
Work and rework reclaiming the land
Farms and orchards, grains and fruit trees
Mark our labor
Now this land becomes grand

Here we are
These Chinese immigrants
The early tenant farmers of America
Our story untold
Our words scattered
Like the fruits forgotten seed

One day-one dollar
Our memoir
For the bittersweet struggles
Of a hundred years gone by

Where have our delta Chinatowns gone?
Only our pictures remain
Tattered and yellowed
Waiting to be seen
Our Forgotten work
This panorama of Delta farm land

References

Chan, Sucheng. *This Bittersweet Soil: The Chinese in California Agriculture, 1860-1910*, (University of California Press, Berkeley and Los Angeles, California, 1986)

Leung, Peter C. Y. *One Day, One Dollar: The Chinese Farming Experience in the Sacramento River Delta*, California (Second Edition, 1994, the Liberal Arts Press)

Leung, Peter C. Y. "When A Haircut was A Luxury: A Chinese Farm Laborer in the Sacramento Delta, *California History*, Summer 1985

Leung, Peter C. Y. and Ma, L.Eve Armentrout. "Chinese Farming Activities in the Sacramento-San Joaquin Delta: 1910-1940 "(*Amerasia Journal*, UCLA, Vol. 14, No. 2, 1988)

Lydon, Sandy. *Chinese Gold: The Chinese in the Monterey Bay Region,* 1985, Capitola Book Company

Chinese Pioneer Farming Families in Suisun Valley (1870-1980) [1]

Peter C. Y. Leung
and Dr. Tony Waters

---

[1] We would like to give our special appreciation to Robert Tim Quan, Jennie Tim, John Tim, Lewis Tim, Julian Timm, Christopher Yee, Eva Yee, Mr. & Mrs. Andrew Lowe, Michael Bow, Edward Lum, Charlie Lum, Ivy Fong, Nira Wong whom we interviewed for this article between 1986 to 1996. Their relationships to the Pioneers: Chun Tim, Go Long, Lum Foon and Yee Eng are illustrated below:

Roberta Tim Quan: Youie Tim's daughter, Chun Tim's Granddaughter.
Jennie Tim: Youie Tim's wife, Chun Tim's daughter-in-law.
John Tim and Lewis Tim: Youie Tim's sons, Chun Tim's grandsons
Julian Timm: Chun Mon Gum's son, Chun Tim's grandson
Christopher Yee: Yee Eng's son
Eva Yee: Yee Eng's daughter
Andrew Lowe: Lin Tim's husband, Chun Tim's son-in-law
Lin Tim Lowe (Mrs. Andrew Lowe): Chun Tim's second daughter
Edward & Charles Lum: Danny Foon's sons, Lum Foon's grandsons
Michael Bow: Danny Foon's grandson, Lum Foon's great grandson
Ivy Fong: Go Long's second daughter
Nira Wong: Ivy Fong's daughter, Go Long's granddaughter.

Today you need to look closely to see Suisun's Chinese "Big Camp." All that is left is a patch of asphalt here and there next to a quiet stretch of Suisun Creek in Suisun Valley. Perhaps if you dig with your toe, a few bricks of uncertain vintage will turn up. The old wrecked cars are more recent relics at the site, perhaps the 1980s, some 50 years after Big Camp was abandoned. In some ways, the cars seem to be a desecration of the site where there once was a thriving Chinese farm-camp which had a population as high as 1,000, complete with an active KMT (Kuomintang: the Chinese Nationalist Party) branch, Chun Ying Association building, clapboard farmhouses, drying fruit ovens, stable yards, labor movement organization, stores, meeting and ancestor halls, gambling rooms, and even an opium den hidden in the riverbank of the Suisun Creek.[2]

The ranchers who owned the area, the A. T. Hatch family, built bunkhouses for their workers, which were long wooden sheds with a few small windows and wooden floors. Many single men who were seasonal fixtures in the camp used these. These sheds had built-in bunkbeds, and a space at one end where a hired cook might be found cooking in a wok over a wood fire for as many as one hundred men. During the peak harvest season in August tents might augment the bunkhouses. In the beginning of the early 1900s, Dr. Sun Yat Sen himself visited the Chinese community in Suisun to raise money while travelling among California's Chinese communities.[3]

There are no known photographs left of the thriving Big Camp, and indeed it exists primarily in the legends still told by the descendants of its residents--and in the

---

[2] Christopher Yee's note, July, 1988

[3] Interviews with Jennie Tim, Roberta Tim Quan, 1986

memories of the few surviving citizens. The basic facts though are clear: Big Camp existed on the Hatch Ranch from about 1870 until 1929 or so, and was a thriving center for Suisun Valley's Chinese community. In August 1928, 11 Chinese were brutally murdered by an itinerant Chinese laborer.[4] Jennie Tim points out that the residents were so frightened by traditional beliefs about the evil spirits associated with violent death that many residents fled to surrounding ranches and San Francisco within six months. Later descendants also recall hearing about this terrible day in their childhood. Some older residents prefer not to talk about what they called " bad history."[5]

However, the small Chinese community that started at Big Camp and extended to neighboring ranches has unique historical interest for five reasons. First, it is central to the memory of one of the few surviving rural Chinese communities in California. Second, it was one of the few areas of Chinese settlement where rural Chinese immigrants were able to begin as laborers, advance in the agricultural sector as foreman supervising Chinese as well as others, and finally became independent ranchers. Several of these descendants eventually become the most prosperous farmers in Suisun Valley. In addition, because most of these farms also engaged in the fruit-drying business, children who grew-up in the valley had to help sorting fruits for drying.[6] Most of the Chinese in Suisun Valley did not engage in sharecropping; instead, they were hired as foremen to supervise farming for the landowners. This is in contrast to other rural areas like the Delta where the

---

[4] Randy Bechtel, " Hatch Ranch: Site of long ago Chinatown massacre eerie", *Daily Republic*, Fairfield, October 30, 1985.

[5] Interviews with Jennie Tim, 1986

[6] Interviews with Roberta Tim Quan, Eva Yee, Michael Bow.

majority of Chinese preferred sharecropping arrangements with Caucasian landowners.[7] Third, the number of Chinese children born in this area was so small that the local school did not have a segregation policy to deal with the race issues in those days. Fourth, the Chinese who settled in the Suisun Valley all came from the same district of Loong Doo, Chungshan County, Guangdong, China, while the majority of Chinese who settled in the Sacramento River Delta were from other parts of the same county. This immigration pattern was determined by the first pioneer who arrived in the area. Fifth, the Chinese laborers worked for A. T. Hatch, a rancher who became the largest grower of deciduous fruit in the state in 1880s. He was the first to use the refrigerator car to transport California fruit to the East in 1889.[8] Part of his success should be credited to the Chinese foreman and the laborers. Although the Chinese community declined rapidly, its involvement in farming in the Suisun Valley should have been documented.

The Suisun Valley is located north of Suisun Bay in Solano County. A 10-mile wide strip, this valley extends from Suisun City, bounded by rugged hills on the west and on the east by the Vaca Mountains. The clay-loam soil could store up moisture from the winter rainfall, making it suitable for the support of vegetation. Many growers in the Suisun Valley were also involved in drying fruits as a source of revenue for Solano County.[9]

---

[7] Peter C. Y. Leung, *One Day One dollar: Locke, California and the Chinese Farming Experience in the Sacramento Delta*, 1984

[8] Rosa Lee Baldwin, "Old Timers" *Solano Republican*, Fairfield, Oct. 15, 1936, p. 2

[9] Tom Gregory, *History of Solano & Napa Counties, California*, Historic record Company, L.A. California, 1912, pp. 130-131.

Census records show that by 1850, the first Chinese had arrived in Solano County. By 1870, there were 920 Chinese men in Solano County, but only one Chinese woman. Of these Chinese men, 261 of them lived in Suisun as farm laborers, about one third of the total Chinese population of Solano County, 13 laundrymen in Suisun City, 171 Chinese laborers in Vacaville, and 182 Chinese in Vallejo. There were 14 farm laborers in Montezuma Township, 53 woodchoppers in Rio Vista Township, and 90 woodchoppers in Green Valley. Other Chinese were scattered in Benicia, Dixon, and Tremont.[10]

At that time, Suisun City was the shipping point for the interior of Solano County, including the towns of Fairfield and Vacaville. There was a steamer which passed down the narrow creek, plying a regular route to San Francisco. The town itself included solid brick buildings from one to three stories high, and boosters bragged that 75-100 students were attending the public elementary school. There was also a macadamized road to the county seat, Fairfield, one-quarter mile away. Although Fairfield was half the size of Suisun City, it was on the line of the California Pacific Railway, and since 1850, had been the county seat.[11]

The early population was supported by wheat farming in the Suisun Valley while the reclamation work was supported by the fertile farmlands of later years. Wheat farms, the mainstay of the valley's economy, began to give

---

[10] United States Census 1850, 1860 and the California census of 1852. Chinese population for Suisun City comes from U.S. census. The 1871-2 Solano County yearbook (Pettis Brothers, Vallejo) describes Suisun City as including 700 residents.

[11] Bill Lawrence, " Suisun Hidden in Fairfield's Shadow", *Sacramento Bee*, June 9, 1986

out by the early 1870s as the continuous cropping began to take its toll on the soil.

A fruit boom emerged out of these conditions in the 1880s and proved to be the answer to the Suisun Valley's economic woes. Centered around the Hatch Ranch, which was just north of what is now Solano Community College on Suisun Valley Road, the boom was propelled by the new markets opened up by the introduction of the refrigerated rail car. Planting began in the 1870s and progressed over the next 30 years using Chinese labor. The importance of the Chinese in the orchards was described in the Pacific Rural Press of September 16, 1893. "The Chinese are the mainstay of the orchardist and thus far it must be said, form the only supply of labor which he can depend upon. They are expert pickers and packers of fruit. It is difficult to see how our annual fruit crop could be harvested and prepared for market without the Chinaman."[12] Evelyn Lockie said, " In Suisun Valley practically everyone (ranch) had a "Chiny" cabin, usually kept for the (Chinese) bossman."[13]

In the Suisun Valley, small towns like Rockville were established, and quickly became rural centers. Much of this labor was under the direction of the foreman, Chun Tim, from the Loong Doo District of Guangdong Province. By 1910, there were some 1,000,000 fruit trees in the entire valley, with the Hatch Ranch owning the most. Peach, pears, prunes, apricots, cherries and almonds were all planted and thrived. Chinese farm labor played an important role in the development of these ranches, first as laborers planting the orchards, then as ranch foreman and labor contractors coordinating harvests and pruning, and

---

[12] Quoted in *Factories in the Fields*, by Carey McWilliams, p.73

[13] Evelyn Lockie, "The Village that Vanished , A Suisun Valley Tragedy", *Solano Historian*, Dec. 1985.

finally as independent ranchers leasing and owning substantial portions of the valley.[14]

To understand how the Chinese community emerged in Suisun Valley, oral interviews were conducted between 1986 and 1992 with surviving third generations of members of the Tim and Yee families, two of the families which have continued to live in the area as well as other knowledgeable individuals. At the time that these interviews were conducted, only a few of the surviving children or wives of the original pioneers continued to live in the area. What follows is the history of how this small community began in California. Because no formal study had been conducted with the Chinese in this area before, this article will document their lives and memories together. Hopefully, several hundred descendants of these pioneer families remember the big winds and hot sun as their ancestors' worked on sorting fruits for drying and cutting thousands of fruit trees as part of their legacy in Suisun Valley.

The Pioneer Chinese Family of Chun Tim (1851 - 1923)

It is not clear what the proportion of Chinese farm labor was in Solano County in the 1870s, but if the rest of the state is any indication, the work force peaked at between 70% and 90% of the farm labor force in 1882. We also know what had begun to happen on a piece of land measuring several hundred acres owned by A.T. Hatch, a wealthy Bay Area resident who had made a fortune in the Nevada silver fields, and later a substantial name for himself as an innovator in California agriculture. Shortly after purchasing the ranch in Suisun Valley in 1871, he had

---

[14] Rosa Lee Baldwin, "Old Timers", *Solano Republican*, Fairfield, Oct.15, 1936, P. 2, Interviews with Jennie Tim, Mrs Andrew Lowe.

hired a cook and servant, Chun Tim, a 20 year-old Chinese immigrant from the Loong Doo region of Guangdong province. Tim soon began to manage the Hatch Ranch. But he was also important because of all the hundreds of Chinese laborers who passed through the Suisun Valley in the 1880s, he was the first to marry and raise children in the area.[15]

Because Chun Tim was able to do this, the ancestors of three pioneer families, the Tims, the Foons, and the Go Longs have been able to establish themselves permanently in the Suisun Valley. In addition, a fourth family, the Yees, arrived at the turn of the century to work for Chun Tim, and was able to establish a permanent presence. Chun Tim's descendants, as well as the descendants of the other Chinese farm families in the area, cite his arrival as being the origin of the permanent Chinese community in the Suisun Valley.

Chun Tim, at the age of 18, made his own way to San Francisco from his native village, Gong Bui in the Loong Doo district of Chung Shan County, Guangdong Province, China. Today, there are over 140 descendants bearing his direct family line into four kinds of surnames as " Tim", "Timm", "Chan" and "Chun" living in the United States.

Mrs. Andrew Lowe, Chun Tim's second daughter, recalled hearing about how her father arrived when she was interviewed in 1987. "He thought that everyone was going to mine gold, but it's not easy. Working in the railroad was not good either. He wanted to learn English, so he may have a better life in the future...[these English skills meant that my father was able to get a job with Mr. Hatch] driving to San Francisco for shopping and going to the church on

---

[15] Interviews with Roberta Tim Quan, Jennie Tim and Mrs. Andrew Lowe.

Sundays. In those days, they were using a surrey, pulled by a horse."

Chun Tim proved to be an effective organizer, and his English skills meant that he could be more useful to Mr. Hatch. Soon, he was a well-known labor boss for the Suisun and Green Valley areas in addition to becoming the on-site boss for the Hatch Ranch. Unlike the other Chinese labor organizers Quong Shing Lung and Company from Vacaville, Tim went beyond the San Francisco labor market for single Chinese men, and recruited directly from his home village in China by correspondence. Mrs. Andrew Lowe continued, "at first he worked with Mr. Edward, an American foreman, who came to see Chun Tim once in a while and told him what to do. Chun Tim brought lots of Chinese over from China to work at Hatch Ranch. Mr. Hatch encouraged the Chinese workers to build their own houses that eventually evolved into 'Big Camp.'

Julian Timm, one of Tim's grandsons remembers living in Big Camp as a small boy in the 1920s:

"We moved to a very small house in a settlement which was originally started by Grandfather Tim; it was large and was called "Dai Cum" translated as "Big Camp" located adjacent to Suisun Creek. I grew up in the Suisun Valley, which at that time had many, Chinese from the Loong Doo region of Chungshan, Guangdong Province, China.... I remember the farm [where Sam, my father worked at] was staffed by year-round workers, about 10, which were also from the Loong Doo region. In the summer during the fruit picking, cutting and drying, migrant Portuguese and Spanish speaking families also swelled the work force...I learned my first words in English during the first day [at school] when I played tag during recess and said "can't catch me."[16]

As with the rest of California, the Chinese population of Suisun Valley area reached its first peak in 1870-80. The 1882 Chinese Exclusion Act limited further immigration of Chinese into the United States, which led to an immediate decline in the total Chinese population.[17] Organized harassment of the Chinese men, and the limitations on their re-entry to the United States if they visited China led to immediate declines in California's Chinese population. Because California's Chinese population was largely composed of male sojourners, most young men came to California in order to make enough money for a dowry, return to China, and settle down as farmers on family-owned lands there. A very few then were able to find a wife, perhaps in San Francisco's Chinatown, or take advantage of one of the few loopholes in the Exclusion Act which permitted a businessman to return to China on a short trip to arrange for a bride with whom he might legally return.

Mrs. Andrew Lowe described how her father found her mother during a trip to San Francisco: "After Chun Tim had worked for Mr. Hatch for about twenty years, he wanted to go back to China to start his family. He went to

---

[16] Jilian Timm's personal essay "My Life in Suisun As a Young Boy", Sept. 1992

[17] Peter C. Y. Leung and L. Eve Armentrout Ma,"Chinese Farming Activities in the Sacramento-San Joaquin Delta: 1910-1941," *Amerasia* 14(2):1-18, 1988. They go on to note that the Chinese Exclusion Act, passed in 1882, caused a drastic reduction in Chinese activity in the agricultural labor sector. By 1890, only 8 years after passage of the Act, the proportion of the agricultural work force that was Chinese was already down to 20%. Consequently, California agriculture imported Japanese farm labor, the second largest group of immigrant labor at that time.

San Francisco for rice and Chinese food at a shop called 'Wo Kee', where eventually he met his wife-to-be'."

Another family member, Jennie Tim, daughter-in-law, relates how this had happened:

At age 36, in 1887, Chun Tim was preparing to return to China to select a wife. A brewmaster from San Francisco's Chinatown learned of his quest and introduced him to his 17 year-old daughter, Ding Shee, who came to San Francisco when she was six. They were married, and Chun Tim moved his bride to the "wilderness" of Suisun Valley...Ding Shee was the only Chinese woman for miles around in 1887, but despite that fact, she remained cheerful and helpful. Because of her optimistic outlook, she was a great inspiration to her husband and her family. The success of this small group of Chinese attracted others. Soon a bona fide Chinatown existed at the edge of Suisun creek on the Hatch Ranch.

By the early 20th century, the demographics of the Chinese population in California were unique. There was a large group of aging men who had begun to die off, along with a small group of families who had started small towns which were able to replicate at least some of the traditions of their home country.

Mr. Christopher Yee whose grandfather was recruited as a cook on the Hatch Ranch from 1908 placed Chun Tim at the center of Suisun's early Chinese community. He focused on the role that Chun Tim played in developing Suisun Valley Chinese community from an all-male work force to a community, which began to include women and children.

He points out that Chun Tim's daughter, Moy Chun, born in 1888, was the first Chinese born in the Suisun Valley. However, when son, Chun Mon Gum, was born on August 25, 1890, at the Hatch Ranch in the Suisun Valley, the whole Chinese Community was elated because he was the first Chinese male born in the Suisun Valley. More pleased was his father, Chun Tim, because now he had a son to carry on the family name. His mother was also happy that she was able to present her husband a son.[18]

This role was recognized not only by the Chinese community, but also by the elite portions of the white community, which had hired the Chinese laborers to manage their ranches. Using the voice of her day, Rosa Lee Baldwin, resident of a neighboring ranch in 1936 described Tim in her biography of rancher A.T. Hatch in 1938 in this way:

It is not fitting to close this historic career for the Hatch family without a few brief remarks concerning Tim, the Chinese, who for so many years held forth as Patriarch over a thriving Chinese settlement on the banks of Suisun Creek, located on the Hatch ranch. Tim came to work for Mr. Hatch at the age of twenty (in 1872). He saved enough to enable him to go to San Francisco, and bring back a shy but lonely little Chinese bride. Here for over 60 years [sic] the couple continued to live, rearing a large family and gathering around them several hundred countrymen until they formed a typical Chinatown.

Tim not only supplied the labor for harvesting crops on the Hatch Ranch, but on adjoining ranches as well. He not only gave to his descendants the heritage of thrift and honor, but a love for the art and culture of the Old World as well. It has been the writer's observations to marvel at the magic touch which time has wrought to a Chinese descendant, reared in simplicity and obscurity in this settlement--to be endowed with an almost palatial home and social positions among the aristocrats of a large

---

[18] Christopher Yee's personal note, July, 1988

city. Surely there must have been culture and refined tastes hidden in the background of that crude Oriental village.[19]

Such views are in stark contrast to the situation found in the Sacramento River Delta where Chinese had little authority on the ranches of whites, and labor was concentrated in sharecropping and unskilled labor.

The labor boss formed a key link between the owner of the ranch and the laborers who tended the orchards, and harvested the fruit. As a result, the labor boss, not the land-owning rancher, was the central person in the Chinese farm worker's life. This situation was necessitated by language, but also reflected the concern of the local white community with maintaining a racially segregated society, and the concern of the Chinese laborers for maintaining familiar cultural institutions. Among these institutions was the patrimonial interest that the boss took in the affairs of his workers and their affairs. Consistent with the nature of such relationships, Mrs. Andrew Lowe recalls nostalgically that her father not only was the boss, but also was well respected as the "big brother" of the workers he had brought to Suisun from China. "My father was very kind, everybody trusted him. Whenever there was an argument, they brought it to 'Big Brother Tim', and he solved everything for them. He was well-respected in the whole camp."

The role of the bilingual labor boss included not only duties as an employer, but as a mediator he could also be called upon to settle disputes, protect the laborers from thieves, engage in labor negotiations with the rancher, as well as hire, fire and maintain discipline within the workforce. A great deal of mutual trust was necessary between the worker and boss, a situation that was facilitated

---

[19] Rosa Lee Baldwin, "Old Timers", *Solano Republican,* Fairfield, October 15, 1936, P.2

by similar roles brought from patrimonial Chinese society. Two legendary examples illustrate the ideals that shaped such relationships between workers and their "boss." Christopher Yee recalls hearing about Chun Pun Leen, a relative of Chun Tim's.

"Just before World War I, Chun Pun Leen farmed.four parcels of land in the Mankas Corner Section of Suisun Valley. Believe it or not, Chun Pun Leen was heavily in debt in 1917 to his Chinese workers and to the Chinese grocery store in San Francisco [from whom he had purchased food for the workers' kitchen]. Although he owed his workers three years of back pay, his workers were still loyal to him. All of a sudden came World War I. He had acres and acres of Bartlett pears which he sent east. Prices were sky high. He made a fortune, consequently. As a gentleman, he paid off his debts to the grocery store in San Francisco, paid off all his workers in full, and in 1921 he returned to his native village in Loong Doo as a rich man . . . his nephew, Chun Buck Inn remained behind to continue farming." [20]

In another example, in 1927, Hatch Ranch foreman, Wong Gee,· also known as Wong Fook Hong, was confronted by a worker "run amuck" in the Big Camp. As the boss, whose implied duties included law enforcement, it was up to him to confront the individual, and shoot him. This he did. The Solano County sheriff had Wong Gee arrested for investigation for murder, but Gee was released the next day after crowds of loyal Chinese crowded around the courthouse demanding Wong Gee's release for what they considered to be justifiable homicide. The sheriff recognized the importance of having Gee play this role, and

---

[20] Christopher Yee's personal note, July 1988.

subsequently, the request of his workers was recognized as being legitimate, and he was released. [21]

Pioneer Families of Go Leung (Long), Lum Foon and Yee Eng

Chinese residents of the Suisun Valley remember their history not as one of dry statistics, demographics, or a shift in agricultural production, but as the rich lives of their family and friends. Although not much information is available about these families, an account of these families is still necessary to provide a brief history of the Chinese in the Suisun Valley.

Go (Leung) Long (1846-1937); Mrs. Go Long (1877-1972)

His Chinese family name was "Leung." However, later it was changed to "Long", because his landlord named his ranch after him as "Long Ranch". His descendants knew the fact, but nobody knew the reason. Mr. Go Long definitely had done something right that earned the respect of his landlord. Long Ranch is near the Mangel Ranch on the south side of the Suisun Valley. Go Long and his wife lived there all their lives and raised sixteen children, seven sons, and nine daughters. He liked his children and worked very hard to raise such big family. Today, Mr. John Pavlina owns this ranch and his foreman William Fong farms it.[22]

---

[21] See *Sacramento Bee* September 17, 1927 and Randy Bechtel, " Hatch Ranch: Site of long ago Chinatown massacre eerie", Daily Republic, Fairfield, October 30, 1985.

[22] Interviews with Ivy Fong, Nira Wong, and Christopher Yee's personal note, July 1988.

Although Go Long was the only child in his family, he migrated to California in 1860's, leaving behind his parents and the comforts of a middle class family in China. He worked on the railroads in Marysville for a short time before he found work in the Suisun Valley.

Mr. Go Long never owned the "Long Ranch" where he lived all his life. He managed the ranch for over sixty years until it was sold. In this ranch, he was able to raise a huge family with sixteen children. The first-born was Willie, then came Albert, Bill, George, Harold, Henry, and Howard. The daughters were Eva, Ivy, Mildred, Gertrude, Grace, May, Mary, Lorraine and Margaret. He adapted many American customs in the family. Nira Fong, one of the granddaughters, recalls that the family always used forks together with their chopsticks at the dining table. Each individual used his own fork to serve food from the different dishes whereas the chopsticks were only used for eating. The children and grandchildren in Long's family not only received "Lucky Money" in red envelops for the traditional Chinese occasions, but also received them for all American festivals, such as Christmas and New Year, as well.

Go Long had a live-in- tutor who taught his children to read Chinese. All of his children could speak and understand their Loong Doo Village dialect. Besides learning Chinese, his children also attended Rockville School. They remembered well their teacher, Mrs. Bauman.

Some of the family members branched out to other areas from Suisun. In 1930s, under his children's names, Go Long purchased two parcels of land in Winters. One was a 30-acre parcel with apricot and peach trees. The other one was a ten-acre tree orchard with a five-bedroom house. The house was surrounded by orange and grapefruit trees. Two of his sons remained active in farming until the 1980s. George farmed in the Winters area. His main crop was apricots, and he farmed as many as 160 acres at one point. The other son Howard farmed on a smaller scale and also dried some apricots each year. Both retired in the 1980s. However, one of the Go Long's grandsons, Melvin Fong is still involved in farming on Abernathy Road, Suisun Valley.

Other children married and moved to San Francisco, Oakland, Watsonville, Bakersfield, and Sacramento areas. His second daughter, Ivy, first married Walter Low and bore three children, Ruth, Wilber, and Tom. Unfortunately, Walter died very young. Several years later, on October 1923, Ivy married Jim Fong. They have two sons, Melvin and Robert, and three daughters, Nira, Elizabeth, and Barbara. Jim Fong was a farmer in Suisun. In 1950s, they bought Shelly Ranch, which was sold in 1980 and now is the site of Fairfield West Plaza.

Ivy Fong was born on February 14, 1900. She was the oldest surviving member of the Chinese farming pioneer families in Fairfield in 1990s. Ivy still states the horse and buggy days, when her father took them to Sacramento to shop for Chinese goods. They would leave early in the morning, and did their shopping quickly. When they returned home, it was dark already. Ivy also remembers a visit to her home by Dr. Sun Yat Sen. Her brother Albert sat on Dr. Sun's lap. Ivy passed away on August 14, 1996 at the age of 96.

Today, there are over 200 Long's descendants who are located all over different parts of California. Although they are engaging in different professions, they were nourished in the Suisun Valley.

Lum Foon (Although not much of Lum Foon's experiences are available, he deserves to be recognized as one of the pioneer Chinese in Suisun Valley).

Lum Foon first worked in Winters, California. Later, he moved to the Miller Ranch in Suisun Valley.[23] Many of his nine children were born there. Although the family was very poor in the early years raising the children, all his boys were engaged in farming. Today Fred Foon still farms with his son Tom on Rockville Road near Interstate 80. Another son, Henry, farms on Abernathy Road. The oldest son, Danny, who passed away at age 75, was also an outstanding farmer. Danny's two sons, Edward and Charles, and even their children became Suisun Valley's top, largest, and most successful farmers in 1980s.

Yee Eng (1890-1977) [24]

Yee Eng's father is Yee Chew Yong, who came to United State from Loong Doo District, Chungshan County. He worked first as a farm laborer in the Sacramento River Delta. Later, he rented land to farm for himself until World War II and returned to China to retire. His son, Yee Eng, joined him in 1908 at the age of 18. He came over on the S.S. Siberia. He obtained his first job as a Chinese cook for the foreman, Lum Mon Inn, of the Pierce Ranch in Suisun Valley. There was a crew of 300 Chinese laborers whom Lum Mon Inn was responsible for feeding.

On February 16, 1923, Yee Chew Yong returned to China to bring back a bride for his son Yee Eng. Before the arrival of the bride, Yee Eng rented a 20-acre orchard from Mr. William Rye in the Mankas Corner area. On this fruit ranch, Yee Eng and his wife raised a family of four sons and one daughter. Later, Yee Eng rented many acres of fruit

---

[23] Interviews with Edward Lum, Michael Bow, and Christopher Yee's personal note of 1988.

[24] Interviews with Christopher Yee and his two personal notes of 1983 and 1988.

orchards to farm besides the Rye Ranch. Yee Eng also served as president of a Chinese land company, Wing Chong Land Company. Yee Eng and his wife lived on the Rye Ranch from 1908 until their death. Yee Eng passed away on November 19, 1977 and his wife died on April 9, 1980. The family fruit-drying business still operates very successfully today.

Marriage and Family of Second Generations

Chun Tim had four daughters and three sons. Only the third son, Youie, remained active in farming. He farmed his entire life. His account is also a focus of this study.

Youie Tim (1895-1978) is a typical story of how a few from the second generation were able to move out of laboring positions and into supervisory roles.[25] He first attempted to follow in his father's footsteps in 1909 as a fourteen year-old. With a friend, Low Lum, he began a ranching venture in Sonoma. After two years, due to an untimely drought, his first venture failed. In 1913 at age 18, he returned to the Suisun Valley to manage the Baldwin Ranch. Youie was inducted into the military during World War I until 1917 when the 24 year-old began to manage the Scholl Ranch. He kept several account books from this period which are still available, and some ideas about life in the Suisun Valley orchards can be gleaned from them. He kept a meticulous rainfall account from 1937 until his death in July 1978 because he believed rainfall had direct impact on his farming activities.

---

[25] Interviews with Roberta Tim Quan, Jennie Tim, John Tim, Lewis Tim

Although Youie Tim continued to live in Chinese Big Camp, the ledgers he kept show that the majority of his workers between 1917-1919 were Anglos and Spanish and not Chinese. Between late 1917 and 1918, Jack Lawrence worked for 187 days at $2.25 per day; another employee, Jack Leonard, worked 72 days at $2.00 per day. In addition, there were 17 employees who were paid at $2.00 per day for 179 days. Total wages paid were $ 922.00. However, in 1919, the four major employees, including Jack Lawrence, George Caldwell, and Modesto Astoga, George Buchert worked 168, 75, 72 and 55 days respectively. In addition, 23 laborers worked between three to 25 days, some even worked overtime. The pay rate went up from $2.00 in 1918 to $4.00 per day in 1919. The total wages paid were $3348. The wage at $4.00 per day was relatively munificent for that time.[26] By comparison, wages for Chinese laborers in the Sacramento Delta during the same period were under $2.00 per day for the same type of labor.

Roberta Tim Quan reflects hearing her mother Jennie describe how she first met her husband, Youie. Youie Tim, Chun Tim's third son and a World War I veteran who had been stationed at Fort MacDowell, was delegated to bring the body of his father back to Loong Doo for burial in the family shrine in 1923. As part of the trip, he also arranged a bride for himself. He found a pretty 16 year-old bride who later came to call herself Jennie. Jennie remembers wondering aloud to her parents about the identity of the strange man from America and asking her parents the reason he was around the house so much. She was surprised to find out that the man was her husband-to-be, but nevertheless soon accepted the situation. In 1924,

---

[26] Youie Tim's farm ledgers,1917-1921.

she was on her way to a clapboard house in the small "Big Camp" on the A. T. Hatch Ranch.

In 1935, at the age of 40, Youie moved his family to the 160-acre Peabody Ranch. He and his partners, Wong Mun, managed it for Mr. W. C. Robbins. A varied product line of apricots, peaches, pears, prunes, and walnuts made the working season almost endless, but this was what Youie loved doing best. During harvesting season, many fruit pickers were hired. Youie had a life-long affiliation with Mexican and Filipino workers and their families. He was well respected, and everyone addressed him as "Boss." A quiet, competent, well-organized man, Youie kept records of workers' hours, wages, and farming expenses. He loved to sit at his desk and pursue his hobby of calligraphy. Town merchants would readily accept his cheques as they were so highly recognizable and distinctive.

In 1948, Youie managed Danielson Ranch for Mr. Robbins. Twelve years later, in 1960, at the age of 65 finally he had an opportunity to purchase the 40-acre Bransford Ranch. He and his two sons, Lewis and John, finally became independent farmers. Nevertheless, with the onset of his age, labor problems, and a poor market in agriculture in 1970s, Youie sold the property to Ambusher Busch, thereby ending three generations of farming in Suisun Valley.

Danny Foon (1900-1975) was the oldest son of Lum Foon, who had nine children. Danny was born in Winters in 1900, but grew up in Rockville, as recalled by his grandson, Michael Bow in 1987. [27] When Danny was 10 years old, he found a job in Isleton making pear boxes for harvesting. Isleton is about 40 miles from Suisun, and

---

[27] Interviews with Michael Bow who is Danny Foon's grandson

Danny's only means of transportation was a bicycle. Danny worked in Isleton during the week, and came home only during the weekends. Because the family was very poor, Danny didn't have enough food to eat. One time about half way returning to Isleton, he was so hungry that he could not continue his trip. Fortunately, a lady took him home and fed him a sandwich. His grandchildren recall the story even today.

Danny only attended elementary school in Rockville for several years. He didn't attend high school. He worked very hard so that he could save enough money to return to China as a young man of 22. To find a bride, he began to ask his friends for advice. In China, he became particularly interested in a picture of a beautiful 16 year-old girl who was later to take the name Elsie. He later married her and brought her back on the *President Coolidge*, steerage class.

Finding wives became a major goal for many Chinese bachelors. The ideal was to return to China and settle there once their fortunes had been made. At least some, at least, must have met this ideal. Often, though, this did not work out, and a number of other alternatives were attempted. Residents in Solano County today recall that their families began with marriages arranged between the more successful farm workers who returned to Loong Doo District, China on short trips to find a wife who could bear children as well as manage their household affairs. Several of the women who arrived under these conditions continue to live in Solano County, honored and cared for by their children.

This system worked because one of the few loopholes in the Chinese Exclusion Act permitted the entrance of brides of shop owners until 1924. Thus, Chinese bachelors would return to their home village in Loong Doo where they would arrange for a traditional bride. Of course,

American families began only by those who returned to California with their husbands. This situation involved a number of complications, including suspected prostitutes, finances, and objections of the brides' family. The difficulty in overcoming each of these situations is reflected by the fact that there were only three Chinese families in the Suisun Valley by the turn of the century, despite the presence of a Chinese population which in the 1870s had numbered in the hundreds.

Although arranged marriages seem strange in modern times, they provided a basis for a stable Chinese community, which was once again growing. However, this time, growth was due to young families rather than an expanding pool of young immigrant agricultural laborers. Jennie Tim remembers that when she arrived in 1924, there were three extended families living in the Big Camp, but as many as 20 Chinese families living in surrounding ranches in the Suisun Valley. Still, it was a male-centered society in the 1920s, and the population was still disproportionately male.[28] Jennie Tim remembers that one consequence of

---

[28] Ivan Light, in " From Vice District to tourist Attraction: The Moral Career of American Chinatowns, 1880-1940, "Pacific Historical Review, 1974, pp.367-394, compiled a table showing the number of males per 100 females for all American citizens, foreign-born whites, and Chinese from census data. The data is as follows:

Year	All Persons	Foreign-born White	Chinese
1880	103.5	115.9	2106.8
1890	104.9	118.7	2678.9
1900	104.6	117.3	1385.0
1910	106.2	129.2	925.7
1920	104.1	121.7	405.7
1930	102.6	115.7	296.4

this was that social life was dominated by male-oriented events such as the harvest festivals of the Suisun Valley and the Delta. She explains that these festivals attracted men from San Francisco as well as the surrounding ranches. Even though she did not go on the harvest festival circuit, Jennie Tim remembers the season as being one of great joy. Usually, the women did not formally attend these festivities.

A close look at a photo of Suisun family Chinese community taken at the memorial ceremony of Dr. Sun Yat Sen in 1925 in Big Camp illustrates who was part of the community. Fully one-third of the people pictured are children. There is still an apparently large proportion of adult men to adult women, but the presence of children indicates that a new type of California Chinese society was emerging in the 1920s.[29]

Third Generation's Memories Growing Up on the Farms
During Depression Era

The children who were born in the 1920s and 1930s, meaning the grandchildren and children of the early

1940	100.8	111.5	224.4
1950	98.7	103.8	161.1
1960	97.1	103.5	133.2
1970	94.8	n.a.	110.6

What these statistics indicate is that foreign-born populations in the United States have had disproportionately large numbers of males. Even given this fact, though, it is clear that Chinese immigrants, particularly in the late 19th century have had even higher proportions of males than other immigrant groups.

[29] Jennie Tim's family photo albums.

pioneers, recall the hard work of their immigrant predecessors with a mixture of nostalgia and envy for an era that was somehow "more interesting." "Those old-timers were real characters," recalls Eva Yee, the daughter of Yee Eng. "They had interesting lives, not like us today; we're kind of boring." She recalls nostalgically the two-mile walk to the Suisun District School where she attended through the eighth grade in the 1940s. One of these interesting stories was recounted by Julian Timm whose mother found herself without a home in Suisun Valley as a result of a prolonged stay in San Francisco:

"Our resourceful mother found that there was an empty wooden gas station that was clean and habitable, and she though it would be a nice house if repaired and with my Uncle Gum's permission, it was bought for $25 and moved to Uncle Gum's farm nearby on Russell Road. Like an old time barn raising in the mid-west, all the Chinese farm workers came by, and helped raise the structure, now a house and had it repaired. In appreciation, my mother fed them all a big dinner..."

Eva Yee also remembers stories about the old days when the old-timers gathered at night. They would talk about the hard times, the parties, and young brides from China. Perhaps they also played the gambling games for which the Chinese community was so well known. Through the eyes of her own childhood, she also recalls the thrill of wading in the slough as a young girl to catch the large "sucker" fish that were at the bottom. Considered too bony by others in the community, she remembers that her parents would chop the meat up, bones and all, to make a tasty fish paste.

Eva, however, has less nostalgia for the hours she spent in the 1940s in the summer or after school slicing and pitting fruits in the drying shed of her father's ranch. "During the season we would work well into the night," she recalls. Special lights were installed in order to permit the after hours labor. Roberta Tim Quan has a slightly different view:

"I always looked forward to summer even if I knew the physical labors such as cutting fruit, picking prunes and walnuts would bring sheer exhaustion. Summer meant the itinerant workers and their families would be encamped to help with the harvest. After a full day of labor, the children would gather to play baseball, "kick-the-can," or "hide-and-seek" until it was dark. I loved their company as the rest of the year, I only had my three older brothers for companionship. I envied the Mexican and Filipino families who lived in temporary shelters erected with wooden trays and canvas tent on a dirt floor....it was so exotic!...We had one of the more "comfortable" camps as Dad had built two shower rooms for the workers. The single men lived in a separate bunkhouse and a cook was hired to feed them. I remember that the Filipino workers didn't care for the showers, but preferred to soak their weary bodies in a hot tub. They dug a hole in the ground and lined it with large rocks leaving room for a pit. A large wooden tub was placed above and filled with water. The entire structure was wood enclosed [as a] bath house! Logs were placed in the pit to heat the water . . . a precursor to today's sauna!"

Julian Timm recalls visiting his uncle Youie's house: "During fruit harvest time mother and I would cut fruit. My father, Sam, worked picking fruit and Mother and I would cut fruit. Father also helped supervise the Spanish and Portuguese seasonal workers that my uncle hired. This was right in the middle of the Great Depression, and the seasonal help moved their entire families in, pitching tents to live on the farm during summer school vacation. Farm life was hard; my mother cooked Chinese full course meals three times a day besides working out on the farm; in summer she picked wind blown fruit--it was stoop labor--in between cooking. During fruit cutting time she also cut fruit consisting of apricots, then peaches, and finally pears. Peach cutting was a miserable chore because the fuzz got into your skin and you were always itchy. When mealtime came, my mother rang a small "church bell" which could be heard a mile away. The workers would come in from the field and dry yards to eat, and they were always hungry because of the physical labor of fruit picking and yard lifting of the fruit-laden trays. My mother cooked big meals to keep the workers happy; the meals were always tasty. We had chicken for many of our meals as they grew semi-wild on the farm and protected themselves by roosting in some walnut trees at night..."

This is an important period in the history of Suisun Valley's Chinese community, because it includes the death of Chun Tim and the massacre at Big Camp. The Youie's account books for 1932-34 provide another indication of the changes which had occurred in the larger community in the interim.

At this time, Youie was foreman on the Scholl Ranch. Because this period was at the height of the Great Depression, wages had fallen to $2.25 for a 10 hour day. This hardship is reflected not just in the entries Youie made with his neat English calligraphy before the name of each farm worker, but also in the $300-$400 losses that each of the six Chinese partners from the ranch suffered.[30] For Youie's daughter, Roberta Tim Quan, such problems were reflected in the personal deprivations of Depression-era childhood.

Toys were few and far in between as money was not to be wasted on such frivolous items. Thus, we were most ingenious with our creative endeavors with the resources available. A discarded metal can lid nailed to a

---

[30] Youie Tim's farm ledgers, 1932-1934.

stick was something to roll along the ground. Nail wheels on a box, add a handle, and you have a wagon. A handkerchief folded correctly and tied with a string produced an instant doll. Y-shaped branches and a piece of rubber made for hours of slingshot entertainment. After Dad (we affectionately addressed him as "Pop") dynamited dead trees, it always left a giant hole in the ground. Brother Lewis and I spent hours in the pit running little metal trucks and cars over the fresh dirt and bugs.

John Tim was born in 1927 at China Camp. When he was a child, during the 1930, there was not much social life on the ranch. He notes "We didn't have radio, no telephone. All we got was newspaper, but my grandmother (Chun Tim's wife Ding Shee) would tell us Chinese fairy tales and old times stories sitting next to the stove after dinner. My grandmother came from China in 1868 about six years old. Before she got married, she earned a living by sewing at home in San Francisco."[31]

Andrew Lowe came to join his father in America in 1939 at age 14 and remembers his first job picking in the orchards:

"My father [who was foreman on a ranch in Winters] was worrying that I could not stand the hot weather [in Winters]. He sent me to work in Suisun. More than ten Chinese 'labor farmers' worked on that ranch. My pay was two dollars per day, and included three meals. What I remember is that on one summer night in August, there was a heavy rain. We were told to put out the drying fruit at two [in the morning]..I earned $120 for the whole season."[32]

---

[31] Interviews with John Tim, Youie Tim's son

[32] Interviews with Andrew Lowe who married Chun Tim's second daughter.

The nature of the workforce also changed as the next group in California's succession of immigrant farm labor arrived. Many of the workers names in the account books of the 1930s are Mexicans, reflecting the Filipino and Mexican origins of the farm workers. Due to the hard times, several Chinese names also appeared in the column of farm laborers hired for the harvest. Many of the Chinese were older men who had been unable to find work elsewhere. Andrew Lowe emphasizes that at 14, he was by far the youngest. "Most of the workers working with me were a generation older, around thirty to seventy."

As with other ranches in California, Scholl Ranch ran a company store from which workers could purchase essentials. As foreman, it was Youie Tim's responsibility to maintain the accounts for the store. Here, we get an indication of the goods that the meager wages were able to purchase. Perhaps the most consistent item is the ubiquitous Prince Albert tobacco. But the other interests of the farm workers from the 1930s are reflected in the newspapers they bought. However, they still managed to send the occasional $20 remittance to family in China.[33]

Community Life and Schooling:

The emerging community life reflected not just the problems of elderly migrant farm workers, but the children of the third generation Chinese in the community who went back and forth between the American world of their schools. The Chinese world they found at the ranch quarters were also affected by trade with the outside world. Roberta Tim Quan recalls,

---

[33] Youie Tim's farm ledgers, 1932-34 .

"We rarely needed to go to town to purchase food as so many travelling peddler wagons arrived at our doorsteps. I can recall the fish wagon, a meat truck, and a vehicle filled with delicious baked goods. Everyone carried a variety of convenience items as well. I would save my coins and purchase a ten-cent box of Cracker Jacks for the coveted prize inside. Frequently it was a metal toy, NOT plastic!"

Unlike the Sacramento River Delta Region, separate elementary schools for "Orientals" were not established in the Suisun Valley, despite the substantial Chinese and Japanese immigrant communities. Indeed, each of Chun Tim's seven children was sent to the local school in Rockville. Mrs. Andrew Lowe (Chun Tim's daughter) remembered attending Rockville School at the turn of the century. "It was a long way for walking. We didn't have a car...it was difficult in winter and on rainy days." In 1992, she continued: "I loved to attend school... always looking forward to getting a library book to take home to read on Fridays. I graduated with the highest average of 98 [students]." She stayed at Rockville School from age 10 to 16 before going to San Francisco for high school. Notably, this was an opportunity that her older brother Youie did not share. After finishing eighth grade at Rockville School, he began his work in the orchards. [34]

The stability that the elementary schools afforded is described by Julian Timm, who had particularly warm feelings for Mrs. Bauman, who taught him 5th through 8th grades in the 1930s. She was also taught his father, Sam, some 20-odd years earlier. "Mrs. Bauman was an excellent teacher and I learned math and geography from her and from reading the small library which held books on Greek

---

[34] Interviews with Mrs. Andrew Lowe (Lin Tim, Chun Tim's second daughter)

mythology, Rafael Sabatini, and Zane Grey adventure novels besides others. It was a happy time for us; we were together as a family."

Photographs of the one or two room rural school show that the classes with Caucasian, Chinese, and Japanese students quickly lead to integration into American society. Among the Caucasian students, old-timers remember there were Spaniards and Mexicans. Inevitably, such education oriented the children of Chinese immigrants away from their home culture and towards the new American culture. And as with many immigrants, this was a tendency both encouraged and discouraged by parents.

Thus, Jennie Tim proudly recounts that each of her five children have gone to college and embarked upon conventional American lives. She also recognizes that this was not without cost, though, and at one point in the 1930s attempted to curb it by sponsoring a weekend Chinese school on the Wang Chern Ranch. However, Chinese education has always been problematic for the immigrants to California. Her husband Youie and the other children of Chun Tim were lucky and learned their Chinese characters informally from their father's bookkeeper/accountant. Today, Jennie Tim proudly recalls that her first son, Lund, was one of the best students in the weekend Chinese class at the Wang Chern Ranch in the 1930s. But she also knows that the school was open for only about two years. As a result, her younger children were not able to attend and cannot read or write Chinese.

Retirement and Home Country Politics

Retirement inevitably came for the Chinese men persistent enough to spend their careers in California agriculture. Before the Communist revolution in 1949, that time also brought a choice: whether to return to their home village to retire or remain in the United States. Marriage and children often dictated the decision. For example, Yee Chew Yong arrived from Loong Doo as a single male in about 1890, shortly after his young wife gave birth to his son. His son, Yee Eng, joined him at age 18 in the United States in 1908. Yee Chew Yong then returned to China in 1923 to bring a bride back for him. War prevented him from returning to China until after the end of World War II when he retired to China. His son, though, was not able to return after the Communist Revolution, and partly as a result, the family has become firmly established as Americans.

In many respects, the firm alignment of Suisun Valley with the Chinese Nationalist (Kuomintang) Party of Chiang Kai Shek forced what was an emerging social fact: the emergence of Suisun Valley's community as an American society. The Communist victory in 1949 meant that the regular trips back to China, whether for brides, retirement, or to pay respects to the ancestral shrine in Loong Doo, were stopped from 1949 until the late 1970s. While some contact was maintained by letter during this period, the ardent KMT Nationalist stance of the old-timers precluded the more intimate relations which had existed between about 1900 and 1949.

While it is uncertain how or why the ardent anti-Communist stance of the Suisun Valley Chinese emerged, it is apparent that there were strong KMT Nationalist feelings at a very early date. Ivy Fong recalls Dr. Sun visited her home and Christopher Yee claims hearing about the visit of

Dr. Sun Yat Sen to the Hatch Ranch's Big Camp during his visit to the USA in 1909.[35] At the time, Sun was one of many anti-Manchu agitators canvassing support for the Nationalist effort to overthrow the Ch'ing dynasty. When Dr. Sun Yat Sen visited Suisun, accompanied by Chauncy Chew from Courtland in 1909, the Chinese hosted a big party for him at the Hatch Ranch. He was here to canvas support to overthrow the Manchu rulers of the Ch'ing Dynasty. Dr. Sun Yat Sen was the first Chinese allowed to sleep in an American Hotel in Suisun City, the Arlington, although racial discrimination prevailed at that time. Chinese also found that their living quarters in China camps was not convenient to host him so they made special arrangements for him to stay overnight in an American hotel."[36]

Evelyn Lockie wrote about visiting a Chinese "bossman" on the Towner Ranch about 1912. "I used to make regular visits [as a young girl] to the bossman who lived n the Towner Ranch. Once he had a brand new picture up on his wall, and he told me that it was Dr. Sun Yat Sen, the new president of China and that he was a great man." [37] One of the reasons for Dr. Sun's continuing support was his ability to stimulate anti-Manchu interest among the overseas Chinese communities in Hawaii and California which were largely from the same small area of Guangdong province in which he himself was born. Indeed, Dr. Sun himself had a personal connection to California. Two of his uncles had died during sojourns to

---

[35] Dr. Sun visited Suisun Valley was confirmed by Ivy Fong, Christopher Yee, and Jack Chew. Jack Chew said his father Chauncy Chew accompanied Dr. Sun to Suisun from Courtland.

[36] Interviews with Christopher Yee and his personal note.

[37] Evelyn Lockie's letter to the author, Peter C. Y. Leung, Jan. 8, 1987.

the California Gold fields in the mid-19th century. In Suisun Valley history, Dr. Sun's fund-raising visit to the Hatch Ranch was especially memorable.

The KMT politics of Dr. Sun, and later those of Chiang Kai Shek, have always been central to the maintenance of loyalty in the small Chinese community in the Suisun Valley. KMT fundraisers were continually rewarded in their trips through the Suisun Valley, reflects Jennie Tim, who continues to be a strong supporter. She indicates several of the extensive fund-raising efforts during the 1930s and 1940s to which the Suisun community loyally subscribed, and she proudly recalls donating a gold necklace to the cause. There was also $10,000 donated to defend China during the war with Japan and bigger yet, there was a $75,000 war bond purchased from the KMT. The Chinese of the Suisun Valley also contributed to a memorial to the martyrs of the Chinese revolution during 1910s in Canton City.[38] She asserts this interest, was due to the common origin of the Loong Doo villagers and Dr. Sun in Chungshan County of China. And despite the fact that several of her children have visited her home village since 1980, Jennie refuses to go back for a visit "as long as the Communists are in power."

Moving into American Society: The Purchase of Land, and the Third Generation Enters the Professions

In the 1880 agriculture census manuscript, a 978-acre farm owned by Chinese, Ah Wing and Hong Tong Vey, was already recorded in Suisun Township.[39] Despite laws prohibiting the ownership of land by Chinese, Chinese

---

[38] Interviews with Jennie Tim.

[39] Sucheng Chan, *This Bittersweet Soil*, p. 265.

in the Suisun Valley were still able to obtain ranches sporadically. Mrs. Andrew Lowe remembers that several Chinese who owned Loong Doo Ranch. She recalled that one of the partners, Mr. Ching, bought a ranch during World War I because he did not want his sons to become soldiers.[40]

The Yee family claims that they owned land as early as the 1910s, although Christopher Yee admits to being confused about how this was possible given the legal status of Chinese in those days. Sucheng Chan indicates that there were 60-70 legally filed leases in the area during 1900-20.[41] Although it is not understood how the laws were circumvented, it is clear that by the turn of the century, there were at least two Chinese-owned land companies farming pears in the Suisun Valley. In addition, American-born sons of the Chinese immigrants also owned land.

Gradually, as the years passed, the second generation of Chinese was able to rise among the ranks of the major farm owners of Solano County. However, just as surely as the second generation had occupied the farmland, the third generation began to sell out. Armed with college degrees and tempted by the financial offers of Fairfield developers, the actual time in outright ownership of the land was often relatively brief. Chun Tim never actually owned a farm. The one son who followed him into farming, Youie, was not able to purchase his own fruit ranch until 1960 at age 65. Even then, his purchase was not to remain a farming venture for long. In 1968, Youie's ranch was sold to Anheuser Busch for the construction of

---

[40] Interviews with Mrs. Andrew Lowe.

[41] Sucheng Chan, " Chinese Livelihood in Rural California: The Impact of Economic Change, 1860-1880," *Pacific Historical Review*, 1986, pp. 282-83. And Christopher Yee's personal note, July, 1988.

the brewery, which now can be seen from Interstate 80. The proceeds from the factory were adequate to purchase a suburban home where Youie continued to live until his death in 1978, and his widow, Jennie, lives to this day. Another example is the second wife of Chun Mon Gum, Fong Wai Yee. Her son, Lloyd, continues to supervise the 13 acres of fruit trees that remain.[42] Like his siblings and cousins, his main work has been as a professional, first as an industrial chemist and then was Solano County deputy sheriff.

Roberta Tim Quan reminisces her own break with the rural life nostalgically:

"After years of this established pattern of farm life, I was very excited to move away and attend an institution of higher learning at the University of California, Berkeley. But in retrospect, I had many rich and fond memories of a special childhood and experiences that today's children will not know. We are no longer an agrarian society with a definite set of inculcated values. ... In terms of materialism, it was sparse. In terms of a unique childhood, it was rich. It was well worth the journey."

Despite the one-time presence of thousands of Chinese in Suisun agriculture, about twenty families actually established themselves. In 1990s, only two families, the Yees and the Foons, continued in agriculture. Both families have developed enterprises in the agribusiness model of the rest of California agriculture. The Foon family holdings are today among the largest in Solano County and include not only fruit trees, but also row crops where orchards once grew.[43] The Yee family has survived

---

[42] Interviews with Lloyd Chan (Sam Tim's son, Chun Tim's grandson)

[43] Interviews with Edward and Charlie Lum and Lawrence Clement, Solano County Experimental Station Farm Advisor.

by carving a niche for itself in the dried fruit market. In addition to selling fruit to the large packers such as Del Monte and Sunsweet, Cal Yee farms has a drying and packaging business that specializes in marketing Chinese-style dried fruits among the West Coast's rapidly growing ethnic Chinese communities.[44] Several of the third generation pioneer families continue their family legacy in farming. With their family's full support, these children obtained their higher education at the best universities. They returned to the valley to expand the farming enterprise. With the farm they already worked on and the knowledge and decades of practical experience, the young generation no longer had the obstacles that their parents had to face.

John Tim earned his B.S. degree from University of California, Davis in Agricultural Economics. John remembers that "after I graduated, I tried to find a job in the cities, but it was difficult. My father needed help, so I decided to come back to the Suisun Valley to become a farmer, since it didn't seem to be such a bad life. Although at that time we were still using manual labor." John Tim continued, "All business decisions were made by my father. I learned new farming techniques from the university, but my father followed his traditional ways. Sometimes I found it very frustrating. For example, we were spraying by hand, I asked why didn't we buy equipment that did it automatically. He wouldn't have anything to do with it. But after several years when all other farmers started to switch over, he finally relented."[45]

The four sons of the Yee family all attended college. First son, Christopher, has a Master's Degree in

---

[44] Interviews with Christopher Yee and his personal note, July 1988.
[45] Interviews with John Tim.

Business Administration from University of California at Berkeley. Second son, George, studied Industrial Arts at San Jose State University; third son, Peter, studied Pomology at University of California, Davis; and the fourth son, Donald, studied Gasoline and Diesel Mechanics at a university in Los Angeles.

Christopher and George started a fruit drying business in 1948 when they were in college. Their plan worked well because fruits are dried in the summer months when college was out. The two brothers learned the art of drying when they were young helping their father. By 1951, the two brothers were doing a substantial volume of business, drying apricots and pears. The Mankas Corner section of Suisun Valley is ideal for fruit drying because it is hotter here than other parts of the valley, with excessive winds, and lacking excessive dew in the mornings. The family finally purchased the fruit orchard from Mr. William Rye in 1951 and built this place into a modern drying plant for fruits. The first thing that the family did was to build a new cutting shed and sulphur houses. As time went by, a garage and equipment shed, labor camp for Mexican laborers, tray storage shed, and pear dehydrator were built. Lastly, a new house and office were constructed by 1955.

Yee Eng's wife knew how to make preserved dried fruits with Chinese spices. The Chinese style dried fruits are consumed as candy in the United States. Her son, Christopher, began to conduct market research for preserved fruits to determine whether there was a market for this Chinese-type of preserved fruits. As a result, Christopher found that Hawaii was the best market for Chinese style preserved fruits. The first shipment of the new product from Suisun to Hawaii left on August 12, 1958. Not only did he conduct research on preserved fruits, but also he made salted pumpkin and squash seeds. His results showed that squash seeds are superior because the

Chinese prefer the ones with the larger seed. By December 22,1958, their first shipment of seeds left for Hawaii. Today, the product is still viable and popular throughout the United States and Canada.

The family formed the trade name "Cal Yee." With their success, the "Cal Yee" firm has a capacity to dry 3,000 tons of fresh fruits per year. They have handled about 1,000 tons of apricots, 1,100 tons of peaches, 500 tons of pears, and 400 tons of nectarines. At this volume, the family can maintain quality and cost control. One-half of the fruits dried is kept for their company to pack, and the other half is sold to independent packers.

The responsibilities and functions of the firm have been divided among the four brothers. Christopher was in charge of administration until his death in 1991 at age 66, George was responsible for all the machinery, equipment, and buildings. Peter was in charge of the fruit orchards, retailing, and wholesales. Donald was in charge of repair and maintenance of the machinery and equipment. Christopher was active in community service. He had served on the Mario Sengo Museum Board of Directors and was actively involved in many business associations. The Yee brothers are truly a uniquely successful example to be proud of by those pioneers who first set foot in Suisun Valley.

Conclusion - An Ethnic Farming Community in California

Studies of ethnic immigrants tend to speak of the culture or community as being monolithic and isolated from the rest of society. Particularly prior to World War II this was at least partly true in the Suisun Valley. Customs and laws insured that new immigrant groups, and particularly non-whites, had carefully defined positions within society. These norms played an important role in defining what the Chinese of Suisun Valley did with their time, including where they lived and the jobs they could hold. On the other hand, despite the presence of such norms, relationships did occur across the ethnic boundaries that shaped both the Chinese community in Suisun Valley and other communities as well.

Such relationships developed first in the context of work--the Chinese were in Suisun Valley to work in the orchards, and had to have a relationship, directly or indirectly, with the white owners of the land. A second area was through the administration of justice. Self-regulation was permitted and subsequently developed in the small Chinese camps. Conventional wisdom among the white community of the day indicated a belief in the omnipotence of these communities' leadership, and as a result a great deal of internal regulation of social norms was permitted.

But it is also true that in other cases, such as situations involving outsiders or more serious crimes like murder, the sheriff and courts quickly became involved. Particularly in the earlier parts of the 20th century, opium use was not limited to only the Chinese community, but there were substantial numbers of whites entering the dens to smoke and gamble.

Sociologist Ivan Light has written extensively about the vice-oriented relationship that the Chinatowns had with surrounding mainstream society and claims that this emerged because it was an effective way to isolate such activities from the surrounding society.[46]

Nevertheless, in the days of prohibition, the attention of the authorities was often directed at controlling the opium. This attention shaped white-Chinese relations as is reflected in the comments of Solano County resident Fred Salesman in a 1985-newspaper article. Salesman apologetically stated that the white community feared the Chinese due to the wide acceptance of stereotypes that emphasized the role that vice played in the relationships between whites and Chinese. "When we thought of Chinese in those days we thought of dope peddlers -- dope fiends," he recalled." We didn't think of Chinese people as humans in those days. They were absolutely forbidden to own property. They were chattels. They were merchandise . . . I was taught to beware of the heathens." Ironically, as sociologist Light points out, the opium dens were frequented by whites as well as Chinese, and this was a point of contact between the older Chinese male community and the surrounding community of white males.

This was not the whole story, though. Particularly as the all-male society slowly began to gain women and children and the proportion of single males declined, different types of relationships began to emerge in the schools and between individuals. Christopher Yee fondly

------

[46] Ivan Light, "From Vice District to Tourist Attraction: The Moral Career of American Chinatowns, 1880-1940," *Pacific Historical Review* 1974, pp. 367-394. An opium raid on the Wilson Ranch near Vacaville in September 1928 resulted in the arrest of two Chinese proprietors, and the flight of 22 persons of unspecified race were "hitting the pipe or gambling." (*Dixon Tribune*, p.1, 9/7/28).

remembers Mr. Pierce, a man who owned the second largest ranch in the Suisun Valley. Yee's father, Yee Eng, obtained his first job in the Suisun Valley on the Pierce ranch after World War I where he was the Chinese cook for the foreman on the ranch. "As far as the Chinese laborers are concerned, Mr. Pierce was the best boss. He treated the Chinese with dignity and respect." In a 1985 newspaper article, Lewis Pierce III stated having particularly close relations with the Chinese who lived on his father's ranch and claimed that he "grew up" with the Chinese.[47]

Evelyn Lockie, who remembered visiting the small "Big Camp" to sell pigs from her father's ranch as well as to buy rice, tells a similar story. During her visits, the ranch foreman, Wong Gee, would buy her bottles of strawberry soda pop from the town store. She also recalls that her best friend's little brother used to run away to live with the Chinese laundrymen who lived in Suisun City. Evelyn Lockie herself maintained a lifetime relationship with Chun Tim's son, Chun Mon Gum, until Gum's death at age 91 in 1978.[48]

The emergence of families also meant that children were raised to both honor Chinese customs while seeking to accept the responsibilities of American citizenship. As with many Americans, the demands of military service proved to be an important. Chun Tim's son, Youie, served in the military during World War I. In honor of his service, Youie, became a lifetime member of the Fairfield Branch of the American Legion and he attended meetings faithfully. A grandson of Chun Tim, Lock entered the military as an

---

[47] Christopher Yee's personal note, July, 1988

[48] Evelyn Lockie's personal letter to the author, Peter C. Y. Leung, October 15, 1986

officer after graduating from UC Berkeley and died in the invasion of Normandy during World War II. [49]

Many of the second and third generation attended universities. They used this education as an entry into the work force, whether in managing family orchards, or more frequently, as professionals in non-agricultural careers.

Status in traditional Chinese culture is measured by how many of your descendants continue to honor you after death. For the early Chinese in California, this meant returning the ashes of the body to China for internment in the ancestral shrine. Chun Tim's immediate family followed the same practice. After Chun Tim died in 1923, his son, Youie, brought his ashes to China. However, time and conditions of such practices changed a great deal for the Chinese-Americans in the 1970s. Efforts were initiated to return Chun Tim's ashes to Suisun Valley, California where it seemed his descendants would remain. At the time, this was a complicated process since the United States and China began to redevelop a new diplomatic relationship. Nevertheless, in 1978, the ashes of Chun Tim were returned to his adopted country. He was interred in Rockville Cemetery in Suisun Valley, not far from the Hatch Ranch. Next to him were his wife, Ding Shee, and their three sons, Gum, Sam, and Youie.

The Chinese pioneers and their descendants are buried in Rockville Cemetery, Suisun Valley. There was no segregated policy of burial sites for Chinese and whites in Suisun Valley. Many early Chinese laborers were buried in unmarked graves near the foothill of the Rockville Cemetery. Chun Tim and other Chinese tombs are nearby A. T. Hatch's tomb.

---

[49] Interviews with Roberta Tim Quan and Jennie Tim.

The Chinese pioneers are always remembered in a unique way. Every year during Ching Ming, a traditional Chinese Memorial Day, a multitude of descendants gather together in the Rockville Cemetery. Consistent with Chinese tradition, a whole roast pig, flowers, and fruits are displayed in front of the tombs. Ceremonial paper money and incenses are burnt for sending off the dead to heaven, and firecrackers are lit to ward off evil spirits. Reverence is shown by kowtowing three times in front of the tombs by children, grandchildren, relatives, and friends. It is the last remaining folk ritual that continues to be practiced by the Chinese descendants in Suisun Valley, California. It is the Chinese Pioneer families' legacy and a vital chapter of Chinese American history in the Suisun Valley.

Honoring
Dr. March Fong Eu
Cliff and Vicki Beaton

From a Daughter of Laundry Operator to an Educator, Legislator, California Secretary of State, U.S. Ambassador and Artist

Introduction

Dr. March Fong Eu (photo on page 95) served as the California Secretary of State for five terms lasting two decades from 1974 to 1994. When she was first elected in 1974, she received over three million votes. In her third election in 1986, her vote totaled nearly five million. In her fifth campaign, she received over 75% of the votes. She became one of the first women and the first American of Chinese descent to serve in the California Legislature in 1966. She has changed the face of California politics for Chinese-Americans by representing Chinese American interests. Her distinguished legislative record of more than 400 bills reflected Dr. Eu's wide spectrum of expertise and interest.

Prior to her election as an Assemblywoman to represent parts of Oakland and Castro Valley, Dr. Eu served three terms on the Alameda County Board of Education and was president of the Board during her third term. She received a bachelor's degree from the University of

California at Berkeley, a master's degree from Mills College, and a Doctorate of Education from Stanford University. She taught and served as an educational consultant in the Oakland, Alameda and Santa Clara County Public Schools. She also taught at Mills College.

Dr. Eu is a third-generation Californian of Chinese descent. With a distinguished career in California politics, she deserves a place in California's history as well as in Chinese and Asian American history. Historians, political scientists, biographers, writers and researchers must go through thousands of documents and records during her tenure to understand her contributions and accomplishments. Her dynamic involvement in constitutional, administrative duties, Voting Rights Act, voter registration, getting funding for a new building for California State Archives and promoting the export of California agricultural and industrial products across the country and around the world needs to be documented.

In this book, we honor her as the Chinese American who reached a highest position in the state government. Our accolades will not be adequate to illustrate her achievements as well as her leadership in California's political arena. She is our inspiration and is leading us continuously to build a better California for future generations. She is not only highly respected in the Chinese American communities across the United States, but she is a true Californian and American with the qualities of the Chinese. She encourages us not to be intimidated by American political parties who have often manipulated and made Chinese-Americans scapegoats to advance their agendas. We must continue to build a visible Chinese American identity and image that will not be contaminated by biased American politicians and media. In addition, we must fight for our rights as Chinese-Americans in California and the United States. We will respect both great nations (U.S.A and China) when governments are negotiating their own interests and rights in the stage of world politics, but we should not be treated unfairly as American citizens.

Highlights of Dr. Eu's Contributions

The following is a summary of Dr. Eu's accomplishments and contributions during her 45 years of public service.

Elections and Political Reform

Ensuring the right of Californians to have elections conducted fairly and efficiently was a hallmark of Secretary of State Eu's administration. Since 1975, she conducted 17 statewide elections without a problem. Her reforms have been a model for the nation. These reforms include:

Voter Registration by Mail: Dr. Eu sponsored legislation in 1975 to allow voters to register to vote by mail. Voter registration hit an all-time record of 14 million in October of 1988.

Chief Election Officer: Also in 1975, legislation proposed by Dr. Eu led to the designation of the Secretary of State as California's chief election officer.

Political Reform Act Implementation: In January 1975, Dr. Eu established the political Reform Division to handle the filing responsibilities dictated by the voter-approved Political Reform Act of 1974. Lobbyist and campaign-related disclosure reports are made available for public inspection within 48 hours of receipt.

Absent Voter Ballots: In 1978, legislation supported by Dr. Eu eliminated the requirement that a voter must provide a specific reason when requesting an absentee ballot. She established an absentee voting task force to examine ways to ensure that voting by mail is both safe and convenient.

Voter registration Drives and Outreach Programs: In August, 1984, Dr. Eu launched an toll-free voter registration line (1-800-345-Vote) which proved to be a highly effective program to register voters. A TDD line for hearing impaired was added in 1986 and in 1990, the audio service was expanded to include a separate line for Spanish-speaking voters.

Implementation of the voting Accessibility for the Elderly and Handicapped Act: Dr. Eu sponsored legislation and established programs that allow elderly and handicapped voters access to all phases of the democratic process.

Elections Investigator: In 1986, Dr. Eu hired the first elections investigator to crack down on elections fraud.

Automation of Campaign/Lobbyist Reporting Information: In 1990, Dr. Eu implemented an on-line computer system for lobbyist and campaign filer information that provides access to the complete list of candidate and ballot measure committees filed with her office. In 1994 elections, her office included use of optical scanning technology to make contribution and expenditure information available on-line.

Notaries Public

Dr. Eu spearheaded the first major revision of notary public laws since the program began in 1859.

Notary Law Revision: Legislation sponsored by Dr. Eu in 1977 brought the first substantial changes in the way notaries are governed. It created the toughest law in the nation, and earned Dr. Eu the 1979 National Notary Association's Achievement Award.

Notary Investigators: Dr. Eu secured budgetary resources in 1977 to hire the nation's first full-time notary public investigator to weed out the relatively few notaries who were abusing their seals and violating the public trust.

Dr. Eu also established the Notary Liaison Committee, New Notary Examination and Regulation of Sale and Manufacture of Notary Seals. Notaries have to obtain a certificate of authorization from the Secretary of State to purchase a new seal bearing the ID number.

State Archives

Push for New Archives Building: Dr. Eu finally convinced the Legislature and Governor to enact legislation to provide the authority and the funding for construction of a new archival facility, which began in 1991 and was completed in 1994.

Travelling and Stationary Exhibit Programs: During Dr. Eu's tenure, California established the only travelling exhibit program in the nation. Exhibits are also featured in the Archives Exhibit Hall, State Capitol Museum Archives Room, and in the State Building in downtown Los Angeles.

Governor's Papers: In 1983, Dr. Eu supported legislation requiring that the public papers of every governor elected after 1986 be placed in the State Archives when the governor leaves office. Its enactment ensures that an important body of public policy history remains part of the public record in the Archives.

Corporations

Legislative Changes: Legislation in 1975, supported by Dr. Eu, revised the laws governing stock corporations in California. Similar legislation in 1980 revised nonprofit corporation laws. The Secretary of State was also given added power to suspend corporations that fail to comply with statutory requirements.

Satellite Offices: A Los Angeles office was opened in 1972 to handle the corporate-related needs of the area. In October of 1982, Dr. Eu opened a San Francisco Office, and in 1986 she opened an office in San Diego. All offices are self-supporting through special handling fees.

Information Automation: In 1986 the corporate files in the office were fully automated and in 1990 were made available via computer.

Limited Partnerships

After pushing bills for several years to establish a statewide limited partnership filing program, Dr. Eu finally secured passage of legislation to open a Limited Partnership Division, the first major change since 1949.

Program Implementation: The Limited Partnership Division was established in 1982 to provide for the transitional filing period. In July 1990, the office accepted the filing of California's 100,000[th] limited partnership.

Full Automation of Records: The Limited partnership Division is the first fully-automated division within the office. All information is entered "on-line" into an ITT computer system.

Uniform Commercial Code

Dr. Eu emphasized the need for improved service in this unit, and succeeded in speeding up turn-around time for providing information to the public.

Increased and Improved Service: She increased training staff, acquiring new equipment, revised office procedures, and renewed employee commitment to provide prompt, efficient service.

Implementation of Prepay Accounts and a No-billing Policy: A computerized "charge-to-my account" type of accounting system for frequent-user clients provided faster service. Combined with a new policy of requiring advance payment for reproduction orders, the Secretary of State saved thousands of dollars annually.

Judgment Liens: In July of 1983 legislation assigned the duty of accepting and filing judgment liens against debtors to the Uniform Commercial Code Division.

Trade Promotion

Legislation sponsored by Secretary of State Eu created the California State World Trade Commision in 1983. The Secretary of State served as an ex-officio member of the Commission, a role she relished as it enabled her to continue her efforts to increase California's export markets overseas and to maintain a long-standing commitment and association she had with the state's agricultural community.

Conclusion

Dr. Eu has received numerous awards and recognition from local communities, professional and political organizations, state and federal governments, from the United States to other world nations. Although she retired as U.S. Ambassador to the Federated States of Micronesia in 1997, she has not disappeared from the Chinese American community or American politics. While she continues to mentor a new generation of Chinese-Americans into American politics, she has found time to be a devoted learner of Chinese brush painting and Chinese calligraphy. She also begins a new phase of her art development into oils as influenced by her Chinese brush paintings. Her paintings have been widely exhibited in California, Taiwan and China.

The Sacramento Chinese Culture Foundation salutes Dr. Eu in this book in the spirit of *150 Years of Chinese Presence inCalifornia: Honor the Past, Engage the Present and Build the Future.* We are proud of Dr. Eu. The Organization of Chinese-Americans and many other organizations will continue your legacy in California as we enter a new century.

LEGENDARY RESTAURATEUR FRANK FAT (Dong Sai Fat)

Peter C. Y. Leung

It would be misleading to dwell on the limitations of Puritan ethics without emphasizing (their) enormous contribution ... to political freedom and social progress ... The virtues of enterprise, diligence, and thrift are the indispensable foundation of any complex and vigorous civilization.
-- Richard Tawney, *Religion and the Rise to Capitalism*

Two blocks from the State Capitol Building in Sacramento is a long-standing mealtime mecca for governors, legislators, lobbyists, state workers, professionals, businessmen and tourists -- the restaurant known as Frank Fat's. When its owner announced his retirement in 1971, California lawmakers honored him with a joint commemorative resolution of the Legislature for being a legendary host and acknowledging his restaurant as "Sacramento's Second Capitol."

Frank Fat, a Chinese immigrant who arrived in America in 1919, would be 93 years old (1904-1997).

Though he and his restaurant have enjoyed sustained coverage in the local press for more than 30 years, many significant aspects of life in China and the United States have yet to be told. This is a story that matters, because it not only encompasses experiences common to many early Chinese immigrants but also provides America's rapidly-growing Asian population (including many unskilled immigrants who still work in restaurant-related businesses) with a vivid example of what still can be achieved by a poor immigrant short on formal education but long in a willingness to become involved with and to learn to understand his new American community. Racism exists in all societies, and Frank Fat's positive efforts to deal with the societal racism he encountered by fostering deep human understanding, had earned the respect and support of many of his important friends. His positive approach had been highly effective in resolving conflicts in multi-ethnic society, an approach worthy of our study and emulation -- although of course Frank Fat himself maintained modestly that he was "only an ordinary restaurateur who worked hard and had a bit of luck."

From China to Gold Mountain

Frank Fat was born May 12, 1904, as Dong Sai Fat in WuLong village, Toishan County, Guangdong. His great-grandfather was an upper-class landowner with several wives and 15 children. His grandfather, the second eldest of those 15, was an official during the Ching Dynasty who often left his family to work in the city of ShunDak (about 45 miles northeast of Toishan), where he started a wine and rice wholesale and retail business. It was into this business that both Frank and his father were born.

When Frank was only a small child, his father left for the U.S. so that Frank as a young boy was especially close to his grandfather. An only son, Frank had one elder and one younger sister. He spent 14 years in tiny WuLong village, with only about 200 residents. The school was also small, but large enough to accommodate the children of several nearby villages. The students learned Chinese calligraphy and the "Four Classics" as well as Chinese literature. Frank recalled, "I wasn't the best student, but I wasn't dumb either."

Although the Republic of China was established in 1911, Chinese civil wars and peasant movements continued thereafter and during Frank's childhood his native Southern China was a battleground for warring military, peasant unions and local secret society leaders. It was not the responsibility of the local government to protect life and personal property and robbers often plagued Frank's grandfather, stealing wine and pigs from his store, once even attempting to kidnap the old man. Finally, the robbers forced Frank's grandfather to close up the shop and return to his village. Frank recalled that when he was 14, "One day my grandfather, who was 73 years old already, asked me whether I wanted to stay home, continue to go to school, or go overseas." At the time, Frank was like so many other Chinese with dreams of fortune who'd heard of the United States as the Gold Mountain, so he decided to go to America. He remembered that "Neighbors actually went there and came back loaded with gold coins. They always talked about good things."

But when he actually came to Gold Mountain, Frank was also like the other Chinese immigrants in that he had to endure the hardships and somehow circumvent the Chinese Exclusion Act of 1882, which was not repealed until 1943. Like most Chinese who came to the United States, Frank traveled under so-called "paper documents" -- false identities enabling Frank and others to become "paper sons" of citizens or merchants eligible to enter the U.S. So Frank, beginning at 14, worked for two years with no pay other than room and board at a store owned by his maternal uncle in a small village near Canton while his grandfather looked for a "paper document" for him. When Frank was 16, his "paper" was obtained through an arrangement that, Frank estimated, cost his grandfather more than $1,000.

Frank, sailing third class aboard the ship Nanking, suffered from seasickness as well as found his "paper" father to be cold and rude. He finally arrived in San Francisco in 1919, at the age of 16.

Frank's paper father, Mr. Wong, was allowed immediately on shore. After the fires of the 1906 earthquake burned all the records, Mr. Wong, like many other Chinese immigrants, took the opportunity to claim that he was a "native." Frank, however, was detained at Angel Island, the immigration headquarters for Chinese, for more than one month. Frank recalled, "I could only go to certain places on the island. I didn't even know what Angel Island looked like until the 1980s, when Angel Island was restored and opened up as a historical state park; my family and I went over there for a picnic." When Frank was approved to enter the U.S., Mr. Wong took him from San Francisco to Sacramento to join Frank's uncle, who had pervasively immigrated.

Though Dong Sai Fat had become "Wong Bing Yuen" on paper to get to America, once arrived Frank continued to use his "paper name" only on an official basis. In Chinese circles, however, he was known as Dong Sai Fat, then later established "Fat" as his new family name. In the 1930s, he chose an American first name, "Frank," and began using his middle name, "Fat," as a surname. The character, "Fat," in Chinese means to prosper or to flourish, making Frank's surname a fortuitous choice.

Frank's 36-year old uncle, who had immigrated several years earlier, had already established a restaurant in Sacramento's Chinatown -- the Hong King Lum, dating back to 1906, and one of the capitol's oldest restaurants. Unfortunately, the Hong King Lum restaurant was unable to hire Frank, and his uncle's house was too small to accommodate him in addition to his uncle's family, so the poor, unemployed and homeless Frank slept on the stone stairs in the restaurant's basement. He remembered, of those days, that "It was good enough for me." In exchange for his spot on the stairs, Frank helped out at Hong King Lum, doing odd jobs wherever he was needed.

Finally a friend of Frank's uncle's found the youth a job at the Sutter Club as a dishwasher. In less than two weeks Frank had seriously cut his hand on a platter, an injury that cost him his job. While recovering, Frank studied some English from a family in a Chinese church downtown.

Frank's next job earned him only $3 per week, filling hair tonic bottles at the Ivy Beauty salon. "One Sunday, the salon owner and her daughters brought me my coat, and gestured towards the door," Frank remembered, smiling, "I thought I had been fired again, and ran quickly back to Chinatown. Later I learned that actually the ladies wanted to take me on a picnic. My English was so poor at that time," he said, laughing.

Frank worked through the summer in an orchard near Courtland during the 1920 harvest season, associating with other teenagers, and living in a bunkhouse on the ranch with several Chinese college students. Most of the fruit farmers were from the Chungshan clan in China, and, naturally, allowed their own clan members the first pick. This meant that pickers from other clans, such as Frank (whose clan was the Toishan) got the less accessible, smaller fruit, making their jobs more difficult and their pay less. Nevertheless, Frank earned about $70 by season's end, enough money to travel to his next destination: Ohio.

When a cousin of Frank's decided to start a laundry business in Akron, Frank went with him. At that time, according to the 1920 U.S. Census, of the 45,614 Chinese workers in this country, 11,438 worked in restaurants and 12,599 were laundry workers. Though he hated the work, Frank was grateful to be able to stay with his cousin. While in Akron, Frank located his real father, Dong Ngai Long, who was living in Cleveland, working as a cook in a Chinese restaurant. After his father persuaded the owner to hire Frank as a kitchen helper, father and son worked side by side in the kitchen and slept in the small basement of the restaurant.

After they had worked together for a short while, a friend of Frank's father convinced Frank's father to use his small savings to buy a restaurant in Youngstown, Ohio. But economic conditions were poor and like many businesses of that time, the restaurant went broke after a few months. Frank's father, unfamiliar with American laws and procedures, simply locked the door and walked away. During this emotionally difficult time, young Frank felt uncertain where he should turn, and from where his next meal would come.

"The manager at my father's restaurant gave me $75 and told me to go to Detroit where the manager had some friends," Frank recalled. The next year he worked at a succession of jobs in restaurants in Grand Rapids, Chicago and other mid-western cities. In Chicago, Frank, not yet 17, roomed with some Chinese college students and was able to improve "my English skills and understanding of American culture, along with my skills as a restaurant busboy and waiter."

His father, who was about 50 years old at the time of the failure of his restaurant in Youngstown, Ohio, eventually made his way back to China. Because his wife had died in 1923, he remarried, then later, he returned to Sacramento (before Frank arrived). Tragically, the hardships of the Great Depression in 1930s pushed Frank's father into suicide when he was in his 60s, perhaps explaining why Frank's strongest emotional attachment to his grandfather rather that his father.

A Return Home and Back Again

When Frank turned 20, his grandfather persuaded him to return to China for a visit. Once there, he learned that his mother had also died. A year later, a traditional marriage was arranged for him. Although he wanted to return to school, he complied with family wishes, and on 18 December 1924, Frank and Yee Lai Ching, who never knew each other previously, were married in a large, formal ceremony appropriate to the Yee's family status of wealth in Hong Kong.

Yee Lai Ching was born on November 27, 1908, in Hoiping County, Guangdong. The youngest of seven children in a family which owned the San-Li architectural company in Hong Kong, Lai Ching recalled that "My family was a large, extended family; we were rich and had many servants. For example, when I married, I had two maids with me as dowry from my family."

The young couple remained in China for another year during which their son Wing Kai was born in 1925. Frank also spent several months of that year in the company of his wealthy, politically minded cousin, Dong Cho-Long, who was a member of the Kuomintang (KMT) party.

Dong Cho Long, a retired merchant from the Philippines, worked in a financial department in Canton. Though Frank no longer remembered why, his cousin took a particular liking to him. After Frank married, Dong invited Frank to follow him to Canton. Frank, recalled of those times that "I accompanied Dong to parties many times. We met different types of peoples and ate various delicious foods; it was time rich in experience as well as a welcome vacation." But he still intended to return to America, and did.

After working in the United States for several years, Frank realized that life in the States was not easy. Although he sent some money home several times a year to his grandfather on Chinese festivals or on relatives' birthdays, he saved as much as he could and spent money very frugally on himself. His cousin Dong had taught him well the "power of money" and the extravagant lives politicians led. Many parties were held in the nunneries located at Kwan Yin Mountain in Canton, or on boats along the Pearl River, during which the young orphan girls sheltered by these nunneries were made available by their guardians to entertain the wealthy politicians and military officials. Frank said today "I knew many of the rich and powerful people who were involved in politics and corruption, yet I was young and obviously an outsider." At the many parties to which he was invited as well as those he hosted, Frank found that he was having a very good time and that people seemed to enjoy his company. No doubt Frank began losing his frugal attitude toward money during this period, as well as developing the public relations skills necessary to move in social circles of the wealthy and influential.

When Frank had returned to China in 1923, he had a total of $1,500 -- not enough to live on and to entertain friends. Fortunately, Dong generously loaned him money as needed. Later, when Frank owed his cousin approximately $7,000 Hong Kong dollars, Dong fell ill and died. Because they only had a verbal agreement, Frank could have ignored the debt, but instead began repaying his late cousin's family as soon as possible. To earn money to repay his debt to Dong and to support his family, Frank returned to the United States in 1926, without his wife and newborn son.

In Chicago during the 1929 crash and beginning of the Great Depression, Frank labored as busboy and waiter in a series of restaurants both Chinese and American. The times being what they were, many restaurants went under and in many that were able to remain open some waiters received no wages, only tips, room and board. Frank and 11 other waiters pooled their resources and purchased a laundry to help each other survive. When one of them became unemployed, he would work and live temporarily at the laundry. Frank never did work at the laundry, but nevertheless took some responsibility for the business. During the same period, Chinese tongs (gangs) were fighting among themselves to gain control of territories for survival and power. "When the tongs discovered the seller of the laundry owed them money, they demanded repayment from me and my partners and threatened to shut down our business," Frank recalled. He immediately went to the tongs and managed to settle the case without additional cost, although he said, "I didn't understand how I had such courage and skill to resolve that problem at that time."

In 1930, after four years in Chicago, Frank relocated to Sacramento to work for his uncle in his newly remodeled Hong King Lum restaurant on "I" Street. Hong King Lum, with a bar and a dancing floor, was considered one of the most elegant restaurants in Chinatown, as well as in downtown Sacramento. Working as manager, host and occasionally waiter, Frank earned less than $100 per month but developed his fine skills in managing and hosting as well as friendships with many important California political figures.

These governors, legislators, judges, lobbyists and businessmen provided Frank with valuable insight into the dynamic and fascinating world of the American political process. Frank said proudly, "I have known all of the governors of California from Jimmy Rolph (1931-1934) to the present governor Gray Davis."

Harold Powers, former California Lieutenant Governor (1954-1960), who met Frank when he first came to the Legislature in 1933, remembered that "Frank was waiting tables and he seemed to know most of the legislators. I think probably no one knows more people than Frank does statewide. Frank's remarkable memory for names, his humor and courteous manner made him well liked by his customers."

When gambling was still legal in California, the basement of Hong King Lum offered Chinese Keno games, which most Chinese played. One day, a prestigious state official came in for lunch and expressed his interest in buying several Keno tickets in the basement. He marked the tickets, and Frank went downstairs to pay for them. A 50-cent ticket won $900 for the gentleman, but he left before the game started. Frank saved the winnings and gave them to the man the next time he came in for dinner -- as act of honesty earning Frank the everlasting friendship of that gentleman. When Frank decided to open his restaurant, this man provided the necessary business loan.

Before the immigration law was amended in 1965, Chinese males commonly came alone to the United States, Frank's wife Lai Ching recalled that "at that time, few merchants were able to bring their wives and children to the U.S. for economic reasons as well as immigration regulations." Frank was no exception, and consequently was separated from his family for 10 years, during which Lai Ching and their eldest son, Wing Kai, alternated living with Frank's family and her parents in Hong Kong.

Lai Ching was not eager to immigrate to the United States: her father had returned from New York with unpleasant experiences and opposed her immigration. As time passed however, she worried that ever-changing immigration laws that only allowed children up to a certain age to immigrate would permanently exclude their 10-year old son, Wing Kai, from entering the country. So, in 1936, with this concern and at Frank's urging Lai Ching and Wing Kai joined Frank in Sacramento.

Frank had to use the name Wong Bing Yuen when he prepared the documents to bring his wife and son over. Despite the certificates' legitimacy, immigration officials, who were becoming wise to the "paper" system, might have given Lai Ching and Wing Kai a difficult time. Not realizing that Chinese women frequently married at age 15 or 16, they thought Lai Ching looked too young to have a 10-year old son. But Frank's many important political friends at the State Capitol expedited the process so Lai Ching's recollection was that "The stay at Angel Island and interrogation were brief and simple; the officials allowed us to leave Angel Island and to enter the United States officially."

After arriving in the U.S., Lai Ching who adopted the American name of "Mary" did not have domestic help for the first time in her life. She had to learn to perform household chores as well as adjust to the new environment. During summers, she also worked in the Del Monte cannery downtown for seven years, during which she also gave birth to two more children, a period she considered "the hardest time" in her life. After seven years and two more children, Frank suggested that his wife should stop working in the summers so that she could take care of their growing family. However, her labors were far from over. As a housewife, Mary cooked and cleaned house, cared for the children, grew Chinese vegetables in the backyard and also raised chickens for the family. Frank and Mary eventually had six children -- four sons and two daughters.

The Beginning of Success

In 1939, a restaurant known as the Truckadero, at 806 L Street in Sacramento, went up for sale. The site was a former Italian restaurant that had doubled as a speakeasy during Prohibition. The area was so seedy, Fat later recalled, "they said even a dog wouldn't go there." Although the place was run-down and rough, Frank wanted to purchase it. "My friends thought I was crazy," Frank said, "but I knew this place had a better location than Hong King Lum because it was only two blocks from the State Capitol." Frank also was confident in his hosting skills and friendships that he had cultivated for years working at Hong King Lum. His family's meager savings combined with a business loan from the gentleman whose Keno winnings Frank had returned gave him enough money to buy and renovate the Truckadero, which he renamed Frank Fat's. Putting in 16 hours daily alongside his 12 employees, Frank gradually established the business. He served a full lunch for 35 cents, dinner for 85 cents and gave ladies fresh gardenias on Friday nights. Frank installed a window between the dining area and the kitchen so patrons could see the sanitary meal preparations themselves, effectively squelching the common rumors of dirty Chinese restaurant kitchens. After eight months Frank Fat's was turning a profit and attracting a clientele from the Capitol and other businesses. Therefore Capitol denizens did, lured mostly by Frank's unfailing graciousness and willingness to accommodate his clientele. After hours, lawmakers and lobbyists could forget the differences of the day and indulge in drinking and gambling.

The ambience was particularly hospitable to politicians and lobbyists. Harold Powers says that "If I'd just come to town, I'd go to Frank Fat's and if any of the legislators had been in town, Frank could tell me who'd been there. It was just like a homecoming." Not surprisingly, much political maneuvering went on in such an atmosphere. Norva Muse, who worked in the Legislature for more than 27 years, confirmed that Frank Fat's "is where bills were born and passed for almost all the years I was in the Legislature." As Larry Liebert wrote in the San Francisco Chronicle, "At Frank Fat's, lobbyists liked to thrown lavish banquets for legislators. Any new legislator would be introduced to Frank Fat by a lobbyist as his initiation to Sacramento soul life." Other patrons even addressed Frank as "Senator Fat." His reputation as a discreet, non-partisan person grew and increasingly made him privy to information that helped him to understand the American political process well enough to use it.

"Fat's was a place where we could get together after work and forget political differences," said University of California Regent Bill Bagley, a former assemblyman. "And you're not going to be vicious and nasty to someone you just had dinner with the night before. Frank really set the tone for the place, and the value of that contribution to the state of California was very high."

Asked to explain his acceptance by the California State government's most elite and powerful circles, Frank explained. "I am a restaurateur and I listen a lot. I never repeat any conversations heard here. That is why patrons feel absolutely comfortable and secure to conduct their meetings, negotiations and parties here." Though always careful to separate politics from his food business, Frank shrewdly took advantage of what was open to him. More importantly, he never forgot how important it was to return to support to public officials and friends. These years finally provided Frank with a sound financial foundation for his business as well as a unique linkage with many important and powerful patrons. Entering his middle age thus equipped, Frank reached a new milestone.

The year 1939 not only marked Frank's entrance into his own business but also the year in which he began to use the American political system as a "self-appointed lobbyist" for the general welfare of his people and his motherland. That year, Frank recalled, "I read a news article about a Chinese demonstration at the San Francisco waterfront protesting the shipment of American goods to Japan. I felt strongly that I should do something similar in Sacramento." He conveyed his opinion and feelings to his friend Senator Jack Metzger from Red Bluff and soon Senate Joint Resolution No. 10 was introduced and passed on January 24, 1939. The Resolution stated in part:

"Whereas, in utter disregard of its obligations as a signatory of the Pact of Paris of 1928 and the Nine Power Treaty of the Washington Conference of 1921-22, the government of Japan has been waging an unjustifiable war on the Republic of China and ...

Resolved that the Legislature of the State of California hereby respectfully urges the President and Congress of the United States to declare an embargo against the shipment of arms, munitions, and materials of war from this country to the government of Japan..."

Encouraged by this success, Frank began to get involved in other critical issues that affected his fellow Chinese-Americans.

When World War II came, Frank's business slowed down a bit: supplies were harder to get and sometimes he did not remain open full-time. When he left Sacramento to explore other business opportunities, he entered another community where he was unknown and found himself face-to-face with a difficult situation.

Ernest Babcock, the district attorney of Sacramento, had invited Frank to lake Tahoe to consider opening and managing a restaurant there. Frank took his family to visit Lake Tahoe for a few days. Babcock had arranged accommodations for the Fats at Bijou Motel in Lake Tahoe, but Frank and his family stayed only one night. The next morning the motel manager apologetically explained that Chinese could not stay in the motel. The humiliation angered Frank. He left the motel and returned to Sacramento before Babcock had even found out what had happened. Frank recalled, "When Mr. Babcock found out about the incident, he asked why I did not sue the motel owners. But I know what was going on in society -- discrimination was alive. Suing would also have cost a lot of money that I did not have at that time." But Frank did respond to the basic injustice: this experience made him determined to help change the American image of the Chinese, and he vowed to return to Lake Tahoe. The very next year, Ernest Babcock and three other friends each invested $25,000 in a casino-restaurant with Frank in Lake Tahoe. They appointed Frank to be in charge of operations. For the next three years every weekend Frank would drive to Lake Tahoe to inspect and supervise operations, making a point of going up one and returning via the other of the two highways linking Sacramento and Tahoe. En route, he stopped at as many restaurants, bars and coffee shops as he could to introduce himself and to acquaint himself with other businessmen as a fellow businessman as well as a Chinese man.

"My point," he recalled, "was to make personal contact with as many Americans as possible, so that Americans also have the opportunity to interact with Chinese personally. I believe that Chinese have many good characteristics, but Chinese must help the American people understand more about Chinese."

But the demands of managing two restaurants five hours apart proved to be too much. During World War II, Frank's eldest son, Wing Kai, was drafted and sent to the

Pacific, so Frank was managing both places alone. Mary Fat remembered those many sleepless nights when she held her four children in bed, worrying about Frank driving back and forth to Lake Tahoe. After three years, Frank and his partners sold the Lake Tahoe business. Frank refocused his energies on his Sacramento restaurant, which became increasingly popular for leisure and "off the record" time of California's legislators and lobbyists. Frank agreed that "In those years, my wife took care of all the children while I devoted so much time, at least 16 hours per day, to my business. My wife has all the credit for bringing up the kids."

In addition to supporting and nurturing her family, Mary Fat had interests of her own and got involved in the Chinese community during the 1940s. She was an active member of the Chinese Women's Association, founded in 1943 in Sacramento to support the Republic of China against Japan. In 1943, Madame Chiang Kai-Shek came to the United States to address the U.S. Congress regarding the Sino-Japanese War, and to raise funds from Chinese communities in U.S. to help the Chinese government. Mary recalled that "I carried my baby on my back to help the Chinese Benevolent Association prepare the fundraising program. I even donated all my newborn child's gold chains and lucky money to show my support to the Republic of China. I love my motherland and people. Today, I am old and not active any more in the Chinese Women's Association. This organization needs some new blood and direction to address the needs of the community."

Frank met Governor Earl Warren when Warren was California's State Attorney General from 1939-43. Warren was one of Frank's favorite governors. Frank said, "When Governor Warren came to the restaurant, he would always order Chicken Chow Mein. Governor Goodwin Knight was colorful, but Governor Warren was friendlier. He mixed with all the customers in the restaurant. However, Governor Reagan was not so much fun."

In 1957, the Sacramento Chinese Benevolent Association chose Frank as one of two delegates to attend the National Conference of Chinese Communities in America. The Organization of Chinese-Americans held the conference in Washington D.C. to lobby for the welfare of Chinese regarding changes in immigration laws. While in Washington, Frank visited his old friend, then U.S. Chief Justice Earl Warren (1953-69). On the invitation of the Chief Justice, Frank "went to the Supreme Court Building where the U.S. marshals were waiting to escort me inside. When I inside, they seated me in the first row. Chief Justice Warren wanted me to see how the Court operated. There I saw nine Supreme Court justices with Chief Justice Warren in the middle with two other attorneys. They were dressed in full regalia. They discussed a case without a single argument. I have never seen a court so quiet in my life. After a half-hour recess, the marshals escorted me to Warren's office. He pulled out a bottle of whisky and two cups. We drank and talk for a while. I felt extremely honored."

Success in Two Worlds

As early as 1852, there were 814 Chinese residents in the city of Sacramento. Chinatown, first located in the I, J, 5th and 6th Street blocks, grew in population to 2,331, and by 1860 settled between 3rd and 6th Streets along I Street, which would remain the center of Chinese life until the redevelopment of Sacramento's new Chinatown in 1968. For roughly a century, Sacramento's Chinese could only obtain housing in the overcrowded old Chinatown area. In the late 1950s, several prominent Chinese families, including Frank's wanted to move out of Chinatown. When he identified some locations into which he wanted to move, he was either told that no housing was available, or that the house could not be sold to Chinese. This type of situation no longer shocked Frank. When he told his white friends, a dentist succeeded in helping Frank buy a house outside Chinatown. Other Chinese also found ways to solve similar personal and business problems through their American friends -- this was the way of life for Chinese in those days.

Hoping to improve the housing situation for his fellow Chinese, Frank proposed the formation of a non-profit organization to buy some land outside of Chinatown. He hosted a meeting at the Hotel El Rancho in West Sacramento and invited many Chinese merchants to disucss the idea. Frank's proposal, however, was too radical for others in the Chinese community: they had been intimidated by social and political conditions for such a long time that they could not overcome their conservative instincts overnight. Furthermore, some people suspected Frank's motives for the project. His idea was neither seriously considered nor supported. Several decades later, Frank would reminisce that "Looking back, the value of the land which I had in mind was only about a couple hundred of dollars per acre, but today, this land had already become a high-value suburban residential area."

All his life Frank regarded his lack of formal education as a handicap. His ability to provide education for all his children, and watching them become professionals in their own right, had been a source of great pride to him: "I told my children that in this country, I myself am not an educated person. I know I can succeed in business; however, there are some limitations. I told them what is important is to be educated for the future. I know how I feel. I know how difficult it had been for me all these years."

As part of his children's equally important informal education, Frank never dictated the direction they should choose regarding marriage or career, yet saw to it that each child -- even some grandchildren -- spent time working in the restaurant. Starting from the bottom rung of busboy, the Fat children worked their way up and were treated like all other employees, to acquaint them with the business and encourage discipline in operating the family enterprise.

He also tried to educate the Chinese community, bringing his growing knowledge of the American way to bear, "I understand the critical and essential features of American politics. We must be involved in civil and community activities. We must donate money to support the statesmen who can lobby in the Legislature; otherwise, no one will speak for us or know us. That is why I always encourage young Chinese-Americans to be involved and to be organized. The Chinese community has many small groups, but still does not have a strong and effective organization to deal with many social and political issues facing the Chinese. In the past, many laws that discriminated against the Chinese were passed. We must kill the bill before it is passed. I am very upset, because we Chinese-Americans still do not understand this common practice in American politics."

Throughout his years of urging Chinese-Americans to become involved politically, Frank approached the Chinese-American community through organizations such as the Chinese Benevolent Society, for whom he lobbied for the improvement of immigration laws for Chinese in 1957. But perhaps the strongest appeals to Chinese-Americans were made as an individual rather that through formal organizations. One example was his attempt to convince Sacramento's Chinese merchants to form a non-profit group to buy land outside Chinatown to circumvent housing discrimination. In 1972 and again in 1986, he sent letters to Chinese members of the community regarding his dream of forming "an association of Chinese people who would exert greater influence in the world of business, economics and politics." His letter asked others to attend a meeting to help get this association going. And he has of course, approached his goals by setting an example of participating in mainstream American organization life. He belonged to restaurant associations, both local and nationwide, as well as the Lions club and other community groups. The recognitions the mainstream American community has accorded him are too numerous to list, but include his appointment to the Greater Sacramento Business Hall of Fame and the boards of such businesses as Federal Home Loan Bank of San Francisco. Senator Bill Campbell and Assembly Speaker Willie Brown presented even "The Great Seal of the State of California" to Frank.

Retirement and New Beginnings

When Frank Fat retired in 1971, 32 years after opening his restaurant, his son Wing Kai became Frank Fat's new host. Other sons as well as his daughters-in-law and even grandchildren gave up their former jobs to expand and create a family-owned enterprise on the foundation established by Frank. Since 1975, the family has opened two new eating places, China Camp and Fat City in Old Sacramento, as well as branches in San Diego during the 1980.

For Frank himself, retirement did not mean slowing down but merely redirecting his energies to other areas. After President Richard Nixon opened the way in 1972, Frank visited China several times to promote exchanges in trading, cultural and educational activities, which he also actively worked for once back in America. His pride of his motherland becomes clear whenever he spoke of China:

"Several hundred years ago, foreign countries were taking advantage of China. During the Cultural Revolution from 1966-76, Chinese were afraid to do anything. But since the government has changed its national policies, it has restored all the properties it took away from the overseas Chinese. Now China realizes she has to work hard in order to catch up with the rest of the world. The Chinese have tried to build confidence in themselves once again."

He said, "I am proud to be a Chinese in the United States. Although there are cultural differences as well as different ways of life, the second generation of Chinese should also be proud of their ancestors. I sent all my young relatives to China, so they could know some their Chinese heritage."

Besides his work as director of the New Chinese Education, he contributed funds to a small project personally. One such a project that began in Guangdong Province and ended in Sacramento, when Frank "donated some money to rebuild the school that I attended in WuLong village in China."

But Frank made far greater contributions than just keeping politicians well fed. In 1991, he established the Frank Fat Foundation, designed to enhance understanding between Chinese and American people through educational and cultural projects. The Frank Fat Endowment Fund followed, to aid research into cures for kidney and urinary tract diseases.

In 1993, he came up with an idea "to get all these people together and celebrate their cultures with each other and with people of other backgrounds." The idea became the annual Pacific Rim Street Festival, which draws tens of thousands to Old Sacramento to sample tastes of more than two dozen Asian and Pacific cultures.

He died in 1997, the patriarch of a family that has become a dominant player in area restaurant circles and in the Asian American community.

"If you ever wanted a splendid example of the importance and contributions of immigration to California," said Bagley, "Frank Fat is it."

Epilogue

After 45 years of business in the same understated, dark, and homey restaurant, the family corporation agreed to renovate Frank Fat's. Following a six-month closure for remodeling, on 18 June 1984 the "new" restaurant opened with a lavish 8,000-guest street party, hosted by Frank and his family -- and event selected by the Sacramento Bee as one of the year's 10 special events.

In a bold departure from the original classic Oriental look, the magenta, rose, and moss green décor was a calculated risk, but also is regarded by Wing Kai Fat as gift for the pleasure of the people whose patronage helped his father create a successful business. There are precious Chinese art and artifacts, including a royal guardsman's uniform (circa 1880) emblazoned with dragons, lavish screens, carved panels, a massive gold Laughing Buddha head and, most spectacular of all, an 11-foot-tall, richly-hued silk tapestry suspended behind the polished brass and rose-hued bar. (The tapestry once belonged to a Mexican president's wife and at another time, hung as a curtain in a Beijing opera house.) Some view the new look as a symbol representing the life of its originator, mingling contemporary and traditional, American and Chinese.

Like other ethnic groups of immigrants to the United States, Chinese settlers represented people whose livelihood in their country was disrupted by economic depression caused by war, famine and natural disaster.

Historians and demographers often describe the patterns apparent in waves of immigration by applying economic or political analyses. But each numerical increment in such a census represents the life of an individual who chose to leave the homeland and venture into a new and foreign culture. Frank Fat's story provided insight into American's social and cultural patterns and lends further understanding of her pluralism.

Before Peter C. Y. Leung passed away in 1999, he expressed his gratitude to Frank and Mary Fat as well as their family for having assisted and supported to this article of the book project. He also expressed his appreciation to Marion Franck, Kelly Young, and Ellsi Sung. He wished to give his special thanks to Janet Perkins and his wife, Eileen, for their critiques. He had conveyed his gratitude to the Department of Applied Behavioral Sciences, and to Dorothy Suhr for her typing of the manuscript. This article was based on 10 interviews with Fat's family conducted both in Cantonese and English between 1984 and 1986, and Frank Fat's personal documents, supplemented by some press accounts. There were many excellent general works concerning the Chinese in America including the following which he used as references: Him Mark Lai, Genny Lim, and Judy Yung's "Poetry and History of Chinese Immigrants on Angel Island 1900-1940" (HOCDOI Project, 1980); H. Brett Melendy's "The Oriental Americans" (Twayne Publisher, Inc., 1972); Mary and Adrian Praetzellis' "Archaeological and Historical Studies of the IJ56 Block, Sacramneto, California: An Early Chinese Community" (Anthropoloigcal Studies Center, Sonoma State University, 1982); Charles H. Duncan's "Cathay in Eldorado: The Chinese in California-Sacramento" (Keepsake Series, No. 2, 1972, The Book Club of California); John T. C. Fant's "Yee Fow: The Chinese Community in Sacramento" (Chinese Publishing House, 1961); June Namias' "First Generation: In the Words of Twentieth Century American Immigrants" (Beacon Press, Boston, 1978) and Melford S. Weiss' "Valley City: A Chinese Community in America" (Schenkman Publishing Company, Cambridge, Massachusetts, 1974). -- Editor: A.Y., July 26, 2000.

Wong Family Realizes the American Dream: The Bel Air Supermarket Story

Dr. Alex Yeh and Romy Jue

T his book is to commemorate 150 Years of Chinese Presence in California. It is fitting their success stories be told. The story of the Wong family from the pioneer generation to the present one is detailed chronologically as follows:

First Generation

The county of Toishan was among the poorest in southern China. Only 10 percent of the land were suitable for farming; drought and salt-water infiltration from the South China Sea often plagued these areas. As a result, Toishan produced only a quarter of the grain its population required. With mountains on three sides and water on the fourth, the location was also unsuitable for overland commerce (Chan, 19). To escape poverty, the men looked abroad to find work and make a livelihood. Between 1842 and 1943, over 70 percent of Chinese emigrating to the United States came from Sze Yup, or "Four Districts": Sunwui, Toishan, Hoiping and Yanping (Chan, 16-17).

of fifteen, in 1868, he set out across the ocean to America, joining the thousands of other Chinese entering California to fill the labor shortage. Not only were workers needed to build railroads, dig mines, and harvest crops, they were needed to fill the tasks traditionally assigned to women such as laundry and cooking (Sandmeyer, 14). While early Chinese immigrants were primarily miners and traders, immigrants between 1865 and 1870 branched out and found new places in society, serving the community as agriculturalists, manufacturers, cooks, and laborers (Chan, 52-63).

Yon Dung made his way to Newcastle, California, where he found work as a farm laborer, becoming part of the first generation of migrant farm workers. The Chinese workers earned the reputation of being quick learners, trustworthy, and hard working. Growing two-thirds of all California produce in 1872, the Chinese were indispensable to California agriculture (Chan, 84-85).

After twenty-five years in California, Yon Dung finally saved enough money to return to China. At the age of forty, he married eighteen-year-old Tom Shee, a young woman chosen by his parents. His time with his wife would be brief. Within a year of marriage and with a baby girl on the way, Yon Dung was forced to leave his wife and again find work in the US.

Frequent passages between the United States and China, such as that of Yon Dung, were common among early Chinese immigrants. Most of them left their families at home while they worked in America, attempting to earn enough money to pay off family debt or to buy land. They would then return to their homeland after such goals were accomplished. Like many of the Chinese, Yon Dung came as a "sojourner," one who planned to return to his homeland after making enough to assure a good life.

Yon Dung made four more trips between California and Toishan in the following years and fathered two sons: Gim Wong (*Chinese name*) in 1900 and June Wong (*Chinese name*) in 1906. Yon Dung worked over fifty years in the California fields before he was able to retire to Toishan. In 1922, at the age of sixty-nine, Yon Dung returned to China for one last time and bought a plot of land. He spent his remaining years providing for his family and growing rice. He later died in 1931 at the age of seventy-eight. His wife, Tom Shee, died in 1944 at the age of sixty-nine.

Second and Third Generation

In 1914, at the age of fourteen, Gim Wong left his mother in Toishan to join his father, Yon Dung, in California. Like many young men in China, he dreamed of America as the land of gold. Gim had seen money from the overseas Chinese support families, build schools, and gradually pull Toishan out of poverty. It was a matter of filial piety for sons to travel to California to seek their fortunes and improve the standard of life for their families. (Chen, 62)

Forty-six years had passed since Gim's father first entered the United States, and feelings towards Chinese immigrants had changed. Chinese immigrants were no longer welcome as laborers, and several acts had been passed to curtail their immigration, most importantly the Chinese Exclusion Act passed in 1882 and extended until in 1904. This act barred the entry of Chinese laborers for the next ten years, required identifying certificates for all other Chinese immigrants, and denied Chinese immigrants naturalization rights. In order to bypass this law, Gim Wong entered the United States as a "paper son." After visiting their families in China, Chinese US citizens would report fictitious births of sons upon returning to the US. Other families could then buy these slots to bring their own children into the United States (Chen, 189).

In 1916, Gim Wong returned to China to take a bride. His mother had arranged for him to marry Lee Shee (*Chinese name*), a girl from a neighboring village. Within a year, the newlyweds had their first child, a son named Bill (*Chinese name*). In order to support his family, Gim Wong returned to California to continue his work as a farm laborer. In 1922, after five years of diligence, he saved enough money to return to China and bring back his wife and son. Gim and his family settled in Placer County and found work as sharecroppers. Between 1922 and 1942, Gim and Lee Shee increased their family size with nine more children: Gene (*Chinese name*) in 1922, George (*Chinese name*) in 1924, Lillie (*Chinese name*) in 1926, Raney (*Chinese name*) in 1927, Albert (*Chinese name*) in 1929, Evelyn (*Chinese name*) in 1931, Paul (*Chinese name*) in 1933, Nellie (*Chinese name*) in 1935, and Betty (*Chinese name*) in 1942.

Gim and Lee Shee struggled to uphold Chinese traditions in their second homeland. It was customary in China for a male descendant to be present during the last years of the parents' lives and to reside over the burial and later reburial of the remains. As Gim's parents grew older, the need to fulfill filial obligations weighed heavily on his mind. Because Gim Wong was not an American citizen, his absence from United State was limited to one year. Therefore, the family decided to send the first American citizen in their family, their second son, Gene. In 1927, five-year-old Gene left his parents to live with his grandparents in China. He would not return until 1935.

In 1932 Gim and Lee Shee took their small savings plus the borrowed money to acquire five acres of rock-studded land in Penryn, California. Although the California

Alien Land Act of 1907 did not allow Chinese immigrants to own land, many of them were able to bypass the law by putting property titles in the name of their American-born children. The Wong family cleared the land to cultivate fruits and vegetables. Eventually they were able to buy a used red truck, the Chinese color of luck and prosperity, and installed sides that opened out to serve as a mobile vegetable stand. Their sons Bill, Gene, and George assisted their father going door to door in the Auburn area selling their homegrown fruits and vegetables. These young merchants learned early the importance of selling quality products at fair prices, while providing excellent service to their customers.

The third generation had trials of their own to overcome. While their parents and grandparents were focused on survival in their new environment, the third generation had to balance two worlds. The Wong children went to American schools, followed current trends, and learned American slang. At home, they spoke to their parents in Cantonese, ate Chinese food, and were expected to uphold Chinese traditions. Like many children of Chinese immigrants, Bill and George were sent to a Chinese school in Newcastle, in addition to their American schooling, to learn Chinese history, culture, and language. With these influences, the Wong children formed "Chinese-American" identities, adopting American ways while preserving their Chinese heritage.

Turning Point

During the Second World War, even though he was denied naturalization rights, Bill was drafted into the Army Service in 1942. He served in an ordinance company during the Allied troop invasion of Normandy, France. Bill landed in Omaha Beach on D-Day Plus 7. Gene was the second to go in 1943, joining the 13,499 Chinese men drafted or enlisted in the US Armed Forces (Takaki, 373). Gene served in China, Burma, and India as a member of the 14th Air Force (the famous Flying Tigers). Raney was the last son to be drafted in 1945. He would be killed in a tragic automobile accident while serving in the US Navy at the age of eighteen. World War II was a turning point for the Chinese in America. After the bombing of Pearl Harbor, the United States and China became allies in the war. Chinese-Americans mobilized in their war effort. Patriotism ran high, and young men served proudly in the armed services while young women took volunteer positions to support the war effort. Such efforts of the Chinese in America brought attention to the inequality of their situation, prompting the repeal of the Chinese Exclusion Act in 1943 (Takaki, 375-378).

World War II impacted the Wong family in another way. During World War II, the Japanese families living in Penryn were sent away to relocation centers, and their stores and businesses closed. Because of the shortage of grocery stores in the area, Gim saw an opportunity to open a small grocery store in Penryn to serve the community during the war. The family made the switch from being farmers and peddlers to store owners.

Bel Air

After the war ended, Bill and Gene returned home from their distinguished military services. Upon their return, the two brothers went their separate ways to seek work in the business and professional world. For a few years, Bill, Gene, and George independently operated their own grocery stores. From 1951 to 1953, Albert was called to serve with the 1st Cavalry Division during the Korean War. It was in the early 1950's that the supermarket concept was beginning to catch on, so the three oldest brothers requested a family meeting with their parents and siblings Albert, Paul and Lillie. Together the Wong family decided to pool their talents and resources. In 1955 they opened their first supermarket at the corner of Fruitridge Road and 63rd Street, in the newly developing south Sacramento area. They christened their supermarket "Bel Air Market," after the upscale Los Angeles neighborhood.

Following the opening of the first store, they faced many challenges. With limited capital, the Wong Family had to compete against stronger national and regional grocery chains. They drew upon their early fruit peddling days and made up what they lacked in size by continuing the tradition of providing better service and quality products. It was not long before Bel Air Market became a household name in the Sacramento community. Their market chain expanded gradually under the leadership of the family patriarch, Gim Wong. The number of stores increased to seven before he passed away in 1971. And his wife, Lee Shee, saw their eighth store open before she died in 1980. But before they died, they were able to realize their own piece of the "American Dream."

By 1992, the Wongs had opened twenty-one stores and employed over 2,600 employees. Their store sales had reached in excess of one million dollars per day. They partnered with Raley's Supermarkets in their own grocery warehouse distribution ventures (WestPac / Western Pacific Food Warehouse), their own dairy plant (Mid-Valley Dairy), and their own dairy byproduct plant. Their large, modern, and upscale stores were a far cry from the Wong family's humble beginnings. Considered an industry leader, the Wong family initiated or enhanced many innovative and popular features in their stores that are now common sights in today's grocery industry. In the 1960s, there was an in-store United States postal service station. The 1970's saw

Bel Air open floral and bakery departments. In the 1980's, their services expanded to include sit-down cafes, fresh sushi counters, full-service banking, and video departments. Bel Air became the first in Sacramento to open Chinese hot food departments in the supermarket. In the 1990's they launched child play care centers in their stores, the first in the Sacramento area.

From the beginning, the Bel Air Markets had earned the reputation of "The Stores That Care." They cared for their customers by providing the best of products and services at competitive prices. Equally, the Wong family showed its devotion to their loyal employees by treating them like members of their own family. And for the community, they supported charitable programs such as the "Bel Air Fund For the Hungry and Homeless," a permanent endowment fund to assist the less fortunate. In recognition for this community outreach program, Bel Air received a presidential citation. President Ronald Reagan presented George Wong, president of Bel Air, with the "Presidential Award for Private Sector Initiatives" at a White House ceremony in 1987 (picture 2).

The three oldest brothers were also active in the grocery trade industry and involved in community affairs. Bill was the president of the Sacramento Chinese Grocers Association and was a member of the advisory board of River City Bank of Sacramento and of the County Grand Jury. Gene took part in numerous community and charitable organizations. He served on the Board of Trustees of the National Multiple Sclerosis Society and as board member of the Military Selective Service System. Due to his bilingual background, Gene became president of the Wong Family Association of Sacramento and was the founding director of the Wong Center, sponsor of government subsidized rental units for low income senior citizens. He also was an officer of the Chinese Benevolent Association of Sacramento and played a role in fundraising for the construction of Confucius Temple. George participated as director of the Western Association of Food Chains, the Food Marketing Institute, and the Sacramento Metropolitan Chamber of Commerce. In addition, he served as chairman of the Northern California Grocers and the California Grocers Association.

The five brothers Bill, Gene, George, Albert and Paul and sister Lillie represented the nucleus of Bel Air supermarket (picture 3). Each of them contributed to the company their own field of expertise. Bill was the Vice President and headed the produce department. Gene filled the roles of Secretary and Treasurer and was involved in financing, real estate acquisition, and real estate development. From the inception, George served as President of Bel Air Mart. Lillie flourished as Office Manager and Albert assisted as Meat Department Manager and later Director of Merchandising. After returning from his navy service between 1956 and 1957, Paul became a store manager and later the Director of Maintenance and Store Remodeling. The three youngest daughters, Evelyn, Nellie and Betty, each worked at the Bel Air Supermarkets before branching off into their own endeavors

In the early 1990's the founding shareholders, most of whom had already passed their retirement age, reached the "Golden Age" and were now ready to sell their stores and retire. The family considered many suitors to carry on the earned name and quality business. Their highly successful enterprise attracted strong interests from both national and international grocery store chains. In 1992, the family decided to accept an offer from Raley's, one of the largest regional grocery store chains in California. Having worked together in their joint venture partnerships, the two families had established a strong rapport. The Wong family felt the Raley's operation would be the best match for its customers and employees and would continue to build the Bel Air Market name and its legacy. Bel Air stores would keep the Bel Air name and serve as Raley's upscale counterpart. After the Wongs sold their Bel Air Mart stock to Raley's, Bill, Gene, Lillie, Albert and Paul retired after thirty-seven years in the business. George remained as the president of Bel Air to coordinate the transition until 1995, when he eventually retired.

Fourth Generation

All nineteen children of the six shareholders worked in the family business during their lives. They practiced the same hard work ethic that was instilled by their parents and grandparents. Some of them left the business to strike out on their own. Others stayed to help promote and expand the family business. In the 1980's the young Wongs established a new company named Liquor Mart, which sold wines, beer and spirits at discounted prices. These massive "warehouse" stores, seven in all, were revolutionary at the time. They later sold the chain to a national discount liquor chain, Liquor Barn. The young Wongs also ran an interstate trucking company called Transwest Transport. This trucking company provided services to both the Bel Air Markets and other third party businesses. The trucking company was liquidated when Raley's acquired the Bel Air Markets interest. Gary Wong, the son of Gene Wong, is still managing the Wong Family Investors LP, the entity that owns the Wong Family's real estate holdings. Some of those holdings include the shopping centers where the Bel Air Stores are located.

Conclusion

The Wong Family success story is one of hard work and strong family ties. This is a testament that ordinary people can accomplish extraordinary goals. Their achievement of the "American Dream" has paved the way for future generations.

Gene Wong reflected, "Whatever success we have, I think it exceeded our expectations. Our gratitude goes to our forefathers for their courage, sacrifice, and endurance, who persevered against odds to make a better life -- not only for themselves but also for their descendants. They built the foundation, paved the way, and gave us the direction to take advantage of the opportunities America offers. It's like the preceding generation planted the trees for the succeeding generation to harvest."

References

Chan, Sucheng. *This Bittersweet Soil: The Chinese in California Agriculture, 1860-1910.* Berkeley: University of California Press. 1986.

Chen, Jack, *The Chinese of America.* San Francisco: Harper & Row Publishers. 1980.

Sandmeyer, Elmer Clarence. *The Anti-Chinese Movement in California* Urbana: University of Illinois Press. 1973. Reprint of 1939 ed.

Takaki, Ronald. *Strangers From A Different Shore: A History of Asian Americans.* Boston: Little, Brown & Company. 1989.

C. C. and Regina Yin and Their McDonald Enterprise in Solano County

Peter C. Y. Leung

Introduction

C. C. and Regina Yin (see photo on page 164) are
the owners/operators of ten McDonald's
restaurants in Vacaville, Fairfield, and Suisun
Cities: all in Solano County, California. Since the founding
of Yin's McDonald's in 1984, their business has grown
from
$1 million into over $15 million sales each year with 350
employees. Yin's McDonald's is a franchise of the world's
largest fast-food chain, McDonald's Corporation Over 600
million Big Macs are consumed at McDonald's 23,300
restaurants in the United States and worldwide each year.

C. C. and Regina Yin were awarded the 1997
Ronald Award. This prestigious honor is awarded to
McDonald's owners/operators who made outstanding
contributions to the development of McDonald's image
through community involvement. Each region gives only
one Ronald Award each year. This news was reported
respectively in the *Fairfield Daily Republic*, September 2,
1997, and the *Vacaville Reporter*, September 7, 1997, both
Solano County newspapers.

"Congratulations! Regina Yin, our own Regina Yin has been named the 1996 Woman of the Year in the Fourth State Senate District. When volunteers are needed, when work needs to be done, Regina Yin is always there," said Redding Senator Maurice Johannessen in a press release. "Whether she is teaching high school students about the business world or opening her home for a fundraiser, she is always first in line asking, what can I do?"

"It's that kind of unselfish attitude and dedication to giving back to the community that is responsible for making this country great," Sen. Johannessen added. Regina is also responsible for starting the Interact youth club programs at Vanden and Fairfield High Schools, recorded in the *Rotary News & Notes*, International Rotary, March 11, 1997.

In September 1992, the Board of Directors of the Vacaville Chamber of Commerce appointed C. C. Yin, a relative newcomer to Vacaville, owner of four McDonald's franchises to be a new director. In less than four years, C. C. Yin was installed as president of the Vacaville Chamber of Commerce in 1996, with over 700 people attending the event.

From the brief information above, one will easily develop some good impressions and admiration for both C. C. and Regina Yin. For the last fifteen years, this dynamic couple has become well known to the local business circle, community and even political arena in Solano County and California. Their successes and life stories often make the headlines in Solano County newspapers. I had the opportunity to review many articles from *the Daily Republic, The Reporter,* newsletters and other sources about them. But the most important was the privilege for me to interview both C. C. and Regina Yin face to face for several sessions.

C. C. and Regina Yin are Chinese who came to America from Taiwan for their graduate studies in the 1960s. Were their experiences common to that of other Chinese immigrants? What about their personal characteristics, education, family backgrounds, business practices which led to this success? How do they cope with the highly disciplined, competitive demands from the world famous McDonald's fast food enterprise?

Thousands of Chinese immigrants engage in operating Chinese restaurants in their local ethnic communities. There is no doubt that some of these immigrants have also achieved financial success in their business and contributed to their community. Frank Fat, a legendary restaurateur, established Frank Fat's two blocks from the State Capitol Building in Sacramento, California, a long-standing mealtime mecca for governors, legislators, lobbyists, state workers, professionals, businessmen and tourists. Frank Fat's restaurant is acknowledged as "Sacramento's Second Capitol."

C. C. and Regina Yin are different because they were able to break through ethnic lines in entering the mainstream to become part of a successful enterprise such as McDonald's. They uphold the image of McDonald's spirit by being involved in public and community affairs and return part of their profits to the community. This case study explores how they worked through the system, what kind of hardships they encountered, and why their experiences deserve to be documented.

In my earlier studies on the Chinese farm workers, not only did I have to conduct interviews in Cantonese and translate them into English, but I also found it extremely difficult to gather their personal records for verification and review. However, in this study I could use English to interview C. C. and Regina Yin. Both fluently speak English and Mandarin, their native tongue. They are also very conscientious and organized their documents thoroughly for my review and evaluation, thus making it much easier for me to document their life stories.

Family Backgrounds in China and Taiwan

C. C. Yin, age 63, was the youngest son born to Yin Chin-Fu and his first wife, Pun Shee on November 2, 1936 in Chungking, Sichuan Province in southwestern China. Sichuan is rich in minerals and other resources, and has some of the most fertile agricultural land in China. Its remoteness and self-sufficiency made it an ideal base of operations for Chiang Kai-Shek's National Government during the wartime in the 1930s.

C. C.Yin's father was a farmer originally. Because he did well in school and he worked very hard, eventually he became a county head officer in one of the counties in Sichuan Province when he was only 25 years old. Later he became an official in charge of army food supplies in Chiang Kai-Shek's government in Chungking where the family stayed until 1948.

The 1920s to 40s were years of unprecedented national crises in China. Internally there were the warlords and the rise of the Communists led to civil instability and provided opportunities for Japanese expansion. Since the time of the Meiji restoration in the 19th Century, the three eastern provinces of China (Manchuria) had been the target of Japanese aggression. The Chinese not only suffered civil war between the Communist Party and the Koumintang (also known as the Nationalist Party), but they also were terribly torn apart and ruined by Japan's invasion. From 1930, Japan launched several forward moves into North China. On July 7, 1937, the Lukouchiao incident marked the outbreak of the Sino-Japan war. After losing several battles with Japan, the Chinese Government moved her wartime capitol from Wuhan, to Hankow and then in 1938 to Chungking, which is on the upper Yangtze River. On May 3-4, 1939, the first major Japanese bombing raid took place on Chungking. There were horrible losses in civilian life and property. Over a thousand houses were destroyed, four hundred persons lost their lives, and the wounded totaled more than three thousand. Chiang Kai-Shek reflected in his diary: "The enemy is cruel, inhuman and barbarous beyond belief. This is the most horrible scene I have witnessed in my life. May Almighty God punish him (Japan) for such wickedness!" (May 4, 1939)

Fortunately, C. C. was not living in the city, although he was born in the war time capitol of Chungking. When C. C. was only six months old, his mother passed away. C. C. and his sister, who was one year older, were sent to live with a woman who lived on the farm where Yin's father and grandfather had farmed before. The farm was very far away from Chungking so danger from the war was minimized. In addition, although Yin's father was busy working in the city, he provided food and money to this woman to take care of his children. As a child, C. C. neither have any strong recollection about his mother, nor understood what was going on in those days. As long as there was food to fill his stomach and he had his sister as a playmate in the house and in the fields, he was content. The farm and nearby areas were very poor. C. C. and his sister lived without parental care and love, or any schooling. They stayed on the farm for eight years. During those eight years they were lucky to have their father or their older brother and sisters stop by to visit them once in a while. C. C. recalls, "Life without much affection from the family was real difficult in those days; fortunately I got along with my sister, and we survived as a family in these years of turmoil." After his wife's death, Yin's father remarried a well-educated woman and the wife eventually gave three more children to the family. But Yin's father didn't bring C. C. and his sister back to live with them in the city. After eight years of living on the farm, in 1944, his father brought C. C. and his sister back to Chungking where they started schooling. It was the first time that C. C. lived with his stepmother. At the age of eight, C. C. began kindergarten along with his sister. They needed to walk about one hour to attend school. In less than six months, they were transferred to a boarding school. C. C. recalls his teen life in China, and he asserts with humor, "I was not learning and didn't behave well in the school, and often I was disciplined by teachers. I ranked in the bottom of my class; however, my sister always did very well in school. Although I didn't do well in school, I had a good time with my close friends, and we always played ball. We were not bad, just naughty."

C. C. Yin had four years of schooling in China until he was 12 years old. One day, in 1948, his father came home from work and told the family that they had to follow the government of Chiang Kai-Shek to Taiwan. His family had to leave in a hurry and left an older brother, James, behind. "In fact, at that time, my brother, James, who was 22 years old, favored the ideology promoted by Mao Tse-Tung's Communist party. When he was in high school in Shanghai, he had already joined the Communist youth group." C. C. Yin's father found out about this and punished him for his disloyalty to him and his government. James, who disliked the corruption of the Koumintang, left home and never returned. "My father had no choice, and was not able to persuade him to follow with the family to Taiwan. It was difficult for my father, a high official in the Chiang's National Party, to have a son who was active in the opposite party." C. C. recalled that his father was terribly angry and upset with his brother.

A 100-mile-wide Taiwan Strait separates Taiwan, which had been ruled by Japan for 50 years, from the mainland of China. China regained it from Japan in 1945, after Japan's surrender at the end of World War II. After Chiang Kai-Shek's government fled to Taiwan in 1949, the government continued to defend her sovereignty. The government needed to support millions of soldiers in the army forces, another million government personnel and many refugees who fled to Taiwan. The daily bombing between Quemoy and Mainland China frightened all her residents in the 50's. The Chiang Kai-Shek government started to reform land ownership in Taiwan. The education system provided for six years of compulsory education to all citizens; later it was extended for nine years.

C. C. mentions, "After arrival in Taiwan, my father continued to work for the government. My father mainly took care of his new family. Eleanor and I stayed with our oldest sister, Chei-Wen who was eighteen years older than we. Since our mother passed away, Chei-Wen shared the most responsibility to look after Eleanor and me. Chei-Wen married Mr. Sung. He had two children, but he treated us quite generously. Since I was 13 years old, I stayed at their house until I went to college. For the first few years in Taiwan, I had a great deal of trouble staying in school, and I was kicked out of school several times during my junior years. I was very grateful to have had the care and support from my old sister and her husband."

As C. C. grew older, he began to take schooling a little more seriously. He completed his senior year in high school but could not qualify for university entrance or even meet the minimum standard required for a four-year college in Taiwan. Although he didn't make good grades in high school, he made some real good friends who always supported him. C. C. looked at me with his smile and claims, "Friends were very important to me in my early life.

I do well today, because of my sisters and my friends' emotional and monetary support. I make friends easily and I like to treat my friends honestly and sincerely. I also learned 'money' is very important to me. Money brings me security, because, when I was young, I had no money. I was in fear of my future. I begged for help, either from my sisters, two cousins or friends to meet my meager survival needs."

He was admitted to a two-year vocational college where he studied for one year. Because he didn't like to study there, he got some tutoring at night school and retook the university entrance examination. This time he was surprised that he did much better and was admitted to Cheng Kung University in southern Taiwan. He majored in Civil Engineering and graduated in 1960. C. C. indicates, "My college education was also supported by my second sister, Evelyn who was working at that time. I was very fortunate to have three sisters who provided financial and moral support until I grew up."

Regina Yin's maiden name was Chung Fong Huang. She was the third child of Mr. and Mrs. Jen Huang, born on March 8, 1940, in Shanyao, Jiangxi Province, during the Sino-Japanese War. Her father graduated from the Police Academy in the city of Nanjing in 1930 and was assigned to Chongming Island as a patrol officer. Chongming Island is located at the mouth of Yangtze River near the city of Shanghai. A few years later, he was named Wuxi's Chief of Police. In 1937 he joined the Third Regiment as a colonel, under the Kuomintang Party. Because of the war, Jen and his family were constantly on the move. On April 4, 1940, the Japanese bombed the city of Shanyao with a series of air attacks. Mr. Huang wrote in his short autobiography, "Twenty-four airplanes bombed the city in the morning, and 37 came that afternoon. More than 300 people died in the daylong attack. With Chung

Fong (Regina) in arms, my wife and I dove into a small bomb shelter. We had to be together, and the family survived "

Regina reflects on her early years in China, "During the war years, I was a very sick child who suffered from malnutrition. Because we were always on the move, we were never able to stay at any one place long enough to establish a life. We were never anywhere that was 'home.' There was always the understanding that we were going to have to pack up and leave at any moment. We never knew when that would be. I was seven years old and had never had any formal education."

After the Sino-Japan War end in 1945, Chiang Kai-Shek's government faced many defeats by the Communists. In June 1946, the Kuomintang's military was reorganized into four specialized divisions: the army, navy, air force and logistics. The latter was responsible for coordinating the other three and supplying provisions to each. Jen Huang was assigned to logistics and continued to be under General Ku's command. At the end of 1948, Jen Huang was sent as a first stage to relocate the Kuomintang government to Taiwan. In early 1949, Jen Huang arranged for his wife and children to board a freighter to join him in Taiwan.

Regina remembers interestingly, "Our first year in Taiwan was hard, but life improved little by little. As life got a little better, I started attending school. That was my first formal schooling. I wore shoes, but the native Taiwanese did not. They wore the Japanese wooden clogs. Some of my classmates still spoke Japanese."

Regina grew up in a very loving family. Although her mother didn't have any formal education, she was always there to encourage her children to do well in their homework. The father did not just sit back but was involved directly in supporting his children's education. As Regina described " The days of the entrance examinations for high school and college were major days in Taiwan. My father sharpened our pencils, always making sure we had three or four, so that, when one became dull, we would have a sharp pencil at hand. The night before the examination, he made sure we went to bed early. Then, in the morning, he cooked our breakfast himself. On the day of the examination, we always had two eggs, which symbolized 100 percent, a perfect score, in our examination. My father would fix us a big bowl of noodle soup with chicken, eggs and some vegetables in it. Our parents felt having a good breakfast would help us think more clearly and do our best work." Regina was able to attend a good high school, and she also graduated from Taiwan Normal University with a degree in education in 1963.

A New Beginning in U.S.A.

During the 1960s to 1970s, many top university graduate students in Taiwan could study abroad, and the majority of students preferred to go to America. In these two decades, the highest number of foreign students in U.S. universities came from Taiwan.

C. C. and Regina Yin were not immigrants or refugees when they first arrived in the United States from Taiwan. They came with student visas to further their education. Although they were still poor in the sense that they did not have much money to support their graduate studies and live well here, they already had a baccalaureate education degree in their fields, and passed TOEFL, the basic English proficiency examination that qualified them for admission to American universities. Regina came to the United States in 1963, the year President Kennedy was assassinated. She studied at the University of Washington in Seattle, and majored in Social Work.

C. C. Yin's sister, Eleanor, came to the United States to study at the University of Illinois in 1962. One year later she also transferred to the University of Washington. Her motivation in education definitely influenced C. C. Yin who had just completed his two years army service in Taiwan. With a degree in Civil Engineering, no doubt he could find a job and make a decent living in Taiwan. However, he was not happy with the life and conditions there. Being in his late twenties, he was concerned about his future. He looked for a change and always admired Eleanor. C. C. Yin asserts, "If my sister was able to overcome all hardship to go to America, why not me? My stepmother would not support me, and my oldest sister did not have money to give me. She had already lent out a great deal of her money to help Eleanor to come to U.S.A. I was determined to try my luck in America so I borrowed some money from my two cousins and from friends."

In 1964, C. C. Yin boarded a cargo ship and spent about a month's unpleasant journey at sea. He first arrived at Los Angeles. Later he was admitted to the graduate school at the University of Washington. During summer months, he worked two jobs in order to cover his living expenses. Regina earned room and board as a live-in housekeeper and nanny. C. C. met Regina at the University through Eleanor. Eventually C. C. graduated in structural engineering and Regina in social work, and they got married in 1966. Regina states, "We did not have a great deal of money. It was ten dollars for a ring and ten dollars for the church. I paid a five-dollar rental fee to this smart 'business' lady for the bridal gown."

C. C. and Regina worked a couple years in the Seattle area. Then C. C. got an engineering job with the Bechtel Corporation and relocated to San Francisco in 1968. They bought a rundown house in Belmont. In 1969,

Regina's parents moved from Taiwan to live with them. The grandparents took care of their one-year-old child, Mary. Besides C. C. and Regina working very hard in their 8-5 jobs, they moonlighted as well as took courses in real estate. They had to support the family as well as other relatives.

C. C. moved on to the Fluor Corporation, later becoming principal project engineer, overseeing projects for mining and heavy construction. He traveled to foreign countries frequently to supervise and solve problems. Although he got along with his colleagues and did well in his profession, he was excluded socially in the company's inner circle. "I did all the work in my projects for the company, yet I was overlooked when there were opportunities for promotion. I believed my qualifications and my performance in the company were much better than the persons who were selected. This happened to me several times. It hurt me inside very much. At the beginning, I thought that my English skills or my public speaking was not good enough, so I joined the Toastmasters to improve my public speaking. I participated socially in informal lunches or parties. I liked to talk and made jokes. What more do I have to do to be accepted?"

When China opened up in 1970s, American companies, like Fluor Corporation, had several projects in China including a $1.7 billion business deal in copper mining. C. C. was the right-hand liaison person under the senior-vice president. Later, 20-30 Chinese engineers were sent to the United Stated to study American engineering. It took several years to complete these projects. C. C. was also sent to Peru when local engineers or field supervisors could not solve problems there. Working in mining projects required him to live in very isolated areas.

C. C. claims with an emotional gesture, "I learned a great deal from working in American corporations. I learned how to socialize with co-workers. However, as an Asian with my knowledge, skills, dedication and my loyalty to the company, I did not see I had the chance to move up any further to vice-president in the company. Is there a 'glass ceiling' in American corporate culture? Do I lack the ability to become a corporation's president? Should I wait there to be promoted before I retire? I had been working in the company for more than 12 years as a successful principal project engineer."

What C. C. faced was not an isolated or individual case. A case in point is Mr. Li-Pei Wu, President of the General Bank, headquartered in Los Angeles, which was cited as the best and most safe bank in the U.S.A. by the US Banker in 1998. Looking back to Mr. Wu's career path, which was quite similar to that of C. C. Yin, he graduated from Taiwan University and came to Fort Hays, Kansas, for a MBA degree. After he finished his study, he went to Columbia University for additional study in financial business and banking. After he graduated, he got a job in the National Bank of Alaska and moved up to the Vice-Executive Officer. Although, as a vice-executive officer, he turned around the financial crisis of the National Bank of Alaska into profit in late 1970s, the "White" Board had difficulty to appoint him to be the president of the bank. While the board was deliberating their selection, Mr. Li-Pei Wu was hired by the Alaska National Bank of the North as the Acting President of the Board and the Chief Executive Officer. Within one year, under his reorganization of the six branches, the bank also turned profitable. The president of the board resigned to run for public office and highly recommended Mr. Wu to be the president. With the ample evidence of Mr. Wu's achievements in the bank, the board still faced a serious question: "can an Oriental become a president in an American bank." Mr. Wu was very angry, and resigned from the bank to go to New York. Because of his resignation, the stock of the bank dropped immediately overnight. The board had no choice and finally invited him back and named him to be the president of the Alaska National Bank of the North. He was the first Chinese American President in an American Bank. With these two near misses, Mr. Wu no longer felt secure. Two years later, in 1982, he decided to leave the Alaska National Bank of the North and became the President of the General Bank, which handles investment mostly coming from Taiwan.

During this period, the family had two more daughters. Regina was promoted to mental health supervisor from social worker for San Mateo County. Both C. C. and Regina were also active in real estate. C. C. also established an engineering consulting business. Regina joined a multi-level business, Fashion Dynamic, selling products by organizing parties and seminars. C. C. followed her around the country, and he discovered that he liked the business very much and enjoyed meeting people. Although they were selling their products successfully, C. C. realized this kind of selling could not bring in much money.

Financially, they became independent not only from their regular jobs, but from their savings, moonlighting and the rising value of their real estate holdings during the 1980s. They turned rundown properties into high value real estate by fixing them up during their weekends. They learned how to manage property and developed good relationships with tenants. They accumulated real estate with a value of millions. With the success in their professions as well as their investments, both wanted to make more of their lives. As C. C. mentioned, he wanted to have financial security in his future. "I can be fired in my job anytime. Where do I go from there? I am in my late forties now. I felt strongly that I would like to do something by myself," C. C. said.

They started looking seriously into different kinds of business, like Burger King, McDonalds, Taco Bell, Arby's, Sizzler, Denny's, ARCO gas station and even thought about a Chinese restaurant. After they did some marketing surveys, C. C. clearly knew what he wanted to do now. He resigned his Fluor Corporation's job in 1984. He admired the McDonald's fast food business simply because everyone can afford to eat hamburgers. Even if the economy is not good, people still have to eat. He also liked the cleanliness of the restaurants

A Taste of the McDonald's Franchise

While working at Fluor Corporation, C. C. often joined fellow engineers for lunch at McDonald's. He was very fascinated and amazed at McDonald's efficiency and their standards of quality and service. Regina also liked McDonald's community efforts. In 1984, C. C. was accepted to enroll in McDonald's Registered Applicants' Program. Here he had to learn how to clean toilets, to keep the kitchen clean, how to handle food safely according to health and safety codes, how to manage part-time workers, how to deal with customers and a payroll. C. C. completed the program in four months with a high score. He hoped the McDonald Corporation. would sell them a restaurant. However, this was not the case even though he had the money available to invest. At first the company tried to discourage them. First their application was rejected and the company questioned their age, personal communication skills, business experience and cultural backgrounds.

C. C. and Regina were not new immigrants. They have lived in the USA for more than twenty years with graduate degrees from an American university. They had worked in American corporations and government agencies and had successful career records in their professions. They were no longer poor and had made their fortune through wise investments and a hard working ethic. They spoke English and understood the American value system and culture as well as their own ethnic one. The key question remains the same: those from the dominant culture may not know enough about the minority people: their strength, values and skills. Minority people often have to work harder to prove what they can do in order to earn the respect and trust from those who have the power and resources.

C. C. and Regina did not give up their hope because of this rejection. They were still waiting to get the chance to own a McDonald's franchise. One day, C. C. was notified to see a McDonald's restaurant, which was located in downtown Oakland. The restaurant was dirty, and the facility and equipment were old. The place was not maintained to the standard of McDonald's image. The business was losing money. C. C. proudly claims, "I was determined to get into McDonald's business. I signed the deal and paid the asking price of $700,000.00. McDonald's approved my application. I had no basis to compare whether it was worth that much or not. I was really naïve at that time, but I felt I could succeed in my gut feeling. I did not regret what I paid."

To fully understand the development of the C. C. and Regina Yin's McDonald enterprise, the following will be discussed. How did they manage their restaurants? How did they meet the expectation of McDonald's? How did they get involved in their community? What innovative ideas and practices did they contribute to enrich McDonald's image? How did they bring up their family and interact with their own ethnic community?

After purchasing the franchise on Oakland's 68th Avenue near the Eastmont Shopping Center, in the heart of Oakland, C. C. took a bold step to remodel the whole restaurant. He invested another $250,000 to replace the old and broken equipment and make sure the restrooms and the eating area were clean. He hired guards to keep the homeless, transients, and gangs away from his restaurant. He worked closely with the staff and applied the knowledge and skills that he learned from the McDonald's training program. He believed the environment of the restaurant could change peoples' behavior. He stood on his principles and treated his employees and customers with fairness, passion and respect. He rewarded his employees based on their hard work without regard to their cultural background. As a 5' 6" tall Chinese, at first he feared staying in the area, inside or outside of the restaurant. It was so bad that he didn't allow Regina and his children to come to the restaurant. C. C. kept on reminding himself that he could not turn his back on this restaurant. With his positive attitude, hard work, interpersonal communication skills and smile, he earned the trust and respect from his staff, as well as the customers and the community. Within 1-1/2 years, the restaurant doubled sales to rank No. 1 in growth in the chains of San Francisco region. C. C. laughed and revealed a secret "When he first bought the old restaurant, someone in McDonald's remarked that the restaurant would not survive for three months."

C. C. asserts again, "It is a fascinating thing to see how the American system is so good and rewarding for people who wish to serve and excel. You get spiritual, personal and financial rewards in different forms and at different times. It is a very interesting society, you know. A lot of people don't see this."

Golden Arches Mark Golden Opportunity

With this unusual taste of success, C. C. and Regina went on to open four more McDonald's in Oakland

and neighboring Alameda. Regina also joined C. C. by networking with community groups, churches and schools as well as working in those restaurants. They no longer feared to open up a McDonald's in any area. They had the experience and skills to deal with the worst situations.

C. C. is an engineer who is constantly finding ways to solve problems, and Regina is a social worker who has the skills in counseling and to reach out to community. They are truly a unique husband-wife team in this type of business. This time McDonald's did not have to question their cultural background, their experience in fast food, their communication skills and even their financial status. Their plans on buying more restaurants, their financial loans and renovation projects were eagerly approved by McDonald's. They continued to succeed in their restaurants and won all kinds of awards from McDonald's, such as "Outstanding Store Manager Award in 1989"and "AAA Outstanding Store Award" in 1990. C. C. and Regina were active in Oakland with the Youth Conference, the Mayor's Summer Job programs, Martin Luther King Memorial Day, the Marcus Foster Foundation education programs through civic leaders and various school programs.

Working long hours in McDonald's in Oakland and Alameda areas for seven years, CC. and Regina not only reaped tremendous success in their business, they also became part of the large McDonald's family. In 1991, they bought four other McDonald's franchises from a retired friend in Vacaville-Fairfield-Suisun area in Solano County. When they came up to look at the restaurants and surrounding area, they fell in love with the rustic, open environment which seemed the ideal place for them and their young children to live. They didn't hesitate to purchase the restaurants, and sold all five McDonald's in Oakland and Alameda. C. C. and Regina were very thankful to have all kind of support from the McDonald's districts' offices and McDonald's headquarters to make their relocation so smooth and so successful.

Renovation and New Development at Yins' McDonald's in Solano County

C. C. and Regina set very high goals in their business. Although they have several restaurants, the Yins can be seen helping mop floors, stock cups or prepare burgers. C. C. frequently assisted workers in closing up restaurants often past 1 a.m., but he has never missed a 7:30 a.m. Chamber meeting. Their hands-on approach has paid off. Sales at their restaurants earned many awards from McDonald's. They follow and support McDonald's principles in guiding their ventures. In August 1992, C. C. attended "Hamburger University" in Oakbrook, Illinois, where McDonald's owners and managers from around the world receive training. C. C. was elected as the No. 1 – "Most Contributive" student, in a class of 280 owners/ managers. Their Vacaville store is used by the corporation as a "Model Store" for success. "While McDonald's requires only one owner be trained, both C. C. and I attended and graduated. It made us, husband-wife, a stronger team" said Regina Yin.

In 1995, C. C. and Regina opened up their seventh McDonald's at the intersection of Alamo Drive and Marshall Road in Vacaville, where they already have two existing restaurants. The restaurant featured fully enclosed children's playground with a brick façade, the first of its kind at a McDonald's in Solano County. "We wanted to provide something exciting to the community. The play place, which cost $100,000.00, has super fast slides, twisty tunnels, moving caterpillar, ball pit, cliff hanger and toddler play area. It is a year-round fun place," said Regina. The new restaurant also featured the latest generation of

McDonald's high-tech kitchens and supports 48 full-time and part-time employees.

Right after the seventh McDonald's opening in Vacaville, the Yins announced they would build their eighth McDonald's in Fairfield Center. The 2,800-square-foot restaurant is located on the corner of West Texas and Beck Streets. "It caters to an untapped market in Fairfield, and brings additional activity to the area and helps support the stores that have been recently built," said Sean Quinn, Fairfield's economic development director. The other existing McDonald's in Fairfield is located on Travis Boulevard, North Texas Street and at Wal-Mart. One is in Cordelia.

As owners of McDonald's restaurants, the Yins are committed to working long hours in their business and promoting the company philosophy, as well, as their own. McDonald's estimates that one in five young American workers are trained first at their restaurants. The Yins also see their restaurants as a training ground for the community. Regina Yin explains, "While some employees may not stay long, they learn some basic job skills that they can utilize throughout their working lives. For employees who wish to commit to a career with McDonald's, owners pay for advanced training. Top managers earn more than what many college graduates make. We are not just in the hamburger business. In terms of McDonald's relationship to society, the American public has taken an ownership position, so to say, spiritual, emotionally, energywise, we must invest back in the community. That has a powerful result."

Regina Yin claims, "The most important ingredient is the people and your attitude toward the people. She credits their above average profit margin to their company's attention to human resources. We have continuously added to our employees' benefit package, not only the medical

plan but also a 401-K retirement plan and bonuses."
Supervisor Sue Drumheller adds, "The Yins are known as
hands-on owners/operators, energetic and caring. They
appear daily at each location. They would come behind the
counter to assist a customer or offer advice to managers.
The Yins provide a hefty bonus package and took managers
on weekend getaways to Reno for skiing or recreation,
three or four times a year. They are very generous. I have
worked six years for McDonald's, starting as swing
manager trainee."

Whenever C. C. and Regina received awards, they
always share them with their staff and give credit to their
efforts. For example, when they were notified that they
received the McDonald's Award for 1997, they wrote the
following note to the staff: "We want to thank you for
taking care of the restaurants well, so we can have time and
energy to work with the community where due to your hard
work, you have earned a good reputation and good will for
McDonald's," C. C. and Regina, September 9, 1997.

Competition in the fast food business is very keen.
McDonald's 1977 share of the overall fast-food business
has fallen from 17.8 percent to 16.1 percent, according to
Technomic Inc., a market research firm in New York.
Competitors such as Burger King and other new companies
offering everything from rotisserie chicken to bagels to
pizza took away some of McDonald's business. "We do
feel pressure as the world becomes more competitive or
productive, and it's not just our industry. Citing Wal-Mart
and other chain stores, prices keep going down, and quality
keeps going up. Retailing is in the throes of a second
industrial revolution, and this is a part of the change
McDonald's is going through." C. C. added. Fortunately
Yins' McDonald's did not suffer because of their reputation
in their community, and because their friends feel so good
about them.

The Yins' McDonald's is helping to test and implement alternative methods of doing business, such as a new "make-to-order" cooking system. "We are involved in many ways, and we have just invested about $1 million to change our kitchen system totally. That is part of the ongoing change that the McDonald's system is making." The Yins also have developed several nontraditional venues for their McDonald's group, including a mall location and two outlets inside Wal-Mart stores.

New campaigns to promote McDonald's constantly require the district's franchisees' participation. In preparation for the new campaigns, C. C. and Regina have stocked up on products and hired additional workers for their ten local restaurants, bringing in new entertainment, providing new advertisement, in order to make each of the campaigns successful. With additional work and energy, sales go up.

Location	Year	App. Initial Investment $	# of Staff (Full/Part) Time	App. Annual Gross Sale (In 1998)	Special Features
Vacaville #1(#2005)	1991	$800 K	F= 35 P= 12	$2.3 mil.	Decorated with Vacaville High School history
Vacaville #2 (#13226)	1995		F= 37 P= 12	$2.3 mil.	Stamp Collections Signs designed with World War II, Hollywood legend, Disneyland collection, High-tech kitchens and

					children's playground
Vacaville-Wal-Mart (#15011)	1995	$400 K	F= 8 P= 7	$650 K	No
Fairfield #1(#1355)	1991	$800 K	F= 39 P= 11	$2.2 mil.	No
Fairfield #2(#7677)	1991	$700 K	F= 25 P= 9	$1.8 mil.	Travis AFB history Display
Fairfield #3(#8138)	1996	$650 K	F= 24 P= 8	$1.5 mil.	Fairfield High School's celebration with photos over 100 years, high school year book since 1940 and during World War II
Fairfield Wal-Mart (#13197)	1995	$400 K	F= 9 P= 9	$625 K	No
Fairfield Solano Mall (#20066)	1996	$400 K	F= 10 P= 6	$700 K	No
Suisun (#7078)	1991	$800 K	F= 39 P= 11	$2.1 mil.	Decorated with Duck Stamps from 1960 to present
Truxel Wal Mart (#23751)	1998	$400 K	F= 9 P_ 9	$670 K	No
Yin's Headquarter (Central Office)			F= 5 P= 2		

The Yins' ten McDonald's in Solano County from 1991-1998

No Pain, no Gain

It is fascinating and admirable to observe their business growth in McDonald's. But they are facing challenges in their daily operations and new developments. Misunderstanding or unfavorable action could occur. Within a year of purchasing the franchises in Solano County, the manager fired several young black employees of the McDonald's at the Suisun City. Some employees picketed the restaurant, called in NAACP and rallied the black community for support. Frank Jackson, the president of the Vallejo NAACP chapter, after interviewing the Yins' top Oakland restaurant managers and investigating their track record, concluded the Yins were not discriminatory. Roughly 90 percent of their Oakland employees were black. C. C. said. " I don't want to mistreat the kids. We just had some bad management." C. C. handled the incident properly and joined the NAACP Vallejo chapter, becoming a lifetime member, and contributed to its scholarship fund. C. C. participates actively in this organization to this very day. In 1996, C. C. Yin was recognized at the NAACP Tri-City (Fairfield-Vacaville-Suisun) chapter's twentieth anniversary banquet, where he was lauded for "unselfish and dedicated community service" presented an award by the chapter president Griffin Bailey.

When the Yins wanted to open a McDonald's on the corner of Beck Avenue and West Texas Street, as part of a development with Pep Boys, they received complaints from other West Texas Street restaurant owners. City planners originally approved an In-N-Out hamburger restaurant for that site, but In-N-Out didn't like its agreement with the developer. The Yins worked out the deal with the developer. "I wouldn't feel comfortable telling McDonald's, 'Hey, you can't come up here because some people up the street are mad at you.' The good business person will survive, and the bad business person will fail," Chuck Hammond, Mayor of Fairfield told the *Fairfield Daily Republic*, April 6, 1997.

Opening each McDonald's required a great deal of planning and investment as well as support. Not all of Yins' expansion proposals were approved. In 1993, C. C. and Regina Yin wanted to acquire the ownership rights of the McDonald's.'s proposed restaurant in Winters, Yolo County, California. Despite the Yins' track record of excellent operator and heavy lobbying from business and political leaders, the franchise selection committee and the headquarters of McDonald's Corporation at Oakbrook, Illinois, did not favor the Yins' application at that time.

Involvement in civic, local business, community and charitable circles

It didn't take too long for this newcomer couple to be known in the Vacaville-Fairfield-Suisun area in Solano County. Owning four restaurants in 1991 and expanding to twelve in 1999 did not take their attention away from other matters. The couple parlayed their skills and civic interests into local business, community and charitable circles. On October 1992, one year after C. C. arrived in Vacaville, the board of Directors of Vacaville Chamber of Commerce appointed C. C. Yin to be a director. C. C. and Regina actively participated in the Chamber's community activities and fundraising events. Joan Krack, who has worked closely with C. C. at the Vacaville Chamber of Commerce indicates, "They give and they give and they give. It's more than dollars, they give themselves." Vacaville Mayor David A. Fleming notes, "I think they care about people, and that comes through. I have great respect and great regard for them. They are very public spirited. They always come through for any charity drive."

In 1996, C. C. Yin was elected president of the Vacaville Chamber of Commerce. The chamber's 46th annual installation dinner, held at the Yin's Ranch, drew the largest attendance in history. Jean Krack, the Chamber Executive Director said "Two possible reasons for the big turnout were: First, Yin, the owner of several McDonald's restaurant, is well-known in the community and many people wanted to be on hand to see him installed as president. The second reason was a desire to see the Yin's Ranch, a picturesque one-of a-kind estate."

During the years, C. C. has demonstrated his commitment and leadership in the Chamber of Commerce. He emphasized "Teamwork: Working together-Winning Together. Together we can make a difference." Under his term the Chamber organized many activities which included a golf tournament and a Pumpkin Patch in Vacaville. The proceeds benefited many local charitable and civic organizations. The Chamber established an Industrial/ Economic Development Committee, a Marketing Committee promoting Chamber events, created a Past Presidents Council to capitalize on the ideas and knowledge of former Chamber leaders, as well as to recognize their contributions.

The Yins' McDonald's also have "adopted" Vacaville High School by providing financial assistance for the school's music program. They also worked closely with the fundraising efforts for the Eagle Lake Children's camp for children with developmental disabilities. The list of the Yin's accomplishments and recognition is extensive. Their contributions have been invaluable to the welfare and improvement of the community. For example, Regina Yin has played an integral role in resuscitating Interact Clubs at local schools. A member of the Fairfield-Suisun Rotary Club, she asked the principals of Fairfield and Vanden High schools and the superintendents of the Fairfield-Suisun Unified School District for permission to use the yearbook pictures to commemorate local history in one of her McDonald's restaurant in Fairfield. The restaurant's interior was decorated with dozens of historical photographs gleaned from Fairfield and Armijo high school yearbooks dating back to1913. These pictorial collages depict a timeline of different styles and eras in American history. Superintendent Darrel Taylor states, "Younger students would get a sense of the history of the school. The project provided a good strong link between business and schools." Regina reflects, "I got the idea for the project through my community work with local schools. I think the photos will help connect the present to the past and promote traditional values."

In 1997, Regina Yin was named Woman of the Year for California's fourth Senatorial District and was praised by Sen. K. Maurice Johannessen for his "passionate dedication to giving back to her community." In 1998, the Yins' won the McDonald's Corporation's regional Ronald Award for contributions in developing the chain's marketing image and community relations. Both C. C. and Regina were recruited in several capacities to support the chain. C. C. is on the franchisees' purchasing committee, which advises on equipment and food, while Regina is on the advisory board for marketing and operations procedures. She also serves on the board of the Ronald McDonald House, where family members of seriously ill children being treated at the University of California Davis Medical Center in Sacramento can stay.

C. C. wears many hats and has chaired many committees in his community. He is serving as 1. Chairman in Vacaville Police Activity League (PAL), a board of 15 members, serving about 2,000 at–risk children in and after schools by providing sports, recreation and reading programs. 2. Chairman of the Citizens' Advisory Board to the Solano Prisons, a board of 15 members appointed by State Senators. 3. Chairman for the Lungren for Governor Fundraiser Committee. The committee raised $100,000 and brought 1000 people to the event sponsored by Northern California McDonald's and Napa/Solano/Yolo County Group in 1998.

The Yins Family and the Chinese/Asian American Community

C. C. and Regina raised three daughters. Today, Mary works as deputy district attorney in Solano County. Mary graduated in 1991 from University of California, Irvine, where she studied Social Ecology with a pre-law emphasis and minor in English. She then went on to Loyola Law School and graduated in 1994. Following her parents' footsteps, she is active in the local community as well as in the Asian Pacific American legal community. Betty is a family business partner and manager of one of the McDonald's. The youngest daughter, Carol, is attending college in Florida.

C. C. was very close to his in-laws. He remembered when he first got married thirty years ago, his in-laws moved from Taiwan to live with them. While the mother-in-law took care of the children, the father-in-law helped him with the renovation and remodeling of rundown houses and apartments. C. C. especially appreciated his in-laws. C. C. reminisces, "I lost my mother when I was six months old, and my father never stayed with me. Growing up I either lived at schools or with my sisters, so my in-laws' warmth, caring, love and friendship have been very special for me. When I designed my new ranch in Vacaville, I built an additional unit in which they could live comfortably. Also when I designed the yard, I had them in mind. That is why I have ramps on all sides of the house and no steps inside the house, so they could move around easily. Some mornings I liked to accompany the in-laws on a walk on the ranch from their living quarters to the lake. In the middle of the lake is a small island that we have named, "Chongming" in memory of where they were born in China. My father-in-law lived with us at the ranch for more than two years before he passed away in 1997.

Long before C. C. and Regina settled in Vacaville, in the nineteenth century, many Chinese, most from Southern China, came to Solano County for farm work. Census records show that by 1850, the first Chinese had arrived in Solano County. By 1870, there were 920 Chinese men in Solano County, but only one Chinese woman. Records show that 261 of these Chinese men lived in Suisun as farm laborers, 13 were laundrymen in Suisum City, 171 were laborers in Vacaville, and 182 lived in Vallejo. Other Chinese were scattered in Benicia, Dixon, Rio Vista and Green Valley. According to Ronald H. Limbaugh, Vacaville fruit growers, like all other fruit producers of California, depended on Chinese laborers. When the Anti-Chinese Exclusion Law passed in 1882, Chinese laborers became scarce. The population of Vacaville had a handful of Chinese business people who came in the 1950s and afterwards, but few descendants of the early families continue to make their home in the area.

Many new Chinese people who come to live in Solano County today do not know much about the early Chinese experience in Solano County. Few descendants of early farming families were aware of the newcomers. Before the 1980s, the Chinese community in Solano County was almost invisible. Since C. C. and Regina established their McDonald's in the 1990s, the Chinese American community in the area has gotten together again and become more visible.

C. C. and Regina, with a few local Chinese, organized the Chinese-American Association of Solano County. Under the association, Vacaville Chinese School was founded in 1996 with more than 30 students attending the classes. In less than two years, the Association has more than eighty families with 300 members and over 100 students in the school. With C. C. and Regina's networking and full support, the association was able to bring the old-timers and new comers together to form the Chinese American community. Lion Dances, firecrackers, red envelopes, Chinese New Year's greetings, "Gung Hay Fat Choy" and celebrations marked a major step for the Chinese community to share its culture with the public. County supervisors, city officials and many business leaders eagerly come and enjoy these events. The association also took the leadership to sponsor a conference on the History of Chinese-Americans in Solano County in 1997. The event was held in the Yin's ranch with several hundred participants. Scholars, historians and museum staff from the county came together to present their talks. The Chinese American heritage in this county was documented.

C. C. Yin was able to fight for the welfare for the Asian American community. In 1996, when Tele-Communications Inc. (TCI) decided to cancel KTSF, Channel 26 in Vacaville, C. C. Yin formed the "Save Channel 26 Coalition" with about 25 people who rallied support from business and political leaders. Yin said foreign-language channels fill a unique and critical niche for people who speak English as a second language. Newcomers don't understand much of the language here, so they would be cut off from news and entertainment. It would be devastating for the families, yet, they were not given a choice. Coalition members collected almost 2,000 signatures that convinced TCI to retain the Asian programming station. "First we were told it was an impossibility. We were up in arms." C. C. added. "The signatures and the rally really led us to change that decision," said Andrew Johnson, director of communications for TCI in California and Nevada.

"Dear C. C.: Thank you very much for leading the effort to keep Channel 26 on cable television. I was impressed by how fast you worked. The Asian community was also impressed, and several of them asked me to pass on their compliments to you. Again, thank you. You are an asset to the community." David A. Fleming, Mayor of Vacaville, wrote.

The above sentiments speak well about the Yins. They truly demonstrate quality and character as new leaders in Asian American community. They are able to bridge their own community and work very well to connect with the dominant society. It is a new era that the Chinese and Asian American community can enjoy more visibility and recognition in Solano County.

The Yins' Ranch in Vacaville was completed in 1995. Besides serving as their home, it is used frequently for entertainment for their staff as well as a meeting place for the Chinese American Association of Solano County. In 1996, the installation dinner of C. C. as new president of the Chamber of Commerce was held at the ranch. The ranch also hosted the opening of an art and historical exhibit chronicling the Chinese heritage in Solano County in February 1997. In addition, many charitable and fundraising events for political candidates, such as Maurice Johannessen, Mike Thompson and Matt Fong, were also held at the ranch.

Conclusion:

McDonald's is a good business, but obtaining a franchise is very competitive. There are over 20,000 McDonald's Registered Applicants each year, but one hundred applicants will be accepted for training per year and only about 50% of the trained applicants will be offered the opportunity to own a franchise. The average owners/operators who have a McDonald's franchise own 2.3 restaurants. Less than 6% of the 23,300 franchise restaurants of McDonald's Corp are owned by minorities. The number of Asians who are owners/operators of McDonald's is miniscule. C. C. and Regina were very proud to be part of the McDonald's Corporation. They appreciate that they get along well and receive all kinds of support and guidance from the corporation. In 1995, C. C. and Regina also helped to organize the Asian McDonald's Operators Association (AMOA) which has 60 members now. AMOA is beginning to provide mutual support as well as to build better relationships with the corporation, so that their needs and concerns will be heard. There are ample business opportunities with McDonald's, and the markets that can be beneficial to Asian Americans have not yet been tapped. C. C. and Regina Yin are paving a path that may lead to a new prosperity between McDonald's and Asian Pacific communities in the millennium.

C. C. and Regina Yin represent a new generation of Chinese-Americans in California. They are bilingual and bicultural professionals and well-educated in American universities. They are unlike early Chinese immigrants who were subjected to many unfair restrictions and barriers. Chinese-Americans like all Americans are protected from discrimination and have equal rights. They have opportunities to enter different fields and career choices. They can participate in civic, business, political and charitable events. The American dream has become a reality for the Yins and others. They are real assets in many corporations as well as in their community. If Yins can achieve, so can many others. But the Yins' success is not only measured by financial wealth, but also by contributions and positive participation in their corporation, in their community and society.

References

"Board Appoints Yin, Norling" *Vacaville Chamber Comments*, Vol. 11, No. 4, October 1992.

Edwards, Cliff. "McDonald's back on the attack with its Big Mac, *The Sacramento Bee*, September 10, 1998.

Fitch, Mike. " Relishing Hard Work", *Vacaville Reporter*, October 20, 1996.

Furuya, Keiji. *Chiang Kai-Shek: His Life and Times*, Abridged English Edition by Chun-Ming Chang, St. John's University, New York, 1981.

Hostler, Mark and Garver, Mike. *Rotary News & Notes,* March 11, 1997.

Huang, Jen and Regina Huang Yin. *Jen Huang, A Life Story*, Masterpiece Memoirs, P.O. Box 128, Vacaville, California, 1997.

Leung, Peter C. Y. "Legendary Restaurateur: Frank Fat", *The Californians*, Vol. 9, Number 2, 1991.

LaMar, Andrew. "Living the American Dream: Once poor immigrants, local couple gets rich with McDonald's", *Fairfield Daily Republic*, April 6, 1997.

Martin, Richard. " Yin McDonald's: Golden Arches make golden Opportunity for immigrant husband-wife team", *National Restaurant News*, January 1998.

Pully, Michael. " McDonald's restaurant to open in Vacaville", *Vacaville Reporter,* November 17, 1995.

Robin, Douglas. " Fifth McDonald's opens next year", Solano Scene, *Fairfield Daily Republic*, December 6, 1995

Scoggins, Shelly, Hedicke and Associates. " McDonald's Owner/Operators Receive National Recognition for Their Contributions to Building the Business", Press release, August 22, 1997.

Yin Yao. " Li-Pei Wu and the General Bank", *California Sunshine,* October/November, 1998

"The History of Chinese-American in Solano County", Chinese American Association of Solano County, February 1997.

Mecca of Chinese America in California: Dai Fow (San Francisco), Yee Fow (Sacramento), and Sam Fow (Stockton)

Dr. Joe Chung Fong

Introduction

J an Lin's (1998) *Reconstructing Chinatown: Ethnic Enclave, Global Change*, Franklin Ng's (1998) *The Taiwanese Americans*, and Tim Fong's (1994) *First Suburban Chinatown* are a few noted Chinese community studies in the recent past. In Fong's book, his community research departs from the traditional Chinatown in the urban areas. He instead illuminates the first suburban Chinese community in Los Angeles San Gabriel Valley. Fong discusses the new post-1965 Chinese immigrant adjustment, political representation and race relations. Ng's book is the first comprehensive discussion on Taiwanese immigrants in the United States while Lin discusses New York City as localized globalized Chinatown.

Majority of the current studies focuses on the East Coast Chinatowns such as in New York City and Southern California Chinese communities in San Gabriel Valley.

United States. With the mushrooming of studies on Chinese America and its dissimilar approach to examine Chinese communities, it is appropriate to consider the origin of Chinese America.

Dai Fow (San Francisco)

A few contemporary studies of Chinese American community have suggested that other Chinatowns have surpassed San Francisco Chinese community. In this article, we will not debate this issue. It is well documented that the first Chinatown in the continental United States has its roots in San Francisco. For the most part, from 1849 to 1965, the port of San Francisco received more than a significant number of the Chinese immigrants. One example is the Ellis Island of the West, Angel Island. Angel Island represents the "immigrant terminal," which received immigrants entering from the West Coast, particularly the Chinese immigrants. Lai's, Lim's, and Yung's (1980) *Island Poetry and History of Chinese Immigrants on Angel Island 1910-1940* documents that between 1910 and 1940, approximately 175,000 Chinese immigrants came through Angel Island.

More importantly, the social structure of the Chinese community emerged from San Francisco Chinatown. Later, other Chinatowns from the surrounding cities like Sacramento and Stockton modeled themselves after San Francisco Chinatown's social institutions. As pioneer Chinese immigrants migrated to the continental United States' interior, they patterned small and large Chinese communities' social structure after San Francisco Chinatown. It is no accident that even today the majority of the district and family associations' headquarters are located in San Francisco. Even the progressive American-born Chinese civil organization, the Chinese American Citizen

League, started in 1895 in San Francisco. Now this organization has many branches in the United States but the Grand Lodge continues to be in San Francisco Chinatown.

However, San Francisco's Chinatown was and is not an island to itself. Considered by far the largest Chinese community until the 1970's, the community has many supporting environs. When Chinese referred to San Francisco Chinatown in the pre-1965 era, they were actually referring to the Bay Area Chinatowns, which include the cities of Sacramento and Stockton. The Bay Area, particularly San Francisco Chinatown, was and is the Mecca of Chinese America. In the pre-1965 era, every Chinese in America knew that and referred to San Francisco's Chinatown as "Dai Fow," the first city or the "Big City." This label came from the Chinese themselves and says much about the position and the esteem the Chinese place on "Dai Fow." The City of Sacramento is referred to as Yee Fow, the second city and the City of Stockton is referred to as Sam Fow, the third city. These three cities represent the Mecca of Chinese America and the birthplace of Chinese American civilization.

Sam Fow (Stockton)

Of the three Chinatowns, Sam Fow is the smallest. Stockton Chinese community is third in importance to Sacramento and San Francisco Chinatowns. One of the earliest Chinese-American written material on Sam Fow, Wah Yun: The Chinese Community in Stockton (Fang, 1963), reported that "there were Chinese in Stockton as early as 1820, even before the city was established...that the first sizable group of Chinese arrived on a small steamer, the Kate Kearney, in January 1852." Other published materials on Sam Fow are Chinatowns in the Delta: The Chinese in the Sacramento-San Joaquin Delta,

1870-1960 (Chu, 1970), Sam Fow: The San Joaquin Chinese Legacy (Minnick, 1988) and Awakening a 140-year Chinese American Community: A Study of a Local Election (Minnick, 1994).

Yee Fow, Sacramento Chinatown

Yee Fow (Sacramento) is second in importance to San Francisco Chinatown that "To Chinese, Sacramento is an important and commercial center second only to San Francisco, and one of the best place to live...At one time there were more than 10,000 Chinese in the mother lode county." (Fang, 1961) In 1961, Yee Fow had "about 7,000 Chinese in the Sacramento area. About one third of them, directly or indirectly, earn their living through the food business. The Chinese own about 150 groceries and supermarkets, which receive annual revenues of more than $150 million. There are about 145 Chinese restaurants serving Chinese and American food. Less than 300 Chinese still work in the laundry business." (Fang, 1961)

Like San Francisco, Yee Fow has its own environs in the past: The farming townships of Locke, Courtland, and Walnut Grove to name a few. Please see relevant published materials on Yee Fow areas: Valley City: A Chinese Community in America (Weiss, 1974), Report on Locke: Historical Overview and Call for Action (Kagiwada, 1982) and One Day, One Dollar: Locke, California and the Chinese Farming Experience in the Sacramento Delta (Leung, 1984). The freeway construction led to the demise of the Yee Fow's environs. Instead, Sacramento today has three Chinese communities: administrative Chinatown, Co-exist Chinatown, and Indo-Chinatown.

Administrative Chinatown

What is an Administrative Chinatown? Historically, Chinatown between 3rd and 6th Streets along I Street was the center of Chinese life in Sacramento. (Fang, 1961) Due to urban renewal, the Administrative Chinatown replaced old Yee Fow Chinatown in the 1960's. Urban renewal divided the existing Yee Fow where a few traditional associations are still headquartered in the "new" (administrative) Sacramento Chinatown, and others moved to the present day Co-exist Chinese community. For simplicity, the Administrative Chinatown is a symbolic representation of the Chinese people in Sacramento because that particular Chinatown houses the Chinese Consolidated Benevolent Association, a Confucius Hall and few other traditional associations.

The Administrative Chinatown is located in downtown Sacramento. As in any big city downtown, it is hard to find parking. Even though the community is nestled next to a major freeway, unfortunately, the Administrative Community does not attract tourists from the downtown shopping center as in San Francisco Chinatown, and it does not have any Asian supermarkets or grocery stores to attract the Chinese people. Without tourists and co-ethnic clients, the Administrative Chinatown is an urban Locke, an historical rural township.

In the past, the Administrative Chinatown's showcase was the Confucius Hall, an official place where traditional festivals and other important events relating to the Chinese in Sacramento were held to reflect the Chinese accomplishments. Other than a Dr. Sun Yat Sen museum and a few restaurants, Administrative Chinatown followed the footsteps of the nearby rural township of Locke.

Co-exist Chinatown

During the 1960's urban renewal era, many traditional Chinese associations relocated a few miles from the Administrative Chinatown to 12th and J streets, spilling over to 16th and Broadway streets. The area around 12th and J streets is home of the Lim's, Lee's, and other traditional family association headquarters. On the other side near 16th and Broadway streets are the headquarters of the Wong's and the Yee's associations. One of the significant landmarks for locating the Co-exist Chinatown is the Tower Records and Tower cafe.

I use the term Co-exist Chinatown because unlike other urban Chinatowns, this Chinese community is shared by and co-exists with the Japanese American community. In this Co-exist community, Chinese and Japanese shops, restaurants, and mom and pop stores are represented. Similar to the Chinese traditional associations, the Co-exist community has a Japanese Buddhist Church, and many Japanese American festivals are celebrated in the area such as *Obon*. Near 16th and Broadway streets, in addition to corresponding Chinese and Japanese restaurants and shops, there are many American businesses establishments.

There are many obvious differences between the Administrative and Co-exist Chinatowns. Unlike the Administrative Chinatown, people, both Chinese and others, shop, eat, and socialize in the Co-exist community. These social and cultural activities create and recreate a sense of community among the Chinese. The Co-exist Chinese community provides an economic environment for the Chinese to open businesses in the area while the Administrative Chinatown area is not conducive to commerce. Lastly, the Co-existing community is inclusive and accessible to other Americans. Thus, creating community, by and for Chinese, along with economic factors in the form of making a living has generated a true sense of place of belonging. The Administrative Chinatown lacks all these human and economic elements to cultivate a Chinese community.

Indo-Chinatown

The third Chinatown is the newest Chinese community in Sacramento. Most Chinese people in Sacramento consider the third Chinese community as the "real Chinatown." The center of social and economic activities of this newest community is between the crossroads of Stockton Boulevard. and Elder Creek Road. Most of the businesses are located on a mile stretch of Stockton Boulevard. Unlike the other two Chinatowns, the third Chinese community consists of many small and medium size plazas, and each plaza has many different types of business establishments.

From our fieldwork, we have identified more than 6 plazas and as many Chinese and Southeast Asian supermarkets. Besides the typical Chinese noodle houses and restaurants, these plazas have bookstores, video shops, and hair salons. These plazas and supermarkets are self-contained, catering to the whole family, not just merely grocery shopping. During the weekend, the third Chinatown resembles the Oakland and San Francisco Chinese community, bustling with shoppers.

I labeled the community Indo-Chinatown because most of the residents there are from Southeast Asian countries of Laos, Vietnam, and Cambodia. More accurately, Indo-Chinatown represents the ethnic Chinese from Indo-China. However, other Chinese also reside in Indo-Chinatown as well as shop, eat, and socialize in this newest community. The importance of this newest community is reinforced by the location of a branch office of the transnational newspaper *Sing Tao Daily*. Ethnic

Chinese from Southeast Asia too have their own weekly newspaper, *China News*, catering to news about their homeland and about ethnic Chinese in other parts of the United States.

There are several community organizations in Indo-Chinatown but the most respected and well known is the Sacramento Chinese Indo-China Friendship Association in America. This Indo-China Association provides many services to the community. The Association has a temple, catering to the needs of the worshipers. Its Chinese language school is one of the best in Sacramento. In interviews, many former students said they were glad that they went to that school and participated in many of the events in the community such as the essay and speech contests.

Closing Remarks

Few would dispute that Dai Fow, Yee Fow, and Sam Fow represent the mecca of Chinese America in California. The 1965 immigration policy and the 1980's influx of Southeast Asian refugees have impacted these three cities. Each of these three cities now is self-sustaining and more diverse in terms of different ethnic Chinese groups. Now, the Bay Area Chinese communities are home to Chinese from China, Hong Kong Chinese, Taiwanese Chinese, Vietnamese-Chinese and Chinese-Americans. The Sacramento Chinese community reflects these social changes taking place in the Bay Area.

References

China News. A Chinese-Vietnamese Weekly Newspaper.

Chu, George. "Chinatowns in the Delta: The Chinese in the Sacramento-San Joaquin Delta." *California Historical Society Quarterly*, Vol XLIX, No.1. 1970.

Fang, James. *Yee Fow: The Chinese Community in Sacramento.* San Francisco, California: Chinese Publishing House, 1963.

Wuh Yun: *The Chinese Community in Stockton.* San Francisco, California: Chinese Publishing House. 1961.

Fong, Timothy. *First Suburban Chinatown.* Philadelphia: Temple University Press. 1994.

Kagiwada, George. Report of Locke: A Historical Overview and Call for Action. *Amerasia Journal,* Vol. 9, No. 2 (Fall/Winter). 1982.

Lai, H. M., Genny Lim and Yung, Judy. *Island: Poetry and History of Chinese Immigrants on Angel Island 1910-1940.* A Project of the Chinese Culture Foundation of San Francisco: Published by HOC DOI. 1980.

Leung, Peter C. Y. *One Day, One Dollar: Locke, California and the Chinese Farming Experience in the Sacramento Delta.* El Cerrito, California: Chinese American History Project. 1984.

Lin, Jan. *Reconstructing Chinatown: Ethnic Enclave, Global Change.* Minneapolis: University of Minnesota Press. 1998.

Minnick, Sylvia Sun. *Awakening a 140-Year Chinese American Community: A Study of a Local Election. Origins and Destinations: 41 Essays on Chinese America.* A Joint Project of Chinese Historical Society of Southern California and UCLA Asian American Studies Center: The Chinese Historical Society of Southern California. 1994.

Minnick, Sylvia Sun. *Samfow: The San Joaquin Chinese Legacy.* Fresno, California: Panorama West Publishing Company, 1988.

Ng, Franklin. *The Taiwanese Americans.* Westport, Connecticut: Greenwood Press. 1998.

Sing Tao Daily. Every Sunday, *Sing Tao* Daily reports on Sacramento Chinese Community Activities.

Weiss, Melford S. *Valley City: A Chinese Community in America.* Cambridge, Massachusetts: Schenkman Publishing Company. 1974.

Branches Of Chinese Racial Tree
Ethnic Chinese Contributions: Establishing New Chinatown and Indo-China Association in Sacramento, California
Dr. Joe Chung Fong

The term "ethnic Chinese" refers to those people of Chinese descent who escaped from Southeast Asia to the United States during and after the Vietnam War (1963-1975, it began with the US Congress's Tonkin Gulf Resolution and ended as the last Marine boarded a CH-46 helicopter atop the American Embassy in Saigon.) The fall of Saigon government on April 30, 1975 precipitated one of the largest emergency migrations of refugees to America. From April through the end of December of 1975, over 130,000 Vietnamese refugees entered the United States. There are no ethnic Chinese statistics available on the first wave of 130,000 refugees. Their numbers were probably too small to be noticed by the United States government. They were usually lumped together with the Vietnamese people.

Social scientists have identified five major Southeast Asian groups: Vietnamese, Laotian, Cambodia, Hmong, and ethnic Chinese. South Vietnam had the largest Chinese population, 1,400,000; then Cambodia, 310,000;

and Laos, 37,000. North Vietnam had 300,000 ethnic Chinese. It is generally agreed that the ethnic Chinese came in large numbers during the second wave of the influx of Southeast Asian refugees, which peaked in fiscal year 1980 (October 1, 1979-September 30, 1980) with the arrival of 166,700 Southeast Asian refugees, 95,000 from Vietnam. They were the "Boat People." Until August 1979, the ethnic Chinese constituted at least 75 percent (222,870) of the "Boat People" who have fled Vietnam since early 1975.

Within these five major groups, there are many sub-groups. Each established their own social institutions in this new land depending on the time of their arrival, their home social status, and treatment by their host society. Their adjustment patterns in America are well documented. The most recent studies focus on the Southeast Asian children's educational attainments in the United States. However, few studies have adequately addressed their social institutions in terms of their adjustment in their new land and the effect of such institutions on education and social networks.

It would be a Herculean task to examine the social institutions of each of the five groups. This paper more narrowly examines a Southeast Asian Association in Sacramento: The Sacramento Chinese Indo-China Friendship Association. First, we will provide an overview of the Southeast Asian Indo- Chinese in the United States. This will be followed by a discussion on the transplanted as well as the reconstructed social institutions of the Southeast Asians. Lastly, we will discuss the function and structure of the Sacramento Chinese Indo-China Friendship Association.

(1) The Overview of the Southeast Asians History

Ethnic Chinese in some Southeast Asian countries had to change their names for economic survival. Wilbur Gay Lee's Master of Arts thesis (1960), *Overseas Chinese Communities: A Comparative Approach*, states, "In 1956 President Ngo Diem issued an order which granted Vietnamese citizenship automatically to all the Chinese born in Vietnam. Then all aliens were required to register. When the registration was completed, *all aliens* were given Vietnam citizenship papers. Concurrently South Vietnam launched its anti-Chinese campaign. Chinese schools were forced to use the Vietnamese language; Chinese signs in front of the shops were taken down; Chinese born in Vietnam were pressured into Vietnamizing their names; aliens were barred from eleven categories of occupation; aliens were forced to sell their business interests to Vietnamese within on year."

The United States government overlooked the ethnic Chinese among the first wave of Southeast Asian refugees, which were divided into three major official categories: Vietnamese, Cambodian, and Laotian. Later, the government recognized the Hmong tribesmen from northern Vietnam, who were one of the last groups to arrive in the United States. The United States government was either not aware of their existence among these refugees or concluded that it would be simpler to combine them with the rest of the Southeast Asian refugees.

By 1979, ethnic Chinese started being officially recognized among the refugees. A government document entitled *"The Indo-Chinese Refugees Survival; August 1979"* by the House of Representatives indicated and identified that there were, and are, ethnic Chinese in Southeast Asian camps. The population in these camps were--Hong Kong: 12,098; Indonesia: 4,300; and Malaysia:

23, 888. In 1979, the total was 40,286. Nonetheless, some documents barely noted their existence such as the *Hearings before the Subcommittee of Asian and Pacific Affairs Ninety-Sixty Congress, First and Second session.*

By 1986, 138,800 Cambodians, 162,000 Laotians, and 506,700 Vietnamese had arrived in the United States, comprising a total of 809,500 Southeast Asian refugees. As a total group in late 1980's, Southeast Asians represent almost one Asian American in seven. By August 1987, 389,000 of them lived in California. California was, and continues to be, the most popular state for these Asian refugees. They are now concentrated in four California counties: estimated 60,000 in Orange, 93,000 in Los Angeles, 28,400 in San Francisco, and 37,600 in Santa Clara. In Sacramento, the *Needs Assessment of the Asian/Pacific Islander Community in Sacramento County* in 1992 indicates a total population of at least 22,197 Southeast Asian residents: Vietnamese: 9,497; Hmong: 5,470; Chinese-Vietnamese, 3,630; Iu-Mien: 3,000; and Cambodians: 600.

The ethnic-Chinese from Southeast Asia have experienced significant changes during their brief 20 years history in the United States. In the 1990's, ethnic-Chinese community grew and matured with their Southeast Asian compatriots. There are now many ethnic-Chinese communities ranging from self-reliant "Little Saigon" in San Jose, communities Co-existing with African-Americans such as in East Oakland (Fong, 1992), suburban communities in San Gabriel Valley, Los Angeles, New Chinatown or Little Saigon in Sacramento (Fong, 1998), and Indo-Chinatown in San Francisco's Tenderloin district. They are no longer perceived as refugees, living in isolated pockets in the community at large. Now the ethnic-Chinese have emerged as contributing citizens and are an integral part of American society, particularly in the broader Asian American community.

(2)   Transplanted and Constructed Southeast Asian Social Institutions

What do we mean by social institutions? In this discussion, "social institutions" simply means community organizations, associations, and other fraternal groups that more or less represent the community. A more precise meaning is the community's hierarchical social organizational structure such as the Chinese Consolidated Benevolent Association, District Associations and Family Associations in a typical urban Chinatown (Lyman, 1974).

In their research, many social scientists acknowledge the "Mutual Aid Associations" established by the Southeast Asians. But few of these studies closely examine the community social institutions. The coming together of these refugees and the formation of organizations for mutual aid, shared cultural activities, and social networking among co-immigrant fellow strangers, who have shared experiences and commonality in the host society, are significant factors in the Southeast Asians' process of adaptation. When any research discusses the Southeast Asian social institutions, the discussion fails to distinguish the diverse types of community organizations: how many of these organizations are transplanted from their home countries or created in the United States?

It is instructive to examine Min Zhou's article (1997), *Social Capital in Chinatown: The Role of Community-Based Organizations and Families in the Adaptation of the Younger Generation*. It examines the role of how new social organizations created and formed in New York Chinatown were not necessarily replacing the traditional Chinese social institutions, but "promoting adjustment and success of immigrant children." According to her, "Social organizations in Chinatown, whether they are formal or informal, government-funded or community-rooted, have played a vital role in meeting the social and economic needs of the Chinese community."

Among the Southeast Asian literature, Diana Bui's article in 1983, "The Indo-Chinese Mutual Assistance Associations," is the most relevant analysis of the Southeast Asian social institutions. In her article, she indicates that there have been more than 500 mutual aid associations formed in the Indo-Chinese refugee community since 1975 (Bui, 1983). She also divided the Mutual Aid Associations into eight categories in order to give a sense of the diversity of these organizations: social/fraternal; educational/cultural; religious/spiritual; professional political; student; senior, veterans/women; and refugee resettlement organizations.

Bui's discussion is informative and provides general information on Southeast Asian social and political organizations. However, her discussion was not clear and fails to focus on any single Southeast Asian community. Bui's discussion jumps from Southeast Asian organizations in one state to another. In short, her information lacks depth and does not address the social institutional structure of the community. On the other hand, Him Mark Lai's *Chinese Organizations in America Based on Locality of Origin and /or Dialect-Group Affiliation, 1940-1990's* includes the organizations formed by Chinese from Southeast Asia. Lai's discussion is restricted to the Chinese organizations from Southeast Asia but he did contribute to the literature by distinguishing the diversity of Southeast Asian social institutions.

Considering Bui's work was published in 1983, she did a good job informing the general public about the Southeast Asian social institutions. Since then, the Southeast Asian community has matured and continued to grow. Now, the Southeast Asian community manufactures and produces many things for their own consumption. Currently there are many Southeast Asian newspapers, magazines, and videos available in the community. For example, *Saigon Post* covers Los Angeles, Colorado, Florida, San Jose, Sacramento, Washington, and Chicago; *Lang*, a regional Vietnamese language weekly magazine, covers Sacramento, Stockton, and Modesto; and *NGUOI Viet Tu Do* is a local Sacramento community monthly newsletter.

Another source for information about a community's organizations is Asian telephone directories. From our past field work in Oakland, Sacramento, Los Angeles, and San Francisco, each city's Southeast Asian community produces its own telephone directory. A few directories, like *Vietnamese Director/USA 1994,* claim to have a national presence. The Chinese in Sacramento also have a directory: the *Sacramento Chinese Telephone Book/Yellow Pages, 1997-1998.* A typical Southeast Asian telephone directory lists that particular city's Southeast Asian social organizations. The listings in the *Yellow Pages* do not include all of the organizations in the community. Nonetheless, partial listings still provide a window into the inner workings of the refugee and immigrant community.

Among the Southeast Asians, it seems that ethnic Chinese have a much broader range of community organizations, which consist of transplanted, constructed, voluntary, and national types of associations. From Indo-China alone, the ethnic Chinese transplanted at least five major regional and dialectic associations from each country: Teo Chow, Cantonese, Hakka, Fukien, and Hai Nam (Haines, 1985). For example, the Teo Chow Association in San Jose is considered a transplanted organization because there are Teo Chow Associations in

Vietnam, Laos, and Cambodia. The Elderly Chinese Association in Los Angeles is an example of a voluntary association.

The Lao Chinese Association in Los Angeles is considered a national type group because it accepts members based on the country of origin. The national type association is usually developed when a particular group's population is too small in size to form a surname or regional association. Comparable to the national type association is the reconstructed association. The Sacramento Chinese Indo-China Friendship Association is considered a reconstructed group because it replaces and includes the fraternal associations from Vietnam, Laos, and Cambodia. Bear in mind that these organizations may overlap, and the members are free to have dual affiliations. More important, these ethnic Chinese organizations exist in every Asian and Southeast Asian communities, like the Teo Chow, link their organization locally, nationally, and globally.

The City of Sacramento has many diverse Chinese organizations ranging from the Chinese Capital Club to the typical pre-1965 fraternal Chinese Wong Family Association. Within this diverse Chinese community in Sacramento, the two largest Chinese groups are the Chinese-Americans and the ethnic Chinese from Southeast Asia. The Chinese-Americans consist of American-born Chinese and their elders. This group has both the traditional structure dating back to late 19th century and the community service organizations which are usually headed by American-born Chinese. On the other hand, the ethnic Chinese from Southeast Asia are considered the newest Chinese members of the community. Thus, the Chinese organizations in Sacramento range from the pre-1965 associations, which were established in the late 19th century to the new Sacramento Chinese Indo-China

Friendship Association, formed in 1982. The 1997/1998 *Sacramento Chinese Yellow Pages* lists at least 14 Chinese organizations. These organizations cater to, and provide different functions and services to, respective Chinese groups.

(3)   The Function and Structure of the Sacramento Chinese Indo-China Friendship Association

The Sacramento Chinese Indo-China Friendship Association was formed through the coalition of Chinese refugees from Vietnam, Cambodia, and Laos in August 1982. The second President of the Association, Mr. Hao Hau said, "The Association can promote solidarity among the Chinese from Indo-China. For the well-being of the ethnic Chinese from Indo-China, I am ready to spend more time serving them and helping them solve different problems" (Ma, 1998). The main purposes of the Association are representation of ethnic Chinese among Asian groups in Sacramento and establishment of "the bridge that brings benefits to the Chinese Community" (Ma, 1998).

The Association was not formed without many hardships. From our interview with many of the Association's officers, Mr. Wong relates the adversity they faced: "When we first started, we made many mistakes. We do not know the American laws. When we purchased the property for the Association, we do not know about zoning codes to build on the property. We encountered the most mistakes when we built the Chinese School," he said. Their meetings were conducted at members' houses or at members' business establishments. The *Sacramento Chinese of Indo-China Friendship Association 1996* yearbook tells of the early struggles in which the Association had to move from one rented place to another.

A permanent site was established with the formation of the Chung Shan Chinese School.

The permanent site of the Sacramento Chinese Indo-China Friendship Association is located in the heart of the New Chinatown or Little Saigon between Stockton Boulevard and Elder Creek Road. In the 50,000 square feet Association headquarters, there are three major buildings with a huge parking lot for the members (Ma, 1998). The center building is the Kwan Yin Temple. In front of the temple is an open space where the mobile stage can be set-up for performances. Adjacent to the Temple is the Chinese School building, which is divided into approximately six classrooms, with two offices and a large bookstore. In back of the Temple is another huge building with a high ceiling, which often serves as an auditorium for private social and cultural activities.

Currently, the Association has over 533 members. (*Sacramento Chinese of Indo China Friendship Association in America, 1996*) Each member is assigned a number to his or her membership. The assigned number is permanent. As the head of Senior Citizen section, Mr. Von provides a reasonable explanation, "Some members quit. If he comes back, it will create unnecessary confusion to assign him a new number. So every member keeps his assigned number whether he is active or not." If both the wife and husband belong to the Association, they are assigned two separate numbers. We can assume from this information that the 533 membership in the Association may contain some overlapping family members. Assuming some multiple memberships in a family, 400 to 500 members still represent 400 to 500 families in Sacramento.

The structure of the Association consists of eight Directors and Supervisors. The top tier oversees three major components of the Association: The Chung Shan Chinese School, The Kwan Yin Temple, and The Senior Citizens

Recreation sections. Each component has its own governing body and targets the needs of the Southeast Asian Chinese community in Sacramento. Initially, most of the financial support of the Association came from the community and business leaders. For example, the past President Venh Sau Vong raised $400,000 dollars to complete the Kwan Yin temple in 1996 (Ma, 1998). Now, the donations from the Temple and other fund raising activities contribute to the Association's economic independence.

(A)　　Chung Shan Chinese School

The governing body of the Chinese School consists of a principal and senior teachers. They are responsible for the Chinese School. The function of the Chinese School is to expose the young generation of Chinese living in Sacramento to the Chinese heritage. It is this idea, and the concern for the young generation, that propelled the Association's top officers to seek a permanent home for the Association so that there is a place for the young people and a place where Chinese history and language are available to them. As one informant told us, "It is better to have a place for the young people to go to. Before, we saw many young Chinese smoking and hanging (out) around the video machine. We don't like it."

The Chung Shan Chinese School is open everyday except Sunday. Basically, the Chinese School has two operating sections: section one is Monday, Wednesday, and Friday afternoon from 3:30 to 6:30 p.m., and section two is from Tuesday, Thursday, and Saturday afternoon. Like Chinese schools elsewhere in the United States, the Chung Shan School offers up to 8th grade Chinese level schooling. This is because of the lack of interest by the student after the 8th grade.   From our research, most people agree that "from1st to 6th grade, there are about 200 interested students. From 6th to 8th grade, the number of interested students drops dramatically and from 8th grade to high school level, there are few interested students." The student body is made up of American-born Chinese and Chinese immigrants. Besides Chinese academics, the students are also taught Chinese folk dancing and painting. Some students formed their own social clubs such as Table Tennis.

According to an officer of the School, "We are doing this for the children. The tuition is almost free. The books are free. Our goal is to educate the next generation about Chinese culture. We are not here to make money." From interviews with past students, they concur with the officer's statement. If any student does not have the money to purchase schoolbooks, the school provides books for them. The tuition is about $30.00 monthly, depending on the students' economic situation. "The tuition is for the up-keep of the School facility, not for the teachers' salary," said the officer. The School does not discriminate and will accept all children who want to learn about Chinese culture.

(B)   The Senior Citizens Recreation

The second component is the Senior Citizens Recreation section. In this component, a trusted individual is appointed to take charge of this section. The title, Senior Citizen Recreation, means, however, different things to the members and to the public at large. It is not a place like the American Senior Citizen recreation where senior citizens relax and do their exercise. The Ethnic Chinese Senior Citizen Recreation section functions as an informal "departure insurance" policy for the senior citizens. This informal "departure insurance" policy has two purposes: 1.) to ensure a proper burial for the senior citizen and 2.) to guard against financial hardship on the family. This informal "departure insurance" must be examined in the context of America, where government fundamentally replaces the function of the Chinese family in providing traditional obligations and responsibility for the departed.

To be a member of the Senior Citizens Recreation section, one must be a Sacramento resident and over 60 years old. There are other requirements the applicant must meet such as having a legal resident document or passport. However, age is also a factor in this process. Depending on the member's age and the duration of his or her membership, he or she will receive different compensation. Currently, the members are charged a $35.00 yearly fee, plus $2.00 per month (Senior Citizen Pamphlet, 1998). If any of the members die, the rest of the members in the Senior Citizen Recreation section must contribute $15.00 to the departed's financial purse for his or her burial expenses. (Senior Citizen Pamphlet, 1998) If the membership in the section is huge, there may be money left over after the burial expenses. The money left over is then presented to the next of kin of the departed. If there is not enough money after every member contributes $15.00, then the Association will cover the cost of the burial.

When the Southeast Asian Chinese refugees came to America, they faced many adversities along with social and cultural adjustment problems in the host society. One of the worst hardships faced by ethnic Chinese in Sacramento was the death of their elders or family members. At the time of a death in the family, friends, family members, and the community at large can only provide limited financial support. More significantly, a large number of ethnic Chinese came with extended family members as well as family who are separated. Being a stranger in this new country, the family lacked the economic resources for a proper burial. This shared experience confronted the ethnic Chinese community. The community thus started this type of "departure insurance" policy for the Senior Citizen Association. The "departure insurance" policy for seniors could also be sponsored within a large ethnic Chinese organization like the Sacramento Chinese of Indo-China Friendship Association.

(C)   The Kwan Yin Temple

The Kwan Yin Temple, completed in 1996, is the newest addition to the Association compound. The Kwan Yin Temple contains many deities. Besides Kwan Yin, there is also Kwan Kung and the Lady Tin Hau among the deities. With Kwan Kung, the God of War, and Lady Tin Hau in the Temple, this house of worship is for both men and women. As Vong points out, "When the fellow Chinese from Indo-China took to the boats in search of freedom and battled through a shipwrecking storm, they prayed to Lady Tin Hau for blessings and guidance to safe landing. It happened that the overwhelming majority of them did reach their destination"(Ma, 1998).

Similar in structure to the Senior Citizen Recreation section, the Kwan Yin Temple is headed by one responsible person. The Kwan Yin Temple usually serves the needs of the female gender ethnic Chinese community. The doors are always open for those who need to pray and worship. One can also seek advice from observing the "fortune telling stick or paper reading." Typically, people come to worship on the 1st and 15th of each Chinese calendar month. These two dates are the busiest and the most festive where worshipers come and see old friends. On these two particular dates, the Temple provides vegetarian foods for the worshipers.

Of the three components, the Kwan Yin Temple is the most economically active. Its donations from worshipers contribute most to the Association in terms of economic stability. Everything in the Temple is provided by donations, and the people are willing to donate for such items as incense or a prayer. In short, the Temple's frequent visitors on every 1st and 15th of the month ensure continued monetary donations.

The Chinese School, Temple, and the Senior Citizens Recreation section embrace three important segments in the ethnic Chinese community of Sacramento: the youth, the elderly, and the women. These three components reflect the community population and provide services to and fulfil the needs of the community. What distinguishes the Association is its inclusiveness and a sense of belonging. These attributes contribute to the Association's success, growth, and stability. The current President Vong says that, "It is a matter of responsibility which requires our joint efforts"(Ma, 1998). With regards to the development of the Indo-Chinese social groups, he further adds that, "The younger generation only needs to participate and contribute more so these groups can carry on and even grow steadily"(Ma, 1998).

Closing Remarks

The formation of the Sacramento Chinese of Indo-China Friendship Association is not unique. All across the United States, a majority of the ethnic Chinese social institutions are formed in a similar manner. Depending on the needs of the local environment, most ethnic Chinese Associations have comparable structures and functions. In some areas with large ethnic Chinese populations, such as in Los Angeles and San Francisco counties, many social institutions have emerged to reflect the diversity of ethnic Chinese from Southeast Asia. For example, the five major ethnic Chinese groups in Southeast Asia - Teo Chow,

Hakka, Fukien, Hai Nam, and the Cantonese - have transplanted their Associations to Los Angeles.

On the other hand, some urban areas and suburbs may contain only one Association that represents the entire ethnic Chinese community. One good illustration of such community representation is the Sacramento Chinese Indo-China Friendship Association. Whether it is single Association representation or multiple group representation, the ethnic Chinese social institutions generally are linked with each other. Specifically, the transplanted ethnic Chinese social institutions are transnational in nature. For example, the Teo Chow transplanted association in the United States is connected to other Teo Chow Associations in the world, particularly in Asia. In other words, the Teo Chow association here not only has ties and links with local regional organizations, but also with national and global organizations.

In 1993 from September 4 to 6, the Seventh Annual International Teo Chow Association convened at the San Jose Convention Center. From Chinese newspaper accounts, *Sing Tao Daily* & *World Journal*, about 41 Teo Chow associations from around the world participated in this event. It is reported that over 1200 attendees came to San Jose. This international meeting of the Teo Chows was sponsored by nine Teo Chow Associations from the United States: New York City, Northern California, Southern California, Oregon, Southern United States, Washington, Chicago, Hawaii, San Jose.

As far as we know, the only comparable Asian social institutions that are similar to and closely resemble the ethnic Chinese organizations are the Chinatown community structures. This structure starts with the family association, the district association, and at the top tier, the Chinese Benevolent Consolidated Association. One marked difference between these two groups' institutions is seen in their function and the structure. We do not need to reconstruct how it was for the pioneer Chinese community formation. Presently, their function and structure is not nearly as inclusive as the ethnic Chinese. With respect to Sacramento, the ethnic Chinese community is known within and considered by others as the "New Chinatown."

References

* I would like to thank the Sacramento Chinese Culture Foundation for inviting me to participate in this project. In addition, I would also like to thank the Asian American Studies Program at UC Davis in providing the opportunity and allowing me to conduct this study in the Sacramento area while I was teaching there during the Winter 1999 Quarter at Davis.

This article is based on the research project from June 1998 to June 1999. It is, however, a preliminary finding.

Bui, Diana. "The Indo-Chinese Mutual Assistance Associations," in *Bridging Culture: Southeast Asian Refugees in America*. Los Angeles, California: Asian American Community Mental Health Training Center. 1983.

Caplan, Nathan, Whitmore, John K. and Choy, Marcella H. *The Boat People and Achievement in America: A Study of Economic and Educational Success.* Ann Arbor: The University of Michigan Press. 1990.

Mr. Chang. an officer of the Chinese Language School. Interview. 1998.

Fong, Joe C. "The History and Structure of Oakland Chinatown: How Chinese- Vietnamese Impacted the Chinese Community." UC Berkeley Anthropology

Department: Minority Education Project, House Report. 1992.

Fong, Joe C. "The Development of the Chinese-Vietnamese Community in San Francisco: 1980-1988," UCLA: Master Thesis, Asian American Studies. 1988.

** The sources from the History section came from my Master thesis.

Haines, David W., ed. *Refugees in the United States: A Reference Handbook.* Westport, Connecticut: Greenwood Press. 1985.

Haines, David W. "Southeast Asian Refugees in the United States: An Overview," *Migration Today*, 2:10-13. 1983.

"International Teo Chow (Chao Zhou) Convention," *World Journal*, August 10, 1993.

Kim, Illsoo. *New Urban Immigrants: Korean Community in New York.* Princeton: Princeton University Press. 1981.

Lai, Him Mark. Personal Communication. 1987 and 1998.

Lai, Him Mark . "Chinese Organizations In America Based On Locality Of Origin And/Or Dialect-Group Affiliation, 1940-1990's," *Chinese America: History and Perspectives, 1996.* Brisbane, California: Chinese Historical Society of America. 1996.

Lee, Wilbur Gay. "Overseas Chinese Communities: A Comparative Approach," UC Berkeley: Master Thesis. 1960.

Lyman, Stanford M. *Chinese-Americans.* New York: Random House. 1994.

Ma, Quan. *The Story of Ethnic Chinese Immigrants from Indo-China.* Los Angeles, *Chung Hing News*: Leader Publishing Inc. 1998.

Montero, D. *Vietnamese American: Patterns of Resettlement and Socioeconomic Adaptation in the United States.* Boulder, Colorado: Westview Press. 1979.

Needs Assessment of the Asian/Pacific Islander Community in Sacramento County, 1992. Sacramento, California: Asian Community Center.

Park, Kyeyoung. *The Korean American Dream: Immigrants and Small Business in New York City.* Ithaca: Cornell University Press. 1997.

"Seventh Annual International Teo Chow (Chao Zhou) Organizations Friendship Convention," *Sing Tao Daily,* September 3, 1993.

Sacramento Chinese of Indo-China Friendship Association in America, 1996, Year Book. Elder Creek Road, Sacramento: The Sacramento Chinese of Indo China Friendship Association, 1996.

Sacramento Chinese Telephone Book/Yellow Pages, 1997-1998. 6540 Stockton Blvd. Sacramento: Published and printed by Sacramento Chinese Telephone Book/Yellow Pages.

Te, H.D. "Understanding Southeast Asian Students," *Integrating Language and Learning for Inclusion,* edited by L. Cheng. San Diego, California: Singular. 1995.

Trueba, Henry, Cheng, Li-Rong Lilly, and Kenji Ima. *Myth or Reality: Adaptive Strategies of Asian Americans in California.* Washington, D.C.: Falmer Press. 1993.

Zhou, Min. "Social Capital in Chinatown: The Role of Community-Based Organizations and Families in the Adaptation of the Younger Generation," in *Beyond Black and White: New Faces and Voices in U.S. Schools,* edited by Maxine Seller and Louis Weiss. New York: State University of New York Press. 1997.

The Fountain of Chinese American Growth and Development (Community Organizations in Sacramento, California)

Peter C. Y. Leung

For the last 150 years, the Sacramento Chinese community has evolved and emerged as a very diversified community that includes Chinese who are the descendants of second to sixth generations, newcomers from China, Taiwan, Hong Kong in 1950s to 1990s, and even ethnic Chinese who came from South East Asian countries since the late 1970s.

This well-established community has a long history in Sacramento. Immediately following Marshall's discovery of gold at Coloma in 1848, the early Chinatown was established and became large enough to supply groceries, equipment, and other wares to Chinese mining settlements in the "gold rush" camps in the Mother Lode. Part of today's Old Sacramento was the original site for the early Chinese settlement. A new Chinatown Plaza, completed in 1969-72, is located between Fourth & Fifth on J & I Streets.

Collections of early Chinese artifacts and narrative history can be found at the Sacramento Railroad Museum,

Sacramento History Museum, California State Museum, Folsom History Museum, and Sun Yat Sen Memorial Hall. A new and permanent Chinese American historical exhibit "Uncovering Sacramento's Chinese Pioneers" is displayed at the new United States Courthouse at Sixth & I Streets.

Locke, a rural Chinese town, along the Sacramento River Delta, representing the Chinese work forces in building the levee system and farming in the late nineteenth and early 20th centuries has become a national historical site which attracts millions of visitors each year.

Besides the early legislation and laws affecting Chinese and their community development, the social organizations and the community leaders of the Chinese themselves became significant and deserve to be documented. There are over 70 Chinese American organizations plus many church groups in Sacramento Chinese community. There are also organizations that go beyond their own ethnic groups, but Chinese-Americans have played important roles to reach out to other communities. Hundred of events, which represent their perspectives, creative expressions, ideas, heritage, arts and customs, occur each year. It is a very dynamic community that continues to be significant in shaping Sacramento's diverse heritage. The Chinese are well established in Sacramento; they have enriched the areas where they have settled. The following will give a brief description of several major organizations and their activities or individuals who have contributed to the Sacramento Chinese community as well as to the main society.

Due to the limited space and resources available for this project, those organizations and many individuals who are not mentioned here equally deserve recognition and respect, because they are the threads which weave the rich ethnic and cultural fabric of the Chinese American community.

(1) The Chinese Benevolent Association & Family Associations

The Chinese Benevolent Association is the oldest organization in the Sacramento Chinese community. This organization is composted of eight family associations including Gee Duk Sam Duk family, Gee How Oak Ten family, Lim family, Lee On Dong family, Ong Ko Met family, Soo Yuen family, Wong Family and Yee Fung Toy Family and several other groups including Bing Kong Tong, Kuomintang (the Chinese Nationalist Party), and Sun Yat Sen Memorial Hall Association.

Its headquarters is located at " I " and Fourth Streets in the magnificent "Confucius Hall," which is a multi-level complex housing a Chinese language school and a community center. The main entrance features a grand stairway leading into the auditorium which seats 1,000 people. A huge painting of Confucius is on the main wall of the stage. In the auditorium there are two large murals on its walls. One depicts early Chinese immigrants digging of gold and laying railroad tracks. The other shows Chinese entering professions including medicine, law, engineering and even civic leadership. The Chinese school has administrative office and five classrooms that can accommodate a total of 300 students. In the basement, there are the gymnasium and kitchen for sports and community events.

Some of the major functions of the Chinese Benevolent Association include preserving and continuing the cultural and historical identity of the Chinese. Therefore the Chinese language school was established, and language classes were offered. During the Chinese New Year, each of the above family associations sponsors a "Spring Banquet" which is usually arranged on a weekend from February to April. The "Spring Banquet" serves as a means to celebrate the Chinese New Year and renew the contact with the officers of each organization and their members as well as to other organizations. The "Spring Banquet" not only brings economic activities to many local Chinese restaurants and groceries, it is a function to build a bridge of understanding and recognition between the public officials and the Chinese community.

The Sacramento Chinese Benevolent Association and family associations have their headquarters in different cities or towns across the United States and other parts of the world. This forms a traditional global network, which has been a powerful connection among the Chinese and their community no matter where they have settled.

Chinese benevolent associations and the family associations have scholarships for children of members studying in Chinese language schools or in public schools. Many distinguished leaders have contributed generously to their organizations as well as to the welfare of the Chinese community. The Chinese benevolent associations are considered conservative, self-reliant, and hard working. Their struggles and experiences may not be fully appreciated and understood by the new generations. Nevertheless, they will continue to be one of the important resources in the Chinese community.

(2)   Sacramento Chinese of Indo-China Friendship Association

The population of ethnic Chinese from Indo-China is estimated over 15,000. The majority of them are living in the Stockton Blvd. and Lemon Hill area in south Sacramento. In 1975, because of the fall of South Vietnam to the Communist Government, many refugees were sponsored by non-profit organizations and government agencies and settled down in this area. Formation of a new

Chinese community began immediately. A majority of them speak Cantonese as well as Vietnamese or Mandarin.

The Sacramento Chinese of Indo-China Friendship Association was formed in 1982. At that time about 3,000 Chinese already settled in that area. Today, they operate over 100 small businesses. In addition, several big supermarkets and restaurants provide several hundred jobs for their own countrymen. It is considered the second Chinatown of Sacramento, and it is growing fast. The Sacramento Chinese of Indo-China Friendship Association established a cultural center with a Chinese language school and Kwan Yin (Lady of Mercy) Temple at 6117 Elder Creek Road.

Because of various new Chinese business ventures and expansion programs, these efforts have resulted in a substantial amount of new construction, major renovations and employment that have changed the face of the Stockton Boulevard area in Sacramento. The Sacramento Chinese of Indo-China Friendship Association deserves to be commended for its leadership and involvement in many worthwhile community projects, and for taking an active role in supporting civic and charitable programs.

The leadership among the Chinese from Indo-China can be easily understood by the following summary on how they worked together. When the Sacramento Chinese of Indo-China Friendship Association was formed in 1982, the association leased facilities (a 3000 square-foot vacant store) to establish a Chinese Language School with several classes for their children. From 1982-1984, each board member committed to donate $50-$100 each month to pay the rent and other operating expenses for the school as well as to support the Senior Self-help Committee, which provides services to seniors. Board members and volunteers provided all the labor to subdivide a rented place into several classrooms and construct all the study desks and chairs for the classrooms. At that time 300-500 young Chinese attended the Chinese school after their regular public school on weekdays between 4-6 p.m. and weekends in the mornings.

In 1985-86, each board member contributed up to $5,000.00 towards $80,000 to purchase land with three old buildings at 6117 Elder Creek Road in order to provide a permanent location for the association and Chinese language school. The Senior Self-help Committee purchased a van for transportation for seniors. In 1986-89, the language school stopped operation for three years due to the removal of old buildings on site. Fundraising activities extended from Sacramento to San Francisco and Los Angeles. During this period the association raised over $100,000 to remove the three old buildings and purchased a wooden building to be relocated on the site as the school. The Chinese language school was reopened in 1991.

The Senior Self-help Committee has 500 members. It no longer depends on a subsidy from the board members. Membership fees not only support its activities, but are also used to generate funds for the construction of the Kwan Yin (Lady of Mercy) Temple and other site improvements. From 1991-1994, the association made improvements to the parking lot and landscaping. A basketball playground and fences were built too.

From 1995 to present, the association expanded the school by adding additional classrooms, a bathroom and a hall for Seniors' activities. A beautiful Kwan Yin Temple and two magnificent traditional Chinese gates stand at the site which marks their presence and achievements in the American land that they adopted less than three decades ago. Although many of the board members and volunteers do not speak English well, their leadership and dedication to their community show no barriers at all.

(3)   Sacramento Chinese Community Service Center (SCCSC)

Sacramento Chinese Community Service Center was established in 1978. It is a non-profit community agency founded in both the Chinese and American tradition of helping those in need. A member of United Way, the center focuses on serving recent immigrants, Indo-Chinese refugees and elderly people.

The center provides bilingual interpretation and translation services in health, housing and other social problems facing those who encounter language and cultural barriers in obtaining direct services from the public agencies. In recent years, the center also added job training and employment services to limited English-speaking Asians who are on welfare. Besides English language training and citizenship programs, it also provides positive alternatives to at-risk youth through counseling, mentoring and social activities. The center's operation budget comes from United Way, grants, fundraising and donations.

With the leadership of all board members, volunteers and staff, both past to present, the Sacramento Chinese Community Service Center has developed into a mature organization that is able to provide services to the Chinese, and to the Asian and Pacific Islander communities in Sacramento. The center located at 915 T Street has its own permanent building that resulted from generous local individual donations and fundraising within the community. The annual August Moon Night highlights a gala celebration with gathering of community leaders, government officials, professionals, volunteers and staff, who show their support for the excellent services to the community.

(4)   Sacramento Chinese Culture Foundation

Mr. Chih-Yi Wang established the Sacramento Chinese Culture Foundation in 1986. During the past ten years, the Sacramento Chinese Culture Foundation (SCCF) has provided over $20,000 in seed money, materials and human resources to promote the teaching of Chinese language and culture in several public high schools, such as C. K. McClatchy, Mira Loma, El Camino, Luther Burbank in Sacramento area. In 1996, SCCF also helped Kennedy High School start three Mandarin language classes that were expanded to five classes in 1998.

SCCF also provided $3000.00 for a pen-pal program to facilitate one to one correspondence between Sacramento high school students and students in Taiwan and China. This personal exchange between students from different parts of the world will foster better understanding and friendship. In addition, a teacher from Taiwan Shin-Hwa Middle School organized a group of students to visit the California Middle School in Sacramento for three weeks, in 1997 and 1999 respectively. The visits were well received by both the staff and students at California Middle School, where many students have participated in the pen-pal program.

SCCF also became a partner with the Asian American Studies internship program at the University of California, Davis. It donated over $3000.00 to provide tutoring on weekends for the Iu-Mien children in West Sacramento from 1996-1998. The SCCF has attracted many enthusiastic supporters who have helped extend these services to many students.

Besides supporting teaching of the Chinese language, SCCF is the only organization in the area to sponsor Chinese performing arts in the Sacramento community. SCCF sponsored "Songs & Dances from

Tibet" in 1992 and "Chinese Performing Arts Festival" in 1994 and 1996. Finally in 1997 and 1998, the organization was able to reorganize its performing arts programs. Many local musicians and dancers displayed their talent on the stage. These programs have been well received by the audiences. Several new performing arts groups were formed such as Angel String Orchestra in 1997 directed by Mr. Ho Dong who also serves as the conductor for the Chinese Choir.

SCCF participated in many other activities sponsored by other organizations such as Pacific Rim Food Festival, the Sacramento Chinese Community Service Center's August Moon Night, the annual community picnic, the Chinese New Year Celebration.

(5)   Chinese American Council of Sacramento (CACS)

Chinese American Council of Sacramento was formed in 1986. It took seven months of meetings, discussion, research, recruitment, writing by-laws and filing paperwork to become a non-profit organization. Mr. Frank Fat, a well-known restaurateur and community leader, called on a group of his supporters and friends. He expressed his desire to have a strong organization that could influence decision-making in the areas of business, economics and politics. The organization should speak out on behalf of the Chinese American community and encourage the younger people to participate in the political process so the Chinese American community's interests are heard. He also wanted to see the organization have strong financial resources to back up political leaders who supported the Chinese community in local or national level through fund-raising.

Frank Fat's dream has come true gradually. For the last ten years, young, energetic and outspoken professionals have led the Board of Directors. Besides carrying many of its internal activities, CACS is building a stronger voice in advocacy of civic affairs on behalf of the Chinese American community. The historical committee of CACS has sponsored talks on Chinese American history and worked on projects to preserve the early Chinese artifacts found in local sites. The CASC has extended its support by fundraising for the benefit of the Sacramento Chinese Community Service Center. CACS's recent involvement in the Ping Yuen project through the Sacramento Housing & Redevelopment Agency is one of the best examples to prove the organization is going to adhere to its founding mission.

Chinese American Achievements in Education

Dr. Stanley Sue

hinese Americans have made many contributions and achievements in society, despite encounters with racial prejudice and discrimination. Among the many accomplishments is education. Chinese and other Asian American groups have succeeded relatively well in academic endeavors. Among Americans between the ages of 18 to 24 years, fully 66% of Chinese-Americans are enrolled in colleges or universities compared to the national average of 34%. The accomplishments are evident in Chinese American women as well as men. Other indicators, such as qualification for entry into universities, persistence rates, low dropout rates from schools, fulfillment of core academic requirements for college admissions, and doctorates received, also reveal the strong achievements of Chinese and other Asian American groups (J. Hsia and S.S. Peng, 1998). Many Chinese-Americans also receive awards from the National Merit Scholarship Program and Westinghouse Science Talent Search Program. It should be noted that a relatively large proportion of Chinese-Americans who have very little education tempers these findings.

What accounts for the impressive achievements made by Chinese-Americans? Is it possible that Chinese and other Asians come from upper class and privileged families that explain the racial or ethnic differences. There is no evidence that this is a sufficient explanation for the achievements. Perhaps some of the educational achievements can be accounted for by the inclusion of foreign students among Asian Americans or of Asian immigrants who already have high levels of education and subsequently become naturalized American citizens or permanent residents. The available evidence does not support this possibility. Although there is a tendency for foreign born individuals to have higher educational levels, perhaps because of immigration policies favoring the educated, American born Asians exceeded American born Whites in the proportion of those with four years of college education (Sue and Okazaki, 1990).

R. Lynn (1987) advances a genetic hypothesis for the achievement differences. In order to explain why Chinese and other Asians are particularly strong on visuospatial abilities as well as general intelligence, Lynn (1987) proposed an evolutionary theory. In Lynn's view, *Homo sapiens* started migrating from Africa northward into Europe and Asia about 120,000 years ago. Those who populated North East Asia were subjected to severe cold, because the ice ages began to descend on the northern regions. The hostile environment required increased survival skills (constructing shelters, storing food, planning for winters, etc.). Over time selection pressures for improved general intelligence were greater for "Mongoloids" than for "Caucasoids" and "Negroids," according to Lynn. Because of the necessity for improved hunting skills in the cold regions, superior visuospatial abilities developed among the Mongoloids, at the expense of verbal skills. That is, since the brain could not increase its size to accommodate an overall improvement in intelligence, more of the brain's cortex was devoted to visuospatial than verbal functioning.

Lynn's explanation can be challenged on many fronts. Particularly problematic is the assumption that the people in most of Asia were the descendants of those who came from North East Asia. This assumption must be made in order to explain the superior visual-spatial abilities that Lynn found in Chinese from various parts of Asia (Hong Kong, Singapore, Taiwan, etc.) Considerable evidence exists that migration from Africa was not simply confined to the cold regions of Asia. Indeed, migration to warmer parts of Asia occurred simultaneously with that to the north, and remains of early cultures were found throughout Southeast Asia. There is also evidence that the origins of the Japanese people were from diverse parts of the world including Southeast Asia.

While some researchers believe that Chinese and other Asians may be genetically more intelligent that other groups (R. J. Herrnstein and C. Murray, 1994; Lynn, 1987), there is simply not enough evidence to justify the conclusion. To fully address the question of genetic superiority among Asian Americans, it is necessary to demonstrate that they have higher levels of intelligence and cognitive functioning. Unfortunately, few studies have compared these groups on intelligence measures. Some researchers have argued that Chinese-Americans concluded that Chinese and Japanese Americans equal or exceed the national average on intellectual test scores (J. Sowell, 1978; P.E. Vernon, 1982). However, the research studies involving Chinese-Americans had methodological limitations.

Since only small samples of Asian Americans are available, investigators have examined the question of racial differences in intelligence by studying overseas or foreign Asians. Here too, methodological problems were found that do not permit any firm conclusions concerning the genetic superiority of Chinese in intelligence. In fact, H.

W. Stevenson and his colleagues (1985) directly compared Chinese and American students on carefully constructed verbal and performance tests. Their findings revealed a few group differences on subtests (e.g., Chinese scored higher than Americans on mathematics achievement test scores), but no overall difference in intelligence. Thus the evidence for genetic superiority is weak.

In general, the most viable explanations for the educational achievement patterns of Chinese-Americans involve culture and learning. I believe that (1) culture plays an important role in the educational accomplishments of Chinese-Americans, (2) their minority group status has made education a favored means of attaining upward mobility, and (3) Chinese-Americans have found creative ways to enhance their achievement levels.

Culture

Many social scientists attribute the educational success of Chinese-Americans to cultural values that promote upward mobility in this country--values emphasizing hard work, family cohesion, patience, and thrift. I. M. Liu (1986) has adopted the position that socialization to Chinese cultural values enhances academic performance. Chinese are socialized to some behavioral rules that may enhance certain academic achievements. For example, rules such as "respect elders," "memorize lessons," and "practice lessons" facilitate academic tasks requiring memorization and the use of mathematics. The respect-elder rule may also handicap Asians in verbal skills and oral articulation, since a child is taught to listen and obey rather than to speak. Furthermore, respect for education is high among Chinese, so parents frequently stress the importance of doing well in school and getting a good education. It is likely that many Chinese children learn very quickly the importance of education and internalize rules that enable them to function well on some academic tasks, as suggested by Liu.

Relative Functionalism

In the case of Chinese-Americans, R. H. Suzuki (1977) has also taken issue with a cultural interpretation of their success. Although acknowledging that respect for education is a cultural value among these two groups, he also advanced the proposition that Chinese and other Asian Americans came to pursue education because of their status as a minority group. Many labor unions discriminated against Asians, refusing them union membership during the 1940s. In addition, technological advancements and an expanding economy after World War II required educated professionals and white collar employees. Thus, one development limited occupational opportunities for manual laborers, and the other placed a premium on professional-technical skills requiring advanced education. In such a situation, mobility via education took increased significance, above and beyond the contributions of Asian cultural values. Based on these ideas, Sumie Okazaki and I (Sue and Okazaki, 1990) have another theory about why Chinese-Americans show educational achievements. We believe that the academic achievements of Chinese-Americans cannot be solely attributed to Chinese cultural values. Rather, as for other ethnic minority groups, their behavioral patterns, including achievements, are a product of cultural values and status in society (minority group standing). Using the notion of relative functionalism, we propose that the educational attainments of Chinese-Americans are highly influenced by the opportunities present for upward mobility, not only in educational endeavors but also in non-educational areas. "Non-educational areas" include career activities such as leadership, entertainment, sports, politics, etc., where education does not directly lead to the position. To the extent that mobility is limited in non-educational avenues, education becomes increasingly salient as a means of mobility. That is, education is increasingly functional as a means for mobility when these other avenues are blocked. In an early survey of Asian American students at the University of California, Berkeley, C. Ong (1976) found that the students cited as reasons for obtaining an education: to make money, to increase the chances for a better job, and to ease the difficulty in finding other avenues for advancement because of discrimination. C. Hirschman and M. G. Wong (1986) have argued that "Education was a channel for the social mobility of Asians, partly because they were frozen out of some sectors of the economy..." (p. 23). Therefore, education is highly valued because it is a way to find better jobs and to gain respect, especially when one feels that other means of upward mobility are difficult to attain. Chinese-Americans may come to believe that: "If I study hard, I can succeed and education is the best way to succeed." That is, the belief is not only that education is a means of success but also it is the most important way to succeed.

Creative Strategies

There appears to be other reasons for the achievement patterns that we see in Chinese-Americans. I have found that many Chinese use certain strategies to maximize their accomplishments. In one study, Nolan Zane and I (Sue and Zane, 1985) wanted to study the ways that Chinese-Americans have found to enhance their grades at universities. Our interest concerned how Chinese, particularly those with limited English proficiency, adapt to the demands of university life. Because we were especially interested in achievement and adaptation for foreign-born Chinese, the sample was divided into three groups: (a) American-born Chinese students, (b) early immigrant Chinese students (residing more than 6 years in the United States), and (C) recent immigrant Chinese students (residing for 6 or less years in this country). The recent immigrants had relatively poor English skills, although their mathematics skills were superior.

The findings from the study revealed that Chinese-American university students, even recent immigrants, (RI) tended to receive higher than average grades. This high achievement pattern appeared to be enhanced by several strategies. First, the recent immigrant Chinese students take a reduced course load in comparison with American-born or early immigrant Chinese. (RI) Chinese who take a lighter course load even after gaining the class and socioeconomic status.) Because their English proficiency was relatively poor, they took a lighter class load and were able to spend more time on the courses they did take. Second, we found that recent Chinese immigrants were significantly more likely than acculturated Chinese to agree with the statement that their choices of academic majors were influenced by their English skills. Accordingly, the recent immigrant students were more likely to major in mathematics, engineering, and sciences. In these majors, their limited English proficiency but high mathematics abilities would be less of a handicap in these majors than to those in the humanities and social sciences. That is, the students selected majors that minimized their weaknesses and that capitalized on their strengths. Third, recent immigrants tended to report that they studied more hours than American born or early immigrant Chinese did. We now know that Chinese students use certain tactics to maintain their high university grades, even though their English skills may be weak.

Conclusions

We can well be proud of the educational achievements made by Chinese-Americans. As a group, Chinese demonstrate extremely high educational attainments compare to the rest of the nation, and account for a relatively high proportion of persons receiving doctoral degrees--the highest degree possible. Obviously, Chinese-Americans are not a model minority group and we do see a high proportion of them not having much education whatsoever. Furthermore, Chinese American students often complain about the pressures to achieve generated by parents and friends. However, if Chinese initially came to the United States expecting a mountain of gold, they and their children have come away with education as a means of fulfilling dreams.

Why have Chinese-Americans succeeded so well in educational endeavors? We have argued that the explanation is not genetic. There is no substantial evidence that Chinese-Americans are super in intelligence because of heredity. If anything, the evidence points to nurture rather than nature. Chinese cultural values have emphasized education as an important and honorable endeavor. These values have also stressed the importance of memorization, practice, and repetition in learning that, according to Liu, enhances achievements. Furthermore, Chinese-Americans have in the past found it difficult to achieve upward mobility in a wide variety of career areas such as acting, sports, managerial positions, etc. Some of the reasons for the difficulties include limited English proficiency, prejudice, and discrimination. In view of the lack of mobility in some areas, education has proven to be a way for Chinese-Americans to get ahead and to find good careers. Thus in addition to cultural value, education has been a means of overcoming problems associated with belonging to an ethnic minority population. Finally, Chinese American students have shown a great deal of adaptive capacity in succeeding at universities. Many with limited English proficiency simply take fewer courses, study harder, and find majors that capitalize on their skills in order to maintain high achievement levels.

References

Herrnstein, R.J., and Murray, C. *The bell curve: Intelligence and class structure in American life.* NY: Free Press. 1994.

Hirschman, C., and Wong, M.G. The extraordinary educational attainment of Asian Americans: A search for historical evidence and explanations. *Social Forces*, Volume 65, 1-27. 1986.

Hsia, J., and Peng, S.S. Academic achievement and performance. In L. C. Lee andN. Zane (Eds.), *Handbook of Asian American psychology* (pp. 325-358). Thousand Oaks, California. 1998.

Sage, Liu, I.-M. "Chinese cognition", in M.H. Bond (Ed.), *The psychology of the Chinese people* (pp. 73-105). Hong Kong: Oxford University Press. 1986.

Lynn, R. "Japan: Land of the rising IQ. A reply to Flynn,". *Bulletin of the British Psychological Society*, 40, 464-468. 1987.

Ong, C. *The educational attainment of the Chinese in America.* Unpublished manuscript, University of California, Department of Anthropology, Berkeley. 1976.

Sowell, T. (Ed.) *Essay and Data on American Ethnic Groups.* Washington, D.C.: The Urban Institute. 1978.

Stevenson, H.W., J. W. Lee. S., Lucker, G.W., Kitamura, S., and Hsu, C. *Cognitive Performance and Academic Achievement*, 56, 718-734. 1985.

Sue, S., and Okazaki, S. "Asian American educational achievements: A phenomenon in search of an explanation", *American Psychologist*, 45, 913-920. 1990.

Sue, S., and Zane, N. Academic achievement and socioemotional adjustment among Chinese university students. *Journal of Counseling Psychology,* 32, 570-579. 1985.

Suzuki, R. H. Education and the socialization of Asian Americans: A revisionist analysis of the "model minority" thesis. *Amerasia Journal*, 4, 23-52. 1977.

Vernon, P.E. *The Abilities and Achievements of Orientals in North America.* New York: Academic Press. 1982.

New Voices in Chinese American Women's Writing: Recovering the Father-Daughter Stories

Dr. Wendy Ho

. . .what we hold in our heart is what matters. The heart never travels.

Leon Leong, from Fae Myenne Ng's *Bone*

In the 1960s, 70s and 80s, women were vibrantly and fully engaged in critically recovering and examining the stories of women, especially between mothers and daughters. But for many Asian American women writers it was important to reclaim the stories of Asian men, especially fathers, and of their marginalized families and communities as well. In the 'Letter to Ma," Merle Woo (1981) writes about the love, anger and frustration she feels toward her mother, but she turns her personal struggles into a form of social-political activism that embraces a mother, who as a working-class immigrant woman suffered greatly in the United States. At the same time, Woo's activist writing recognizes the multiple oppressions of racism, sexism and classism confronted by her father, and the psychic and social violence that humiliates him in front of his family and community, that grinds him down to the bone as well.[1] Through their stories, many recent Chinese American women writers like Kathy Fong Bates, Lan Samantha Chang, Ying Chen, Sara Chin, Gish Jen, K. Kam, Maxine Hong Kingston, Sky Lee, Mei Ng, Sigrid Nunez, Kit Yuen Quan, Fae Myenne Ng, Amy Tan, and Merle Woo do not leave their distressed families or communities behind. Even when fiercely critical, they return to this site of love, pain and memory to construct their narratives. In their temporary, and sometimes necessary, separations and border crossings, the daughter narrators in these stories remain deeply affiliated to the primary home places of family and community.

The stories of Chinese (and Asian) American men are still wide-open territory for recovery work. Although Asian American history has represented some important stories of Chinese American men, these stories still often concentrate on the working class "sojourner" or "bachelor society" period of Chinese American history or on men's economic work history (Yanagisako 1995). It is crucial to *continue* the stories of Asian American men and women beyond the early period of a predominantly Chinatown male society and its history of prostitution.[2] For example,

---

This essay is an abbreviated, modified excerpt from my forthcoming book *In Her Mother's House: The Politics of Asian American Mother-Daughter Writing*. Critical Perspectives on Asian Pacific Americans series, Vol. 6. Thousand Oaks, CA: AltaMira/Sage Press, 1999.

[1] Ng uses the word "bone" for the title of her novel. It is resonant of a variety of meanings which signify the experiences of many working-class immigrant families in America--to the bone; bone marrow; bone tired, bone raw; bone dry; bone ash; bone dust; bone meal; bone bad; bone picker; bone spirit; bone yard; make no bones about it; have a bone to pick; feel in one's bones; bone of contention; bone china.

[2] For a sampling of recovery work on early Chinatown histories of male society see Chu (1961), Nee and Nee (1972), Siu (1987), Takaki (1989),

it is crucial to reconstruct men's stories from the 1930s through the 1950s, when single and married men were making the adjustment to the presence of and/or reunification with Chinese women, children and extended kin, who were immigrating in greater numbers to the United States and establishing new and more permanent communities in Chinatown.

The late 1980s and 1990s witnessed growing interest in critical examinations of the constructions of masculinity but this new wave of masculinity studies has mainly focused on the white or Black formations of manhood. Asian American constructions of masculinity should also be an important part of this discussion. It is very possible that these marginalized masculinities can suggest more alternative, open-ended or resisting formations of masculinity than have been previously theorized.[3] At this reflective historical turning point, which commemorates the sesquicentennial presence of the Chinese in California, I believe it is important to reclaim the stories of men and women, whose legacies and projects follow us into the twenty-first century.

Chinese American women writers have focused attention on the struggles of women, especially of mothers,

---

Daniels (1988), Cheung (1998), and Hall (1998). See Chu (1976 and 1986), Hirata (1979 and 1982), Asian Women United (1989), Yung (1986, 1990 and 1995), S. Chan (1991a, 1991b and 1998), Dong (1992), Zhao (1996), Okihiro (1994) for some examples of the recovery work on Chinese women's history in U.S.

[3] Besides examining formations of heterosexual masculinities, there is, for example, much work to be done in recovering Chinese (Asian) American queer formations of masculinity and sexuality as well. Such work has begun in earnest. See for instance, work in Hwang (1988), Leong (1996), Hinsch (1990), Fung (1991), N. Wong (1994), Manalansan (1995), Chua (1998), Eng and Hom (1998).

who are situated in the constantly negotiated domestic and familial spaces. They work to tell the frequently silenced, and often neglected stories of women, who raise families and negotiate daily injustice, and attempt to name and work out their own multiple emotional and social tensions and their relationships. In excavating this psychosocial site, they begin to reexamine the nature of their relationships to each other and, in this painful process, to *earn* continuously negotiated and hopeful alliances and histories together.

It is in first learning to grapple with their mothers that the daughters in these stories find the critical tools with which to sustain and expand an empathetic understanding, *which is neither arrogant contempt nor patronizing pity*, to Chinese American fathers, families and communities as well. That is, in doing the intimate heart work and memory work within themselves and with their mothers, they construct a complex, nuanced "vocabulary of feeling," as Leila Fu, the daughter narrator in *Bone*, defines it, that can begin to wrestle with or tease out how it feels to live in new familial, social, economic, and cultural sites in this country. As the mother-daughter texts articulate a new critical "vocabulary of feeling" to name their understanding of their social world, they are sensitive to the "articulate silences" (Cheung 1993) and embodied gestures that can register a woman's range of experiences and perspectives. This emergent vocabulary is part of the on-going struggle to portray more liberating, ethically accountable, and imaginative constructions of identity and community. Such critical narratives of self and struggle enrich our exploration into the dynamics of dislocation, adaptation, resistance and recreation in diasporic spaces.

In portraying the feelings, which are continually negotiated within the daily, practical interactions and sites of Chinese American mothers and daughters in their stories, these Chinese American writers attempt to represent the lives and stories of men as fathers in families as well. Thomas Laqueur remarks that "the history of men and therefore man-as-father has been subsumed under the history of a pervasive patriarchy--the history of inheritance and legitimate descent, the history of public authority and its transmission over generations. Because men are thought to belong to the 'public sphere of the marketplace and women to the private sphere of the family' (a decidedly nineteenth-century perspective on gender roles), men have not been addressed according to their domestic role as fathers" (Clark 1996: 25). Moreover, despite the media hype (popular and academic) which constructs the never-ending division or battle between Asian American women and men, many women writers do not represent men or fathers, as unloved authoritarian patriarchs who are purely oppressive or conservative figures in their lives.

A number of dominant and oppositional masculinist discourses do not substantially represent the fatherhood of Chinese American men, men forced to confront and negotiate terrible social, economic and political violence for the sake of the family, as heroic work. More importantly, such discourses erase or dismiss the potentially democratizing and improvisational political formations of Chinese American masculinity that do not simply duplicate or reify traditional capitalist and patriarchal-nationalist ideals. That is, some men take gender risks by adjusting to dual or multi-income families, to taking care of children and doing housework, to maintaining a nurturing, stable home environment, and being with independent women. Making acts of transition between ways of life and gender systems, becoming a different sort of man may *seem* like being less of a man from some perspectives, but it can also be seen and defined as heroic and ethical work rather than as "dysfunctional," "pathological," "effeminizing," "sell-out" or "model minority."[4]   It would seem more fruitful to seriously engage in the making of practices that have the potential to reconfigure ways of theorizing and articulating new social and political affiliations in American society.

Chinese American (and other Asian American) men as fathers (whether biological or not), after all, are crucial to familial and community building processes, especially considering the long legal and political history of denying them access to women, families, and communities in the United States. "Among most immigrant groups, working-age men tend to precede women, children, or older people to a new land, but in the case of the Chinese, exclusion was imposed just at that point in the immigrant community's development when men might have sent for their wives and children. Exclusionary policies therefore truncated the natural development of the community" (S. Chan 1991: 105). According to Roger Daniels, "as late as

---

[4] The term "model minority" may need to be re-examined as Sylvia Yanagisako (1995) suggests. She believes it too simplistic and dismissive to account for the real successes of Asian Americans in this way.

Furthermore, if one looks carefully, the daughter writers explorations of Chinese American families do not advocate that parents or daughters seek total acculturation or assimilation into dominant white society. They actually create more fluid spaces for families and communities in their stories. What I am saying is that some Chinese American immigrant parents endure humiliation and hard work in order to give their children a better chance at social and economic opportunities and security in life that they themselves did not have after a life of toil. But they do *not* all become model minority types in the process (Chin's "honorary whites"). Many Chinese American families do not forget cultural traditions, or the nature of survival, suffering, racism and resistance in their own lived experiences. We need to find new ways of talking about and theorizing these various sites, all with the hope of furthering more radical and just transformations of society--which was the goal for a number of activists in the Movement.

1920, seventy years after migration began, women numbered fewer than 10 percent of the Chinese American population. During the late nineteenth century, women were even less numerous (1988: 16). Women, children and families were still a rare sight in Chinatown into the 1930s (see Chu 1961). Babies were such a rarity that they were doted upon by single and married Chinese men (Takaki 1989: 254). In 1900, only 11 percent of the Chinese population were American-born, and by 1930, they were 41 percent of the Chinese population and 52 percent ten years later (ibid.). Thus, a majority of immigrant Chinese men-- single or married with kin, wives and families in China-- was denied the traditional markers of heterosexual masculinity in the U.S. well into the twentieth century: fatherhood, providing for women and families, companionship-sexuality, citizenship and naturalization (Naturalization Act of 1790), and ownership of land (1913 California Alien Land Act bars aliens from owning land).

Chinese (and other Asian) American men have not had the opportunity to fit seamlessly into white heteronormative notions of masculinity in America. I believe there is a window of opportunity for Asian American men to seriously engage rather than simply bash Asian American feminisms and to articulate and enact more permeable, transformative notions of masculinity. But rather than substantially engaging with the wide range of Asian American feminist perspectives and with women as potential allies-- a potentially more *radical* form of partnership, considering the racist and sexist oppression suffered by both Asian American women and men-- a number of cultural nationalists identify with the socially and emotionally deforming and exclusionary practices of a white racialized, heteronormative masculinity that have disempowered them as well as women, families and communities. They have tried to empower Chinese

American men by valorizing certain traditional forms of masculinity as heroic or by focusing on the tragedy of not being able to be traditional--for example, that they regret not having been "men" enough to protect their women or to be authoritarian patriarchs in control of their women and children.

Amy Tan's *The Joy Luck Club* is often discussed as a mother-daughter text. Tan herself acknowledges that in concentrating on mother-daughter stories, she did not fully tell the stories of Chinese American fathers or men. However, father-daughter stories are intimately affiliated to her women's stories. As young women in China, Joy Luck mothers certainly speak of their oppressive relationships with Chinese males like Wu Tsing and Tyan Yu (Lindo's boy-husband). But despite their bad experiences, three of the Joy Luck mothers love and marry Chinese men, who can live with clever, practical and independent-minded women. For example, An-mei Hsu and Lindo meet each other in a fortune cookie factory and become friends. In immigrant women's extended social and political networks, women find support, jobs, and husbands. An-mei and her husband George set Lindo up on a blind date with a telephone man named Tin Jong. Both Tin and Lindo overcome their initial ethnic and linguistic differences (Cantonese and Mandarin) and woo each other through a new language, English. They have a delightful, practical courtship--not the silly story Waverly tells. Rather than enduring an arranged marriage, the feisty, pragmatic Lindo chooses the man she will marry this time around, and this makes a difference in her life. She tells Waverly not only to be proud of her mother's Sun clan but also of her father's Jong clan.

The Joy Luck mothers also toil beside their husbands and teach their children the importance of maintaining cultural traditions as well as surviving the cultural minefields of Anglo-American society. The couples travel, play mahjong and socialize together, and learn to pool their resources and invest for their retirement together. This extended social network of husbands and wives extends support to each other's children. The men respect the work of their wives in the care of their children. Re-situated in the United States, these couples both enact more eclectic gendered identities in their relationships and continue a social understanding of self-in-community that is, in part, derived from their early Chinese upbringing. Rather than arranged marriages, most of the Joy Luck mothers find more companionate, fluid marriages with Chinese men. Furthermore, the mothers do not tell their daughters never to marry Chinese men; rather, they tell their daughters to be strong and independent first and to affiliate with partners who will love and respect them in their own right.

Chinese American fathers are represented in *The Joy Luck Club* as dignified, beloved and respected presences in the life of the Joy Luck daughters. Canning Woo, June's father, for example, asks his daughter to take her deceased mother's place in the circle of Joy luck "aunts." June loves the father who cares for her and who honors his wife's story of struggle. Canning keeps her memory alive in the extended family's archives, as a subversive form of ancestor worship that does honor to his deceased wife as well as to himself. He is the attentive partner to her trauma and the one who constructs a narrative of memory that brings mother and daughter together. Through his nurture and respect for these two women in his life, he reveals aspects of Suyuan's stories that will bring June to a closer understanding of her mother. He tells his wife's story to his family in China and to his daughter. And in the telling, he does not skip the *emotional* details--the inner turmoil of her struggle. He lovingly retells her story and their life together.

Suyuan and Canning meet in a hospital in Chungking during the revolutionary war years in China. She is distraught and suicidal, suffering guilt in abandoning her twin daughters, and is sick with dysentery. She loses her soldier husband in the war. Canning Woo nurses Suyuan back to health through these chaotic and nomadic war years in China. She marries him and they search for her children in Shanghai; and after a long period of wandering together through China and Hong Kong, they both make their way to the United States in 1949. Canning Woo is involved in the nurturing of his wife and family as part of his understanding of meaningful manhood. In the final story, it is he who accompanies June to China in order to reunite her with extended family and with his stepdaughters.

Tan reclaims and honors a father's role in building family, community and solidarity not just in public or work sites, but at the crucial sites of the homeplace. Canning Woo does not easily fit into Anglo-American or Asian American cultural nationalist notions of male-warrior identities. He does not rampage like a stereotyped heartless Confucian patriarch or a kung-fu fighter through his daughter's life or his family's. He is also not represented as an effeminate or castrated wimp. Instead, Canning Woo models a construction of manhood that is, I believe, emotionally and socially responsible and nurturant. It is a more democratic and permeable notion of Chinese American manhood which does not need to display or perform a traditional form of masculinity which constantly asserts and re-enacts its repudiation of femininity and which does not need to dissociate from women as a form of manhood (see Kimmel 1996: 318). Furthermore, what needs to be more profoundly healed is not the father wound but the *mother* wound in men (318). That is, the part of the male self which denies or represses a range of emotions, which masks vulnerability, fear, depression but which needs to love and be loved and to nurture and be nurtured as part of the *human condition.* In privileging and reproducing restrictive and debilitating patriarchal binary systems, it seems that some men have "abandoned precisely those emotional skills that were most needed if women were to achieve equality: nurture, sensitivity, emotional responsiveness" (318). Sheila Ruth makes a good point that "the idea that one who is capable of emotion and sensitivity is incapable of discipline and rational [or intellectual] judgement is absurd. . . . It bespeaks no *undesirable* softness (again, the martial belief that "softness" is contemptible), no lack of intellect or strength" (1990: 215). It would be wrong to assume that all Chinese American daughters have a purely antagonistic relationship with Chinese American fathers or men.

In *Bone*, the writer Fae Myenne Ng understands that Chinese American immigrant working-class fathers, symbolic patriarchs that they may be in their own families, do not have privilege, power, or status within a historically constructed racial-ethnic hierarchy that privileged white males and their families and communities enjoy. Chinese American men were often forced to find work in domestic occupations devalued as "women's work"; in popular mainstream and oppositional ideologies, they have often been represented as passive, effeminate, emasculated, and docile. In her work, Ng attempts to recover the more complex and constructive experiences of Chinese American fathers, but even as she does, she does not dismiss their sexist practices, practices which continue to undermine the way in which families can supply and nurture empowering social and political energies. At the same time the daughter Leila Fu critiques sexist (as well as racist) practices, she also sensitively assesses the multiple locations of Leon Leong, telling his stories at the tangled intersections and distances of love and anger. She recuperates his life as a man and as a father from a woman's standpoint, which is attentive to his emotional, social and physical trauma and negotiations within a Chinatown family and community that are variously affected by the institutional inequities of race, ethnicity, class, gender and sexuality. In *Bone,* the complex stories of fathers are recovered in the intimate social spaces of the domestic and familial as a form of grassroots *realpolitik.*

Social and emotional ties and relations are crucial heart work for building--brick by brick--a strong social and political community as well. Political activism is not just about the practice of fighting or about recuperating a narrow masculinist understanding (or a "socially deformed theorizing") of what constitutes privileged "social," "economic," "public," and "political" sites. Over a period of a lifetime, through critical heart work, daughters in these stories come to a critical understanding of their mothers' daily, practical and very "political" activities of negotiating life and work as an individual in diverse familial and social contexts. Fathers and daughters work through their dilemmas in order to begin *to act rather than re-act,* to free themselves to become allies as well.

Raymond Williams makes a very astute observation about how people are sometimes trapped in the discourse and practice of the "old consciousness," which makes a clear division between what is "emotion" and "intelligence." "It is understandable that people still trapped in the old consciousness really do see the new movements of our time--peace, ecology, feminism--as primarily 'emotional.' Those who have most to lose exaggerate this to 'hysterical', but even 'emotional' is meant to make its point. The implied or stated contrast is with the rational intelligence of the prevailing systems... it is in what it dismisses as 'emotional'--a direct and intransigent concern with actual people--that the old consciousness most clearly shows its bankruptcy... But where people actually live, what is specialized as 'emotional' has an absolute and primary significance. . . . If our central attention is on whole ways of life, there can be no reasonable contrast between emotions and rational intelligence" (1983: 266). Furthermore, the "deformed social order," which is, in part, the result of such foundational, binary theorizing about emotion and intelligence, "is not particularly rational or intelligent," according to Williams. "It can be sharp enough in its specialized and separated areas, but in its aggregates it is usually stupid and muddled. It is also, in some of its central drives, an active generator of bad emotions, especially of aggressiveness and greed. In its worst forms it has magnified these to extraordinary scales of war and crime. It has succeeded in the ... improbable combination of affluent consumption and widespread emotional distress " (ibid.).

The point is that social, emotional and personal bonding really matter in our politics, in our theorizing practices, and in building toward our political future together as a community; that attention to feeling and connection is the crucial brick work that builds and sustains a more compassionate world. War as the ultimate meta-narrative and as a *way of life* does not speak to the loss, rage, alienation, terror, confusion, sorrow, guilt, vulnerability, and the need to love and nurture, which are central to the lives of marginalized people and indeed to all people. War and violence as a way of life deforms, represses and destroys the potentially constructive *social and institutional* resolutions of such emotions and needs.

For this reason, the home and family are often constructed by many women of color as one major space in which to nurture skills of survival and political activism. Although "home" is not free of internal physical and psychic struggle and violence or free from the racism and sexism either, "home" has been identified as a source of individual and community strength. I think the cultural critic Bell Hooks says it eloquently in the essay "Homeplace" when she talks about black women who resisted the daily forms of social-economic exploitation and racism by making homes where people could strive to "be subjects, not objects, where we could be affirmed in our minds and hearts despite poverty, hardship, and deprivation, where we could restore to ourselves the dignity denied us on the outside in the public world" (Hooks 1990: 42). Dominant and oppositional discourses and practices can erase or appropriate the radical meaning of subordinated racial-ethnic women's experiences as well as their productive and reproductive labor. That is, they can define the work at domestic and familial sites as women's natural, biological work; they can name self-sacrifice and the care of children (whether one's own or not) as "not reflective of choice and will" (ibid.) "Failure to recognize the realm of choice, and the remarkable re-visioning of both woman's role and the idea of 'home' that black women consciously exercised in practice, obscures the political commitment to racial uplift, to eradicating racism, which was the philosophical core of dedication to community and home" (ibid.) Likewise, Chinese American mother-daughter stories critically forefront women's theorizing of social sites and practices that have often been neglected or dismissed in political understandings of identity and collectivity. Perhaps it is time for women, men, families and communities to re-think the relational discourses and practices that keep us divided and alienated, enemies so close to home, so close to the heart.

Cultural nationalists and other critics rarely make critically visible these men's stories in the work of Chinese American women writers in articulating more expansive, fluid personal and political identities. They do not refer to the tradition of Asian American feminist writing that allies itself with Asian men as it explores the nature of heroism and the nature of male suffering, anger and violence in a racist, sexist world, that acknowledges the contributions of Chinese American men to their families and communities, and that seeks healing, transformative practices, which are *inclusive of* individual and institutional accountability, social change and justice. In making only certain forms of manhood visible or acceptable, racialized, gendered and sexualized masculinist discourses impose a debilitating *invisibility* to this rich area of men's (and women's) experiences. From their restricted rhetorical stance, they cannot see these potentially alternative and resisting men's stories as heroic, but only as "emasculating" or "feminizing." As cultural critic Judith Newton states more work needs to be done at "the site of investigating masculinity," work that links the "economic and political with the familial and personal, the public with the private" (1994: 575). Such links are vital to explore if women, men, families and communities are to enact more liberating and ethically accountable practices as we move into the twenty-first century.

References

Asian Women United of California, eds. *Making waves: An anthology of writings by and about Asian American women*. Boston: Beacon Press. 1989.

Bates, Judy Fong. *China Dog and other tales from a Chinese laundry*. Toronto: Sister Vision, Black and Women of Color Press. 1997.

Chan, Sucheng. *Asian Americans: An interpretive history*. Twayne's Immigrant Heritage of America Series. Boston: Twayne Publishers. 1991.

Chan, Sucheng. "The Exclusion of Chinese women, 1870-1943," *Entry Denied: Exclusion and the Chinese community in America, 1882-1943*, edited by Chan. Philadelphia: Temple University Press, 1991.

Chan, Sucheng. "Race, Ethnic Culture, and Gender in the Construction of Identities among Second-Generation Chinese-Americans, 1880s to 1930s," *Claiming America: Constructing Chinese American identities during the Exclusion Era*, edited by K. Scott Wong and Sucheng Chan. Philadelphia: Temple University Press, 3-40. 1998.

Chang, Lan Samantha. *Hunger: A novella and stories*. New York: W.W. Norton and Company. 1998.

Chen, Ying. *Ingratitude*. Translated by Carol Volk. New York: Farrar, Straus and Giroux. 1998.

Cheung, King-Kok. *Articulate silences: Hisaye Yamamoto, Maxine Hong Kingston, Joy Kogawa*. Ithaca : Cornell University Press. 1993.

Cheung, King-Kok. "Of men and men: Reconstructing Chinese American masculinity," *Other Sisterhoods: Literary theory and U.S. women of color*, edited by Sandra Kumamoto Stanley. Urbana and Chicago: University of Illinois Press, 173-199. 1998.

Chin, Sara. *Below the line.* San Francisco: City Lights. 1997.

Choy, Philip P., Lorraine Dong, and Marlon K. Hom, eds. *The coming man: Nineteenth century American perceptions of the Chinese.* Seattle: University of Washington Press. 1994.

Chu, Judy, Anna May Wong. *Counterpoint: Perspectives on Asian America,* edited by Emma Gee. Los Angeles: Asian American Studies, UCLA, 284-288. 1976.

Chu, Judy, Anna May Wong. "Asian American women's studies courses: A look back at our beginnings," *Frontiers* 8, no. 3: 96-101. 1986.

Chu, Louis. *Eat a bowl of tea.* Secaucus, NJ: Lyle Stuart. 1961.

Chuang, Hua [pseud.]. *Crossings.* Boston: Northeastern University Press. 1986.

Clark, Danae. "Father figure," *Boys: Masculinities in contemporary culture,* edited by Paul Smith. New York: Westview Press, 23-37. 1996.

Daniels, Roger. *Asian America: Chinese and Japanese in the United States since 1850.* Seattle: University of Washington Press. 1988.

Dong, Lorraine. "The forbidden city legacy and its Chinese American women," *Chinese America: History and Perspectives.* 125-148. 1992.

Eng, David L. and Alice Y. Hom, eds. *Q & A: Queer in Asian America.* Philadelphia: Temple University Press. 1998.

Fung, Richard. "Looking for my penis: The eroticized Asian in gay porn," *How do I look? Queer film and video,* edited by Bad Object-Choices. Seattle: Bay Press, 145-168. 1991.

Gee, John. "Life in a Chinese laundry: Interview with John Gee", by Buck Wong. *Counterpoint: Perspectives on Asian America*, edited by Emma Gee. Los Angeles: Asian American Studies Center, University of California, 338-344. 1976.

Jen, Gish. *Typical American*. New York: Houghton Mifflin/Seymour Lawrence. 1991.

Jen, Gish. *Mona in the promised land*. New York: Vintage Contemporaries. 1996.

Hall, Bruce Edward. *Tea that burns: A family memoir of Chinatown*. New York: The Free Press. 1998.

Hinsch, Bret. *Passions of the cut sleeve: The male homosexual tradition in China*. Berkeley: University of California Press. 1990.

Hirata, Lucie Cheng. "Free, indentured, enslaved: Chinese prostitutes in nineteenth-century America.". *Signs: Journal of Women in Culture and Society* , no. 1: 3-29. 1979.

Hirata, Lucie Cheng. "Chinese immigrant women in nineteenth-century California," *Asian and Pacific American experiences: Women's perspectives*, edited by Nobuya Tsuchida. Minneapolis: Asian/Pacific American Learning Resource Center and General College, University of Minnesota, 38-55. 1982.

Hooks, Bell. *Yearning: Race, gender, and cultural politics*. Boston: South End Press. 1990.

Hwang, David Henry. *M butterfly*. New York: Plume Books. 1988.

Kam, K. "The hopeland," *Making waves: An anthology of writings by and about Asian American women*, edited by Asian Women United of California. Boston: Beacon Press, 92-98. 1989.

Kimmel, Michael. *Manhood in America: A cultural history*. New York: Free Press. 1996.

Kingston, Maxine Hong.. *The woman warrior: Memoirs of a girlhood among ghosts*. New York: Vintage. 1977.

Kingston, Maxine Hong. *China men*. New York: Vintage International. 1989.

Lee, Li-Young. *The winged seed: A remembrance*. New York: Simon and Schuster. 1995.

Lee, Sky. *Disappearing moon cafe*. Seattle: Seal Press. 1990.

Leong, Russell, ed. *Asian American sexualities: Dimensions of the gay and lesbian experience*. New York: Routledge. 1996.

Linmark, R. Zamora. *Rolling the r's*. New York: Kaya Production. 1995.

Manalansan, Martin F., IV. In the shadows of Stonewall: Examining gay transnational politics and the diasporic dilemma. *GLQ: A Journal of Lesbian and Gay Studies*. 2, no. 4: 425-38. 1995.

Moraga, Cherríe, and Gloria Anzaldúa, eds. *This bridge called my back: Writings by radical women of color*. New York: Kitchen Table, Women of Color Press. 1981.

Nee, Victor G. and Brett de Bary Nee. *Longtime californ': A documentary study of an American .Chinatown*. Stanford. Stanford University Press. 1972.

Newton, Judith. "White guys (review essay)," *Feminist Studies* 24, no. 3: 572-598. 1998.

Ng, Fae Myenne. *Bone*. New York: Hyperion. 1993.

Ng, Mei. *Eating Chinese Food Naked*. New York: Scribner. 1998.

Nunez, Sigrid. *A feather on the breath of god*. New York: Harper Collins. 1995.

Okihiro, Gary Y. *Margins and mainstreams: Asians in American history and culture*. Seattle: University of Washington Press. 1994.

Quan, Kit Yuen. "The girl who wouldn't sing," *Making face, making soul: Haciendo caras*, edited by Gloria Anzaldúa. San Francisco: Aunt Lute Foundation Books, 212-220. 1990.

Takaki, Ronald. *Strangers from a different shore: A history of Asian Americans*. Boston: Little, Brown and Co. 1989.

Tan, Amy. *The joy luck club*. New York: G. P. Putnam's Sons. 1989.

Williams, Raymond. *Towards 2000*. London: Chatto and Windus/Hogarth Press. 1983.

Woo, Merle. "Letter to Ma," *This bridge called my back: Writings by radical women of color*, edited by Cherríe Moraga and Gloria Anzaldúa. New York: Kitchen Table, Women of Color Press, 140-147. 1981.

Wong, Norman. *Cultural revolution*. New York: Persea Books. 1994.

Yang, Belle. *Baba. A return to Chinaupon my father's shoulders*. New York: Harcoutry Brace and Co. 1994.

Yanagisako, Sylvia. "Transforming orientalism: Gender, nationality, and class in Asian American studies," *Naturalizing power: Essays in feminist cultural analysis*, edited by Sylvia Yanagisako and Carol Delaney. New York: Routledge, 275-298. 1995.

Yung, Judy. *Chinese women of America: A pictorial history*. Seattle: University of Washington Press. 1986.

Yung, Judy. "The social awakening of Chinese American women as reported in *Chung Sai Yat Po*, 1900-1911," *Unequal sisters: A multicultural reader in U.S. women's history*, edited by Ellen Carol DuBois and Vicki L. Ruiz. New York: Routledge, 195-207. 1990.

Yung, Judy. *Unbound feet: a social history of Chinese women in San Francisco*. Berkeley: University of California Press. 1995.

Zhao, Xiaojian. Chinese American women defense workers in World War II. *California History* 75, no. 2: 138-153. 1996.

Saluting Honorable Illa Collin
Dr. Alex Yeh

S upervisor Illa Collin (photo on 243), Member of the Sacramento County Board of Supervisors, has been serving our community for more than twenty-two years (1979 to the present). She represents the Second Supervisorial District, which has the highest Asian Pacific population in Sacramento County. We salute her on our Distinguished Models section Roll as part of this book. This appropriate and timely honor is based upon her outstanding contributions to environmental issues, including transportation and air quality, water and waste management, and to empowering diverse ethnic communities. Citations and recognition of her extraordinary services to the greater Sacramento areas are too many to be counted. We will just present one example of each. (1) The National Association of County Park and Recreation Officials (NACPRO) awarded her the "Outstanding Public Official" award to recognize and honor her accomplishments in various parks, arts and open space issues that have encouraged a livable community during her two decades of service to Sacramento County. (2) She has served as a key member of the Governing Board of the Sacramento Employment and Training Agency, advocating and activating employment programs, Head Start programs, community action and refugee assistance programs. She is a woman of substance far beyond what her political contributions reveal about her as a person (Please refer to the footnotes for numerous awards and recognition for her excellent achievements).

Supervisor Collin is a beloved friend to the Chinese community in the Greater Sacramento area. Her love for the Chinese and their culture can be traced back to her school years when she developed close friendships with fellow students of Chinese ancestry. Those personal friendships, which still continue, add motivation to her commitment to the Chinese community. She has made outstanding contributions to the Chinese community. She definitely deserves a place on our Distinguished Models section. Her contributions and achievements are a reflection of her and the very basic family and human values that are important to us all.

She was born in Rock Springs, Wyoming, attended high school in both Rock Springs and Portland, Oregon and graduated from the University of Oregon. She taught elementary-age youngsters in Portland, Oregon, and in Piedmont, California. Her background in education and early work in grass roots campaigns has given her a unique understanding about the inner workings of government and bureaucracy. And her decision to enter politics years ago marked the beginning of a career filled with determination to work on issues involving education, welfare, women, children, and families. She is full of energy and vision and has an amazing sense of humor and realism. She is a leader in the truest sense. She anticipates potential problems and tries to solve them before they happen. She is also like a favorite aunt who is always loving, loyal, interesting, and supportive.

Affirmative Action is important to Supervisor Collin. She has described it in the same manner that our forefathers must have thought about in creating separate executive branches. They structured our government so we would have innate check and balance systems in place as over time we would need to have some way of re-evaluating our very human decision-making process. She has further explained that "affirmative action is a means of checking ourselves against our own biases, may they be prejudicial or process oriented. And in order to maintain a system of fairness, it is always necessary to examine our motives and the process by which we implement them." She has expressed a sincere optimism for a changing government. She seems to feel that we have a bright future.

Her husband Don, an attorney, was a Lobbyist for the California Building Industry Association and then General Counsel to the Industry before he retired in 1998. They have three daughters, two granddaughters, and three grandsons to share and enjoy. All of her close-knit family members live in the city and county of Sacramento, California.

FOOTNOTES:

1. **Involvement in the Asian Community:**

- Through her affiliation with the Sacramento Employment and Training Agency's Government Board, she has supported funding for Asian Resources and the Sacramento Chinese Community Center.
- She has been an active supporter of the Asian Community Center and the establishment of the Asian Nursing Home.
- She has actively supported outreach services to the Asian community in the social services and mental health fields.
- In 1983, she initiated a Sacramento County Ordinance memorializing the Japanese American experience during World War II, establishing a permanent memorial, and authorizing reparation payments to

County employees who were evacuated to internment camps.

- She represented the Sacramento County Board of Supervisors as the personal representative of the Mayor of Sacramento in a good-will trip sponsored by the Matsuyama Sister City Association to Japan in 1989 and 1999.
- She represented the Sacramento County Board of Supervisors in a good-will trip sponsored by the Sacramento-Jinan Sister City Association of Jinan, China, in 1991.
- She sponsors Sacramento County resolutions honoring Asian Eagle Scouts and attends Eagle Scout ceremonies.
- She has consistently been a avid supporter of honoring the contributions of Asians to the Sacramento region, such as historical status for the Chinese Diggings in Folsom, and the efforts to preserve the town of Locke as a "living tribute" to the early immigrant Chinese in Sacramento County.
- She has given financial support to Asian community efforts, such as the Amanda Chiang Bone Marrow Drive, and the J.A.C.L. Endowment Fund.
- She has sponsored many resolutions for the Asian community, such as the 45th Anniversary of VFW Chung Mei Post 8358, Hiroshima Nikkeijin Kei's 85th Anniversary, Asian Resources Anniversaries, Sacramento Chinese Community Center's Anniversaries, Sacramento Lao Community's Hmong New Year, and welcoming Mayor Zhai Yongbo and the delegation from Jinan, China.
- She has been largely responsible for the appointment of Asians to Sacramento County Boards and Commissions.

- She has authored an article titled, "Important Contributions by the Chinese During the Gold Rush Era" for the Sacramento Historical Society's newsletter.
- She has written letters to Governor Gray Davis supporting the appointment of Chinese American individuals to positions in state government.
- She is an Honorary Advisor to the Sacramento Chinese Community Service Center Board of Directors.
- She has been a member of the Community Advisory Committee for the Chinese American Council of Sacramento.
- She has sworn in officers for the Asian Bar Association and the Asian Chamber of Commerce.
- She has written letters of support for Bill Lann Lee as Assistant Attorney General for Civil Rights.
- She is an adviser to the Council of Asian Pacific Islanders Together for Active Leadership (CAPITAL).

2. Special Awards:

- 1995 "Friend of the Community" Award from the Japanese American Citizens League, Florin Chapter, for her outstanding leadership and service to the community as well as her long standing support of the issues and concerns of the Japanese American community.
- 1995 Community Service Recognition Award from the Japanese American Citizens League, Sacramento Chapter, for her strong support of the Japanese American community and the causes which affect the well-being of the Nikkei Community.
- 1998 Honoree of the Asian Pacific American community for her outstanding contributions. Organizations who honored her include Asian

Democratic Club, Asian/Pacific Southeast Asians Association, Chinese American Council of Sacramento, Organization of Chinese-Americans, Sacramento Chinese Cultural Foundation, Sacramento Chinese of Indo-China Friendship Association, Sacramento Jinan Sister City Corporation, Japanese American Citizens League, Korean American Community Association of Greater Sacramento, Greater Sacramento Taiwanese Association, Council of Asian Pacific Islanders Together for Active Leadership.

3. **Other awards and recognition for her community service:**

- Foster Grandparent/Senior Companion - "Community Friend of the Year Award," 1980
- Mental Health Association - "Presidents Award," 1986
- California Park and Recreation Society - "Political Commitment and Outstanding Service Award," 1987
- National Council of Jewish Women - "Hannah G. Soloman Award for Community Service," 1987
- Alpha Kappa Alpha - "Distinguished Public Service Award," 1987
- Japanese American Citizens League - Special Recognition for leadership efforts in the passage of the Civil Liberties Act of 1988
- Asian Community Center, Inc. - Honoree for "Outstanding Leadership," 1989
- Sacramento Tree Foundation - "Arbor Day Award"
- Sacramento Association for the Retarded - "Albert S. Rodda Award," 1990
- Mental Health Association - Legislative Award, 1991

- National Collegiate Athletic Association - Outstanding Contributions to the Success of the 1991 National Youth Sports Program
- News & Review Magazine: "Best County Supervisor," 1991 and 1992
- Jewish National Fund - "Tree of Life Award," 1991
- Sacramento Magazine "Regional Pride Award for Government," 1992
- Southgate Park and Recreation District - Dedication of "Illa Collin Park", 1992
- United Way - "Distinguished Community Service Award," 1992
- YWCA - "Outstanding Women Award for Government/Law," 1993
- Sacramento Housing Alliance - "Housing Award for Outstanding Commitment to Affordable Housing," 1995
- National Association of County Parks and Recreation Officials' "Outstanding Public Official Award," 1995
- Sacramento Association for the Retarded - "President's Award," 1998
- "Excellence in Public Service" Award from The Democratic Party of Sacramento County, 1999
- "Legislative Award" from the Mental Health Association, 1999
- Special Recognition Award from Health for All, 1999
- Resolution from the Florin Road Partnership in recognition of her contributions to the Florin Road Partnership and Florin Road Improvement Project, 1999

4. **Illa was instrumental in the creation of the following bodies:**

- Sacramento Tree Foundation

- American River Parkway Foundation
- Child Care Consortium
- Blue Ribbon Committee to plan for the future of the Sacramento Science Center
- Florin Road Partnership

5. Illa represents the Board of Supervisors on the following:

- Sacramento Employment and Training Agency, a joint powers agency which administers employment programs, Head Start programs, community action and refugee assistance programs.
- Local Agency Formation Commission, which makes decisions relating to annexation and incorporations.
- Sacramento Metropolitan Cable Television Commission, a joint powers agency which monitors and regulates cable television franchises.
- Sacramento Metropolitan Air Quality Management District, which is committed to protecting public health and the environment by achieving clean air.
- Sacramento Public Library Authority, a joint powers agency which administers the Sacramento Public Libraries.
- Sacramento Transportation Authority, which administers the Measure A program. The voters passed Measure A, the countywide one-half percent Sales tax to be levied from 1989-2009. Proceeds of the tax are used to fund a comprehensive program of roadway and transit improvements.
- San Joaquin Valley Rail Committee, which makes improvements to passenger train service in the San Joaquin Rail Corridor.

6. Illa also serves on the following bodies:

- Center for Fathers and Families, Board Member
- Girl Scouts of Tierra del Oro, Alumni Association Manager
- Sacramento Chinese Community Service Center, Honorary Advisory Board Member

In Her Own Words
March Fong Eu

Dr. March Fong Eu's speech as presented to the Organization of Chinese Americans, Inc, Greater Sacramento Chapter, on May 8, 1999.

I am very happy to be here tonight to share this evening with you to accept the honor that you have bestowed upon me.

I accept this award tonight at a very critical time in my life and life of politic America. I have spent more than 4 decades in public service. I started my political career when women and minorities were a rarity in the political arena. My long tenure in politics signified to me that I had made a crack in the glass ceiling, and I was proud to lead the way.

When I retired two years ago (1997) as the U.S. Ambassador to Micronesia, I basked in the satisfaction that I had done my part in opening the door of politic America to Asians and especially Chinese-Americans.

But, a little over two years ago, that glass ceiling not only cracked wide open but came crashing down on all of us...crushing us, rendering us puzzled and helpless. An "off the cuff" comment by the 1996 Republican presidential nominee that his opponent was financing his campaign with foreign money opened a media frenzy that led to the witch hunt and Asian bashing we find ourselves in today.

Before we knew it, three federal investigative committees, one the Justice Department via the F. B. I., one in the House of Representatives and one in the U.S. Senate, were looking into campaign contributions made by persons with Asian names...more specifically, Chinese names. Persons with Asian names, Chinese names, were telephoned, interviewed, subpoenaed and deposed as to their citizenship, the source of their contribution and their motives in making a campaign contribution.

Persons with Asian and Chinese names had their phone records, business account records and their associate lists subpoenaed or confiscated.

Today, in 1999, loyal Chinese-Americans are being accused, without proof, of being Chinese spies! These are shameful days reminiscent of the early 1880's when Federal, State and local politicians used the campaign slogan, "The Chinese Must Go," to promote the passage of 1882 Chinese Exclusion Act. This ugly past had suddenly became non-American, and the land of their rich heritage became suspect of sinister intent. We are *persona non grata.*

So it is in this political environment that I accept this award tonight at a sad time for Chinese-Americans in politic America. But I ask you not to despair.

Let us continue to work to put more Chinese/Asian Americans into the U.S. corridors of power. Let us denounce in whatever fashion we can the behavior of our government in their obsession to intimidate us. Join me in encouraging Asian Americans to vote and support qualified and dedicated Asian American candidates who are committed to our cause. Support candidates of any ethnicity if they are dedicated to protecting our human and civil rights. Let your representatives know what is happening and that you do not like it.

Let America know that we are all Americans and Americans come in different sizes, shapes and colors. Do not retreat to ghettos, but let us share our rich and varied culture with the rest of America for we are America and America is we.

Honorable Jimmie R. Yee's Story

(An Extraordinary Individual Who Earned an Extraordinary Opportunity)

Dr. Alex Yeh

H onorable Jimmie Yee (photo on 252) is the first Chinese American ever assumed the office of Mayor of Sacramento, the Capitol of the State of California on November 7, 1999. This city is one of the largest metropolitans in the USA. It was founded in 1849, and is the oldest incorporated city of the State. But it is only 150 years young and will continue to prosper for years to come with its resources of land and people.

It took one hundred and fifty years for a Chinese descendant to achieve such a high position corresponding to this book. This extraordinary opportunity has to go back to 1999, when Council member Yee had been asked by the Late Mayor Joe Serna, Jr. to accept the position of Vice Mayor for the 1999 City Council session. Mayor Yee became Acting Major on November 7, 1999. On December 14, 1999, Council member Jimmie Yee was unanimously selected as mayor by the Sacramento City Council to fulfill the remainder of the term of the late Mayor Serna.

In 1992, Councilman Yee was elected to a four year term on the Sacramento City Council representing Council District Four consisting neighborhoods of Eastern Greenhaven, Fremont Park, Land Park, Little Pocket, Maple Park, Poverty Ridge, Richmond Grove, South Land

Park, Southside Park, Upper Land Park and Z'berg Park. He was re-elected to a second four-year term in 1996 and was again elected to a third four-year term on March 7, 2000.

He established a very fair political example by not campaigning for a full term of the mayorship although he had tremendous and available resources of political machine being the sitting mayor.

He is a native of Sacramento and attended local public schools. He graduated from the University of California Berkeley in 1956 with a Bachelor Degree in Civil Engineering. He started his career with the State of California in 1959 and ended in 1965.

He established his own structural engineering firm in 1966. During his 25 years of ownership, his firm had grown to one of the largest consulting structural engineering companies in the Sacramento Valley. His firm designed many of Sacramento's landmark buildings including the Sacramento Convention Center, Capital Bank, Riverview Plaza and Sutter General Hospital.

Honorable Yee is an active member of the Sacramento Optimist Club and the Chinese American Council of Sacramento. He has worked with the Sacramento Chinese Drum and Bugle Corps for more than twenty years. Councilman Yee has raised money for many organizations and efforts throughout the Sacramento community. He organized the first Asian bone marrow drive in the United States in 1989 registering more than 2500 people in that effort. (Please refers to the footnotes about Councilman Yee's great records of achievements).

He has been happily married to his wife Mary for more than 46 years. They have six children, all college graduates with professional achievements throughout proud parents of six children and ten grandchildren.

FOOTNOTE:

Public Service

- City of Sacramento, Mayor (1999-2000)
- City of Sacramento, Vice Mayor (1999)
- City of Sacramento, Member, District 4 (1992-present)
- Mayor's Commission on Development, Chairman (1999)
- Sacramento Area Food Control Agency (1993-1994)
- Water Advisory Board (1993-1994)
- Personnel and Public Employees Committee (1997-1998)
- American River Water Resources Committee (1996-1997)
- Sacramento Metropolitan Cable Commission (1994-1998)
- Sacramento Transportation Authority (1993-present)
- Sacramento-Yolo Port Authority (1996-1998)
- Sacramento City-County Solid Waste Joint Powers Authority (1993-present)
- Sacramento Regional County Sanitation District (1999-present)
- Sacramento Metropolitan Air Quality Management District (1999-present)
- Sacramento-Placerville Transportation Corridor Joint Powers Authority (1998-1999)
- Sacramento City-County Public Library Joint Powers Authority (1997-1998)
- Police Community Relations Advisory Committee (1989-1992)
- Sacramento City Civil Service Board (1974-1977), President (1976)

- Sacramento Citizens Committee on Police Practices (1973)

Honors/Awards

- Sacramento Chinese Community Service Center, "Honoree of the Year" for Community Services (1990)
- National Council of Engineering Examiners, Distinguished Service Certificate (1987)
- California Council of Civil Engineers and Land Surveyors, Distinguished Service Award (1984)
- California Society of Professional Engineers, Distinguished Contributions to the Engineering and Scientific Community Award (1982)
- Society of Manufacturing Engineers, Distinguished Engineering Achievements Award (1982)
- Engineering Council of the Sacramento Valley, Engineer of the Year (1978)
- Structural Engineers Association of Central California, Outstanding Structural Engineer (1977)

Professional Affiliations

- American Society of Civil Engineers, Fellow (1954-present)
- Structural Engineers Association of Central California, Fellow (1959-present), President (1971), Board of Directors (1971-1975), Secretary-Treasurer (1974)
- Consulting Engineers Association of California, Member (1965-1992)
- California State Board of Registration for Professional Engineers and Land Surveyors, Governor's Appointee (1977-1986), President (1981)

- National Council of Engineering Examiners, California State Representative (1978-1986)

Community Service

- Sacramento Optimist Club, Sacramento Asian Concern, Sacramento Asian Community Nursing Home, Sacramento Chinese Community Drum and Bugle Corps, Fundraising and Contributions for Amanda Chiang Leukemia Fund, Sim Yee Crime Reward Fund, and Hate Crimes Unity Fund, Chinese American Council of Sacramento, Asian Pacific Chamber of Commerce, Asian Peace Officers Association, Sacramento Asian Sports Foundation

Education, Registrations, Military Service

- Bachelor of Science in Civil Engineering, University of California, Berkeley (1956)
- California Structural Engineer No. 1404 (1966)
- California Civil Engineer, No. 12703 (1961)
- US Army Reserves, US Corps of Engineers, Captain (1957-1965)

Prolegomenon: The End of the Beginning
Dr. Alex Yeh

The legacy of Peter C. Y. Leung lies in his efforts to preserve certain parts of Chinese American's contributions to California's growth and development for the past 150 years. Though he died two years ago, he would live on through his academic contributions. I referred to this continuance as one of the prolegomena because of his noted worthiness.

The Sacramento Chinese Culture Foundation and the Asian American Studies, University of California at Davis, provided great leadership to publish this book telling the world how Chinese immigrants and their culture enriched this land of opportunities.

It is my sincere wish that this publication will urge all the peoples interested in Chinese culture and heritage to write such Chinese American success stories, in part of significant California history as an important legacy for the USA in general and California in particular.

Since Dr. Kevin Starr, Chairman of the "150 Years California History Celebration Commission", contributed such an eloquent "Preface" to this book, I must yield till this moment to express my sincere appreciation to the individuals and organizations who supported and participated in this effort. The organizations are the Sacramento Chinese Culture Center; Asian American Studies, UC Davis; Chinese Translation Services, San Francisco; Sun Printing, Sacramento; and Sacramento

County Library. My Editorial Board included Vicki Beaton, an outstanding Chinese World Journal reporter, Eileen Leung, UC Davis administrator, and Min Zhu Lin, a Chinese scholar (retired librarian, Solano County, California). Tim Leung, the son of Peter C. Y. Leung, designed the book cover by overlaying the California map over a dancing dragon to depict the symbiotic relationship between California and its Chinese citizens.

For you readers, we earnestly hope that this book signals a beginning, not an ending, to our quest for the integral value of all cultures. Our hopes for you are aptly expressed in the words of the late Sir Winston Churchill:

"Now, this is not the end. It is not even the beginning of the end. But it is, perhaps, the end of the beginning."

INDIVIDUAL DONORS

Steven Bancroft, San Francisco, California
Jack & Valerie Bass, San Francisco, California
Clifford & Vicki Beaton, Sacramento, California
Tina Byrne, Elk Grove, California
Frank & Peggy Chan, Sacramento, California
Chun Kong & Anny Chan, Sacramento, California
Gordon & Mary Chan, Modesto, California
Ruth & Martin Chan, Sacramento, California
Kwai Lung & Elizabeth Chan, Rowland Heights, California
K.S. Chan, Sacramento, California
Rosemary Chan, San Francisco, California
James & Margaret Chan, San Francisco, California
Lloyd & Wai Yee Chun Chan, Suisun, California
Su-Shia & Yung Chen Chang, Sacramento, California
Glenn & Betty Chang, Elk Grove, California
Fung-chu Chen, Sacramento, California
Francis & Lainee Chen, San Francisco, California
S.C. Cheng, Rowland Heights, California
Betty Cheung, Elk Grove, California
Jack Chew, Sacramento, California
Peter & Eleanor Chiang, Sacramento, California
Bernadette Chiang, Sacramento, California
Kenneth & Lisa Chin, New York
Mike & Lisa Chou, Plano, Texas
Darlene Choy, San Leandro, California
Illa Collins, Sacramento, California
Loren Fong, Sunnyvale, California
Robert & Helen Fong, San Francisco, California
Elaine Hun, Cupertino, California
Chen Ai Hsia, Sacramento, California
Peter & Susan Huang, California
Frank Inn, Suisun, California
Burton Jang, San Francisco, California

Yvonne Jang, San Francisco, California
Kenneth Jung, Fremont, California
Karen Kurasaki, Los Angeles, California
Carl & Martha Lai, Sacramento, California
Chun Kit Lai, Hong Kong
Hon Lam, Sacramento, California
Ping Ming Lam, Hong Kong
Ivy Lee, Sacramento, California
Bob & June Leong, Sacramento, California
Tarika Leung, Davis, California
Timothy Leung, Brooklyn, California
Eileen Leung, Davis, California
Toby Leung, Davis, California
Li Ching Lim, Citrus Heights, California
Min Zhu & Grace Lin, Sacramento, California
Hideko Lion, Sacramento, California
Lydia & Tien Liu, Sacramento, California
Betty Liu, Sacramento, California
Kendrick Liu, Sacramento, California
Bob & Linda Liu, Sacramento, California
David & Gerogina Lonney, Harlingen, Texas
Dolly Louie, Sacramento, California
Jim & Chai Louie, Sacramento, California
Worley & Jean Low, Berkeley, California
Henry & Caroline Low, Fairfield, California
Lin Lowe, Laguna Beach, California
Jean Chan Lu, San Jose, California
Wanda Lui, Roseville, California
Dominic Maillard, Paris, France
Albert & Dana Moon, Plano, Texas
Wai & Hon Moy, Roseville, California
Raymond & Robin Muffly, Brisbane, California
Hoa Kim Thai Nhan, Sacramento, California
Gilbert Peng, San Francisco, California
Albert & Eleanor Perez, San Leandro, California
Wing Q. Phong, Sacramento, California
John & Betty Pong, Hong Kong

Cliff & Cindi Quan, Belmont, California
John & Roberta Quan, San Pablo, California
Philip & Jennifer Risken, Walnut Creek, California
Roberta Singleton, Sacramento, California
Stanley & Lollita Siu, Stockton, California
Charles & Wendy Su, Elk Grove, California
Joel Szabat & Chiling Tong, Sacramento, California
Jenny & John Tan, Sacramento, California
Gail & Michael Tanigawa, Honolulu, Hawaii
John & Lois Tim, Pinole, California
Dr. Walter & Kay Tim, Stockton, California
Brad & Robin Tim, Sacramento, California
Julian & Lillian Tim, Sunnyvale, California
Lund C. Tim, Broderick, California
Lewis & Pat Tim, Fairfield, California
Dr. Leslie Tim, Hayward, California
Jennifer & Ron Tim, Vacaville, California
Dr. Michael & Margaret Tim, Lilburn, Georgia
Dr. Richard & Ellen Tim, Durham, North Carolina
Hi Can To, Sacramento, California
Jenny Wong, Sacramento, California
Mandy Wong, Sacramento, California
Ed & May Wong, Sacramento, California
Bill Wong, Sacramento, California
Robert Wong, Fairfield, California
Gene Wong, Rancho Murieta, California
James & Nira Wong, San Francisco, California
Arnold & Effie Wong, Plano, Texas
Raymond & Helen Yee, Sacramento, California
Dr. Alex Yeh, Sacramento, California
Shu Yeh, Sacramento, California
Pearl & Howard Young, Sacramento, California

ORGANIZATION DONORS

All tbe Best Carpets, Sacramento, California
Cal Yee Farms, Suisun, California
East-West Services, West Sacramento, California
Elk Grove Chinese Association, Elk Grove, California
Frank Fat Foundation, Sacramento, California
Happy Garden Seafood Restaurant, Sacramento, California
Hung Sing Martial Arts Assn., Hayward, California
Locke Property Development, Locke, California
Lok Redwood Empire Properties, Petaluma, California
Vin Phat Supermarket, Sacramento, California
Welco Supermarket, Sacramento, California
Wong Family Investors, Sacramento, California
Yin's McDonald's, Vacaville, California
Yuen Kong Foundation, Los Angeles, California

PHOTOGRAPHIC CREDITS

The photographs in this book are reproduced by permission and courtesy of the following:

Sacramento Chinese Culture Foundation Board of Directors by Mr. Lim K. Yee

Asian American Studies Center staff, UC Davis, by Mrs. Eileen Leung

The Locke and the Delta Story by Ms. Vicki Beaton and Lim K. Yee

Chinese Farm Laborers by Professor Peter C. Y. Leung

The Tim Family members, courtesy of Tim family

Mr. Frank Fat's Story, courtesy of Fat family

Bel Air Supermarket Presidential award and its members, courtesy of the Wong family

C. C. Yins' Story, courtesy of the Yin family

Authors' photos, courtesy of this book's contributors

Photos in the "People" section, courtesy of those presented in the book

260 *150 Years of the Chinese Presence in California (1848-2001)*

This photographic version reflects not only the
Chinese traditional heritages but also its cultural
values. It represents some resilient and lively stories of
Chinese immigrant families and individuals for over
the past 150 years with picturesque evidences.

A.Y. (9-8-01)

這組照片，反映華裔在加州一百五十多年生存，生
活與生計的點點滴滴。他們奉獻中華傳統的遺產及
文化價值，促進了加州多采多姿的發展與成長。這
些家族與個體的心路歷程，可為華裔美籍公民，見
證加州歷史的豐盛。

Good Time: [TOP] Traditional New Year celebration of a home.
[BELOW] Cultural Building, Confucius Temple
好年頭：〔上〕傳統農曆新年慶典。〔下〕文化殿堂，孔夫子
廟。

262

Sponsors' key people: [TOP] Sacramento Chinese Culture
Foundation Board of Directors. [BELOW] Asian American
Studies, University of California at Davis.
主辦單位代表：〔上〕沙加緬度中華文化基金會董事。〔下〕
加州大學戴維斯分校亞美系同仁。　、

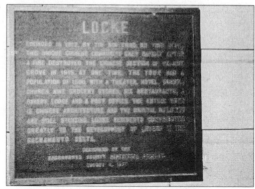

Only town in the United States built exclusively by the Chinese for the Chinese: [TOP] The designated State Park -- Map of Locke. [BELOW] The Locke Memorial.

華人在美建立專供華人聚居的唯一城市：〔上〕加州公園樂居鎮地圖。〔下〕樂居鎮紀念碑。

[TOP] The Chinese School children. [BELOW] The general store
owned and operated by the Chinese
〔上〕中文學校學生們。〔下〕華人經營的華合商店。

The business receipts.

買賣收據。

266

[TOP] Mr. Chun Tim worked from a cook to the site-boss for the Hatch Ranch. He was the ancestor of three pioneer families, the Timm, the Chan, and the Chun. He initiated the recruiting of needed labors directly from China. [BELOW] Mrs. Chun Ding Shee, first Chinese marriage ever consummated in California.

〔上〕陳添從廚師升爲哈親大農場的總管。第一位直接從中國招僱華工來農場。他是當時華人社區的「天理，國法與人情」的代表。〔下〕鄧氏，陳添由舊金山求親而成婚的加州第一對華裔夫婦。她是當時全華人社區的唯一女性。

267

[TOP] Mr. Youie Tim (son) became the assistant site-boss at age 14, kept the rainfall records for farming purposes for 41 years (1937-1978). Lastly, his property was sold to Anheuser Bush. [BELOW] Mr. Lum Foon, site-boss of the Miller Ranch in Suisun Valley

〔上〕于遙，陳添的第三個兒子。十四歲即擔任農場的總管助理。他曾保存四十一年的詳細雨量統計記錄，直接幫助農作收成效果。〔下〕林寬先驅有九個兒女。第三代仍在北加州經營大農場事業。

268

[TOP] Cal Yee Company, one of the largest dried fruits organizations in the world. They used the Chinese dried fruit processing methods and developed their business throughout the world to this day. [BELOW] The reunion of "Cal Yee" families.

〔上〕今日余氏及寬氏家族建立的 Cal Yee 公司，是運用中國乾果製造方法，發展成爲世界乾果事業的龍頭之一。〔下〕余寬兩家子孫團圓紀實。

On Saturday, April 5, 1997 Sacramento lost a great friend and benefactor. Frank Sai Fat passed away as result of failing health. This is a reprint of his obituary as originally published in the Sacramento Bee.

1904 – 1997

Legendary Restaurateur: [TOP] A charismatic character, Mr. Frank Fat. [BELOW] A great family reunion.
加州首府傳奇人物：〔上〕人人敬愛戴的鄧世發先生。〔下〕全家福。

Frank, Mary and Baby Wing pose in 1926 China with Frank's parents and family. Mary is third from the left; Frank, holding baby Wing, is third from the right.

Frank Fat in Chicago

A young Frank Fat

Mary Wing Kai in China

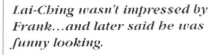

Lai-Ching wasn't impressed by Frank...and later said he was funny looking.

An outstanding seed from a great root.

書香世家。

[TOP]An exemplar community organizer.
Bel Air Supermarket's Story: [BELOW] Mr. Gene Wong at age
five traveling to China on behalf of his parents fulfilling the filial
piety (at the far left).
[上]社區福利機構創辦歷史見證。
柏艾超級市場：〔下〕代親盡孝的五歲黃振滋，返國侍奉頤年，
最左第一人。

272

Bel Air earns presidential citation

by Brian Hoopes

Every year, Bel Air Markets collaborates with various community organizations in the full spirit of giving, the company sought no publicity for its efforts.

On July 23, national attention was focused on Bel Air for its part in the "Fund for the Hungry and Homeless" program.

Over 1,000 programs were reviewed by presidential committee. Of these, 190 were cited for awards, and 20 of those for a Presidential Award for Private Sector Initiatives.

Bel Air was one of those 20 and one of only three supermarket chains which received the Steuben Glass Tetrahedron at the White House Rose Garden by the President.

The award is the highest honor in the country honoring community outreach programs.

"How do I describe it...it's color. It's appreciated to be honored that

continued next pages

Bel Air President George Wong is congratulated by President Ronald Reagan at the White House.

[TOP] The Presidential Award at the White House. [BELOW] The Executive Board of Directors.

〔上〕美國總統頒發「慈濟」特優獎典禮。〔下〕柏艾超級市場董事會。

273

[TOP] C. C. Yins' McDonald's Enterprise. [BELOW] The AAA
Community Award.
〔上〕尹氏的麥當勞企業。〔下〕全國汽車駕駛協會「傑出社
會服務獎」。

274

C.C. Yin
Community Service Award
International Leadership Foundation
Scholarship Awards Dinner
With Jackie Chan
September 21, 2000

[TOP] The "Outstanding Opera Films Award" with McDonald's Corp. leaders: Jock Greenberger (Chairman and CEO), Mike Roberts (West Division President), Rolf Alvarez (Sacramento Regional V.P.), Ray Naslor (Director of Operations). [BELOW] Salute to Jackie Chan, special guest of International Leadership Foundation Scholarship Award Dinner

〔上〕「歌劇影展特優獎」合影者：格林柏（麥當勞公司董事長兼執行長），羅柏德（公司西部總經理），亞菲斯（沙加緬度副總經理），拿斯勒（營業部主任）。〔下〕國際領袖基金會頒獎晚會。主賓：成龍；特別來賓：尹集成。

275

Indo-Chinese Cultural Story: [TOP] The renovated pavilion at
Isleton. [BELOW] The Buddha Temple and Chinese Language
School.
東南亞華裔文化故事：〔上〕Isleton 修繕的中式亭閣。〔下〕
觀音廟及中山華文學校。

276

The fountain of Chinese American growth and development:
[TOP] Dr. Sun Yat Sen's Memorial. [BELOW] Mayor Yee at his
office.
華裔成長與發展根源：〔上〕孫中山紀念館。〔下〕沙加緬度
市長余福慶訪問紀實。

從金山到千禧
的風與雨
(1849-2001)

緬懷先民
齊步今日
共創未來

沙加緬度中華文化基金會
暨
戴維斯加州大學
亞美系聯合出版

美國勞工部長賀辭

美國勞工部部長辦公室
首都華盛頓特區

親愛的朋友們：

　　本人萬分欣悅，邀請對中華文化的愛好者，共同分享這本華裔在加州生根的一項貢獻紀實：「從金山到千禧的風與雨」。它認可慎終追遠，不忘中美族群的根源，它認知齊步今日，珍惜黃金年華時代，它認同創造未來建設另一個千禧世紀。

　　中華兒女以中國傳統與文化，創建不可忽視的政經動力，被澤加州的輝煌成就。他們流汗耕耘的點滴，促進加州繼續發展，是為加州經驗核心主軸之一。因此，在美國偉大的歷史中，加州的豐盛貢獻佔據了重要篇章的地位。這些都是追述華裔對社會基業的奉獻，從藝術建築、電子科學、體育及政治等領域上，不但有高素質的評估，且在數量上，更有超越的記錄。

　　美國機會與希望的光明燈塔，在過去一百五十多年，引導千萬華人奔向自由與民主的樂土，且至今不渝。因為，中華兒女對他們的第二家園，一直貢獻他們的生命活力。

所以，中華兒女及愛好多元文化的同仁，讓我們以浴火鳳凰的志向，來分享及見證多層面的種族生活故事，反思前人的心路歷程，以此為鑒，來建立今天，再創明日。是謂：「萬泉氣象新」。(1)

　　　　　　　　　　　　　　　趙小蘭　賀
　　　　　　　　　　　　　　　一〇〇一年九月

(1) 錄自中國國家主席江澤民先生於二〇〇一年在海南提詩首句。詩文全部如下：「萬泉氣象新，水闊晚風純。四海群賢聚，博鰲更喜人。」

(葉殷　譯及詮)

加州州長賀辭

加利福尼亞州政府州長辦公室
加州省都，沙加緬度 95814
電話：(916) 445-2841

愛護中華文化的舊友新知：

　　希望共來分享"從金山到千禧的風與雨"這本文獻。它緬懷加州華人先民，並祈中華兒女齊步今日，共創未來。

　　歷經一百五十年的華裔社群，發揚移民奮鬥精神，深植東方文化根源·創造"龍的傳人"成功史，增添加州的政經商農錦繡成果，他們的主導力量，將為加州另一千禧豐盛的社稷年華，繼續獻力，獻心。

　　謹代表加州人民，呼籲各方文化愛好者，以明智的視野，深遠的方式，認知與認同加州華裔社群多采多姿文化傳統。

格雷戴維斯　賀
2001 年 7 月 17 日

（葉　殷　意譯）

目錄

歷史

人物

社區

前言

Kevin Starr 博士*

加州圖書館長

這　本書是關於「華人在加州一百五十年的歷史」
（1848-2001），由沙加緬度中華文化基金會和
加州大學戴維斯分校亞美系贊助出版，應可視
為華人在加州生根的一項貢獻。中華文化被澤加州，可
以從六個角度的宏觀定論：中國文化整體、十九世紀華
人移民、加州的崛起、十九世紀的加州、華人在加州的
個人和家庭經歷，及加州作為華裔美國人中心的現況和
未來。

首先，認同中國文化本身的成就和輝煌。中國歷史
悠久，文化深厚，是代表人類發展的重要一環。數千年
來，中國人一直探索的一個重要層面，是人文關懷——

---

* Kevin Starr 博士是加州的總圖書館長，也是加州州長戴維斯在 2000
年任命的「慶祝加州成立一百五十週年委員會」主席。

華人在加州一百五十年的歷史　　　　　　　　　　　1

人的成長和成就。從哲學、文學、藝術、科學、醫藥、技術、農業、公共工程、城市發展、建築和治國之道等方面來看，中國是促成人類成就的三個重要極限之一。

在中國悠長的歷史中，中國人對外界一直保持以和為貴的態度。中國曾經是一個帝國，融和八十多個不同社會和文化代表的族裔和語言團體。從這個角度來看，中國無須假以外援。它本身已是一個文明，一個世界。

但是，在十九世紀，工業革命和強權主義等原因——外國入侵、戰爭連年、旱災飢荒導致人口的流離，促成中國商人階級的興起，開始放眼海外、廣東地區人口的增長，和廣東省經濟萎縮等因素——結合起來，促使大量的華人移民，前往今天的馬來西亞、印尼、越南、加勒比海的一些島嶼（特別是千里達），和加州。華人很快就在東南亞和北美形成一個移民社群，影響了當地的社會發展。

加入美利堅聯邦的加州，就是這個社會的共生樣本。早在一八四八年，兩名華人移民來到當時仍是以軍治政的加州；因此，大量華人從廣州橫渡太平洋來到金山，追尋他們的黃金夢。到一八五二年，已有二萬五千多華人來美，尋找金山世界。今天，在三聖縣（Trinity）雲林寺（Weaverville's Joss House）（現在是州公園的名勝），可以見證當年淘金華人的魄力和生命力。從一八四九年起至一八五零年代，每一年，有數以千計的華人礦工，聚集在雲林鎮（Weaverville），進行堂口比賽以及各

種貿易和節慶。雖然受到礦工稅和其他各金礦地區的白人歧視排擠，華人仍然──藉本身技能和辛勤工作──在主礦（Mother Lode）山脈的谷地和河床中，找到他們橫渡太平洋來美挖金的目標。

因此華人成為尋金熱時期一個固定和重要的貢獻份子。當加州繼續發展時，這個有能力、有精力和勤勞的人源，面對新的挑戰，共同走上成功之路。當一八六四年四大公司（Big Four）開始興建跨美鐵路時，華人更是這個浩大工程的主力。在工程進行如火如荼的時候，超過一萬多華工，在巍然高聳的內華達山，開山劈路，穿鑿隧道，鋪置鐵軌。今天回顧當年，我們無法不將華工這種成就，比美興建中國的萬里長城。感謝華人的勤奮，協助此一巨大工程，終於在一八六九年五月，將美國東西連接通車接軌，運輸之夢成真。

在完成這個偉大的工程之後，加州的華人並未停止他們對加州的貢獻。他們轉向其他重要事業，在沙加緬度谷地，從事農業、灌溉和防洪的工作。這些成就，並不亞於興建跨越美西到美東的鐵路功績。沙加緬度谷地，以前有一大片內海，每年冬天河水氾濫，防洪真是一件重要任務。在一八六零、七零和八零年代，華人與這片廣大內海搏鬥，築成一道堤岸，使沙加緬度谷地，在冬天可以安居樂業，直至今天仍然予人受惠良多。華人並為加州引入數千年的中國農耕技巧，他們改變氾濫的土地，種植收成。從這個角度看，十九世紀中葉和末

期的加州華人，可以稱為加州農業經濟的先鋒，而農業經濟直至今天，仍是加州的重要經濟生命力。與此同時，其他華人在加州的其他地區——三藩市、沙加緬度、士德頓、瑪利斯維爾（Marysville）甚至南面的洛杉磯定居——更而建立自己的城鎮，例如洛克鎮（Locke）。

但是，一八七零年代卻是個生活困難的年代。人們預期當鐵路於一八六九年完成後，必會帶來經濟繁榮，但結果人算不如天算。反而，自一八七三年起，經濟開始蕭條，對移民往加州和加州正在發展的經濟，均帶來苦難的生計影響。在那個時候，很多煽動家，例如三藩市的克尼丹（Denise Kearney）所領導的反華白人，將他們的生活困境，發洩於華人移民身上，將他們變做經濟不景的代罪羔羊。這些敵視行為，早在淘金熱時期已見端倪，這包括從一八五四年至一八七二年，禁止華人在法庭上做指控白人的証人。一八八二年，國會通過排視東方人法案，且在一八九二及一九零二予以延續，不准亞洲人移民美國。也就是說，華人婦女無法合法的移民來美，因而華人移民，要在這裡建立正常的家庭生活殊為困難。有一整代的華人男子，過著孤單的如鰥生活，只希望死後的骨骸能夠回歸梓里，落葉歸根。

事過境遷，這些排外的法律，在二十世紀初期有所修訂，有些並予撤消。這部份得歸功於新成立的同源總會的努力。在第一次大戰及戰後，加州的華裔開始較有家庭生活，有孩子可以共聚天倫。事實上，到了二十年

代，加州華裔的生活已大為穩定和安樂。

二次大戰是華裔社區發展的分水嶺。來自加州的華裔男女，不少服役軍中，派發世界各地，其中不少更表現傑出。回國後，他們的世界觀更見包容和成熟。從二次大戰一代開始，在大城市中，產生了華裔的民選官員和知名人物。加州再次認知到華裔公民的貢獻。

在六十年代，聯邦政府更進一步改革移民法，使華人移民來美，與歐洲人移民有平等機會。在以後的三十五年，加州華人人口大量增加，不少家庭得以團聚，且有不少是第一代從中國大陸和台灣來的移民。在這新的千禧年到臨之際，加州有超過一百萬華裔人口。加州事實上已成為中國以外的中國文化重要中心。在加州生活的每個層面，無論是公共或私人行業，均看到不少才華卓越，勤奮成功的華裔。

因此華人在加州得到最重要的另一層面：家庭和個人已能分享公平而應享的生活經驗。中國文化一向重視家庭價值，包括崇敬祖先。十九世紀的移民最大的艱苦，是因為移民他鄉缺少了家庭生活。可幸的，在二十世紀得以補救。今天，在加州一百萬人口的華裔社區裡面，家庭生活和家庭價值重獲新生。這些華人價值，包括廣為人知的工作勤奮、重視教育、節儉克己、自力更生、和對社區的貢獻等。與此同時，華裔的個人價值亦受重視。這些華人歷史事實，亦充滿了個人成功的故事：他們夢想美好的生活，已步步的在成功實現著。

自一八四八年兩名華人移民來加州後，已經有一百五十年。加州亦承認華裔的經驗，是加州經驗核心主軸。沒有昨日和今日華裔的勤奮性和創造力，加州不會有今天的好景：一個擁抱來自世界各地人口和創造力的聯邦主力。中國文明在加州歷史留下可貴的遺產，促進加州今天農業、交通、防洪、商業、銀行業、文學、藝術、建築、政治、和衛生的盛況。華裔的遺產，已成為加州之夢的一個重要基礎，也是展示加州之夢的一個重要指標。

　　所以，在新千禧年來臨之前，所有的海內外華人，尤其是加州的華裔，必須協力而促進一個更完美的大千世界，來慶祝加州成立一百五十週年之際，再創歷史新章。

致謝感言

崔以聞

身為沙加緬度中華文化基金會主席，為出版紀念加州華人來美一百五十年文獻，向促成這本著作問世的諸君，所給予所有精神、物質、經濟方面支持，致上誠懇的謝意。（請參照圖片緊接的各界捐贈紀錄）。

首先，不容疑問的，要向當時擔任基金會副主席，梁靜源教授表示十二分的感激和追悼之意。因為他所提出出版這文獻的倡議，經過董事會之支持而達成協議。他將數年間努力研討、收集的寶貴資料納入這本著作裡。他認真並執著的態度，令他工作的戴維斯加大亞美系主任司徒永俊博士深為欽佩，因而給予大量人力、物力方面的全力支持，在此，我向亞美系同仁表示感謝。非常令人唏噓的、天妒英才，在著作工作進行當中，梁教授因肝癌突然逝世。此一大打擊，令這項任務幾乎難以繼續下去，擱置了約一年之久。

同時在戴維斯加大業餘進修單位工作三十年餘的梁張愛玲，自從夫君梁靜源教授突然辭世，化悲憤為力量，毅然加入著作工作之隊伍，給以全力精神、人力、以至財力支持，促成梁教授的未了遺志。因此，對她表示萬分之謝忱。

　　幸運的，經大家各方探詢和覓才，終於找到曾在加州政府教育部，擔任高級顧問的葉殷博士。慨允在百忙中，接下這非他莫屬的總編譯工作。中英文俱佳的葉博士，投入的精力與心血令人敬佩。沒有他的支持，這本著作是否能出版，是令人懷疑的。

　　出版本著作之達到成功，要向當時基金會主席尹集惠博士致上深深謝意。她不但對此書給予精神上和實際上支持，更因為她的建言，而影響了兄弟尹集成夫婦與麥當勞集團，不斷在物力與財力方面大力支持，因此本著作才得以問世。不可否認的，因尹氏家族的加入，使這樣一個意義重大的工作，得以順利達成任務。

　　當然，我必需向那些大力資助的朋友們，獻上最大的謝意。沒有大家的慷慨解囊捐獻，這本著作將難以順利出版。（請參照各界捐贈記錄）

　　假如讀者們對這本著作發生興趣，而願意閱讀下去的話，那為我們執筆作序文者功勞不可減。經過梁教授在先，葉博士繼續的邀請後，加州圖書館館長 Dr. Kevin Starr 博士，同時也是慶祝加州一百五十年活動委員會委員之一，在閱讀本著作初稿後，慨允為之作序，令人感

到榮幸及萬分感激。

　最後，也要對我的外子畢頓上校 (Col. Beaton) 給我不斷的教導的、耐心的、竭力不懈的所有支持表示感激。對我所應允及擔當下來，任何有關我熱愛的兩個國家，中國和第二國家的美國每項任務，他都給予鼓勵和協助，因此，我才得以無後顧之憂的完全達成。

「華人在加州一百五十年的歷史」贊助者聲明

加州大學亞美系
司徒永俊博士‧梁張愛齡

此書是前加州大學戴維斯分校亞美系梁靜源教授生前一個雄心計劃的成果。當加州慶賀其成立一百五十週年之際，梁教授想借此機會，紀念華人對加州歷史和發展的貢獻。此書的目的，是紀念過去、齊步今日，建設將來。在他去世之前他完成此書的大部份編輯工作，他的同事、朋友和家庭繼承其志，完成計劃。

此書訂名「華人在加州一百五十年的歷史」，記錄華人移民加州的演變——從一八四九年華人踏足加州尋金的第一個浪潮，到建設跨美鐵路的第二個浪潮，進而建立加州農漁業的第三浪潮，以至今天成為現代的企業家的歷史。與早期歐洲移民來美一樣，華人移民是因為

原居地貧窮內亂，生計有困難而被迫到陌生的土地求生故事。

　　加州大學戴維斯分校亞美系很高興支持此書的出版計劃，因為此書記錄很多時被人忽略的華人移民經驗和貢獻。所以，我們和沙加緬度中華文化基金會合作，贊助此計劃，弘揚中華傳統以肇將來。我們十分感謝所有讓我們闡述他們故事的人。此書當然無法包括過去一百五十年加州不同地區不同行業不同領域的華人的故事。它的目的，毋寧是引起各界分享我們經歷的興趣。

　　我們希望大家閱讀此書，能欣賞歷史、經濟、政治和教育的互為作用，如何可以轉變這些人和我們所有人的命運。

文獻感言

為響應加州一百五十年歷史慶祝委員會
（Commission to Celebrate the California
Sesquicentennial History）慶典活動，本基金
會與加州大學戴維斯分校（University of California,
Davis）亞美系研究所合作，編印華人在加州一百五十年
文獻一種，藉以發揚加州華人移民奮鬥的精神。追溯每
一位成功的「龍的傳人」，深植東方文化的根源，證明華
人社群具有不可忽視的政經與文化動力，全球三千萬華
僑（包括北美四百萬華人）當須有此共識。

文獻中，從一八四零年加州的淘金潮開始，說明加
州華人的奮鬥已有一百五十年的歷史。雖然，當初華人
幹的只是採礦、建造鐵路一類的血汗生涯；到二次大戰
前，一直遭到歧視與排斥，受盡屈辱，但是，仍不可否
認的，對加州的發展與成長的貢獻。其中可歌可泣的史
實，加州各界都應予珍惜。

二次大戰期間，華人且以行動表示忠誠國家；以迄
大戰後，各行各業生根立命的表現，足以改變過去歧視
風氣。在制度上，也已擺脫了「二等國民」，贏得了公民

與選舉權。老僑的第二、三代都已跨出「唐人世界」，走向更廣大的多元天地。所以，華人參政情形，現已日漸積極，排華事件亦見改善。

七十年代後，華人新移民潮，改變了以往的「相安共處」。新移民的高學歷、國際觀，流利的雙語或多語，加上龐大財團，這種多層次，寬領域的條件，對加州參政與經濟發展上，我們所見的企圖心，早已瓦解白人「居高臨下」的心態。

當初老僑來加州，雖然精神上在故國有「連根拔起」的感覺，新移民到此陌生環境，難免產生各種疑慮，真是「夢鄉萬重山，桑梓非故土」。如今時移事遷，排華歷史，當不再於今日重見。

因此，作此文獻，願與僑胞共同勉勵，認清歷史，保持中華民族的榮譽，大家團結，創造新的僑社，期待主流社會能從中悟出，加州的政經錦繡是各族裔努力共創的成果；任何歧視或忽視，都將是一種歷史的歪曲叛離。尤其華人社群要觀摩思考，悟出老僑與新僑，實質上追求著共同理想，大家一起擁抱過去令人珍惜的歷史，引介機會與責任，開創另一個「盛史寶典」。老僑與新僑決不容分裂，更不允許外界力量分割。大家團結，共同努力，學習文獻中鄉親成功的經驗，追求「修、齊、治、平」個人與社群福祉。

沙加緬度中華文化基金會　葉殷

沙加緬度中華文化基金會創辦人－汪治宜先生[*]

葉殷　博士

汪治宜先生和夫人，於一九八六年，捐助一萬元的孳息基金，成立沙加緬度中華文化基金會。他們的善舉，得到沙加緬度亞裔社區和本地校區的大力支持。

　沙市各方的支持，證明了基金會提倡文化的宗旨，極有價值。基金會弘揚中華文化傳統，並為本地學區的學生，爭取和提供學習國語的機會。[**]

　在世界歷史上，中國和埃及都是文明古國，是文化

---

[*]此文資料，由作者向汪先生諮詢及提供。
[**]沙加緬度中華文化基金會服務學校的例子：（一）曾協助沙市數所高中成立可得學分的中國國語教學班，並提供中國國語、史地、及文化有關的教學材料；（二）提供與中國文化／語言有關的書本、字典、參考書及其他教材的資金；（三）中國文化專題介紹；（四）與美國、台灣及中國的學校文化交流。

的搖籃。汪先生及夫人最初倡議創辦沙加緬度中華文化中心基金會，其理念亦在溯源並薪傳這個偉大的文化。

基金會的貢獻廣為人知，但汪先生對沙加緬度的成果現在才開始受到注目。汪先生是策劃基金會的組織，徵募董事，分配招募會員的工作，及擬定基金會會章的主力。當基金會一切上軌道後，他又推出獎學金方案，獎勵有才華的青少年學生成功向學。他及汪夫人且推動了多個文化交流項目，在美國、中國和台灣風行一時，一直推行至今。

汪先生曾為北加州多個慈善、教育及社會服務團體，統籌多個改善社區項目，廣為人知。無可置疑，汪先生的領導和視野，對沙加緬度中華文化基金會的開花結果，功莫大焉。

汪先生二十三歲時在中國昆明被委任為華僑銀行的會計和行內的審核師。其後他加入中華民國的軍隊，從排長升到裝甲兵部隊營長。而後出任中美軍事聯絡官，負責中華民國國防部與美國軍事顧問團的人事和行政。在他的協調之下，成功的設立了除役官兵就業輔導委員會，為退伍軍人安排轉業、就業和就醫等服務工作。他服務超卓，曾當選為「政府優良服務獎」和「事業榮譽獎」的特優公職人員，包括「忠勤、弼亮、績優、克難」等勳章。

汪先生於一九六六年結束軍職，再向會計事業發展。為了更上層樓，他入讀紐約州立大學賓咸頓分校研

究院。在一九六九年取得碩士學位後，他移居佛羅里達州，受僱於 Lake Butler Inmate Reception and Medical Center。因為該處專業發展有限，同時考慮到子女的教育機會，於一九七零年毅然搬來北加州。當他抵達加州羅斯維爾市後，出任當地市府會計師的工作，直至一九八四年退休為止。

汪先生曾任沙加緬度中華文化基金會主席五年，董事兩年，然後於一九九一年辭去所有職務，成為該會的永久榮譽主席。汪先生對基金會的歷任領導人，給予大力鼓勵和支持

汪先生為中國文化在海外薪傳，出力至大；他的貢獻，將為沙市未來世世代代的華裔，流澤久遠。

引言

梁靜源教授・梁張愛齡夫人

慶祝加州一百五十週年的加州委員會，主辦各種紀念她成長的歷史和活動，開始於 1844 年的尋金潮，繼續於一八五零年加入美國聯邦，至到二零零零年的千禧年歷史。加州各級政府、教育和社區機構，逢此盛會舉辦各類慶祝節目，例如「一八四八年柯魯瑪（Coloma）發現金礦一百五十週年紀念」的活動，表述加州的尋金熱，吸引了數以萬計的華人移民來美事蹟。所以華裔社區亦藉此機遇，表述他們在加州的貢獻。

沙加緬度中華文化基金會，加州首府一個活躍的華裔非牟利機構，曾不斷舉辦文藝節，支持公校和大學的中國語文和文化教育，為弘揚中國文化努力，倡議加州大學戴維斯分校的亞美系合作，運用它的專業課程，以及不同團體在美國的共同經驗，例如課業中包括歷史、文化、法律、政治和社會等寶貴資源，合編出版這一本

華人文獻，紀念華人和華裔對加州發展的精神歷史。

這本書包括五個主要部份：歷史、人物、社區、專題，和風雲榜。

關於歷史部份：（一）「加州華裔金礦工一瞥」概述華人來美在金礦工作的因由，以及他們的奮勉的生活。早期加州的華裔移民，在面對極端的歧視性的本地和聯邦法律下，其堅苦卓越，見證了他們的大勇志氣，以及他們對開發加州的重要貢獻。他們的決心和毅力，挑戰了美國的法律制度。（二）「一天一塊錢」，用詩的形式，描繪在沙加緬度河三角洲的華人農工的甘苦共嘗的生活；和（三）「蘇宣谷的華裔農民家庭先驅：一八七零年至一九八零年」，是根據華博士（Tony Waters）（當時是加大戴維斯分校社會系的博士候選人，現任加省大學奇柯（Chico）分校副教授）和我在蘇宣谷與三代華裔農民所做的採訪史實。「蘇」文陳述華裔社區在農村的成立，華工與地主的關係，以及他們在農場的點點滴滴。

關於人物部份：（一）畢庭上校（Col. Cliff Beaton）和崔以聞夫人撰寫的「余江月桂的故事」，表述一名華裔婦女的事蹟，她克服了無數的障礙，成為加州和全國政界的領導人物。（二）「鄧世發：沙加緬度的傳奇餐館東主」是從我在一九九 年發表在加州歷史雜誌的一篇傳記改寫；原文是根據我訪問鄧先生的真實資料寫成。鄧世發的聞名，不僅因為他的餐館是首府有影響力的議員和政治家的聚腳之地，亦因為他鼓勵華裔積極參與社區

的公益和政治事務。(三)葉殷博士及黃家第四代孫女黃周玉笑,號舉穆小姐(Ms. Romy Wong)撰寫的「柏艾(Bel Air)超級市場的故事」,表述了黃氏家族辛勤致富歷史,他們在沙加緬度創辦連鎖超級市場的成功典範;和(四)梁靜源教授及梁張愛齡夫人所作的「尹集成先生(CC Yin)及夫人和他們的麥當勞企業」,介紹了另一家華裔企業家庭,如何通過參與社區、商業和公民事務,在主流社會發揮的影響力。他們慷慨為社區作出回饋,幫助社區成長發展。(承尹集成先生的建議,英文版由蘇緯德女士(Ms. Swett)修編。蘇女士是一位有名的各大報章和雜誌作家)。

關於社區部份:這裡收集多篇學界人士的論文,討論首府的重要社區組織如何在發展階段,豐富了華裔的生活及促進社交網絡的貢獻:

華裔馮宗祖(Joe Chung Fong)是加大柏克萊分校的人類學的博士候選人,一九九九年他是亞美裔系(AAS)的導師。他的第一篇論文「華裔的聖地:大埠、二埠和三埠」,追溯華裔在三個重要加州城市(三藩市、沙加緬度和士德頓)的歷史發展。他討論了三藩市華埠的社會結構,如何影響全國各地華埠的成形成長。他並評論華埠不同功能結構(行政性的華埠、共存性的華埠和印支裔的華裔)的並行互動情形。

他的第二篇論文「新華埠和沙加緬度印支聯合會」,縷述東南亞裔社區的社會機構,如何協助新移民適

應新環境，以及這些機構對教育和社交網絡的影響。

　　這個部份所收集的第三篇論文「華裔發展的泉源」，是梁靜源教授原著，由他太太梁張愛齡夫人（Eileen Leung）修訂，縷述沙加緬度過去一百五十年華裔社區的演變和發展。這個多元的社區包括六代的華裔，以及從中國、台灣、香港和東南亞國家來美的華裔新移民。論文抽樣介紹了五個突出的華裔社區機構的貢獻。

　　關於專題部份：(一)加大戴維斯分校亞美系（AAS）主任兼該校亞裔精神健康國家研究中心主任司徒永俊博士（Dr. Stanley Sue），專題探討「華裔在教育上成就的研究報告」。他的論文，迴異於一些社會科學家對華裔成就所作的爭論性的假設和解釋。他指出華裔不是一個模範的少數民族，沒有充份的證據證明華裔的聰穎是先天遺傳的。雖然華裔在某些領域例如體育、表演、管理方面較弱，但華裔在教育方面的成就，只證明另一個可以出人頭地的成功途徑。例如，那些英文程度能力較弱的，在大學裡可以少修一些課程，加倍努力，和主修一些能發揮他們潛能的科目。此外，他並指出華裔學生和學界人士，必須重視中國文化的價值，適應大學的環境，認識個人在學習、成功和取得成就的上限和潛能。他的論文，數據詳盡，資料豐富，為我們提供　個極好的學術研究模式。無獨有偶，他的論文正如本書的分題「齊步今日」不謀而合。

　　(二)亞美系（AAS）副教授和加大戴維斯分校婦

女研究系何美雲博士（Dr. Wendy Ho）所撰的「華裔婦女作品的新聲：重新發掘父女的故事」，介紹在六十年代至八十年代以婦女為主題，特別是以母女關係為主題的女作家。雖然以華裔母女為題的作品不少，但很少有人留意到作品中的父女關係。身為父親，華裔男人在建設家庭和社區過程中備嘗艱辛，念及他們在十八世紀末期到十九世紀以來因法律和歷史原因，過單身生活，缺乏家庭關係，無法享受妻女情誼、失聯家庭和社區關係，更是如此。她的論文，每多討論華裔男子在家庭的角色。

風雲人物榜：（一）葉殷博士撰寫，表揚長期支持華裔社區的沙加緬度縣議員柯琳夫人（Illa Collin）。（二）余江月桂博士的共勉詞，討論華裔未竟之業。（三）葉殷博士向美國第一位大都會華人余福慶市長致敬，敘述他為政界所標榜的政治選舉風氣。

這本書當然無法完全的介紹華裔在加州過去一百五十年的歷史。其中文章，只提到北加州華裔社區的一些點滴故事。但是，這是一個開始，應可鼓勵我們保存華人的故事，以傳來者。沙加緬度中華文化基金會和加州大學戴維斯分校，希望讀者覺得這些事蹟有興味，繼續為後代建設一個更美好的未來。

念先夫，憶似水長流：

先夫梁靜源一直致力推動紀錄早期加州華人的口述歷史。他六十年代末由香港移民來美，因為在加州大學戴維斯分校的第一份教職，引發起他對華裔歷史的興趣。他那時是加大的粵語導師，發現班上很多學生不只有興趣於學習粵語，並想對他們的文化源頭有更多認識。他的第一個口述歷史計劃，是訪問加州洛克市的華人農工；這些農工很多在年輕的時候從中國南方來美尋找金山之夢，但最後終老他鄉，孑然一人。他和這些退休的農工建立友誼；幸運的是，他們很多都願意講述自己的故事。後來他被邀請參與修復柯魯瑪縣馬歇爾州公園（Marshall State Park）的華合商店時，又和州公園的工作者建立友好關係。他在加大戴維斯分校的學生，大多和他一樣，對移民家庭在美扎掙謀生的經歷，惘環在抱。他在加州各地舉辦的華人歷史照片展覽，向大眾宣傳華人對開拓加州農業的貢獻。加州檔案局在鑒別華人文物時，亦不時向他徵詢意見。此外，

華人在加州一百五十年的歷史

他對緬甸和東南亞裔社區的研究，亦充滿熱情和啟發。
他的家人深受他熱誠服務社區的感染，都志願參與不少
社區工作。這本書是獻給靜源的，為他對社區和對家庭
的一份愛。

── 愛齡

加州華人礦工一瞥

加州淘金熱潮華人剪影——從中國千山萬水來美淘金的辛酸史

梁靜源　教授

在一八四零年至一八七零年間，那遙遠古老的中國，發生了多年來罕見的厄運。天災人禍，以至民間生活貧困，難以生計。加上朝廷中官僚昏庸腐敗作風，令人民對國家感到失望而喪失信心。當時最大的遭遇就是敗於在一八四二年的鴉片戰爭，和一八五六年的英法聯軍後的慘況，在短短十多年中收到雙重傷害，令滿清政府的國運一敗塗地。外交內政兩方面都災難連連，一片大好江山看著就要面臨瓦解的地步。鴉片戰爭引起最大的後遺症還有那大批偷渡而來的鴉片

煙販，帶著毒素，不懷好意的讓那醉人的煙霧，在各地蔓延燃燒。加上一八五一年太平天國反叛清廷，西方的各種文化，就突破性的一一侵染了中國。

一八四八年在美國加州一個叫哥羅馬（Coloma）的小鄉鎮發現金礦的消息，很快的傳到世界各國，更很快的奔走相告的在中國傳了開來。

那些從外地忽然蹦進來的陌生客，都是想在那淘金熱中發財致富。幾個月之間把那本是平靜綠色山谷，搭蓋了漫山遍野的白色帳篷。

在那新來的數千人中，不乏從東方來的中國人。短短的期間，從寥寥可數的幾個而增長到上千人之數。在一八五零年代初期剛來的華人，幾乎都是從廣東省南方沿海地區來的單身漢。他們大都是不想久居下來，而是準備很快的在金礦挖到他們千山萬水來尋求的財富，然後就返回中國，娶妻成家。那些年青人，大部份都來自貧苦之家。他們的家，既無田地，也無養家糊口的工作能力。幾經考慮商量之下，忍痛拋鄉別井，背起行囊上了木船奔向西方。根據一八五五年的沙加緬度聯合日報（Sacramento Daily Union）的資料，在太平洋海岸一帶金礦工作的華人數字高達兩萬人之上。

華人用來開礦的工具是極為簡陋的。除了一個鐵盆和淘金木框外，就是那粗糙的一雙手。華人使用那基本開礦工具的其它主因，是在當時的情況下，山路崎嶇難行，如果再同時搬運笨重工具的話，那就更加困難了。

華工們在陌生的國家謀生不易，生活習慣兩樣，語言不通，迫得他們團結一起抵制外面給予的種種壓力。當然最大的困擾，還是來自那些白人礦工施予的種族歧視。他們看不慣那些亞裔長相，輕視這些穿著不同的華工，對待他們如奴隸，時時加以侮辱，壓迫和給予不平待遇，令人難以忍受。

像所有新來的移民一樣，那早期來淘金的華工，帶來家鄉的許多風俗習慣。他們穿著半身短襖，覓大褲子，寬邊帽和木板鞋。他們也都把頭髮辮成清朝規定的長辮子。

華人礦工們的飲食習慣還是照家鄉時完全一樣生活。每餐都少不了米飯，魚乾，和茶。偶而吃吃豬肉和雞，那也是年節時的豪華大事。

工作在美國河流畔淘金一天的工資，只有幾毛錢。還得忍受那外來施與的種族歧視壓力，最後，華工們亦漸漸的被白人礦工排離礦場。淘金致富美夢破碎，他們紛紛朝其他方面，如做店員，洗衣工等。這些中國人做的小生意，都是當時開礦工人們謀生有限生計。

哥羅馬（Coloma）中失落的中國城

一八五零年在哥羅馬的中國城，是當時加州最大的中國城。不只供應許多礦工所需服務，更是華人的聚居地。中國城裡有華人理髮師傅，中國人種的蔬菜和日用

品，以及用草藥治病的中國大夫等。

　　到了一八五零年代末期，哥羅馬的中國城輝煌盛況已經接近尾聲。淘金的熱潮，很快的就冷卻下來；那曾經擠滿了掘金人的山谷，顯得一片荒涼寂寞如同死城。那曾經是賓客盈門的酒吧，客棧，餐館以及晝夜喧嘩的賭館都無可奈何的釘上門板，宣佈停止營業。淘金客走了，已經沒有生意可做了。他們大都遷移向其它河流或山谷方面去尋金了。

　　中國城之衰落，大約是在一八六零和一八六一年間開始的。因為淘金礦工們另求發展，當地那些應景突發的事業們都難以維持，面臨關門大吉之厄運。一次會議中，為了爭奪產權問題一發不可收拾。例如，不幸的是當時大約有四十個酒醉失態的愛爾蘭人，就此借酒發瘋在中國城裡到處破壞，搶劫又放火。經此浩劫華人被無故毆打甚而傷殘大有人在。令人哀嘆的還有兩個華人，在眾人圍觀下，被打死而無人挺身阻止慘劇發生。在一八八零年一場大火，將哥羅馬的中國城幾乎燒成平地，那些僅存的華人不得不再背起行囊，移地另求發展。哥羅馬的中國城，在今天似乎只是個歷史的記憶古跡而已。

　　今天去哥羅馬參觀的游覽客，在國家歷史黃金公園中，所能看到的只是華合商店（Wah Hop Store），民利樓房以及那賣乾貨的店鋪而已。一九五八年政府為了保存史跡撥款將那曾是淘金勝地的哥羅馬裝修整頓一番，並且正式對外開放為觀光景區。那些在一八五八年和一

八五九年由白人建造的磚瓦建築房舍，曾在一八六零年租賃給華合商店。這家包羅萬象的商店，從日用雜貨，到中國草藥，燒煮食品以至於華人用的骨灰盒，應有盡有。民利樓房則是以販賣五金器材為主的商店。目前用來展覽那些淘金熱潮年代的開礦工具。

從華合商店和民利樓中，可找尋出當年早期開路先鋒華人在哥羅馬淘金的痕跡。那曾經風光一時，加州最大的中國城，在今天觀光國家歷史黃金公園中，所代表的只是一個空空回憶罷了。

西斯谷地帶礦場

華人在美國河畔工作了一陣之後，漸漸發現那裡的金量已所剩無幾，只好另謀發展。加州藏金礦大約可分成三大地區：南方礦區包括 El Dorado、Amador、Calaveras、Tuolumne 和 Mariposa 等縣。北方礦區包括 Plumas、Butte、Sierra、Yuba、Nevada 和 Placer 等縣。第三礦區是 Klamath、Trinity、Del Norte、Klamath、Siskiyou、和 Shasta 等縣。

易采金河流幾乎被掘挖空，所有的美國白人礦工都不願繼續努力並棄它而去。但是那些華工們卻不就此輕易放棄，決定在那已經乾竭的河床中，再接再勵的開掘下去，希望終有一日淘得大量黃金，以圓發財美夢，早日衣錦還鄉。他們有計劃的分工合作，有幾個人更研究

出一種連環的打水機，幫助大量操作。後來，新的水壓開礦法普遍應用了，更多的華工又回到礦場工作。到了一八七零年代，在加州礦場工作的華工，竟高達三分之一的礦工人數。

雖然華人漸漸有能力組織自己的礦業公司，但控制新來工人的大權，仍是操縱在三藩市的華商手裡。華商組織，商家老闆與各地區的總部，隨時保持密切聯繫，對加州，奧里崗，內華達，科羅拉多以至愛達荷等州，總管並指揮各地操作情形。

一八五一年間，一位湯木遜（Abraham Thompson）先生在加州北方一個名為 Black Gulch 峽谷平地發現了金質。消息一經傳開，在短短的六個星期內，從各地踴進大約有兩千人 Thompson Dry Diggings，大作淘金美夢。那時，Shasta Butt 剛剛在一八五一年成立為新市鎮，另外新的縣 Siskiyou 也在一八五二年的三月成立，後來 Shasta Butt City 才改稱為今日的 Yreka 市。

南來北往的旅客們，把新發現金礦的消息很快的在各地傳聞開來。Klamath， Scott， Trinity 以及 Shasta Rivers 河流等處趕來了數千人參加淘金熱潮。到了一八五二年，華人們開始朝 Siskiyou 縣方向發展，因為河流裡測量出大量的金沙粒。據估計，大約有一千左右的華工在一八五三年的四月間到 Shasta 縣地區尋金。似乎傾刻間，數千華人聚集在 Trinity 縣做工，居住。情勢大好，不久就在 Weaverville 鎮興建起一個很大的中國城。到了

一八五三年,有大約三十五個華人從 Shasta 縣趕到 Yreka
城。Shasta 城報紙報導說,有數不清的華人從 Weaverville
來到 Yreka。Siskiyou 縣,據稱是僅次于在 Sierra 山谷的
第二藏金豐盛地帶。

　　在當時的十九世紀年代,長途交通不像今日那麼方
便,去這個山高水遠的地方,更是相當艱難。多數人都
靠驛馬車;記載中也提到當年華人常常用這種交通工
具。但是華人多數乘坐在馬車外面座位,因為車費便宜
很多。還有,當時華人也曾經協助建橋造路。

　　一八五四年至一八六零年間的 Siskiyou 縣,華人礦
工都住在礦區裡或者不遠的地方。除了在礦區裡工作,
有的也兼差做廚子,清洗工或是園丁等。

　　一八六零年所做的人口調查中顯示,大約有三萬四
千九百多華人,居住在美國。根據另外一個調查中的報
告,在一八六零年至一九零零年間,住在 Siskiyou 縣的
中國人數字情形,大約如下:

1860 年	—	515 華人
1870 年	—	1441 華人
1880 年	—	1568 華人
1890 年	—	1151 華人
1900 年	—	790 華人

　　在淘金熱潮時期的人口,流動性很大,因為華人的

語言溝通困難，加上外來的種族歧視壓力，這個數字所代表的真實性很有限。例如：一八八五年太平洋鐵路向各方大事伸展；從三藩市朝北進行遠到奧里崗邊界。在 Siskiyou 山區工作的華人，大約就有四千人左右。這項資料就從未出現在人口調查的報告中。

Yreka 地區，包括當地的中國城，都先後發生過幾次水火災難。一場發生在一八五六年的大火，幾乎燒毀了半個中國城。後來，在一八六一年及一八九零年，先後又被兩次大水淹害得災情相當慘重。華人居住的房屋，受到嚴重的損害，以至於坍瘓到無法修理的程度。不幸的在一八七一，一八八六以及一九二三年間的多次火災都發生在中國城裡。後來受到美國全國經濟大崩潰的影響，華人已經不能再依靠中國城為生，無法繼續在城裡居住。美國建造了無數條重要高速公路，縱貫在加州南北的就是五號公路。這條公路的興建，更消除了那代表華人的中國城存活機會。

在 Klamath 河岸有個快活營（Happy Camp），它是礦區的活動中心。到一八六零年時，那個活動中心已包羅萬象。有兩家大商店，兩家旅館，兩間酒館，兩所舞廳，郵政局，肉店，以及包括華人經營的兩家商店。一家大的中國店是由華人 Ah Ock 所經營。他更擁有自己的礦場，及有權自己招收礦工。有四大商業則由 China Bow 組織直接管理的。一八八零年時，在 Happy Camp 中心有五九七的人口數字。包括二百五十名華人和九十

七名印弟安人。一般人都認為中國人大約只能做些苦力工作，但是，事實上，不單有很多人擁有土地出租也有礦場。就像那很多華人是 Classic Hill 的業主。

藏金最豐盛的礦場就是在 Klamath 河流一帶，靠近 Happy Camp 的地區。如 Richardson 礦場，Gordon 礦場，和中國小溪礦場等都在那裡。在一八八零年間，「China Oak」華人以高價租下了一塊在 Happy Camp 的土地，以五十萬元大量資金大事掘發金礦，並同時招用了大約兩百華工。Richardson 礦場有五十華工。華人以自己能力及知識努力開礦，平均為 Richardson 礦場賺進五萬元的大量業績。Classic Hill 礦場也是 Happy Camp 和 Titus 的產業。大約一百名華人以預付兩萬元現款租下長達九十九年契約，開發淘金事業。在中國小溪礦場工作的華人，大約有上千人數，繼續在那邊作了多年的開採。

一八八零年從紐約來了一位歐文（Charles Owen）的開礦先鋒，他招收了很多華人礦工，在 Indian Creek 礦場工作。那是適合以水力開發掘礦的地區。華工們努力開鑿山洞的酬勞大約是四千元。

李文士先生（Joseph Reeves）在 Happy Camp 擁有最大的礦地，為他工作淘金的華工，都成為他的礦業公司長工。那個名為「中國溪礦場」的主人翁正是華人。在此礦場，他們先後掙掘金量，大約價值十萬至二十萬元的數據。

華人 Ah Ock 在一八九六年向 Siskiyou 礦業公司購

買了以前屬于 Happy Camp 水力礦業公司的一部分產業。後來，在一八九九年時轉售給奧里崗金礦水利公司。

到了一九一零年代，留在 Happy Camp 的中國人大都是些年長者。Quong 是最後還在大街上開店的僅有華人。一九一零年發生在中國城的一場大火，幾乎趕走所有的中國人。到了一九二零年時，只剩下兩個華人。他們是受雇於那礦場業主 Reeve 女士。

在一八五五時期，有大批華人礦工湧進 Salmon 河附近礦場。在一八五零年至一八六零年間更有龐大中國人口紛紛定居在 Petersburg 城的 Salmon 河岸南區，因為那裡有多家中國商店，供應華人日用必需品。但是，到了一八九零年時，卻只剩下數名華人，仍留居在那邊。

Montezuma 礦場以五萬元售給中國礦業公司。在當時的 South Fork 近鄰地區，那是由華人接手的大交易。到一八六六年，A H Denny 搬入 South Fork 時候，那礦區地帶除了兩三百個華人外，甚為熱鬧。那時 Springtown 居民幾乎全是華人。報導上說大約有五百到八百華人居住在那裡。是 Siskiyou 縣城裡，華人最多的地方。

在 Etna 的鄉鎮地區住的華人數字也不小。很多以前做礦工的到這個地方求發展，有的在牧場做雜工，也有的在牧場做佣工為生。

China Hill 的名稱由來，是很多中國人在那邊定居生根。最多曾經有過六棟以上的房屋和一家華人商店。在開礦時期，Scott Valley 地區雇用了很多中國廚師，因

為很多牧場增加了許多在農場工作的幫手。聯邦政府當局發出規定，要所有中國移民必需正式登記。有大約百名華人來到 Etna 辦理登記手續。記得當時有趣的是，有位叫「Chinee Mary」和她的母親，「Old Susie」據說是整個社區僅有的兩名婦女。到了二十世紀的初期，大部份的華人，都已經離開了那個地區，只有少數的在當地旅館，餐館或是大牧場中求生活。

在 Seiad 地區有兩條河流，一條叫 Grider，另一條為 Seiad 溪。有兩家華人礦業公司，大約有十二位員工在那裡努力開發。那家 Lee Yet 水利開礦公司算是規模較大的礦場，共有二十五位員工。另有一家 Hoskins Bar 也是由華人經營的礦場。

到一八九四年間，大約共有四百六十名左右的華工，在 Siskiyou 縣區礦地工作。到了一八九五年間又增加到四八四人。但是到世紀末期，大部份華人都漸漸脫離那些小營地，投向大型水利開礦公司求發展。很多進入 Homestake 礦場，或是 Yorget Bar 場做工。也有的，轉去華人多的其他城市求生存。

現在分析一下，當時的中國人對 Siskiyou 縣經濟方面的貢獻的確不少，主要的因為礦業開發，帶來地方的繁榮。而中國人在礦場有多方面貢獻，有的自己為業主，也有的與人合伙經營礦場開發事業。

淘金熱潮中的暴力與新議案抵制華人

美國當地開礦業主不甘與外來尋金人分享利潤。有時也不願與當地人分享。在一八五零年初期，他們請求加州議會設立一項外國開礦人稅法。該項稅法主要是針對墨西哥人及南美來的礦工。新的稅法，規定外來開礦的人必須以高價申請一張開礦許可才可合法作業。那時，對非白人的種族歧視，以及暴力行為，是非常明顯的。受不了這種漫天高價的稅法，一些從歐洲，中南美洲或墨西哥來的人，只好放棄開礦，無可奈何的被迫離去。

　　在一八五一年時，加州人對少數的中國人的態度尚算溫和。但是後來大量踴進來來淘金人時，他們的忍耐度量，開始有了改變。在一八五一年，一年之中的華人人口從四千人，一下激增兩萬五千龐大數字。這個華人人潮，令美國白人開礦業招架不住，深為不滿。次年，很快的又增加一項新的礦業法案，來抵制外地來的開礦人潮。這項實際為針對華人法案，規定凡外籍不能歸化為公民，每月必需繳納一項特別稅。這項明顯的排華稅法，暢行無阻了二十多年，為加州金庫中增加了五百多萬庫存，是當時全州三分之一的年度財務稅收。

　　這項高稅法，並未阻擋那些對華人礦工施壓的行動。偽裝收稅人到華工家裡招搖撞騙，偷搶華人辛苦掘到的金子。令人遺憾的是，有些真的收稅者也是惡性敗類，欺辱華人以至于殺害那些拒絕付稅人。可憐的中國人，當時是活在毫無保障的環境裡，自生自滅，忍辱圖

存。

在一八五三年八月間的 ALTA CALIFORNIA 報導說,「一個無恥的美國人,昨天毆打一個中國人。那施暴狂徒抓住那長辮子華人,拳打腳踢,一直打到沒有力氣為止才住手。」這類暴行在很多地方都有發生。據稱在一八五二年春天,在北方礦區就已經有驅逐華人礦工的情形。最初報導中曾提到,在 Yuba 市的 Foster 和 Atchinsons Bar 礦地有集體行動表決,拒絕發給華工領取采礦權利。並且在一八五二年五月三日要求所有華人離開工地住處。

一八五二年間的五月,在南方礦場區域的 Columbia 礦場,開了一次大型集會,幾番討論後,決定將華人排除在礦區的所有活動。在 Calaveras 縣則規定華人開礦所得必需登記報備。一八五五年的時候,在 Shasta 縣的礦場也有排擠華人的事件發生。其他的縣城地區,在發生暴動後,白人就藉故將華工集體趕出礦場營地。這些大小事件,迫得華人不得不逃走,另找其他生路。

在淘金熱潮裡,沒人能計算出究竟有多少華人受到傷害,甚至慘遭死亡。情形嚴重到許多地區根本將華人趕出礦區。更有無可理喻的事件,在一八五三年時,加州最高法院規定有色人種,不能在對抗白人案件時出庭作證。加州州長 John Bigler 還正式下令,不准華人在礦區工作,也不准任何華人有采礦權。

雖然在一八五二年以前,Siskiyou 縣城並沒有中國

人，但是縣政府方面卻已對排華行動有所準備。同時鼓勵很多縣鎮的礦場地區，一起抵制華人工作機會。這種情形也發生在 Yreka 縣。在一八五四年間，Siskiyou 縣政府通過一項新的議決：法規中指出對華人的種種限制，共有：

1. 中國人沒有權利在美國國土取得居民權益，
2. 華人永遠無法配合美國社會生活，
3. 華人破壞了美國勞工制度，
4. 華人在金礦裡所得運回中國去，
5. 加強了一八五四年的稅務，
6. 加州因中國人的大量流入，而遭受就業機會威脅，
7. 凡是有華人居在地，就發現經濟不景氣現象，等等。

一八五六年的美國國慶日，舉行大遊行慶祝。許多礦工在華人居住地區任意滋事尋釁。在華人房屋門外狂踢，搗毀家具，毆打男人以及侮辱婦女等。令人悲哀的是，在當時的美國國會，對白人礦工施與華人的暴行已經是天經地義行為。一八五六年，規定每個外國礦工，必須繳納六元的苛刻開礦稅金，迫得華人離開淘金區。很多中國人乘坐驛馬車，出走到遠遠的奧立崗的 Jacksonville 城，另謀發展。

一八六二年時，一項新稅法規定，非礦區工人，所有華人亦須每月交付二元五角的合法工作權稅。Yreka 一個地區，每月就在這方面輕易得到一千元稅收。根據這項數字，看出當時住在 Yreka 地區的華人就有四百人交此「不義稅金」。有些華人因不願屈就為廚子或雜工，只好付苛刻重稅，再回礦場工作。

　　到了一八七零年代，Yreka Union 報紙的主編社論，對華人發表明顯的偏見。報社對全州的排華活動表示支持，一直到一八八二年，促成國會通過排華法規，正式公布施行。

　　一八五零年代，當金礦裡的含金量已經漸漸減少時，那些美國礦工，加上一些北歐來的移民起哄和煽動，都對華人引起憎恨。在一八六零到一八八零年的二十年中，由於當時發生的許多事件，他們對華人的厭煩不滿，演變成了敵視暴力的情況。南北戰爭對東部的工業方面，有不良影響。發生在一八六零年的經濟大不景氣，慢慢的延展到加州，已經是一八七零年的初期了。無形之中，華人就為了這些不幸事件，做了待罪羔羊。

　　這些種族歧視性的法規，增加那些反抗華人的勢力。一八六零年時，從三藩市港口下船登岸的華人，被大群白人譏諷，用石塊加以擲擊攻打。很多礦場也有層出不窮的暴行發生。在一些小地區的中國城，則隨時有被丟火把，或用槍威脅著他們趕出中國城。許多大小城市以至遠到洛杉磯地區，時時有白人殺害中國人的事件

發生。

　　自從華人踏進美國國土以後，多年來命運坎坷的他
們，除了在礦區時時受到多種打擊外，在城市裡也有多
種被歧視事件。從十八世紀末期直至二十世紀初，美國
各方，從地方到州政府以至於高至國會，隨時有數百種
法案來抵制中國人。中國人幾乎沒有任何權利，不能發
言，任何事件發生，也只能默默的接受命運的安排，逆
來順受。

結論

　　早期來美淘金的華人，帶著淘金致富夢默默耕耘，
但求早日衣錦還鄉。但是未料這異鄉訂立的種種不利華
人法規，以及其他種種風俗習慣的適應困難，迫得他們
的歲月是在艱苦中度過。最後能讓那些淘金華人存留生
活下來的原因，最重要的還是那傳統中國人堅忍不撓的
民族性，鼓勵著他們勇往直前，繼續奮鬥下去。

　　從歷史的記載中來看，許多歷史學者或作家認為，
在美國西部十九世紀時的華人，多數為受苦受難者，但
是如果我們從好的一方來看，他們是在苦難中，掙扎出
來的成功者。他們跟隨白人乖乖的去開礦。他們願意在
無人肯做的丟棄礦區裡尋活。他們從不與白人競爭，只
會扶助。他們用自己發明的「China Pump」（中國打水機）
開礦。主要的，他們在適應著那對他們不同的文化而生

存，而不是以對抗的態度去改變別人，因為他們知道，他們並沒有一個強大的政府在支持他們。他們這種忍辱求存的情形也曾得到少數白人的同情，願意對他們給予保護，雇用他們。有幾個幸運者，也會在努力多年積存不少資產，而擠入高階層的社會中。因為這些人是堅忍的好榜樣，使得後來的千萬新移民在美國生根安樂的生活下去。

在讀到當年那段華人歷史，今天，雖然對有關種族和文化的情形多少有理解，態度也有轉變，但是難免仍感到憤憤不平，為那早期華人遭受到的種種災難，只是因為他們是「中國人」。

華工田園生涯

梁靜源　教授

今天，所謂「華工」幾乎已經在美國勞工市場銷聲匿跡，蕩然無存。想當年，大約在一世紀前，華工在農業方面需求的情形，是跟其他如礦業，鐵路工程，土地開墾，漁業及輕工業等方面一樣的重要。當年美國千方百計的抵制華人，又定出各式法案排遣華人。但華工在沙加緬度三角洲地帶，多方面卻扮演著非常重要角色。不管是建造堤坊，土地開墾，以及農業都佔了不可被忽略的份量。這些華人是代表來到三角洲亞洲移民熱潮的重要一環。他們的生活經過等，在歷史中應佔據重要的篇幅。

黃祐先生在沙加緬度三角洲做苦力，一周工作七十小時，一天的辛勞代價，只得一元。「美國華工田園生涯」書中所描寫的是十九世紀到二十世紀初期的華工們的不屈不撓，艱苦奮鬥結果建造出今日的沙加緬度河流域，以及聖河昆河流一帶的農業蓬勃情形。當一八六九年的

鐵路工程完畢後，很多華人向三角洲地帶求發展，那時正在修建河堤，需要大量的工人。華工們挖掘多條河溝，建造數百里長堤防，到一八八零年間，從沼澤地帶開發出了八萬八千平方畝良田。當那項工程結束時，許多華人還繼續留下工作或為佃農。

　　數以千計的華人，漸漸的分散定居在葛侖，樂居鎮，汪古魯，埃靈頓以及里奧威士打等社區裡，忍受著外來的壓力，做勞工過活。多年來的幾次火災摧毀了三角洲的幾處中國城，剩下僅存的只有一個樂居鎮。鎮上的很多建築，雖然現在只是空蕩的房子，可是美國政府還是將此鎮劃定為北加州國家紀念華人歷史性景點，為中美文化與歷史添姿。

築堤墾壤　廣闢田園
勤栽穀果　勞績永延

A HUNDRED MILES OF LEVEE BUILT
THE TULE MARSH MADE FERTILE
GENERATIONS OF KNOTTED HANDS
WORK AND REWORK RECLAIMING THE LANDS
FARMS AND ORCHARDS,
GRAINS AND FRUIT TREES
MARK OUR LABOR
NOW THIS LAND BECOMES GRAND

工農華裔　奠基美洲
散見史籍　民罕傳流

HERE WE ARE
THESE CHINESE IMMIGRANTS
THE EARLY TENANT FARMERS OF AMERICA
OUR STORY UNTOLD
OUR WORDS SCATTERED
LIKE THE FRUITS FORGOTTEN SEED

田園生涯　可歌可泣
集匯成冊　前功確立

ONE DAY - ONE DOLLAR
OUR MEMOIR
FOR THE BITTERSWEET STRUGGLES
OF A HUNDRED YEARS GONE BY

華人在加州一百五十年的歷史　　　　43

流域華埠　萬頃良田
旨此展覽　憶昔當年

WHERE HAVE OUR DELTA CHINATOWNS GONE?
ONLY OUR PICTURES REMAIN
TATTERED AND YELLOWED
WAITING TO BE SEEN
OUR FORGOTTEN WORK
THIS PANORAMA OF DELTLA FARM LAND

早期華農在加州蘇宣谷地（**Suisun Valley**）的生活史料

梁靜源教授・東尼戈特士
譯者：崔以聞

今天，如果要了解當年蘇宣（Suisun）谷地華人大農莊的情況，那遺留下可供參考的東西並不很多。只剩下一些東一塊，西一塊的破舊柏油路躺在寂靜的蘇宣（Suisun）的溪畔。腳踩下去時，也許會將那一塊塊破碎的柏油翻動起來。遺棄的一些舊車，已經是五十多年前留下的一些見証。那些舊車，本是當年興旺的華人農莊的農作中心動力。那時蘇宣當地人口最多時的數字，曾高達千人，多數是由當年甚為活躍的國民黨員所組成的團體。如今俊英會館（Chun Ying）社團樓房，板牆建造的農莊房屋，水果烘乾爐，馬房，

勞工運動遺蹟，商店，祖先會堂，賭館和那鴉片煙房等，都被埋沒在蘇宣（Suisun）谷地的溪邊了。

整個地區的主人原是哈親（A. T. Hatch）的大家族。他們建造了好多農莊房屋給他們的工人。用長長木板建造的簡陋房子，除了搭了地板外，就只有幾個小小的窗子。那些房子，都是供給一批批季節性單身男工住用的。裡面搭造了許多木板床鋪。在房子的一角是廚房用的大鑊可為數十人煮食。在最忙碌豐收季節的八月，還得加搭帳棚，多增臨時工人住宿。

在 1909 年，國父孫中山先生，為革命奔走到加州時，也到過蘇宣谷地的華人社區籌款，並得到當地華人的熱烈支持。

在曾是興旺的華人社區中雖沒甚麼照片留下，但當年發生過的那些點點滴滴，仍時常被一些少數僅存的居民談起，他們還清晰記得當時的喜慶哀樂。

1870-1929 年代中，哈親（Hatch）農場地區華人團體，一直是很興旺的一個社團。但在 1928 年的八月，突然，有十一個華人，被一個外來的華工殘殺。一生都住在那兒的陳（Jennie Tim）女士在回憶著述說：那時當地的居民都被這件突發的凶殺案嚇昏了。他們一致認為那是幽靈作祟，魔鬼詛咒所致。就在短短的六個月中，紛紛逃離到其他地區，還有遠走到三藩市躲避。有些人仍記得在孩童時，聽到過那可怕的事件。但那些老一輩的則不願多談這件他們認為這是「不幸可怕的歷史」。那段

經過，也是加州僅存的農工記憶中的大事之一。是華人在農莊發展非常特殊的經歷。

　　其他可以陳述的，有下列的五點：第一、他們是少數華人移民中，能靠農耕本領而生存的。他們以後更能升遷為農場工頭，不只管理華人，還包括其他種族的人。更有些人，最後成為自立農場主人。當年的農耕華人，經多年的努力而變為許多成功的農業專家，今日仍活躍在蘇宣谷地社區。

　　第二、當年的一般農場工人，都是以烘製乾果為生，他們的後代，也是在童年，幫助家人採割水果烘焙中長大的。不同於三角洲地帶的華農，都願與白人分地為佃農。而在蘇宣谷地區的華農，都是努力而得升遷為農場工頭。

　　第三、在當地出生的孩童不多，被送到不同學校就讀，談不上種族隔離的影響。

　　第四、在蘇宣谷地社區定居的華人，幾乎全來自廣東中山縣的隆都區，而在三角洲地帶的華人，則大多來自廣東中山縣石歧區一帶。

　　第五、哈親（Hatch）農場的主人，在 1880 年代是第一位種植桃、李、杏與蘋果樹的最大農商。在 1889 年他也是第一位使用冷凍火車從加州將水果運往東部的果農。令他成功的原因之一，就是為他工作的農工管理陳添領導及其他華農的合作結果。雖然近年來在蘇宣谷地的華人社區日漸縮小，但他們的成就在農耕的歷史

上，增加了土壤的適耕性。

蘇宣谷地（Suisun Valley）位於蘇拉諾縣（Solano County）以北的蘇宣灣（Suisun Bay）。這裡從蘇宣市（Suisun City）伸展出來的十平方哩寬闊山谷地帶，在西面及東面被崎嶇的屈架（Vaca）山分隔著。這裡黏質土壤藏了冬雨的滋潤。這些肥沃的土壤是最適合耕種的。大多數在蘇宣的農民不單以種植果園為生，他們還以曬乾水果事業為蘇拉諾縣（Solano County）帶來更多的經濟利益。

人口普查資料指出，在 1850 年已有華農來到這蘇拉諾縣（Solano County）。到 1870 年，男性華人已達九百二十人之多。但女性華人就只得一位。而在九百二十位男性華工當中有三分之一，約有二百六十一人是在蘇宣谷地從事農耕事業。而十三名華工在蘇宣市以洗衣工作為生。還有，約一百七十位華工在屈架威拿（Vacaville）工作，及一百八十二位華人在離開屈架威拿不遠的華理豪（Vallejo）謀生。而在小鎮之望地索瑪（Montezuma）農工約十四人，更有五十三名在理奧威打（Rio Vista）鎮及九十名在青青谷地（Green Valley）以木工為業。其餘，中國華工分佈在附近的本尼士亞（Benizia），滴臣（Dixon）及處理芒（Tremont）各地求生。

當年的蘇宣市已是蘇拉諾縣內的運輸主站，而這主站並包括通往啡飛（Fairfield）和屈架威拿兩地。因為這裡有往來的蒸氣船，從這長而狹窄的河道直達三藩市。

市內建有一至三層高的堅固磚樓。還有，公共小學為當
地七十五名至一百位學生授業。這裡有一條碎石道長達
一又四分之一里至縣府啡飛。雖然啡飛市的面積只是蘇
宣市的一半，而啡飛已是加州太平洋鐵路（California
Pacific Railway）的重要聯絡站，在 1850 年已是縣府所
在地。

　　早期住在蘇宣谷地內的人民是以種植小麥為生。並
有些居民以開墾荒地以作日後農耕目的。種植小麥為蘇
宣谷內的經濟支柱。但直至 1870 年代初期，土壤因長期
種植小麥以至土壤貧乏而終止。

　　到 1880 年代，由於水果農業的迅速發展，改變了
蘇宣谷地內經濟衰落的情況。位於蘇宣公路旁，環繞著
哈親大農場為中心以北一片土地，現今已成為蘇拉諾縣
學區校址。開發果園是因冷凍火車運輸事業的發展，從
1870 年起的三十年內僱用了很多華工。

　　中國農民在果園農業上貢獻頗多。實際上他們也是
果園農業的最能信任的主力。經年累月工作經驗，竟成
為一流的採摘與包裝水果專家。這些難以估計的全年水
果收成與進銷到市場各處的過程，完全有賴於這些中國
農工勤勞工作。洛奇女士（Evelyn Lockie）更說過：「在
蘇宣谷地內每一個大農場都設有小房子，專為中國農民
工頭所建造。」在蘇宣谷地內有很多小村鎮像樂威拿
（Rockville）迅速成為農村的中心。很多村內的農民，
都曾在來自廣東省中山縣隆都區的農場工頭陳添（Chun

Tim）手下工作過。1910 年代，這裡種植了大約一百萬株的水果樹。這些茂盛的果樹包括桃、李、梅、杏、櫻桃，及杏仁。在這水果農業發展史上，中國農民扮演了最重要的角色。最初，農民只種植果樹，後來成為農民工頭及農工包商管理，及所有一切收割及修剪農務。最後他們還成為大農場的園主，並在蘇宣谷內擁有不少農地。

要得知中國農業區在蘇宣谷地內的發展。這就要從陳氏（Tim）和余氏（Yee）及他們第三代兩家人口述中求証。從 1986 至 1992，以口述形式訪問這兩個家庭在蘇宣谷內的生活情況。這兩個家族至今仍住在那個地區。這些訪問對象包括一些最初農民先驅者的遺孀及仍然居住在這裡的子孫們。下面將述說的是這些農民社區在加州的發展。這是值得我們關注的問題。這些資料是記載他們的記憶中的生活點滴，因為過去沒有正式研究資料。希望早期農民先驅者的數百位後代，能夠明白昔日農民在蘇宣谷地內種植水果的辛酸史。

開發先驅之家陳添 Chun Tim (1851-1923)

在 1870 年代，並沒有資料記載中國農民在蘇拉諾縣市農工的人數比率。但在 1882 的最高峰期，中國農民佔百分之七十至九十比的勞工率。我們知道這片數百畝土地是屬於大農場哈親（A. T. Hatch）所有。他是因開

發內華達州的銀礦致富的，而成為灣區富有居民。其後，他更成為加州農業的革新派。在 1871 年他購買了在蘇宣谷地內的大農場，並聘請了廚師和傭人。當中有一位年約二十歲的中國移民名叫陳添（Chun Tim）。他來自廣東省中山縣隆都區。陳添開始就擔任管理大農場工作。因為在 1880 年代，有數百人來到蘇宣谷地為中國農工，而令他的地位更顯重要。陳添是蘇宣谷地最早結婚而成家立業的華人。

因陳添能幹引導，其餘農民先驅的家庭，包括林寬（Foons）及高梁（Go Leung）和其後來的余氏（Yees），也能在蘇宣谷地建立基礎。余氏也是早期來到這裡為陳添工作過的。陳添和這幾位農民先驅家庭的後裔，都在蘇宣谷地開枝散葉，並成為華人社區的核心家族。

陳添在他十八歲，離開他的故鄉崗背（Gong Bui）。這是中國廣東省中山縣隆都區的小村莊。現今，他的一家共有後裔一百四十多人，以下列的英文四姓（Tim、Timm、Chan 和 Chun）分佈散居在美國。

盧（Andrew Lowe）太太是陳添的第二位千金。她在 1987 年接受訪問時，回憶他父親來美的經過。她說，「他誤以為每個從中國來到美國的人都是開採金礦的。但那並不正確。中國移民也在鐵路工作。我父親來美，渴望並能有機會學習一些英語，這才有能力為他帶來好一點的生活。（例如，他可以在 Hatch 先生那裡找一份工作），並在星期日為他駕車到三藩市，買一些雜貨及上教

堂。那時大都是用馬車來往的。」

陳添的英語能力，不但大大的幫助 Hatch 先生的農業，而且有助於他成為能幹的主管。不久，他除了在蘇宣，青青谷地聞名外，後來搖身一變更成為整個 Hatch 大農場的主管。他不像廣盛隆（Quong Shing Lung）和屈架威拿的農工主管，只從三藩市找一些未婚男性為農工。陳添更遠自他家鄉，招聘大量男工直接來為他工作。盧人太（Andrew Lowe）繼續說，「他父親最初是為 Edward 先生主管工作。那時他偶而來探望陳添，並給他不少寶貴意見。陳添為 Hatch 大農場帶來很多直接來自中國的農工。Hatch 先生並鼓勵中國工人，建造他們的房子和組織他們的社團。就這樣，中國大農莊(Big Camp)日漸形成了！」

Julian Timm 是陳添的一位孫兒輩。他憶述當年（1920 年代）當他仍然是孩童時在中國大農莊的生活：

「最初我家居住在這裡的一間小房子。這農莊地方很大，並以鄉下土語名為『大農莊』。這就是現在的華人社區。這裡隔鄰是蘇宣溪。蘇宣谷地帶是我成長的地區。當時很多華人，也是來自廣東省中山縣的隆都區。我記憶家父的果園，有大約十個長期的華工也是來自隆都區。在炎炎夏日裡，採摘、修剪、及乾曬水果。最忙碌的季節，一些西班牙及葡萄牙的農工也來參加工作。我還記得我最早學會的英語，是去學校時在玩遊戲時所說的一句『捉不到我』。」

在 1870-1880 年代，加州的蘇宣谷地的中國人口第一次達到高峰。1882，美國政府實施排華法案後，引致整個華人人口下降。這些排華法案，包括限制華人回國探親，或再次進入美國境內，也是造成華人人口直線下降的主要原因。因為寄居在加州的華人以男性為主，他們來美國的目標是賺錢回鄉定居，養兒育女。但在美國，很少人能找到女人結婚，除了在三藩市的中國城。在排華法案下，也有一些漏洞，就是讓一些中國商人媒介而結婚的女人，從中國再次合法進入美國境內。

盧（Andrew Lowe）太太描寫她父親如何在三藩市找到她母親的經過：

「陳添為 Hatch 先生已工作了二十多年了，他希望回國組織他的小家庭。有一次他為 Hatch 先生去三藩市買中國雜貨及米糧等。就在『和記』雜貨店認識了他的妻子，我的母親。」

另一位家庭成員，珍妮（Jennie Tim）是陳添的媳婦追述。1887 年，當陳添三十六歲那年，他準備回鄉娶妻。但有一位媒婆得知他的心意，為他尋覓一位年約十七歲的鄧氏（Ding Shee）嫁給他為妻。鄧氏在她六歲時已來到三藩市。她有開朗樂觀的性格，協助丈夫工作，為她的丈夫及家庭帶來喜悅。在蘇宣谷全鎮，鄧氏是唯一的華人女性。他們為蘇宣谷地的華人社區，踏出了成功的第一步。

在二十世紀初期，在加州華人人口情況非常特殊。

這裡有大量單身老華僑,漸漸撒手塵寰,而只有少部份有家室的家庭,開始在不同的小市鎮居住。幸好在他們的家裡,仍傳習中國舊有的風俗人情。

Christopher Yee 先生的祖父在 1908 年被哈親(Hatch)大農場雇為廚師,是早期進入蘇宣谷地農莊工作的先驅。余先生更提及陳添在蘇宣谷地的華人社區的發展,擔當了很重要的角色。從開始時清一色男性農工,到後來漸漸出現女性及兒童人口等情況。

他指出在 1888 年,陳添的第一位千金出生,叫 Moy Chun,也是第一位在蘇宣谷地出生的華裔女嬰。1890 年 8 月 25 日,陳添的第一個兒子 Chun Hon Gum 出生在 Hatch 農場,竟是第一位在蘇宣谷地出生的華裔男嬰。他為這裡華人社區帶來一片興高采烈的氣氛。陳添很興奮,因他的兒子能承繼他的姓名,在蘇宣谷地開枝散葉。而兒子的母親,也高興地能為丈夫帶來喜悅。

當時不只華人社區,認為聘請華人來管理大農場的重要,白人社區也同意聘請華人來管理他們的農場。大農場的鄰居的 Rosa Lee Baldwin,在她的傳記中也提及陳添在 Hatch 大農場在 1938 年的情況:

這個中國男子陳添對 Hatch 大農場,可說是影響深遠,並繼續詳細言述。陳添經過多年努力,為蘇宣溪兩岸帶來大量華人集居。陳添在他二十歲(1872 年)時已為 Hatch 先生工作。當他存夠金錢,便從三藩市帶來一位怕羞年青的中國新娘子。他們居住在這地區已有六十

年，建立了一個大家庭，與其他數百華人共同努力，日漸建立了中國城。

陳添不但只為 Hatch 大農場，提供中國農民耕作及收割農務，他更負責聯繫各大小農場。他的後裔繼承了他的節儉美德和榮譽，並且熱愛祖國傳統文化。作者觀察中，從華人社區聚居單純的生活方式，到日漸形成高水準的家庭生活，在城鎮裡建立了華人的社會地位。這些當然也是原有鄉村的文化背景所融合形成的。

這裡情況完全與沙加緬度三角洲（Sacramento River Delta）一帶的中國人的社區情形大大不同。他們在白人農場裡佔有很少的權力，他們大多數是以分耕為主，或只有做低層粗工的機會。

農工主管是聯繫果園工人及大農場東主的重要人物，結果，這農工主管雖不是農場主人，卻形成為華人農工生活的中心人物。這種情形多是因語言障礙所造成。還有，這樣也反映出白人社會對其他種族有所分隔心態。而華人農工也因保守自己傳統文化。在這祖傳世襲社區裡，農工主管對華工的習俗也有所尊重。盧（Andrew Lowe）女士懷念地回憶當年她父親不只是工人主管，而且是中國的農工尊敬的長兄。

「我的父親非常友善，每個人都信任他。任何時候發生什麼爭論，只要眾人尊重的長兄到場，就把事情解決。他是整個華人社區最受敬重的調解人。」

身為雙語工人主管的工作並不輕鬆。他不單只為大

農場主人工作。他時常為工人排解糾紛，並為工人與農場交涉工人權益，保障工人不被偷竊，處理聘請及解僱，賞罰等。工人與農場主管之間互相信任的關係，還是傳自中國傳統的方式。以下舉兩個例子，說明工人與主管之間的關係。基利斯杜化（Christopher Yee）回憶起一位親戚名叫陳本倫（Chun Pun Leen）的舊事。

第一次世界大戰前，陳本倫在蘇宣谷地的文卡（Mankas）一帶耕作。信不信由你，他在 1917 除了欠下很多中國工人的巨債，還在三藩市的中國城市場購買中國食物時所欠的債。雖然他三年沒有發工資，但工人仍對他信任，不加懷疑。後來第一次世界大戰爆發，他運往東岸的果梨價錢暴漲，突然他因此致富。結果，他能一次付清工人債項並還清在三藩市雜貨店的欠債。他在 1921 年回歸故鄉隆都，成為當地財主，但他的侄兒陳北燕（Chun Buck Inn）並沒有隨他回國，留下繼續農業工作。

另一個例子，發生於 1927，Hatch 大農場主管黃朱，又名黃福康（Wong Fook Hong）。一次，黃碰到一個農工失去理性亂殺人，因他主管的地位有法律制裁的權，所以他就開槍殺死那工人，警局立刻逮捕黃朱並加以調查謀殺罪，但第二天就把他釋放了，因為有一群華人集會在法院外面要求放人，他們說黃朱的射殺是出於公平的制裁。最後，警察當局認為黃朱的地位重要，處理此事件合理，就將他釋放了。

早期農民家庭先驅高梁（**Go Leung**）、林寬（**Lum Foon**）及余英（**Yee Eng**）：

在蘇宣谷地華人社區居民的回憶裡，並不只是呆呆板板的數字，人口，及農民生產量的資料而已。而是農民先驅家庭及朋友在生活上一些活生生的彩頁。雖然他們的資料並不詳細。但他們的歷史片段，也可編織出昔日蘇宣谷地華人社區的情況點滴。

高梁（**1846-1937**）及高梁女士（**1877-1972**）的故事：

他的中國姓原為梁（Leung），後來改為 Long。主要原因是 Leung 姓的地主把農場名叫 Long 農場。他的子孫雖然知道這件事，但沒有人知道祖先為何把原姓改掉的真實原因。但肯定的高梁先生一定為 Long 農場主人翁所尊重的。Long 農場在文真（Mangel）農場附近，並在蘇宣谷地以南。高梁先生及他的妻子一生都住在這裡，並養育了十六位孩子，包括七男九女。他極痛愛他的孩子，並為這大家庭辛苦工作。現在這個農場已為約翰柏連拿（John Paulina）所有。但由威廉方（William Fong）管理。

雖然，高梁是家中獨子，他在 1860 年代離開雙親及在中國舒適的中等家庭生活，來到加州。他首先在馬利允（Marysville）做短暫性的鐵路工作，以後他才在蘇

宣谷地找到工作。

　　高梁先生並沒擁有 Long 農場的土地。但他在該農場工作了六十年之久，直至農場被賣掉。在這農場內，他能夠養育了十六個孩子的大家庭。他的第一位孩子名叫 Willie，繼後有 Albert，Bill，George，Harold，Henry 及 Howard。而千金的名字 Eva，Ivy，Mildred，Gertrude，Grace，May，Mary，Lorraine 及 Margaret。在家裡他們接受了不少美國式的習慣，他的孫女黃拉娜 Nira Wong 在記憶裡提及，在他們的家庭，吃飯是以筷子和叉一起並用。每位也有自己的叉來取菜，而非筷子。筷子只是給每人自己吃用。在梁氏家庭裡的孩子及孫兒，不單在中國傳統節日裡得到紅包利是，並在美國節日裡也收到不少禮物和利是。例如，聖誕節及新年等節日。

　　高梁在家有駐家的老師，教導他的孩子學中文，所以他的孩子都能學會隆都村的方言。他們除了學習中文外，他們也到樂威拿（Rockville）學校上課。他們並對鮑文（Bauman）老師印象尤深。

　　及後他們的家庭成員從蘇宣谷地內不斷延伸到外地。在 1930 年代，高梁以他的子孫名義在溫提（Winters）鎮內選購了兩塊土地．一片土地是三十畝之大並種植了桃及杏樹。而另一片是十畝的果園，另有五個房間的房子。房子外面全是橙及西柚樹所環繞。而高梁先生的其中兩個兒子一直在果園耕種一直至 1980 年代。而兒子

華人在加州一百五十年的歷史

George 則在 Winters 地區耕作。他的主要種植為杏果。他所種植最豐盛時期佔有 160 畝之大。而另一個兒子 Howard 種植佔地較小。而他每年也曬製乾果。在 1980 年代，他們都退休了。而其中一位高梁先生的孫兒名叫 Melvin Fong 在蘇宣谷地的亞白拉提（Abernathy）地段繼續農耕業務。

其餘的兒女結婚移居到三藩市、屋崙、屈巨威拿、北加菲、沙加緬度各地。高梁先生的第二位千金愛榮，她第一次嫁給窩打盧先生（Walter Lowe）並育有三位子女，名叫露扶（Ruth）、域卡（Wilker）、及湯（Tom）。不幸地，窩打先生英年早逝。在數年後（1923 年的 10 月），愛榮再婚，並嫁與占美方（Jim Fong）。他們育有兩位兒子，名叫墨雲（Melvin）及羅拔（Robert），及三位千金，拉娜（Nira），依利沙伯（Elizabeth）及巴巴拉（Barbara）。占美方曾在蘇宣務農。在 1950 年代，他們購入了些利（Shelly）農場，並在 1980 年賣掉。這是現今在啡飛 Fairfield 西區廣場（West Plaza）的地址。

Ivy Fong 出生於 1900 年 2 月 14 日。在 1980 年代，她是在早期農民先驅家庭成員最為年長的生存者。她仍然住在啡飛。Ivy 仍然記憶尤深，也描述出當年父親帶他們到沙加緬度（Sacramento）選購中國貨物的情形。他們每次是很早離家去市場，迅速選購物品。但每次回家時天色已晚了。她也提及孫中山博士到訪她家的情況。而她的弟弟亞拔（Albert）還坐在孫博士的膝頭上

的有趣情景。

到了今天，他們的後裔多達兩百多人，分佈在加州不同地區。雖然他們從事不同業務，但他們都是在蘇宣谷地培養出來的。

林寬（**Lum Foon**）（雖然對林寬的歷史資料不多，但也應該被提出列為其中一位早期農民先驅）。

林寬首先在加州溫提（Winters）市內工作，其後，他去了蘇宣谷地的米拿（Miller）農場工作。他的九位孩子中，多位是土生土長。雖然他們的家庭早期很貧困，又養育這麼多孩子，但是他們的男孩都為家庭出力幫助耕作。今天費納（Fred Foon）仍與他的兒子湯（Tom）在樂威拿（Rockville）附近八十號州際公路以耕作為生。另一位兒子亨利（Henry）在亞伯拉提路耕種，而他的長子丹尼（Danny）在七十五歲那年過世，也是一位出色的農民。丹尼的兩位兒子愛德華（Edward）與查理（Charlie），和他們的子孫在 1980 年代，成為蘇宣谷地內最為成功而出色的農主。

余英（**Yee Eng**）（1890-1977）

余英的父親余超陽（Yee Chew Yang）從中國中山縣隆都地區來到美國。他的第一份工作是在沙加緬度河

三角洲（Sacramento River Delta）為農工。後來他租用了一塊土地自己耕作。直至第二次世界大戰，他退休回歸中國。他的兒子余英在 1908 年，十八歲那年跟從他父親來美。他來時是乘西伯利亞號（S.S. Siberia）船的。他的第一份工作，是在蘇宣谷地的比亞士（Pierce）農場，為農工主管林滿燕（Lum Mon Inn）做中國廚師，並為三百多位華工煮食。

　　在 1923 年 2 月 16 日，余超陽回到中國為他的兒子余英帶回了新娘子到美國。在余英的新娘子還未到達美國時，余英已從威廉萊茵（William Rye）先生在文卡角（Mankas Corner）那裡租下二十畝的果園。在這果園裡，余英及其妻育有四子一女。其後余英更租用了多畝地在 Rye 農場旁邊果園土地種植水果。余英也為榮昌土地（Wing Chong）及中國土地（China Land）公司的總裁服務。余英與其妻子從 1908 年一直居住在萊茵大農場，直到他們去世。在 1977 年 11 月 9 日余英過世，而其妻在 1980 年 4 月 9 日隨其而去。但他們的乾果業已很成功的繼續下來。

第二代農民先驅的婚姻與家庭

　　陳添育有四女三子。只有排行第三的兒子，于遙（Youie）從事農耕業務。他以農務作為他的一生職業。他對農業發展的貢獻，也是我們所研究的主要歷史。

于遙（Youie Tim）（1895-1978），他的一生傳記也是典型農民先驅家庭的第二代故事。他們的第二代，大多數由工人階級進升為主管級。在一九零九年 Youie Tim 只有十四歲，已跟從父親以繼承他的農務。他與他的朋友盧林（Low Lum）在索羅馬縣（Sonoma）開創他們務農的工作。兩年後的一次乾旱，使得他的投資農業失敗。在 1915 年，當他十八歲的那年，他再次回到蘇宣谷地為寶棠（Baldwin）大農場擔任主管工作。當第一次世界大戰時他被召從軍。而在 1919 年當他二十四歲時，他再次為士高（Scholl）農場工作。他珍藏了不少蘇宣谷地果園內生活的統計資料。他也保存了從 1937 年直至 1978 年 7 月他逝世為止的詳細的雨量統計。他相信了解水量，能夠直接幫助他農作失收或豐收。

　　雖然，Youie Tim 一直住在華人社區，他的資料指出，在 1919 年，他的大多數工人，包括英裔美國公民及西班牙人。這裡工人薪金大約二元二十五分至二元二十七分一天。以當時平均工人薪金計算，也可以算是可觀的收入。比較之下，一些在沙加緬度三角州的中國工人做一樣勞力，也只得兩元一天。

　　關女士（Roberta Tim Quan）回憶起她母親珍妮，描述她怎樣與他父親相識。他的父親丁遷是陳添的第二個兒子。他曾在第一次世界大戰，服役於福麥當勞基地（Fort MacDowell）。在 1923 年，他被委派運送其父親的遺體回故鄉隆都陵墓。在這旅程中，他為自己找到一

位新娘子。這美麗的新娘子名叫珍妮（Jennie）。只有十六歲的她，曾奇怪問父親為何于遙時常到她家裡來。後來，她驚訝地得知那人將會是她的丈夫。在 1924 年，她跟從丈夫來到 A.T. Hatch 大農場的華人社區。

在 1935 年，于遙年近四十歲的時候，他們舉家移居到一六零畝的碧波地（Peabody）的大農場。他與他的合伙人，黃滿（Wong Mun），一起為魯賓（W.C. Robbins）先生工作。他們的生產種類繁多，有杏、桃、李、梅及合桃等，使收成季節忙得不可開交。雖然在收割季節時，工作忙碌，但于遙非常喜愛這份工作。在收割季節，于遙聘請了很多水果採摘工人。于遙並與這些來自墨西哥，菲律賓工人及家屬有深厚的交情。他獲得所有工人的敬重。他的冷靜、組織力及能幹地處理工人的工作時間、薪俸及農場各樣的收支事務。他閒時也愛坐在他的書桌上練習書法。他的名聲遠播，他開出去的支票都樂被接受，因為他是受所有商家所信任的人。

在 1948 年，于遙為魯賓先生在丹尼臣（Danielson）大農場作總管。十二年後，在 1960 年，他六十五歲那年，他終於有機會購得了四十畝的白蘭福特（Bransford）大農場。他和兩個兒子，路易（Lewis）及約翰（John）也成為獨立農戶。可是在 1970 年，因農工問題及農業不景氣的情況下，于遙決定把土地賣給安輝沙啤酒廠（Anheuser Busch）。這樣子便終斷了蘇宣谷地維持三代的農耕工作。

丹尼寬（Danny Foon）（1900-1975），他是林寬的長子。林寬有九名孩子。丹尼出生於 1900 年在溫提市（Winters）。但他成長於樂威拿。在 1987 年，他的孫兒米高布（Michael Bow）口述他祖父十歲時已在埃靈頓收割包裝果梨工作。埃靈頓離開蘇宣約四十哩。而他的祖父丹尼以單車做往返工作地的交通工具。丹尼天天在埃靈頓工作，而週末才回家一聚。由於家境貧窮，丹尼時常吃不飽。有一次在半路回家途中受不了而暈倒。他得到一位女士帶他回家及給與食物。這個故事仍然在孫兒的回憶中時常轉述。

丹尼曾在樂威拿上過小學，但他從沒有唸高中。因為他日夜勤勞地工作，希望他年二十二歲時，存有足夠金錢回中國。他計劃找一位新娘子。他更向他的朋友查詢如何找一位妻子。在中國，藉著照片，他特別喜歡一位年約十六歲的女子。其後他們結為夫婦。那女子名叫伊絲（Elsie）。她跟從丈夫一起來到美國。

很多未婚男子回歸中國最主要的原因，是尋找一位適合他們的妻子。如果這種方法不成，他們也有其他辦法。現今一些居住在蘇拉諾縣（Solano County）的一些居民，回憶起有些家庭是藉婚姻介紹成功的。這些較為成功的農民回鄉（降都），尋找願意生兒育女及照顧家庭的女子為妻。有不少婦女在婚姻介紹情況下來到蘇拉諾（Solano）縣居住下來，照顧丈夫和養育下一代。

這種婚姻介紹是美國政府排華政策的藉口，只批准

商店老板的妻子進入美國，直到 1924 年止。所以一些中國單身男士可以回鄉（隆都），尋找適合傳統女子為妻。在這情況下，也有一些複雜的個案，在天使島的移民官，也發現有一些娼妓來美的情況及新娘子的家人反對個案。在這世紀前的蘇宣谷地，只有三個中國農民家庭。直至 1870 年代，中國人口才增至百多人。

　　現今很多人認為婚姻介紹是不合時宜，但這種制度建立了華人社會在蘇宣谷地的根基。現在這裡的華人增長，非靠大量海外移入的農民工人，為本地華人新一代家庭的擴展。珍妮女士回憶起當初在 1924 年到達這裡時，只有三個中國家庭居住在大農莊。但在整個蘇宣谷地鄰近共有二十多個獨立中國家庭居住。在 1920 年代，這裡是以男性為社會中心。所以造成人口性別不平均。珍妮指出這種以男性為中心社會情況。例如，在蘇宣谷地和三角洲慶祝收割聯歡節日，她記起這些節日吸引了很多男士從三藩市來到這裡一帶的大農場。雖然她並沒有參與這些收割聯歡節日，但她很享受這節日氣氛，而她之所以沒有參與節日，因為女性很少公開參加這種慶典活動的。

　　從拍攝於紀念日的照片中可以反映出，在 1925 年孫中山博士與蘇宣谷地的華人家庭社區關係密切，促成社區成長。而照片中也反映出有三分之一的是兒童。還有，從相片中明顯地展示也有大部份年青男女。因此，說明了在 1920 年代，在加州的新一代中國華人社會漸次

成形。

第三代華農記述在不景氣時代農場長大的情形

在 1920 年及 1930 年代出生的兒童是早期華農先驅的子孫。他們回憶起祖先移民來到這裡複雜心情，是懷念故鄉但也分享這裡的新事物。余英的女兒指出，昔日生活並非如現在的沉悶。她懷念在 1940 年代，當她升讀十一年級時，步行二哩到蘇宣谷地區學校上學。朱利英（Julian Timm）更說出其中一個有趣的故事。他的母親因在蘇宣谷地找不到房子而使她留在三藩市。

我們機智的母親發現一間用木造成的空著的油站，她覺得這地方也頗為清潔，只要打掃及修理一下也可以居住。所以她向錦（Gum）叔叔借了二十五塊錢，買下那木造的空油站，搬到錦叔叔在羅素路（Russell Road）附近的農場暫住，並得到很多華農的幫助，修補了這間像中西部古時的木屋。完工後，Julian Timm 的母親以大宴來答謝各位幫助她修建房子的人。

余亞娃（Eva Yee）也說出當年的老一輩，在晚上談到當年的艱苦情形，和慶祝會等。他們口述當時的生活瑣碎和從中國帶來的新娘子。有時，他們也說及在中國華人社會的賭博情況。Eva Yee 回想起昔日孩童時在沼澤捉魚的趣事。有時候他們收獲豐富。她的父母用魚連骨頭剁碎來燒出鮮味魚湯。Eva 並不太懷念在 1940 年代，

在夏天放學回家，要幫助父母親在果園收集已曬乾的水果的情形。她說當時大多在晚上工作。而要特別按裝燈火，工人才能在晚上工作。而 Roberta Tim Quan 卻有另一種看法：

「我非常渴望夏季的來臨，雖然我也明白很多工人在仲夏採摘李子和桃子，是非常辛苦的工作。但農民工人一家大小一天忙著收割時，兒童們大多數一起玩皮球，捉迷藏遊戲直至天黑。在這季節裡我除了有三個兄長作伴外，我還有不少小朋友為我作伴呢。我也很羨慕那些墨西哥及菲律賓家庭，居住在非常簡單的木建帳篷內，帳內地下非常污垢，頗有異樣風味。比較之下，我們擁有一所舒服的居所，父親建了兩間沐浴室給留住的工人使用。而單身男士，都住在隔壁而設的床鋪。還有，父親聘請了廚師，負責給大家煮食。我也記起菲律賓工人並不重視沖澡，只喜歡在浴盆內浸濕疲倦的身軀。他們在地下開鑿了一個大洞用作煤爐，並在上面按放木盆及裝滿水。這樣子整個構造成木製的洗浴室，也就是今日的流行的三溫暖蒸氣浴（Sauna）！」

Julian Timm 回憶到探訪 Youie 叔叔的家：

「當水果收割季節時候，我與母親負責切割水果，而父親（Sam）採摘水果。他還負責監督季節性的西班牙及葡萄牙工人。在經濟不景氣時候，季節性的工人全家移居到大果園居住，農民生活非常艱苦，母親除了在果園工作外，還負責一日三餐的煮食工作。在切割水果

時，她也幫助切開杏桃、桃、及梨，而以切割桃最難受，因為桃的表皮上有一些小毛，插入皮膚內使人奇癢。當開飯時間，母親搖響大鈴，以傳達一里之內的工人來到乾果棚進食。他們常常都非常饑餓，因為他們整天做採摘水果，及搬運一箱一箱水果的體力勞動工作。母親也為討好他們，烹調很多好吃的飯菜給他們享用。我們多數吃自養的雞，因雞的生長很快。牠們在晚上多集合在合桃樹下休息。」

在蘇宣谷地華人社區的最重要的歷史包括陳添之死及大屠殺。在 1932 至 1934 年，Youie 的記載也顯示出，這個華人社區在兩大事變後而有所不同的情況。

在那時，Youie 正在士高（Scholl）大農場為總管。由於當時正是經濟不景氣的高峰，所以一般的工資下降為 $2.25 元的一天十小時工作。這種情況不單只完全反映在 Youie 的詳細英文記載中。還有，其他六位中國合伙人也損失三百至四百元左右。Youie 的女兒 Roberta Tim Quan 反映出在蕭條社會長大的一代的問題。

Julian 說：「當時玩具很少，我們也沒有把錢浪費在這些算是奢侈的項目上。所以，我們對利用廢物來創造玩具獨有特別的天份。例如，我們用被棄置的鐵片造成車殼，加上鐵釘造成的車胎。這樣就成了一部玩具車了。而用紙手巾仔細地摺疊好，一串起來就造成一個洋娃娃；丫字形狀的樹枝加上橡皮膠，就造成射彈弓箭了。而爸爸燒毀枯樹後地上留下的一個大洞，是哥哥和我最

好的小型汽車跑道場。」

John Tim 出生於 1927 年的中國華人社區裡。在 1930 年代的孩童時，在大農場裡並沒有如此多姿多采的生活。他說他們並沒有收音機和電話。而所有的新聞，完全是依賴報紙。他們幼年時幸得祖母在飯後時，坐在火爐旁說一些中國故事及一些民間傳說，作為我們閒暇的節目。祖母在 1868 年從中國來到這裡，當時她只有六歲。在她還未結婚時，家在三藩市以縫製衣服為生。

在 1939 年，盧先生（Andrew Lowe）十四歲時來到美國與父親團聚。他還記得在果園採摘水果的第一份工作。他說：

「我的父親在 Winters 市為農場主管。他知我受不了 Winters 市的酷熱，所以把我派到蘇宣那裡工作。在這個大農場，中國農民工人大約有十個以上。當時我的薪金是兩元一天，包括一天三餐。我還記得一個八月的晚上，忽然下大雨，早上兩點鐘，我們被指派把乾果收入柵子裡。在那個季節裡，我的收入大約有一百二十元。」

農工的情況，隨著一批批陸續來到加州的新移民農工而有所改變。在 1930 年時的記錄簿的引証，農民工人大多為墨西哥及菲律賓族裔，只在繁忙的季節裡，也偶然有一些較年長的中國農民幫助收割。他們大都是在別的地方找不到工作而來農場的。盧先生 Andrew Lowe 在他十四歲那年，記得大多數與他一起工作的是較年長的農民，大約三十至七十歲之間。

士高大農場與其他在加州大農場一樣，他們擁有屬於公司的商店，為農民工人提供一些生活必需品。而Youie Tim 除了是士高農場的總管，他也是商店的負責人。他負責店裡的一些財務支出。發了工資後，農民可以用微薄的薪水，任意選購生活所需，而當時最受農民歡迎的是 Prince Albert 香煙。但在 1930 年，報上記錄了有一些農民，除了買一些日用品外，他們也匯款廿元給中國的家庭。

中國農民社區及學校的生活

中國華人社區生活，不但反映出年老的移民農人的情況，更是影響到在社區內的第三代！這些第三代的子女生活，介於美國社會與中國學校間。他們所學到在農場中的知識，漸漸地因與外界社區交往而有所改變。Roberta Tim Quan 如此回憶著：

「我們很少到市鎮去選購物品，因為很多四輪運貨車，時常到我們的家兜售。我還記起有一些賣魚肉，也有的是盛滿美味的烘焙麵包貨車等。當然，他們另外還帶了些日常所需用品。我有時候也因儲蓄的一些零用錢，用來買十仙的 Cracker Jacks，因裡面藏有獎品。那多是一些金屬製的玩具，而不是像今日塑膠製成的東西。」

蘇宣谷地的學校不像沙加緬度三角洲地區，把東方

學生和當地的學生分開，雖然中國和日本裔的移民也很多。當然陳添的七個孩子，都是送去當地 Rockville 學校上學的。盧女士（Andrew Lowe）（是陳添的其中一位女兒）憶述當年上 Rockville 學校的日子。她說：每天步行很遠的路才到那所學校。我們並沒有汽車‧‧所以在天氣寒冷及下雨天的日子就相當困難。在 1992 年她說:「我非常喜歡上學的日子。我時常渴望在星期五到圖書館那裡借一些書籍回家閱讀。當我畢業時的平均分數，是學生中最高的九十八分。」她十歲至十六歲就讀於 Rockville 學校，其後轉到三藩市的中學就讀。明顯地，她的長兄，並沒有這樣幸運，有機會去學校上課。在他讀完第八年級後，他就到果園工作了。

在 Julian Timm 就讀小學的生涯中，他印象尤深的是鮑文 Bauman 老師。在 1930 年代，她曾教導他從五年級至八年級。她在廿多年前也曾教過 Julian 的父親 Sam。她說:「Bauman 老師是一位極為優秀的老師。我從她那裡學數學及地理。我也學會了在圖書館那裡借閱書籍。有希臘傳說書本，也有 Rafael Sabatin，和 Zane Emery 的冒險小說。那真是快樂的時光。在學校我們一起相處就像一家人一樣。」

從鄉村學校的兩間教室掛著的照片看出，那裡漸漸融入美國社會的方式。有白人、華人、及日裔學童。在這白人學童中，一些年長者還記得這裡也曾有西班牙及墨西哥裔人。所以慢慢的，一些華裔學童已疏遠故鄉文

化,而接受一些新事物。正像許多移民一樣,這種趨勢有的被一般父母鼓勵,也有的加以阻擋。

　　Jennie Tim 自豪地表示,她的五位子女都上大學唸書,接受美國生活與文化。她還說接受教育並不是免費的。在 1930 那時,Wong Chern 農場就曾贊助週末的中國學校。但是,華人教育,對一些加州華裔移民常常帶來問題。她的丈夫及陳添的子女非常幸運。在不正統的學習下,從父親的會計部那裡學會了一些中國字。今天,珍妮引以自豪地憶述,她的長子 Lund 在 1930 年代的 Wong Chern 大農場所開設的週末華人學校中,是最優秀的學生。但可惜這所學校只開辦了兩年。所以,在這樣的情況下,造成下一代年輕的子女,並不太會書寫及閱讀中文了。

退休及對母國政治情結

　　不可避免的,退休是對一些在加州務農為終身職業的挑戰。在 1949 年共產革命後,他們大致有兩個選擇。第一個選擇是回到他們的故鄉退休,或選擇留在美國。而這些決定也因他們的婚姻及子女的關係有所影響。例如,Yee Chew Yong 在 1891 年單身從鄉間隆都到達美國。而他留在中國年輕妻子卻為他誕下一位男嬰。他的名字為 Yee Eng,於 1908 年十八歲時來到美國與他父親團聚,且在 1923 年 Yee Chew Yong 回到中國為他兒子,

娶回一個妻子。但因戰爭關係而阻止他回到中國。直到第二次世界大戰終結後，他退休回鄉。而他的兒子就在共產革命後又不得回鄉，這樣的情況下，他們就分隔兩地，而其兒子就只得留在美國了。

很多方面來看，在蘇宣谷地裡大多數華人，是和蔣介石為首的國民黨的關係非常密切。但 1949 年，共產黨戰勝後，一些華裔移民不能回鄉娶妻，退休，及參加在隆都祭祖活動。直至 1970 年代末期才有改變。

也不知道什麼原因，在這個時候，蘇宣谷地的華人，全是滿腔熱誠的反對共產黨的成員。很明顯地，強大的國民黨勢力在很早就形成了。Christopher Yee 憶述孫逸仙博士在 1909 年到訪 Ivy Fong 與 Hatch 農場的中國社區情形時，在那時候，孫先生是鼓吹革命，反對清朝。在 1909 年，孫逸仙博士到訪蘇宣谷地同行者，更有從 Courtland Chauncy 來的林粲士 Chew。Hatch 大農場的中國同胞，還為他舉行了一個重大的歡迎會。孫先生在這裡大力推動反清政府。孫逸仙博士是第一位中國人，入住在蘇宣市美國大旅館 Arlington 客人。雖然這時候已有種族歧視，但孫先生的政治地位，也受美國人所敬重。並且一般華人也覺得，安排孫博士入住美國旅館，比住在華人的農場宿舍中較為適合。

Evelyn Lockie 女士談起她在 1912 年時，常去探訪住在 Tower Ranch 的大總管情形。一次他指著掛在牆上的一張大照片說，那就是孫中山先生，他是中國的新總

統，是一位偉人‧‧‧。那麼多人追隨孫先生，因為他有能力，鼓吹革命，得到海外對滿清政府不滿的中國人的支持。尤其那些住在夏威夷和加州的華裔移民，大多數和孫先生一樣是來自廣東省同一地區的同鄉。當然孫先生自己更有和加州密切的關係的因素；他兩個叔伯，是在十九世紀的淘金潮時逝世的。在蘇宣谷地大家的記憶裡，孫先生曾到過 Hatch 農場，而都是為了革命籌款而來。

孫博士領導下的國民黨與日後蔣介石政府，也維繫著在蘇宣谷地裡的小小華人社區良好關係。國民黨籌集資金時，每次都在蘇宣谷地社團的獲得良好成果。Jennie Tim 是一位國民黨的支持者，憶述起在 1930 至 40 年代，蘇宣谷地華裔社區更成為籌集經費的重要地點。她更自豪說起她捐出金頸鍊作為支持。還有，這裡為中國對抗日本捐出金錢高達一萬元，及向國民黨以七萬五千元高價，來採購了戰爭公債。在 1910 年代，蘇宣谷地華人，為紀念中國革命的殉道者，而對廣州市認捐了不少善款。她說，對它發生興趣原因，可能是大部份的社區華人故鄉是隆都村民，而孫博士也是屬中國中山縣緣故。雖然她的子女從 1980 年開始也曾有回鄉之行，但她仍然拒絕回隆都，因為故鄉一日在共產黨的政治領導之卜，她絕不回去。

打入美國社會，購買土地及第三代成為專業人士

在 1980 年農業統計資料指出，在蘇宣鎮內有兩位華裔擁有九百七十八畝農地〔亞榮（Ah Wing）和康唐威（Hong Tong Vey）〕。其後，雖有法律禁止華人擁有土地，但在蘇宣谷地的華人還是斷斷續續擁有耕地。盧太太（Andrew Lowe）還記得隆都大農場就是由數位華農所有。她也憶起她其中一位合伙人，Ching 先生在第一次世界大戰時買了一個農場，因此兒子不必參軍。

Yee 氏家庭指出，他們家族早於 1910 年代已擁有土地。雖然 Christopher Yee 有時也懷疑，為何在當時的法律地位上如何能成為土地的擁有者。Sucheng Chen 指出在 1900 年至 1920 年代有六十至七十個合法租用案件存檔。雖然，這裡並未明確記錄法律是怎樣被矇過的，但我們清楚知道本世紀初時，在蘇宣谷地這裡，最少有兩個華裔擁有的農業公司。他們是以生產梨子為主的公司。另外，在美國出生的華人移民子女也能擁有土地。

日漸地，華農的第二代在 Solano 縣成為主要農田的主人翁。雖然第二代擁有很多農地，但華農的第三代，開始慢慢又把這些土地賣掉。擁有大學學位的第三代，嘗試成為在啡飛 Fairfield 一帶的發展商。陳添本身未曾擁有過一塊田。但其中一位兒子 Youie 也繼承他的農務工作。但直至 1960 年，他時年六十五歲時才有足夠資金購買一個自己擁有的果園。在 1968 年 Youie 的果園賣給 Anheuser Busch 先生改建為啤酒廠。以他賣掉園地所得，Youie 在郊區購買了一幢房子居住，直到 1978 年逝

世時，其遺孀 Jennie 至今仍居於同一地址。另一個例子，余芳惠（Fong Wai Yee）是陳滿錦（Chun Mon Gum）第二位妻子。她的兒子 Lloyd 也繼續管理十三畝的果園，好像他的手足弟妹，堂兄弟姊妹，他的主要職業已是專業的了，首先是工業化學師，及後來轉為 Solano 縣的郡警員。

Roberta Tim Quan 懷念她往昔在農村的生活：

「經過在往日多年典型的農村生活，我當初是很興奮地離開鄉村，走到繁華都市，並到高等學府的加州 Berkeley 深造。但是回想起來，我還是非常緬懷往昔的童年時光，及一些現今孩子沒辦法理解的生活經驗。我們不再是社會中有限的價值存在的佃農。至於物資方面雖稀少，但在童年記憶中卻是富有充足的，那些往事可以追懷享受一番情趣了。」

當初，一段時光有二十多個家庭及千多名華人在蘇宣谷地從事農場。但在 1990 年代，只剩下余氏 Yees 及寬氏 Foons 兩家仍然繼續農耕工作。這兩個家庭建立的農業企業，成為其餘加州農業事務的好榜樣。Foon 代家族農務在今天來說，成為 Solano 縣之內規模最大的農商。他們不單只出產水果，更有乾果穀物。余氏家族以生曬乾果為生，在乾果業已爭得一席之地。除了他們把水果賣給大包裝商，例如 Del Monte 及 Sun Sweet，Cal Yee 農務主要是生曬及包裝水果農業，最特別是他們專注以中國式的生曬水果方式打入市場。在美國西部是成

華人在加州一百五十年的歷史

長最快的華人社區。現今仍有一些早期農民先驅家庭的第三代，仍然繼續他們家族的農業事務。在他們家庭的支持下，他們接受大學以上最優秀高等學府的教育。所以，他們學成後回到村谷，成為農耕業務上大企業家。以他們多年前祖先遺留下來的實際經驗，加上新學到的現代知識，這新的一代不再遇到當初他們父母面對的一些阻礙了。

John Tim 在 UC Davis 得到農務經濟學士學位。他回憶起說：「我畢業後，我想在城市中找尋工作，但很困難，因為當時我父親需要幫助，所以我決定回到蘇宣谷地，成為農夫。自開始，我並沒有覺得農夫生涯是很差的生活。雖然在那時候仍然以人手操作。我父親是農務上的決策人。我在學校接受了不少新的農業技術，但父親按照他的傳統方法操作，所以我有時候也覺得迷惑不知如何是好。例如，我們以人手灌溉，但我提議購買自動灑水式噴射機來灌溉。可是被他拒絕。直到數年後，有很多其他農家改用它，他才答應。」

余氏家庭的四位兒子都上了大學。長子 Christopher 在加州的 Berkeley 大學獲得工商管理碩士學位。二子 George 在 San Jose 州立大學進修工業美術。三子 Peter 在 UC Davis 選擇果樹栽培學，而四子 Donald 在羅省進修柴油及機油工程師學位。

Christopher 與 George 在 1948 年，他們仍就讀大學時，已經開始乾曬水果事業。他們工作與上學時間正好

配合。因為乾果業繁忙時，正是暑假季節。他們早年已從父親身上學會了乾曬水果的技巧。在 1951 年，他們兩兄弟所生產的乾果，以梨及杏在蘇宣谷地的 Mankas 一帶是為最理想的乾曬水果。因為這裡比其他在蘇宣谷地區較為炎熱，而風力較強。在早上並沒有很多霧氣。在 1951 年，他們一家決定從 William Rye 先生買下一個果園。並在這裡建製了現代化的乾曬水果工場。首先他們建造的是一座切割小屋及硫磺房子。漸漸貯藏間及工具房，墨西哥裔工人的營地，貯存托盤的小棚屋，及梨子脫水機等增加收成。最後，在 1955 年，新的房子及公司也都一一建造成功。

Yee Eng 的妻子知道怎樣以中國香料醃製乾果。她在美國這些中國口味的乾果市場中加以開發調查及研究。結果 Christopher 知道這中國式的醃製乾果以夏威夷為最理想市場。在 1958 年 8 月 12 日第一批新產品，就是由蘇宣谷地運到了夏威夷。他不但只推出醃製乾果。他還以鹽醃製南瓜及西葫蘆瓜子。結果報告指出南瓜子較為受大眾歡迎，因為中國人喜歡大的南瓜子。在 1958 年 12 月 22 日，他把南瓜子運到夏威夷。今天這些產品頗風行整個美國及加拿大。

這個大家庭以 Cal Yee 為商品名字。他們 Cal Yee 公司的成功，是生產量每年可以由新鮮水果曬成乾果達三千噸。他們大約處理一千噸的杏，一千一百噸的桃，五百噸的梨，及四百噸的杏桃。這些家族的產量，仍然

保持優良品種及成本控制。一半的生產量，是以自己公司負責包裝出售水果，另一半交給獨立包裝公司負責推銷。

日常公司的運作與職責，分配給四兄弟管理。Christopher 是策劃行政的，直至 1991 年他逝世，時年六十六歲。George 是負責所有的機械，機件工具及工場。Peter 是打理果園、零售及批發事務。Donald 是負責維修及保護機械及工具。Christopher（1925-1991）非常活躍於社區的活動。他曾是 Mario Sengo 博物館的董事。他也活躍參與多項商業組織。Yee 氏兄弟是在蘇宣谷地內，獨一無二成功的早期先驅華農後代。

結論：加州一個移民族裔的農村社區

一般對種族移民的研究，多是認為某個種族文化及社區的團結和外界社會有所隔離。尤其在世界第二次大戰前，情形更為明顯地在蘇宣谷地中表現出來。法律及習俗等也確定的分割出在社會中的地位。這種的情況在蘇宣谷地中國的生活居住地區及工作圈內存在很普遍。相反的蘇宣谷地的華人雖有隔離，但很多種族自然的越過界限對其他社區改變有所融合。

這些關係從工作方面開始，這些華農在蘇宣谷地的果園工作。日漸地，他們與這些白人農主直接與間接建立了關係。再者，就是地方法律。在這華人社區形成有

自我控制的守則。一般的相信，才智在白人社區中有強烈表現出全能性的社區領袖概念，這樣造成很大被接受的社會道德標準。

但也有一些真實個案，涉及區外嚴重罪行，例如謀殺案件。郡長及地方法官也很迅速地參與解決，特別是在二十世紀早期，鴉片煙在華人社區是不遭禁止的，連一些少量的白人也從這法律漏洞走入煙館及賭館。

社會學者 Ivan Light 寫了一些有關於華人雜處對附近社會的關係。他指出這樣是較為有效地阻隔社區外的一切活動。

但是，在排華日子裡，鴉片煙館也被政府有關部門所察視及控制。這些注視華人與白人的有關情況，在 1985 年 Solano County 內居民 Fred Salesman 有所評論。Salesman 感到歉意地道出，一些在白人社會對中國人的驚怕及一些誤解觀念。這些強烈性情況，反映出當時白人與華人的關係與理解。他說：「當時我們認為華人是賣鴉片的魔鬼，而且，我們並不視他們是人。他們是商品。我也認為他們是異教徒。」社會學者 Light 指出這也是極為諷刺的，因為鴉片煙館也同樣有白人與華人。還有，這一點顯示出老一輩的男性華人社區是與在附近社區的男性白人有所接觸。

但這些並不是故事的全部。特別是從以前單身男性華人社區日漸加入女性及孩童。和單身男性的比率下降。這樣的不同人際關係就開始形成。在學校及個人與

華人在加州一百五十年的歷史

個人之間，Christopher Yee 也坦率地回憶起 Pierce 先生。他是擁有在蘇宣谷地第二大的農場場主。Yee 的父親，Yee Eng 就在蘇宣谷地 Pierce 的大農場開始他的第一份工作。其後世界第一次大戰，他在農場為華廚。「Pierce先生為所有華工所敬重。因為 Pierce 先生對華人有尊嚴和敬重。」在 1985 年報張上記載 Lewis Pierce 三世，他之所以與華人有如此密切的關係，是因為他從小就在父親農場中與華人一起長大之故。

　　Evelyn Lockie 也道出她一個同樣的故事。她記得關於到訪小華人社區賣豬給他們和同時來買米的情況。當她到訪時，農場主管 Wong Gee 買了罐從市場得來的草莓汽水給她。她還記得她的好朋友小弟弟，時常到住在蘇宣市的華裔洗衣店的人一起居住。Evelyn Lockie 一生與陳添的兒子 Chun Mon Gum 維持友好關係。直至 1978年 Gum 九十一歲逝世時。

　　這些不同家庭之間的關係，也說出他們的子女除了中國傳統文化外，也負起為美國公民的責任。他們與其他美國人一樣非常重視軍中的服役，所以在軍事服務需求時，也獻出一份力量。陳添的兒子就在第一次大戰時服役。他的功績是被肯定的，Youie 更成為永久性美國榮譽軍人，並在 Fairfield 的分支會時常熱心參加各種社區福利活動。而陳添的孫兒 Locke 畢業於 UC Berkeley後加入軍隊，並在第二次世界大戰諾曼弟戰役時為國犧牲。

很多早期農民家庭的第二及第三代都進入大學，接受高等教育。畢業後他們以這些所學技術，幫助自己成為專業人員，或為家庭管理果園，或有很多從事非農業職業。

　　傳統中國文化以人死歸故土。所以很多早期加州華裔，死後也把其骨灰，運回故鄉家族陵墓入土為安。陳添的家庭也依照習俗。在 1923 年陳添死後，其子 Youie 也將其骨灰帶回中國故鄉入土。但在 1970 年後，新一代的美籍華裔，因時間與環境關係，當他們準備又把陳添骨灰由中國帶回美國，其後代子孫對此亦有所新理解。加上當時美國與中國開始發展新的政治關係，最後，在 1978 年，陳添的骨灰被帶回美國加州。最後，他的骨灰被安葬在蘇地的 Rockville 墳場。這裡距離 Hatch 大農場不遠。他的墳旁還葬有其妻 Ding Shee，及三個兒子，Gum，Sam 及 Youie。

　　很多早期中國農民先驅及其後裔也被埋於 Rockville 墓地。在這蘇宣谷地並沒有任何規定分劃中國人與白人的埋葬地方。很多早期華工被埋在 Rockville 墳場下的一些沒有立墓碑的山坡。而陳添及其他華裔墓碑就距離在 A.T. Hatch 的不遠的墓。

　　這些早期農民先驅者時常為後人所懷念。每當清明時節，也就是每年傳統的中國掃墓日。不同家庭的後代子孫，集合一起到這 Rockville 墳場拜祭一下，依照傳統慣例，以全隻燒豬，鮮花，水果當祭品，一一排列在墓

前，更以香燭，紙錢，等燒給已逝去的親人，希望他們在天有所享用。並且燃燒起鞭炮驅走魔鬼，孝子兒孫也恭敬地在祖先墓碑前叩頭三次，以示敬意。這些傳統是僅存的一點點華人習俗，仍然為加州蘇宣的後代華裔子孫所遵行。這些是華裔早期農民先驅家庭在蘇宣谷地祖先所遺留下的精神，又是美國華裔歷史在蘇宣谷地的重要一頁。

向余江月桂女士致上敬意

畢庭上校・崔以聞

「從一個洗衣坊工人的女兒，到教育家，立法議員，加
州州務卿，美國大使到一個藝術家之過程」

介紹

余江月桂博士在加州政府擔任州務卿五任，從一
九七四年到一九九四年長達二十年之久。一九
七四年，當她被選為加州州務卿時的選票，高
達三百萬張。在第三次連任時，投給她的選票已經超過
五百萬張之多。當她連任到第五任時候，投票給她的擁
護者顯示，已是全部選民的百分七十五至七十八之間的
數字了。她是加州歷史上，第一位女性更是第 位華裔
美人在一九六六年參政的加州立法議員。她的參政就此
將加州政壇改觀，更代表了華裔人士的心聲。由她倡議
四百件以上的立法議案中顯示她博學多才的特殊智慧才

華。

　　在她未當選奧克蘭和卡斯楚谷地區市議員前，余江月桂博士曾連續被選為三任阿拉米達學區委員，和最後第三任委員長。

　　她在加州柏克萊大學取得學士學位，在 Mills 大學取得碩士學位，並在史丹福大學讀得博士榮銜。她曾於奧克蘭市學區，阿拉米達學區以及聖他克來若學區任教，並擔任教育督導。更在母校 Mills 大學任職授課。

　　余江月桂博士是加州第三代華裔美人。以她超越不凡在加州以至於美國的政治經歷，她都應在加州以及亞裔美人的歷史上，佔著一席重要地位。一些歷史家，政治學家，傳記學家，著作家以及考察學者們在她在任時風光一世時，都極盡能事的搜集資料去了解她的貢獻和成就。她以充沛的精力運用在行憲和行政方面，並在選民之權益法，選民登記，為建設加州文獻庫大樓籌款奔走，為促進加州農作物出口到全國以及全世界各地而建立功效，是有目共睹共應大書一筆的。

　　在本書中，我們頌揚她為華裔美人在加州政府獲得最高權位者。我們對她的贊揚不是只限於她在政治領導方面的成就，而實際上她是給我們大家的靈魂啟示，並帶領我們繼續發展，共同建造更好的加州下一代。她不只在美國社會中深受愛戴，而且代表華人民族特色的真正加州及美國人。她鼓勵大家，不要被時常壟斷華人作代罪羔羊的美國政黨們脅迫而卻步，並不能放棄的為爭

華人在加州一百五十年的歷史　　　　　　　　　　85

取華人的地位及形象而努力。不要屈服在一些偏激的政客與媒體下。此外，我們更應為做一個真正在加州的華裔美人之權益而奮鬥。在談判雙方的利益和權利時，我們應同時敬愛中美兩個國家，身為華裔美人，應有公平的判斷態度。

結論

余江月桂博士得到的獎狀無數。從當地社團到學術或政治機構，從州政府到聯邦政府，更包括美國國內到世界各地區等。她雖於一九九七年從駐麥克尼西亞大使卸任回國退休，但是卻從未在華人社區以至美國政壇消失。她除了繼續循循善誘華人下一代多多參政外，更以十年時間，抽空努力學習中國水彩畫與書法。她還更上一層樓的，以她在中國水彩畫所學基礎，發展到油畫方面去而開創新天地。她的作品曾公開在美國加州、台灣以及中國各地展覽過。

沙加緬度中華文化基金會以出版「紀念加州華人來美 150 年——緬懷先人，共創未來」向余江月桂博士致敬。我們深以余博士為榮。相信所有華裔美國機構以及其他組織等，都將跟隨您偉大的精神，共同邁向新的世紀。

加州首府傳奇的餐館業巨子—鄧世發先生（1904-1997）

梁靜源　教授・梁張愛齡

　　Frank Fat 餐館距州府大樓僅兩街之隔，多年來顯貴富商雲集，從歷屆州長、議員、游說者、政府要員、社會名流、乃至觀光客莫不以在該餐館用膳為樂為榮。該餐館的老板是鄧世發先生。一九七一年當他宣佈退休時，加州首府的政要與知名商界人士紛紛前往祝賀。加州議會兩院通過一項不同凡響的議案，稱頌鄧先生為「傳奇的餐館主人」，嘉賞「Frank Fat」為加州首府的第二政經中心美名。

　　鄧世發先生身為中國移民，他于 1919 年來到美國，他的餐館業在過去六十年來常為報章報導，他的為人與經營餐館更受人津津樂道，雖然他受教育不多，英語能

力有限，加上在六十年代以前的華人地位低微，而他能扭轉不良的情況，奮力經營，以他的言行創出卓越成就，已成為華裔與新移民的典範。作者謹從各方收集資料，並訪問了鄧先生數次整理成文，以保存華人在美的一點史料。

鄧世發一九零四年五月十二日出生於廣東省台山縣護龍鄉。他的曾祖父是地主，妻妾成群，共生子女十五人。他的祖父排行老二，曾任清政府官員，在順德（約在台山以外四十五哩）工作，後來在順德開辦酒米的生意。鄧的父親和鄧自己都曾在這個環境下生活。

鄧還是小孩子的時候，他的父親前往美國謀生，所以兒童時代，鄧特別得祖父關愛。鄧是唯一的兒子，他有一個姐姐一個妹妹。他在鄉間住了十四年，那裡大約有二百名居民。鄉村的學校很小，但足夠容納附近各鄉的孩子上學。學生在學校學習中國書法，讀四書，以及中國文學。鄧世發回憶說，「我不是最好的學生，但也不是最笨的。」

雖然中華民國在一九一一年建立，但內戰和農民運動一直未已。鄧孩提時代的華南，就是軍閥、農會和本地秘密會社爭據的地方，當地政府無力保護人民的性命和財產，而盜賊猖獗，經常偷竊他祖父商店的酒，豬；有一次甚至想擄綁鄧的祖父。最後，鄧的祖父只有結束生意，回到鄉間居住。鄧世發記得他十四歲那一年，「有一天，我的祖父，他那時已經七十三歲了，問我到底想

留在家中，還是上學，還是去海外。」那個時候，鄧世發像很多中國人一樣，聽過不少在美國金山發財致富的故事，夢想有一天也會發達，所以他決定去美國。今天他仍記得「鄰里事實上也真有人從美國滿載而歸的。他們經常只提到美好的一面。」

但當鄧世發真正來到美國後，他就像很多中國移民一樣，捱盡艱辛，並且要迂迴的避過一八八二年通過的排華法案規定，用「假紙」入美——那是一些假的身份證明，證明入美者是美籍公民的兒子或可合法入美的商人。排華法案直至一九四三年才予撤銷。所以，鄧世發在十四歲開始，先在他舅父廣州的商店工作兩年，除住宿外並無薪水。而他祖父則為他找一張假紙來美。在鄧世發十六歲時，他祖父終於給他找來一張假紙，估計花費一千元。

鄧世發於是乘坐南京號的輪船來美。他坐的是三等艙，一路暈船，而且發現攜他來美的「假紙父親」冷酷粗暴。一九一九年他終於來到三藩市，那年他十六歲。

他的假紙父親黃先生立刻准予登岸。因為一九零六年大地震，很多紀錄都被焚毀了，所以黃先生也像很多中國移民一樣，利用機會，說他是「土生」的華裔。但是鄧世發就被扣留在天使島超過一個多月。「我只准在島上一些地方走走，我甚至不知道天使島的全貌是怎樣的，直至八十年代天使島修葺過以州歷史公園開放後，我和家人才有機會前往那裡野餐，」鄧世發回憶說。當

他最後准予上岸後，黃先生就帶他從三藩市去沙加緬度找他的叔叔。他叔叔先已移民來美。

雖然鄧世發是以「黃炳元」的假紙名字來美，並且繼續在法律文件使上用這個名字，但在華人的圈子裡，大家都知道他叫鄧世發。後來他並以「Fat 發」來做姓氏。三十年代，他選了一個美國名字法蘭克（Frank），然後開始用發字來做姓。「發」在中文是發財興旺的意思，他選來做姓氏，亦屬喻意吉祥。

鄧世發三十六歲的叔叔早在幾年前移民來美，在沙加緬度開設一家名為杏瓊林的餐館。這家餐館在一九零六年開業，是省府歷史最悠久的餐館之一。但是，杏瓊林無法聘請鄧世發工作，而鄧的叔叔家中又太小，無法容納鄧世發，所以無錢無職業和無家可歸的鄧世發，只好睡餐館地庫的樓梯。鄧說，在那些日子裡，「它對我來說已足夠。」換取在餐館樓梯棲身，鄧要留在餐館幫忙，做各種雜務。

後來他叔叔的朋友為這個年輕人在瑟打會所（Sutter Club）找到一份洗碗的工作。但兩個星期不到，鄧就被碗碟割傷，結果也無法保住職業。在復元期內，鄧在商業區一家中國教會內學習英文。

鄧的第二份工作，那是在長春藤美容院 Ivy Beauty Salon 入洗髮水，每星期週薪是三元。「有一星期天，老闆和他的女兒拿來我的外衣，並指著門外，」鄧回憶當年，笑著說，「我以為再次被人解僱，所以就一氣走回華

埠。後來我才知道她們是想帶我一起去野餐。那時我的英語太差,無法明白。」

一九二零年收成季節時,他在近 Courtland 一個果園工作了整個夏天,與其他青年人工作,並與幾名華裔的大學生,住在果園的簡陋工人宿舍裡。大部份的果農都是來自中國中山縣,因此他們都會先照顧自己的鄉里。來自其他地方的摘果工人,例如鄧世發(他是台山人),就被派摘一些難摘的,果實細小的生果,使他們的工作較難,收入也較少。但是,在收成季工作結束後,鄧世發仍然賺到七十元,夠他前往下一個目的地俄亥俄州了。

當鄧世發的一個表兄決定在 Akron 開一家洗衣店時,鄧世發就跟他工作。根據美國一九二零年的人口普查統計,在美國 45,614 的華工中,有 11,438 在餐館工作,12,599 在洗衣店工作。雖然鄧世發不喜歡洗衣的工作,但仍然感激,有機會留在表兄處。在 Akron,鄧找到他的生父鄧毅龍 Dong Ngai-Long。他父親那時住在奇里夫蘭,在一間中餐館做廚師。在他父親說服餐館老闆,在鄧世發做廚房幫工後,父子二人一起在廚房工作,晚上就在餐館的地庫睡覺。

做了一個短時期後,鄧父的朋友說服鄧父拿出他數目不大的積蓄,買入俄州 Youngstown 市一間餐館。但因為經濟不景氣,像很多生意一樣,餐館在幾個月後無法維持下去。鄧父對美國法律和程序並不熟悉,把門關上

就此離去。在這段情緒艱難的日子裡，年輕的鄧世發頗有不知何去何從感覺，也不知道下一頓飯是否有著落。

「我父親餐館的經理給我七十五元，叫我前往底特律，那裡有一些他的朋友或可幫忙，」鄧回憶說。第二年他先後在 Grand Rapids、芝加哥和其他中西部的城市多個餐館工作。在芝加哥，年齡未足十七歲的鄧世發，與一些華裔的大學生同住，有機會改善自己的「英語能力和了解美國文化，及改善做收拾盤碗和侍者的工作能力。」

他父親在俄州 Youngstown 經營餐館失敗時年約五十歲，最後決定回國。因為他的妻子在一九二三年去世，鄧父再娶，然後再回到沙加緬度。悲哀的是，三十年代大蕭條，生活迫人，迫使六十多歲的鄧父走上自殺的道路。

鄧世發二十歲時，他的祖父叫他回國一行，回到中國。回國後，他知道他母親亦已過世。一年後憑媒妁之言家裡為他娶來妻子。雖然他想回校讀書，但他成全了家中的願望，在一九二四年十二月十八日，他和互不相識的余麗清結為夫婦。余來自香港的望族，所以結婚典禮十分隆重正式。

余小姐在一九零八年十一月二十七日，於廣東開平縣出生。她是家中七個兄弟姊妹中最小的一個。余家在香港經營三里建築公司。余回憶說，「我們是一個大家庭，有錢，有很多僕人。例如，當我結婚時，我有兩個

侍女陪我入鄧家，是我的嫁奩之一。」

　　新婚的年輕夫婦留在中國一年，在一九二五年他們的孩子榮啟出生。在那幾個月裡，鄧也有機會和他有錢的，有政治興趣的表兄鄧卓龍 Dong Cho-Long 一起；他表兄那時是國民黨員。

　　鄧卓龍是從菲律賓回來的退休商人，在廣州財政部工作。雖然鄧世發已經記不起是什麼原因了，但他表兄特別喜歡他。鄧世發結婚後，他表兄請他和他一起往廣州。鄧就跟他一起，「我陪他出席很多聚會。我們認識不同的人，有機會嚐試各種美味食物；那是一個增廣見聞，也是很適意的假期。」但鄧世發最後仍然是決定回美。

　　在美國工作七年後，鄧世發知道在美謀生殊不容易。雖然每年逢年過節時他都有匯錢回鄉給他祖父，或寄錢給親戚慶賀他們的生日，他自己則儘量節省，非常儉用。他的表兄曾教導他關於「金錢的力量」，及告訴他政治人物的奢華生活。這些達官貴人很多時在廣州的觀音山尼姑庵內，或在珠江的花艇上宴會，一些被尼姑收養的年輕孤女，就要出來招呼客人娛賓。鄧世發說「我知道很多有錢有勢力的人都參與政治，腐敗不堪，但我那時年紀輕，而我也實在是局外人。」在他參加或自己做主人的很多聚會中，他都感到適意開心，而人們似乎也樂於與他交往。所以那段時期，他開始改變省吃儉用的態度，開始發展公共關係的手腕，打入有錢有影響力的圈子。

華人在加州一百五十年的歷史

一九二三年鄧世發回到中國的時候，他帶回一千五百美元——那是不夠用來又要生活又要與朋友尋歡作樂的。幸運的是，他表兄在他有需要時都願意借錢給他。在他欠他表兄七千多元港幣時，他表兄患病去世。因為這些借貸都是口頭協議，鄧世發可以不負責任，但他還是儘快還清借款給表兄的家人。為了要還債，鄧世發在一九二六年回來美國，留下妻子和出生不久的孩子在國內。

　　在不景氣年代的芝加哥，鄧世發在多家中國和美國餐館任收拾盤碗工。那個時候，很多餐館關閉，能夠繼續營業的，做侍應的無薪水可拿，賺的是小費和住宿而已。鄧世發和其他十一名侍者傾盤所有，合資買了一間洗衣店。如有人失業時，就暫時在洗衣店內工作和棲身。鄧從未在這店內工作，但他需負照應生意的一點責任。也在同一時期，華人堂口（幫派）都在爭地盤以求生存。「當堂口發現洗衣店的賣主仍欠他們錢時，他們就要我和我的合伙人還錢，並威脅如不還錢就倒閉我們的生意，」鄧回憶說。他立刻前往堂口解決事件而無須多花一文，雖然現在他說，「我實在不知那裡來的膽量和能力，居然那時能解決此事。」

　　一九三零年，在芝加哥工作四年後，鄧世發再回到沙加緬度，為他叔叔重新裝修位於「I」街的杏瓊林工作。杏瓊林有一個酒吧和舞池，是那時被認為華埠和商業區最富麗的餐館之一。鄧任經理、招待，有時也做侍

應，每月收入不足一百元，但他的管理能力日見幹練，又與很多加州的政要培養出友誼。這些州長、立法議員、法官、游說者和商人，幫助鄧世發認識美國政治變化多端的奇妙世界。鄧世發驕傲的說，「自 Jimmy Rolph（1931-1934）起至現在的州長止，我認識所有歷任的加州州長。」

　　前加州副州長（1954-60）Harold Powers 在一九三三年初任加州立法議員時認識鄧世發。他記得「鄧負責招呼我們的桌子。他看來認識所有的政要及議員們。我想整個加州沒有人比他認識這麼多政要了。他記得每個人的名字，有幽默感，有禮，客人都喜歡他。」

　　那時賭博在加州仍然合法。杏瓊林的地庫有玩基諾的牌戲，聚賭的大多是中國人。有一天，一名有名望的州政府官員前來午餐，說有興趣買一張基諾票。他劃票後鄧世發就拿到地庫為他付錢。結果這張五角錢的博彩票為他贏得七百元，但這名官員在博彩未開始之前已離去。鄧世發為他留下贏得的金錢，等到第二次他回來晚飯時交回給他──他這種誠實的作風，為他贏得那名官員畢生的友誼。後來鄧世發決定自己開餐館時，這名官員就借錢給他。

　　在一九六三年移民法修改之前，華人男子通常都是單身來美。鄧的妻子余麗清回憶說，「那時很少有商人可以攜同妻兒來美，因為經濟的考慮，也因為移民法的規定。」鄧世發也無例外，他和妻子分開有十年。他妻子

和長子榮啟，那時就輪流住在鄧家或香港的娘家。

余麗清並不熱衷移民來美：因為她父親是從紐約回去的，在美有不愉快的經驗，所以反對她移民。但日子一天天過去，她開始擔心不斷更改的移民法可能影響孩子，因為孩子到某一個年歲就不准移民，她怕她十歲大的兒子榮啟無法進入美國；所以在一九三六年，在此憂慮下，以及在鄧世發的敦促下，余麗清和榮啟最後來美與鄧世發在沙加緬度團聚。

鄧世發在申請妻兒來美時，用的是黃炳元的名字。雖然證件是合法的，但移民官員對「假紙」制度已有認識，所以余麗清和榮啟入美時可能受到刁難。他們不知道中國婦女很多在十六、七歲即已出嫁，所以認為余年紀太輕，無可能有十歲的兒子。但鄧世發在沙加緬度很多政界有力的朋友都力促移民局早日批准她和孩子入境，余回憶說，「在天使島的查問時間非常簡短；官員很快就讓我們上岸，正式入美。」

來美後余麗清改了一個美國名字叫「瑪莉」，這是她一生中第一次家中沒有傭人幫手。她需要學習自己做家務，並適應新環境。在夏天，她又在商業區的 Del Monte 罐頭廠工作，做了七個夏季。在這段期間，她多生了兩個孩子，她認為這是她一生「最辛苦的歲月」。經過七年及多了兩個孩子後，鄧世發建議她不要再在夏天工作，以便能專心照顧家庭。但她的工作並未減少：身為主婦，她要煮食和清潔房子，要照料小孩，要在後園種中國蔬

菜和養雞。鄧和她最後共有六名子女——四男二女。

　　成功的開始。一九三九年，位於沙加緬度 806 L Street 的 Truckadero 餐館出售。雖然餐館殘舊不堪，但鄧世發仍想把它買下來。「我的朋友都以為我發瘋了，」鄧說，「但我知道這間餐館的位置比杏瓊林好，因為它距離州府只有兩個街口。」鄧並且對自己在杏瓊林工作多年，招呼及攏絡客人的能力有自信。他用自己的儲蓄，加上那名他將 Keno 獎金送還的官員的借款，使他有足夠的款項把餐館買下來並進行裝修。他將餐館改名 Frank Fat's。開張後，他與十二名伙計每天工作十六小時，慢慢把生意做開來。他的午餐賣三角半，晚餐八角半，又在星期五晚給所有的女士每人一朵白蘭花。他用玻璃將廚房和餐廳間開，以便客人可以看到廚房的清潔運作，因而有效的打破人們認為中國廚房污穢不堪的傳言。八個月後他的餐館開始賺錢，吸引了州府和其他商業界的客人。

　　餐館的環境，特別使政客和遊說者感到賓至如歸。Harold Powers 說，「如我來沙市，我會到 Frank Fat's 去，鄧會告訴我什麼人來了沙加緬度。就像回家一樣。」在這個氣氛下，在餐館內進行了很多政治活動是不足為奇的。在州議會工作二十七年多的 Norva Muse 說，「在我任職州議會時，很多提案都是在 Frank Fat's 餐館內誕生和通過的。」Larry Liebert 在《三藩市紀事報》中寫道，「在 Frank Fat's，遊說者都喜歡設宴招待立法議員。他

們都將新議員介紹給鄧認識，就像是前來沙加緬度的入會儀式一樣。」有些客人並稱鄧為「鄧參議員」。愈來愈多人知道他為人慎言慎行，不偏不倚；此外，他也有機會知道一些機密的資料，加深了他對美國政治運作的認識和運用。

當問及為什麼加州政府的精英和有力人士都接受他時，鄧說，「我是經營餐館的人，我聽到很多東西。但我從來不會將聽來的話傳出去。所以我的客人在這裡開會、談判和聯歡，都感到舒服安全。」雖然鄧一直小心將政治和經營餐館生意分開，他也機靈的利用資訊從中得益。更重要的是，他從來不會忘記感謝支持他的官員和朋友。經營餐館多年，使鄧打下穩固的經濟基礎，也聯繫上不少重要和有力的客人。鄧世發在進入中年時期開始了人生新的里程碑。

一九三九年不只是鄧開始創業的一年，也是他開始利用美國政治制度，以「自我委任遊說者」的身份，為同胞和祖國爭取福利的一年。鄧回憶說，那年，「我在報上讀到三藩市碼頭上有華人示威，抗議美國將貨物運往日本。我強烈的感到，我亦應該在沙加緬度做些類似的事。」他向代表 Red Bluff 參議員 Jack Metzger 表示看法，不久，州參院即提出聯合決議第十號並在一月通過為241939 決議。決議說：

鑒於，日本身為一九二八年巴黎和約及一九二一至二二年華盛頓九國條約的簽署國之一但不履行其責任，

無理的向中華民國宣戰，

決議，加州立法議會敦促美國政府禁止將武器、彈藥以及戰爭材料從美國運往日本‧‧‧。

鄧取得這個成功後，受到鼓舞，開始介入影響華裔重要問題的活動。

二次大戰開始後，鄧的生意稍為淡下來：因為供應不足，所以餐館不是天天營業。他要在沙加緬度外探索新的商業機會，於是進入了一個他不熟悉的世界——面對一個困難的局面。

沙加緬度的檢察官 Ernest Babcock 邀請鄧世發前往太浩湖 Lake Tahoe，考慮在那裡開業經營餐館。Babcock 安排他在太浩湖的 Bijou Motel 下榻。但他和家人只留在那裡一晚。第二天早上，旅館的經理抱歉的對他說，中國人不能入住該旅店。這個侮辱，使鄧感到憤怒。在 Babcock 仍未知道發生什麼事之前，他就回到沙加緬度。鄧說，「當 Babcock 知道情況後，他問為什麼我不控告旅店。但我知道社會的情形——歧視是存在的。打官司要用很多錢，而且我也沒有這樣的時間。」但他對基本的不公仍然有所回應：他決意要改變美國人對華人的形象，所以決心回太浩湖。第二年，Ernest Babcock 和三個朋友每人投資了二萬五千元在鄧開設的賭場—餐館。他們推舉鄧負責主持一切。以後三年每個周末，鄧都開車前往太浩湖查察業務。連接太浩湖和沙加緬度有兩條公路，他去時走一條，回來時走另一條。在途中，他會

在很多餐館、酒吧和咖啡店停下來，認識同行，介紹自己也是同業，而且是一名中國人。

「我的想法，」鄧回憶，「是儘量與愈多的美國人有個別的接觸愈好，以便他們有機會認識中國人。我相信中國人有很多良好的品格，但中國人必須幫助美國人認識我們。」

但管理兩家車程相距五小時的餐館，實在是太大的負擔了。在二次大戰時，鄧的長子榮啟被召入伍，遣派到太平洋，所以鄧只有一人負責經營兩間餐館。瑪莉記得有很多個無法入睡的晚上，她抱著四個孩子在床頭，擔心鄧開車來往太浩湖的安全。三年後，鄧和他的合伙人將太浩湖的生意出售。他重新將注意力集中在沙加緬度的餐館。餐館愈來愈受歡迎，成為加州立法議員和遊說者的消閒和「非正式接觸」的地方。今天，鄧同意「在那些年，我的妻子負責照顧孩子，而我則專心照顧生意，每天最少工作十六小時。孩子長大成材，全是妻子的功勞。」

瑪莉除照料家庭外，也有自己的興趣，在四十年代參與華裔社區的活動。她是在一九四三年在沙加緬度成立的中國婦女會的活躍會員，該會支持中華民國抗日。一九四三年，蔣宋美齡來美在美國國會演說宣揚中國抗日，及從美國的華裔社區籌款支持中國政府。瑪莉說，「我背著孩子幫助中國慈善協會籌備籌款活動。我並將所有孩子的金鏈和利是捐出。我愛我的祖國和人民。今天我

年紀大了，不再活躍於中國婦女會了。這個機構需要一些新血和新方向，服務社區。」

鄧認識州長華倫 Earl Warren，是一九三九年至四三年華倫任加州檢察總長時。鄧說，「華倫州長前來餐館時，經常叫雞炒麵。Goodwin Knight 州長生動多采，而華倫州長則較為友善。他與餐館所有人等均打成一片。但雷根 Reagan 州長就不是很有趣。」

一九五七年，沙加緬度的中國慈善會推選鄧世發為兩名出席全美華裔大會的代表之一。美華協會在首都華盛頓開會，討論遊說促進華人福利修改移民法事宜。鄧在華盛頓開會期內，走訪他的老朋友，現在為美國大法官的華倫（1953-69）。在華倫邀請下，鄧世發「前往高院，典禮官已在等候，陪我內進。進入法庭後，他們讓我坐在第一排。華倫想我看看法院的運作程序。我看到九位高院法官，華倫坐在正中，還有兩名律師。他們都全身禮服，討論一宗案件，但沒有辯論。我從來沒有看過這樣肅靜的法庭。半小時後，典禮官陪我入華倫的辦公室，他拿出一瓶威士忌兩隻杯。我們對飲談了一會。我感到非常光榮。」

在兩個世界的成功。早在一八五二年時，沙加緬度有八百一十四名華裔居民，最早的華埠是位於 I、J、五街和六街的街口，後來人口增至 2,331 人，到一八六零年，華埠已擴展至沿 I 街從三街至六街的地方，這是華人生活的中心，直至一九六八年重建華埠為止。差不多

有一個世紀，華人只能在這狹小人口過份擠迫的地方居住。在五十年代，一些富有的華人家庭，包括鄧家，希望搬出華埠。當他找到一些想搬入的地區後，人們告訴他不是沒有房子出售，就是房子不會售給華人。鄧世發對此已不感到驚訝。他告訴他的白人朋友，有一名牙醫幫助他在華埠外面找到一間房子。其他華人亦找到方法，通過他們的美國朋友，解決類似的個人和商業問題──這是當年華人生活的情況。

鄧世發希望改善華人的居住環境，建議成立一家非牟利機構在華埠以外購買土地。他在西沙加緬度的 Hotel El Rancho 主持一個會議，邀請很多華裔商人共商大計。但是他的建議對華人社區的其他人來說太前進：這些人長期受到社會和政治情況的威　　，無法在一夜之間克服他們的保守意識。此外，亦有人懷疑鄧世發的動機何在。所以，沒有人認真考慮或支持他的建議。數十年後，鄧回憶說，「回想當年，我有意購買的土地價格不過是每畝二百元，現在這塊土地已經成為高級住宅區的所在了。」

鄧以未曾接受過正式教育引為一生憾事。他為孩子捐書教學，看著他們一個個成為專業人士，引以為傲：「我告訴我的孩子，在這個國家，我是一個未受過教育的人，我知道我可以做生意成功，但有限制。我告訴他們教育對他們未來的重要。我知道自己的感受。我知道這些年來沒有受過教育的艱辛。」

對孩子來說，非正式的教育也同樣重要。鄧世發從

來沒有規限孩子走的人生路，沒有規限他們在婚姻和事業上的選擇。但他要每個孩子──甚至一些孫兒孫女──在餐館工作一些時間。從收拾盤碗做起，像所有其他的伙計一樣，讓他們熟習生意，鼓勵他們經營家庭企業的紀律性。

他也嘗試教育華人社區，分享他對美國文化的認識：

我明白美國政治的重要和主要特色。我們必須參與公民和社區活動。我們必須捐款支持政治家，可以在立法議會上遊說；否則，無人會理會或重視我們。所以我經常鼓勵年輕一輩的華人，參與公共事務，組織起來。華人社區有很多小的組織，但仍未有一個強力的機構可以處理很多華人面對的社會和政治問題。過去通過很多歧視華人的法案。我們必須在提案未通過之前消除它。我很不安，因為我們華人仍未能明白在美國政治上這些做法。

多年來他一直敦促華人參與政治，他通過像中國慈善協會一類的組織鼓勵華人參政，並在一九五七年遊說改善移民法。但他最大的號召力，可能還是他本人，而不是通過正式機構的號召。例子之一，是他曾嘗試組織沙加緬度的商人成立一個非牟利機構，在華埠以外購置土地，對抗白人在房屋上的歧視。較近期的是在一九七二年，然後是一九八六年，他發信給華人社區的成員，表示他有意成立一個華人的組織，加強華人在商業、經

濟和政治方面的影響。他的信件請大家出席會議幫助成立這個組織。而他自己本人亦有以身作則,加入主流的美國組織。他是本地和全國餐館業協會的會員,也是獅子會和其他社區團體的會員。主流社會對他的承認,例子不勝枚舉,其中包括被選入大沙加緬度區商業名人錄,及出任像三藩市聯邦房屋儲貸會的董事等。州參議員 Bill Campbell 和議會議長 Willie Brown 亦曾向他頒發「加州州章」。

退休即開始:一九七一年在創辦餐館三十二年後,鄧世發退休,他的兒子榮啟成為 Frank Fat's 的新經理。其他的兒子和媳婦甚至孫兒孫女,都放棄他們的工作,投入擴大這個家庭生意,並成立一個基金會。自一九七五年起,鄧家多開兩家餐館,那是在舊沙加緬度的 China Camp 和 Fat City;後來在八十年代,又在聖地牙哥開分店。

鄧雖然退休,但生活並沒有閒下來。他不過將精力放在別的方面。當尼克遜於一九七二年訪問中國後,鄧曾數次前往中國,推動兩國的貿易、文化和教育活動,並在美國這方面努力推行。每次提到中國時,他就充滿驕傲:

數百年來中國受盡外人的欺凌。在一九六六至七六年文革時期,中國人不敢做些什麼。但自從政府改變政策後,它歸還部份以前徵收的物業給海外華僑。現在中國明白要努力迎頭趕上。中國人努力再度重建自信。

我是一個美籍華人，對此引以為榮。雖然在文化和生活上我們有不同，但第二代的華裔應該以他們的祖先為榮。我讓所有年輕的親人都回訪中國，讓他們認識本身的傳統。

除了是新中國教育基金的董事外，鄧世發很多時都資助一些小型計劃。其中一個計劃是始自廣東，但最後在沙加緬度終成其事，那是鄧世發捐錢「重建小時候在鄉間上過學的學校。」

尾聲。四十五年來，Frank Fat's 是一家樸素、深沉和充滿家庭氣氛的餐館。一九八四年六月十八日，餐館經過六個月的關閉裝修後重開，煥然一新，在街外舉行盛宴，由鄧世發和家人親自招待八千多名來賓──一時傳為佳話，被《沙加緬度蜂使報》Sacramento Bee 選為當年的十大新聞之一。

與舊"Frank Fat's"強調東方色彩的風格迥然不同，新"Frank Fat's"的洋紅、玫瑰紅和苔綠色的設計，是一個經過深思熟慮的大膽創新，但鄧榮啟認為這也是一個增加食客歡愉的設計，是一個酬謝多年來幫助他父親餐館得到成功的顧客的禮物。新餐館有名貴的中國畫作和文物擺設，包括一件有龍紋的皇家侍衛（約一八八零年製）制服，美侖美奐的屏風，精雕鑲板，和一個大型的金製笑口佛。最引人矚目的，是一張十一呎高垂下的絲織錦。（這幅織錦，曾經為墨西哥總統夫人所有，後來曾懸掛在北京劇院）。有些人認為新餐館代表了創辦人生命的新

樣貌，揉合傳統和現代，中國和美國。

　　像其他族裔移民一樣，中國移民因為戰亂、飢荒和天災以致生計困難，最後離鄉別井。歷史學家和人口學家分析移民潮時，每每從經濟和政治因素著眼。但每個移民數字的增加，亦代表了個人離開自己土地在新文化冒險奮鬥的心路歷程。我希望鄧世發的故事，可以讓我們從美國的社會和文化的角度加以了解，從而更深認識美國的文化多元面貌。

黃家的美國之夢：
Bel Air 超級市場的故事

葉殷　博士・周玉笑

這個故事是為紀念華人在加州一百五十年而編寫的。敘述黃家成功的經歷頗為合適。以下是按編年方式，描出黃家從第一代開始直至現在的苦與甘。

第一代

　　台山縣是中國南部最窮的一個縣城，只有百分之十的土地可以耕種，且常遭旱災或海鹹水的入滲，災難連年。因此，台山種植所得，僅夠支持縣中四分之一的人口生活。它三面是山，一面向水，和內陸做生意更為困難（Chan， 19）。為了逃避貧窮，縣內的男子逼而出外謀生。由一八四二年至一九四三年的一百年，移民來美

的華人，有百分之七十以上是來自四邑：新會、台山、開平和恩平（Chan，16-17）。

　　為了追尋較好的生活，黃遠宗一直計劃出外謀生，所以離開家鄉中國廣東省台山縣的牛黃（Nun Hung）村。一八六八年，他十六歲橫渡太平洋，加入數以千計的華工行列，登陸進入勞工缺乏的加州。當時加州不只需要勞工建築鐵路、掘礦和在農田收成，而且需要勞工從事一些傳統上婦女擔任的工作，例如洗衣和煮食（Sandmeyer，14）。雖然早期的華人移民，主要是礦工和做生意，但自一八六五年至一八七零年間，這些移民散佈各個地方，有種田的、從事製造業的、掌廚的，和做礦工的（Chan，52-63）。

　　黃遠宗來到加州新堡鎮（Newcastle）佃農為生，成為移民農工的第一代。華人因為很快學會務農技巧、且以信實和辛勤工作得到工作機會。加州農業因華工的努力，以一八七二年為例，加州的農產品中，有三分之二是出自華人農工的成果（Chan，84-85）。

　　黃遠宗在加州工作二十五年後，終於儲夠旅費返回中國。在四十歲時，才和十八歲的譚氏結婚，這是他父母為他安排的年輕媳婦。他和妻子相聚的時間很短，結婚一年後，當妻子仍懷著他女兒的時候，黃遠宗再次離開家鄉和妻子，重回美國求生。

　　早期華人移民中，像黃遠宗一樣，經常來往美國與中國的不少。他們很多人都將家人留在家鄉，自己在美

國工作，一心準備賺夠錢，償還家中的債務且能置田買地。在達到這些目標後，他們就會返國回鄉。像很多華人一樣，黃遠宗也是以一個「暫時旅客」的遊子身份，準備賺夠錢後，能夠回鄉享受美好的生活。

黃遠宗先後回國四次，生了兩個兒子：榮光（一九零零年出生）和榮宗（一九零六年出生）。黃遠宗在加州務農近五十年才回台山。一九二二年，黃遠宗六十九歲，他回到中國，買地置產過活。他的晚年，就在照顧他的家人和種田為業。他在一九三一年去世，享年七十八。他的妻子譚氏在一九四四年去世，享年六十九。

第二及第三代

一九一四年，長子黃榮光十四歲，離開母親到加州尋找父親。像中國很多年輕人一樣，他夢想美國是一個金土。他看到海外華僑賺錢養家、興建學校，最後將台山帶出貧困。前往加州賺錢改善家人的生活，是孝順兒子份內的事。

在黃榮光父親踏足美國以來，已經有四十六個年頭。美國人對華人移民的態度，大多反感。他們不歡迎華工，且政府通過多條法例，阻止華人移民潮。其中最重要的，是一八八二年通過在一九零四年加重的排華法案。這條法例規定，十年內不准再有華人登陸，規定所有移民必須持有居留證件，並不准華人有公民權。為了

要避開這條法例，黃榮光只有用「假紙」身份來美。很多美國華裔公民，在中國探親後回美時，均訛稱他們在中國生有兒子，出賣「假紙」的那些有意要兒子來美的家庭，借機移民美國（Chen， 189）。

　　一九一六年，黃榮光回國娶妻。她的母親安排他和鄰鄉的李氏結婚。在一年內，新婚夫婦生下第一個孩子黃百進。為了要養家，黃榮光再次回到加州，繼續在農田工作。一九二二年，經過五年辛勤工作，他儲夠金錢返鄉，把妻兒帶來美國。他們一家住在含金（Placer）縣，以佃農為生。一九二二年至一九四二年，榮光夫婦再生下了九名子女：振滋（一九二二年出生）、佐治（一九二四年出生）、翠娥（一九二六年出生）、兆棠（一九二七年出生）、兆南（一九二九年出生）、翠眉（一九三一年出生）、守才（一九三三年出生）、翠月（一九三五年出生），和翠容（一九四二年出生）。

　　榮光和李氏在第二個家鄉，要秉承中國的傳統極為困難。在中國，當雙親年老的時候，身為兒子的應該留在他們身邊，侍奉頤年。當榮光的父母年紀日老的時候，要履行這個責任就越見困難。因為榮光不是美國的公民，他最多只能回國一年。所以，榮光一家後來決定讓他們家中第一個美國公民，送第二兒子振滋回家代父盡孝（見圖片），他直至一九三五年回美。（一九二七年，年方五歲的振滋離開父母，回中國與祖父母同住。）

　　一九三二年，榮光和李氏，用他們儲蓄的一點錢，

加上借款，買下加州平陽鎮（Penryn）五畝草木叢生的
荒地。當時（一九零七年）的加州土地法不准華人買地，
他們很多人，卻能避開法律規定，用他們在美國出生的
子女名義購置土地。黃家將土地重新施肥，用來種水果
和蔬菜。後來他們買了一架舊的紅色貨車——紅色在中國
代表好運而富旺的意義——在兩邊加上可以開起的陳列
貨物板，用來做流動的果菜攤子。他們的兒子，百進、
振滋和佐治，跟隨父親同心合力，在安邦（Auburn）區，
沿門叫賣水果蔬菜。這些年輕的商人，在那時候就學懂
了以合理價格，提供超卓服務的重要性，出售高質量產
品。

　　這第三代所學習的考驗和刻苦精神，認知他們的祖
父母和父母的努力，要集中精力在新環境下求生，而他
們就要在這兩個世界中求取平衡。黃家的孩子在美國的
學校讀書，跟隨潮流，學會了美國的生活條件。在家中，
他們和父母親講廣東話，吃中國餐，父母亦期望他們能
秉承中國的傳統。像很多華人移民的孩子一樣，除了上
美國學校外，百進和佐治都被送往新堡鎮（Newcastle）
的中文學校學中文、中國歷史和傳統習慣。在這些影響
下，黃家的孩子都成為「華裔美國人」，接受美國生活方
式的同時，又能保持中國的文化。

轉捩點

二次大戰時，雖然百進沒有入籍的權利，但在一九四二年卻被徵召為陸軍服務。他在盟軍進入諾曼弟時，在連隊任職。D-DAY 盟軍反攻日之後的第七天，他登陸 Omaha。振滋是家中第二名被徵召而參軍的，。一九四三年，他是 13,499 名徵召或募召而成為陸軍的華人之一（Takaki, 373）。他曾在中國、緬甸和印度服役，是著名的第十四空軍聯隊（即飛虎隊）成員。二次大戰是美國華人的轉捩點。在日軍轟炸珍珠港後，美國和中國成為戰爭的盟友。中美共同動員應戰。當時愛國主義高漲，年輕人都以參軍為榮，而年輕的婦女亦參與各種志願工作，支持戰爭。華人在美所遭受到不平等，備受注意，促使在一九四三年撤銷排華法案（Takaki, 375-378）。

　　二次大戰在其他方面對黃家亦有很大影響。在二次大戰時，住在平陽鎮（Penryn）的日裔家庭，都被送往安置中心，他們的商店和生意都被迫關閉。因為這個地區缺少雜貨店，榮光因此在平陽鎮（Pcnryn），開設一家小型雜貨店，在戰爭時期變成店東。於是黃家從農民和小販，轉為商店東主。

柏艾（Bel Air）超級市場

　　戰爭結束後，百進和振滋光榮退役回歸後，兄弟二人在商界和專業工作中各有發展。在幾年間，百進、振

滋和佐治均獨自擁有自己的雜貨店。一九五一年至五三年韓戰期內，兆南被召加入第一偵察師（Cavalry Division）服役。那是五十年代初期，超級市場的概念正在成熟期，三名長兄和父母，及兆南、守才、翠娥開了一個家庭會議。他們決定聚集全家的人才和財力，向超級市場進軍。一九五五年，他們在果壟路（Fruitridge Road）和六十三街，開辦他們在沙加緬度新發展南區的第一間超級市場，以洛杉磯高尚住宅區柏艾（Bel Air）為超級市場的店名。

在第一間超市開張後，他們面對不少挑戰。他們資本有限，需要和強大的全國及區域性連鎖超市競爭。他們從早期叫賣生果的經驗中，繼續以更好服務，更高質素的傳統，來補償規模問題。很快柏艾（Bel Air）超市，就得到沙加緬度家傳戶曉的好名聲。在榮光的領導下，他們的商店逐漸擴展。黃榮光在一九七一年去世，那時柏艾（Bel Air）已經擁有七間分店。榮妻李氏則還眼見第八間分店開幕，她在一九八零年去世。夫婦二人都在去世之前，實現了他們的「美國之夢」。

到一九九二年，黃家共開了二十一間超級市場，僱用員工超過二千六百多人。他們商店每天的生意額合起來超過一百萬。他們和 Raley's Supermarkets 合作，有自己的貨倉發貨生意（West Pac/Western Pacific Food Warehouse），有自己的牛奶廠（Mid-Valley Dairy），和自己生產牛奶產品的工廠。他們現在這個龐大的、現代的、

高級的商店系統，比起黃家早期的小本生意，真是不啻天壤。黃家被認為是業界的領袖，他們提出或加強很多創新和風行的商業特色服務：在六十年代，他們在超市內增加美國郵政局服務站；在七十年代，他們在超市增設花店和餅店；在八十年代，他們的超市，增設可以入坐的咖啡店，壽司吧；提供全面服務的銀行，和錄映帶部門。柏艾（Bel Air）也是第一家在沙加緬度出售中國熟食的超市。在九十年代，他們在商店內增設托兒服務，也是沙加緬度區的第一創舉。

自開辦以來，柏艾（Bel Air）超級市場，一直以「服務週到」而稱譽。他們重視顧客，以更合理的價格，提供最好的產品，最佳的服務。同樣地，他們對待長期顧客，就像家人一般。在社區，他們支持各種慈善計劃，例如「柏艾（Bel Air）飢餓和無家可歸者基金」方案，是一個永久性的基金，幫助一些較為不幸的人。為表揚柏艾（Bel Air）這個回饋社區的計劃，總統特別頒與特嘉獎狀。一九八七年在白宮一個典禮中，里根總統頒給柏艾（Bel Air）總裁黃佐治一個「褒揚私人企業公益行動總統獎狀」（見圖片）。

三名長兄，都活躍於雜貨業和社區事務。百進是沙加緬度華裔雜貨商協會的主席，又是沙加緬度河市銀行（River City Bank）的顧問委員和縣大陪審團成員。振滋參與多個社區和慈善機構的工作。他是全國協助硬化症協會（National Multiple Sclerosis Society）和軍人徵召

委員會（Military Selective Service System）的董事。因為他能通雙語，成為沙加緬度黃氏宗親會的主席，又是黃氏中心的創辦董事（該中心是一所政府補助出租給低收入者英的住宅大廈）。他並擔任沙加緬度中華會館的幹事，在籌款與建孔子廟時，出力良多。佐治是美西超市協會及其食品市場研究學院（Western Association of Food Chains、Food Marketing Institute）和沙加緬度大都會商會的董事。此外，他並擔任加州超市協會（Northern California Grocers）和加州超市分會（California Grocers Association）的主席。

百進、振滋、佐治、兆南、守才五兄弟和翠娥，是 Bel Air 超市的核心份子（見圖片）。他們各有所長，各有貢獻。百進是副總裁，負責農產部。振滋是秘書和司庫，負責財務、物業收購與物業發展。自成立以來，佐治一直是柏艾公司（Bel Air Mart）的總裁。翠娥是辦公室經理，而兆南則先以肉食部經理，後以貨品總監的身份，各表才能做出貢獻。一九五六至五七年間，守才服務海軍；退伍後，他任維修及商店裝修總監。

在九十年代初，這些創辦董事都已經超過退休年齡，進入金色晚年，所以，準備出售商店，真正打算退休。他們考慮了不少可以有意接手經營的公司行號，可以秉持商店聲譽和質素。他們商店的成功，吸引了全國性和國際性的雜貨連鎖店。一九九二年，黃家接受了加州一家最大的雜貨連鎖店 Raley's 的收購。兩家公司曾合

作多次，彼此建立深厚的關係。黃家認為 Raley's 的經
營，最能配合他們顧客和員工的需要，並會繼續將柏艾
超市（Bel Air Market）的名字發揚光大。它將繼續保持
原名，屬於 Raley's 旗下一家重要份子。在出售柏艾超市
（Bel Air Mart）股份給 Raley's 之後，百進、振滋、翠娥、
兆南和守才，在經營這家商業三十七年後退休。佐治留
任柏艾（Bel Air）總裁協調過渡工作，直至一九九五年
才退休。

第四代

　　黃家六名股東的十九名孩子，均曾在這個家庭的商
業中學習工作。像他們的祖父母和父母親一樣，都同樣
的辛勤工作。有些離開這個行業，追尋自己的事業。有
些留下來幫助推進生意。在八十年代，黃家年輕的一代，
創辦酒市公司（Liquor Mart），以優待價售賣烈酒、啤酒
和各類紅白酒。這個龐大的貨倉型商店，最多增至七家，
開始時是頗為革命性的構思。後來他們將這系列商店，
出售給全國性的特價酒商 Liquor Barn。黃家年輕的一
代，並經營一家稱為泛西方運輸公司（Transwest
Transport）的州際貨運公司。這個公司同時服務柏艾超
市（Bel Air Markets）和其他商業運輸工作。該公司在
Raley's 購入柏艾超市（Bel Air Market）的股份後解散。
振滋的兒子黃家利先生（Gary Wong），仍然負責主管黃

氏投資機構（Wong Family Investors LP）業務，這是完全由黃家擁有的物業控股公司。公司的控股，包括柏艾（Bel Air）商店所在的一些購物中心地產。

結論

　　黃家的成功故事，是一個辛勤工作和團結家庭合作的典範。這是一個普通人都能成就大事業的明証。他們實現了「美國之夢」，為未來一代鋪下發展的指標。

　　黃振滋這樣反省：「無論我們取得什麼成功，都是在我們預期之外的。我們要感激祖父母父母的勇氣、犧牲和忍耐，他們含莘如苦，目的在使生活更為美好一點；不只為自己，也為了下一代。他們奠定基礎、鋪好路，並給我們指導，把握美國各種機會。就像前人種樹後來乘涼一樣。」

來源：

Chan, Sucheng，苦樂土：加州農業的華人，1860-1910
　　（柏克萊：加州大學出版社，1986）
Chen, Jack，美國華人（三藩市：Harper & Row
　　Publishers， 1980）

Sandmeyer, Elmer Clarence，加州的反華運動（Urbana：
    伊利諾大學出版社，1973），一九三九年重印本
Takaki, Ronald，來自彼岸的異鄉人：美國亞裔史（波士
    頓：Little, Brown & Company， 1989）

尹集成及尹黃春芳夫婦
建立蘇拉諾縣 (Solano County)
麥當勞快餐事業的成功故事

梁靜源 教授・梁張愛齡
崔以聞譯

導言

尹集成及尹黃春芳夫婦擁有十二家麥當勞
（McDonald）快餐館，衛星式地分布於加州
菲克谷（Vacaville）、肥田市（Fairfield）、瞭
望鎮（Suisun City）和純陽市擁有十二家麥當勞
（McDonald）快餐館。他們從一九八四年創業以來，業
務蒸蒸日上，從當初每年一百萬營業額直線飛升到每年
一千五百萬的業績。今日，在尹氏旗下工作的員工，已
經高達三百五十位。尹氏的事業，是全球成長最迅速的

麥當勞速食連鎖店。這個全球性的連鎖餐館延伸擴展全美及世界各地，且已超越兩萬三千三百多家餐館，銷售了億萬個漢堡餅。

他們夫婦贏得了一九九七年朗龍（Ronald）獎。這個最高榮譽是獎勵傑出麥當勞的業主，或是負責人在社區中有優異貢獻人士而設立。這份獎狀限在每個特定地區裡，發給一名得獎人。他們的榮譽得獎新聞，分別以巨大稱幅登載在一九九七年九月二日的肥田市共和日報（Fairfield Daily Republic）和一九九七年九月七日的菲克谷記者日報（Vacaville Reporter）兩家報紙上。

在一九九六年，加州州議會的第四選區選出尹春芳為一九九六年度的模範婦女。尹春芳對熱心公益，是有目共睹的。在記者招待會中，北加州紅顏城（Redding）州議員張迺傑先生（Maurice Johannessen）表示，任何地方需要義務人員，何種事務需要處理，她總是隨叫隨到，不令人失望。這位議員繼續說，不管她是在學校教導高中學生有關生意業務常識，或是在自己家中舉辦籌款活動，她總是第一名舉手發問，「有什麼我可以效勞的嗎？」

Johannessen 議員又補充說，她的不自私的慷慨作風，充分說明一些在社會中有成功者應對社區回饋的表現，這也是國家美好的原因之一。

在一九九七年三月十一日的國際扶輪社新聞報導中，詳敘尹春芳諸多貢獻，表述她發起並成立萬蒂

（Vanden）和肥田市（Fairfield）兩所高中的「青年交流
社」，領導青少年參加正常有益的活動。

一九九二年九月，菲克谷（Vacaville）市商會推舉
在當時還是資淺的新會員尹集成為董事。他那時已是擁
有四家麥當勞連鎖速食店。在後來四年中，他很快就當
選為菲克谷市商會的會長。在新會長的就職典禮上，嘉
賓顯要紛紛光臨致賀，車水馬龍的出席人數高達七百多
人。

根據上述幾個簡短的例子，就可見一般為何大家對
尹氏夫婦的愛戴和尊敬。在過去的十五年來，這對精力
充沛神采四射的夫婦，在加州的 Solano 地區的商業場
合，社區活動以至於政治集會等，所到之處無不深深引
起大家的好感，從此他們的名聲，遠近聞名。他們夫婦
的的成功故事，生活點滴等，時常成為當地幾家報紙的
重要新聞。但是，最難得的卻是他們夫婦給我幾次與他
們面對面親切專訪的機會。

尹集成及尹黃春芳兩位都是一九六零年代從台灣
來到美國攻讀研究院的中國留學生。他們的留學和移民
經過與一般人有何分別？他們能有今天的成就，是否與
他們的家庭背景、個性，所受教育以及原來的職業有關
係？他們是怎樣從世界聞名，系統作業計劃高超的麥當
勞速食連鎖餐館，競爭劇烈中生存並征服出來而成功
的？

尹集成及尹春芳兩位，與一般美國華人不同的是他

們都能衝破種族隔離界限，在美國主流的麥當勞連鎖餐
館企業中生存，並發展成功。他們認真的遵循麥當勞的
經營精神，介入廣大的社區人群中，參與社區各種活動。
並且，時時將獲得盈利回饋社會。這次我有機會，在數
次專訪中，了解尹氏夫婦是怎樣的辛苦努力，去認真學
習適應麥當勞世界的特別系統，才能在高度的競爭中生
存下來。在創業的過程中，他們遭受到多少困難阻礙，
那些外人不知的經過情形，是絕對應該記錄下來，與大
家分享。

　　早年，當我在研究加州華人農工的時候，我只能以
粵語進行采訪做記錄，然後再將它翻譯成英文。我遭遇
到的最大困難就是，那些個人資料非常不完整，也無法
找到證實的來源。但是，這次卻沒有這方面的煩惱。他
們夫婦非但能說流利的英語和國語，而且還非常有組織
的，將全部有關資料供給我寫作時參考。這方面讓我省
去不知多少時間，和精力找尋資料去書寫尹氏夫婦的事
跡。

尹氏夫婦當年在中國和台灣的背景

　　六十三歲的尹集成，是尹靜夫與原配妻子所生的最
小的兒子。他於一九三六年十一月二日生於四川省的重
慶市。四川省的礦業豐富，農產地在中國更是非常肥沃。
因為它的地理環境隔離，都能自給自足，促成蔣介石領

導的國民政府，在一九三零年代的理想作戰指揮總部。

　　尹集成的父親出身農家，但是他在學校努力用功，成績優良，不久就在當時的縣政府找到了工作。更是因為他勤奮工作表現，得到上級的賞識，在年方二十五歲時就已經當到主管。經過繼續努力，幾年後，他就得到一份令人羨慕的軍中糧食補給主管職位。他帶著家人，在蔣介石領導的國民政府裡，一直工作到一九四八年。

　　在一九二零至一九四零年間中國遭受到空前的災難。國內的戰爭煙火遍地，共產黨那時又應時興起，令民間更加混亂。這樣，就給日本增強侵略中國的大好機會。自從十九世紀的日本明治維新以來，中國的東北三省，成為日本侵華的大好目標。不幸的華人，不但在國民黨，共產黨的內戰中苟延殘喘生活，還要同時對付日本人的侵略暴行。自從一九三零年以來，日本進軍侵略到中國北方地區很多次。到了一九三七年蘆溝橋事變發生後，引發了不可避免的中日戰爭。不幸的中方節節戰敗，不得不向南方撤退，先後放棄了武漢，漢口，和一九三八年間，遷移到揚子江畔的重慶為戰時陪都。一九三九年五月三、四日，日軍連續轟炸重慶市區兩天。民間財產損失無法統計，老百姓傷亡慘重。大約千戶房屋被炸毀，四百餘人死亡，傷殘人數高達三千人的龐大數目。蔣介石在他的回憶錄中如此記載著說：「敵人的殘暴，不人道的野蠻行為令人難以相信。這是我一生中親眼看到最可怕的事件。我請求上天給予他們（日本）應

得的懲罰。（一九三九年五月四日）」。

　　雖然尹集成生在戰亂的重慶，但是他並未住在城裡。當他只有六個月大時，母親就已經過世。他和他只有一歲多大的姐姐——尹集惠，同被送到以前他們祖父、父親的農場，交給一個陌生婦女照顧。幸運的，那個農場離市區很遠，所以那烽火連天的重慶戰亂災情，並未波及到年幼的尹氏姐弟身上。

　　他們的父親雖然在城裡工作忙碌不堪，但是，他還是定期供給他們姐弟的生活費用。年幼的尹氏，對父母沒有太多印象，也不清楚為什麼時常都是兵荒馬亂的。反正，吃飽了，有姐姐陪他在屋裡和農場上玩遊戲就滿意了。農場地區附近很貧窮，他們姐弟兩人過著沒有父母親情，也沒有關愛的日子。當然也沒有進過學校，讀過一天書。就這樣的，他們在那個農場，度過了八年的時光。在那長長的八年中，父親和哥哥偶而會來看看他們姐弟。「在沒有親情的日子裡過活，是外人難以想像的痛苦；幸好，我們姐弟二人感情很好，我倆緊密的團結著，度過了那段坎坷的難關。」

　　尹氏的父親在髮妻過世後再婚，娶了一位教育程度高深的女士為繼室。她不久，連續生下三名子女。可想而知的，尹集成姐弟二人，沒有很快的接去與父親他們在重慶城裡重聚。終於在一九四四年間，他們姐弟被父親接到重慶家裡，他們得以入學像一般孩子們一樣的讀書。他們那時才第一次見到他們的繼母，並開始與大家

同居在一個屋簷下。八歲時，才第一次到幼稚園上學讀書。每天他們姐弟倆步行一個小時的路去上學。但過了大約六個月，他們又被送到學校住讀。「那時，我根本沒有好好讀書，時時都是班上最後一名，又常常被老師叫去聽訓。但是，我姐姐卻是個用功的好學生。雖然我不是個好學生，可是在學校卻交了幾個好朋友。我們在一起打球，玩耍其樂融融。其實我們也不是壞孩子，只是很頑皮罷了。」他笑著追憶當年的快樂時光。

在十二年生活中，他只讀了四年書。當一九四八年的一天，父母回家後，忽然對大家宣佈他們立刻要準備整理行李，趕快追隨蔣介石的國民政府撤離到台灣去。他們全部都在短短時間內，準備好跟隨父親離開。但是，大哥尹集鈞卻未來得及趕到，被迫留下來。

其實，那時我二十二歲的大哥，已經思想有些左傾，偏向毛澤東的共產主義。當他在上海讀書時，他就早已參加所謂的「讀書會」為一份子。他被父親得知以後，大為震怒，並責罵他不知好歹的做叛徒。但是當時的國民黨的腐敗作風，令許多年青人感到灰心失望，包括熱血方剛的尹集鈞在內。所以他就在被父親責罵一頓復，離家出走未再回頭。「父親當時的處境也相當困難，自己在國民政府中為中堅份子的高級官員，但卻出了一個擁護敵對共產主義的兒子，他實在無可奈何。」既然不能說服年青的兒子，時間不容多作考慮的帶著全家妻小奔走台灣。

台灣與中國大陸之間距離，只有一百哩的台灣海峽航程，遭日本人統治長達五十年。一直到一九四五年，日本在第二次世界大戰投降後回歸。由蔣介石領導的國民政府接管，但因內戰被共產黨打敗，不得已將政府全部遷往台灣。那段時期的國民政府，是在水深火熱中生存著。除了緊急不懈的訓練龐大的百萬兵團，以備隨時攻打返回大陸外，更要照顧那同時從大陸跟隨政府遷台的人員與家屬。一九五零年初期那日夜被轟炸的前哨——金門和馬祖，令老百姓感到非常恐懼，不能安寧。所以，政府得時時刻不容緩的嚴謹設防衛台。

　　國民政府被迫遷台的教訓，令執政者漸漸朝著革新振作方向成長。不論外交與內政方面，都在盡量設法大事整頓。其中的耕者有其田，以及六年免費國民教育兩項實行後，尤其深獲民心。人民對政府的信心，逐漸重新建立。六年免費國民教育實施後，各方反應極佳，後來更延展為九年免費國民教育。至今仍在實行。

　　「我們到了台灣後，父親仍為政府忠心的公務員。同時他也有能力照顧他的新家庭。我和尹集惠兩人，則住在比我大十二歲的大姐尹集雯家。大姐集雯自從母親過世後，負擔著大部照顧我們姐弟兩人。她與大姐夫宋先生結婚，自己養育兩名子女，仍繼續對我們姐弟大公無私的照顧有加。我從十三歲那年開始跟大姐住，一直到考入大學住校為止。我剛到台灣的初期，在學校惹了不少麻煩，上初中時候還幾次被趕出學校。」尹氏無奈

　　　　　　　　華人在加州一百五十年的歷史

的回憶著說。不可否認的，對當年那段不懂事歲月中的往事，感到萬分悔恨，因此，更加對那如母般的長姐和姐夫敬愛和欽佩不已。

尹集成年紀漸漸長大以後，開始知道用功讀書。他高中畢業後，但是卻未能立刻考入大學。雖然在校成績一直不太理想，但卻接交了幾個知己好友。他的朋友們一直給他最大的鼓勵，和不斷的精神支持。他有感而發的說：「朋友是我一生日子裡最重要的一部分。假如今天我有成就的話，那是因為我的姐姐，和我朋友們給予的精神和經濟兩方面的不斷支助。我很容易交到朋友，我對朋友總是以誠相待。」他對著我微笑的繼續說：「我也領略到錢的重要性。金錢給予我一種安全感。因為當我年輕時，我沒有錢。那時，我總是對我未來感到恐慌。為了起碼的生活所需，我得向姐姐，兩個堂兄妹或是朋友們求幫助。」

後來，他進入一家職業訓練學校上課，讀了一年，他發現並不喜歡在那種環境讀書，所以他同時做重新考大學的準備加強補習。可喜的結果，得以考入台灣成功大學。他選擇土木工程系，努力進修。終於在一九六零年間學成畢業。「上大學時，曾經得到我另外一個正在工作的姐姐 Evelyn 很多幫助。我非常幸運的有這樣好的三位姐姐，她們不斷的給予我經濟和精神上的諸多支持，」尹氏感慰的訴說著。

尹集成的賢內助黃春芳女士，是黃仁夫婦的第三名

女兒。她於中日戰爭時的一九四零年生於江西省的上饒縣皂頭鎮。她父親在一九三零年間，畢業於南京的警官學校。畢業以後被分發崇明島，擔任巡查官。崇明是一個距離上海市不遠的長江出口關卡。幾年後，他就被調升為無錫市的警察局長。到了一九三七年間，他再晉升為國民黨第三軍團的上校團長。戰亂時期，黃仁先生一家時時不停的東移西遷。一九四零年的四月一天，日軍轟炸上饒縣皂頭鎮，一連幾天都是在躲警報中度過的。黃仁先生在他的回憶錄中寫著：「有一次，早晨有二十四架飛機炮轟城裡，下午又來了三十七架繼續轟炸。那次的災情非常慘重，一天中死亡人數，大約有三百多人。那時春芳還是懷抱中的嬰兒，我們全家都緊緊的擁抱在一起，在防空洞裡躲警報，但求都能度過這場浩劫，生存下來。」

尹黃春芳無奈的如此回憶說：「當我年幼時，是非常體弱多病的，主要因為生活困難，造成營養不良。似乎我們從不知道，究竟何處為家。隨時都得準備整理行囊，離開到另外地方。我到了七歲多，還沒有進過學校。」

一九四五年，中日戰爭終於結束了。蔣介石領導的國民政府，又被新興起的中國共產黨摧毀得損失慘重。在一九四六年的六月間，國民黨軍團分割為四大部門：陸，海，空外加上補給司令部。黃仁先生在顧總司令領導下，主管與其他三軍聯絡關係，供應軍中所需。那個部門，幾乎是在一九四八年間第一批被遣送到台灣的機

華人在加州一百五十年的歷史

構。到了一九四九年間，大致安置好了之後，才把妻子兒女們接到台灣團聚。

「剛剛到台那段日子，大家都過得很苦，但是慢慢地就日漸好轉了。我也在那時開始正式入學。令人非常興奮的，我可以天天上學校讀書。他們本地同學，習慣穿木板鞋，我們這些大陸來的穿鞋子去上學，」尹春芳面露微笑的回憶著。

她是在一個非常和睦可親的環境裡長大的。母親雖然未曾受過高深教育，但是總在一旁鼓勵子女努力用功讀書。父親因為工作繁忙，雖未直接的教導子女讀書，但對他們的教育，也是盡量給予全部支持，並時時加以關懷鼓勵。

尹春芳接著說：「當時的台灣，入學考試是一件大事。我父親一定為我們一個個削鉛筆。每人都會帶三四枝在書包裡，以免鉛斷了隨時有鉛筆用。考試前晚，父親會叮囑我們早點上床休息。而第二天早晨，父母都會早起來為我們準備早餐，那一定是兩個煮蛋，象徵考試得一百分的好預兆。另外還有一碗可口的熱雞湯麵。父母都認為，吃一頓豐富的早餐會令人思想敏銳，考試成績良好。那也許就是為何我能在台灣最好學校讀書，成績優良的在台灣師範大學畢業，出來為人師表。」

開始美國的新生活

在一九六零至七零年代，台灣的各大學的高材生畢業以後，都申請出國深造。而大部份學生都希望到美國攻讀。據說，在那十幾年中，在美讀書的外籍留學生中，來自台灣的數字是最高的。

　　尹集成和黃春芳都不是以移民，或是難民身份申請來美的。而是以留學生簽證入學深造的。雖然他們的經濟狀況都不富裕，也都是在捉襟見肘的，維持著那起碼的留學生活。他們同時在國內得到主修學位，並通過「托福」考試才進入美國大學深造。黃春芳在一九六三年甘乃迪總統遇刺那年來美，到華盛頓大學主修社會福利學。

　　尹氏之姐，尹集惠於一九六二年先到伊利諾大學，一年後轉學到華盛頓大學。她的好學不倦，影響了還在台灣的尹氏。那時，他剛剛從軍中服役回來。已經畢業並有土木工程學位，在台找份工作是不成問題的。但是，二十幾歲的他，對當時現況並不太滿意，時時為自己前途顧慮。他看到集惠姐能一步步克服所有難關，去美國學校求深造，為什麼我不能呢？但是，繼母決不會給予他任何支持，而那照顧他多年的長姐已無力為他的出國留學設法了。他不死心的，到處奔走求助，向他的兩位堂兄和幾個好友，籌得足夠的路費，踏上美國之路。

　　一九六四年，尹氏隨著眾人，擠上一艘貨輪，用了整整一個月時間，在海上航行，來到美國洛杉磯。

　　他終于也得以進入華盛頓大學攻讀。暑期中，他同時兼差兩份工作，才可積存足夠的學費以及生活所需。

而黃春芳則找到一份供食宿的管家兼保姆工作，為她的下學期學費作準備。他們兩人，終于在尹集惠姐姐的介紹下，千里有緣的認識了。尹氏苦讀下拿到土木工程師碩士學位，而黃春芳也順利的修得她那份社會福利學學位。他們在一九六六年，有情人終成眷屬，結為夫婦。

黃春芳回憶說，「我們當時仍很貧困。十塊錢為我買了一個戒指。又用十塊錢租了教堂。我用五塊錢找到一件便宜的婚紗禮服，就這樣的結了婚。」

尹氏夫婦在西雅圖，連續工作三年，直到一九六八年，尹氏得到舊金山的一間有名工程公司 Bechtel 聘為工程師。他們在附近的小城 Belmont 買下一棟破舊的房子，安居下來。一九六九年間，岳父母從台灣來到美國與尹氏同住。在孫女瑪莉（Mary）誕生後，祖父母立刻負擔起照顧孫女責任。尹氏夫婦得以無後顧之憂，分別早出晚歸的上班。此外，他們並雄心勃勃的上課，準備做業餘房地產經紀人。他們認為除了要為自己打算，更得幫助親人。

尹氏努力工作，一再向上升職。他幾年後，在另一家知名公司 Fluor Corp 找到更理想的職位，為專案工程的總工程師。他負責礦場以及重工程方案。他時常因公到國外出差，解決困難案件。

他與同事之間相處融洽，在工作上表現良好，但是，他總覺得無論如何，別人還是把他當做局外人來看。他說：「大家都知道，我工作表現優良，為公司努力建立

業績。但如有升遷的機會時，公司主管總是在多方考慮我的條件而失敗。我相信我的資格並不比他人差，但是最後那職位總是讓給比我條件不如的人。這種情形發生了不只一次。它給我的打擊很深。起初，以為我的英語不如人，我還去上加強語言訓練的 Toastmasters 的社交活動。我也時時參加其他社交活動。我喜歡聊天，結交朋友。我也會說笑話。我不知要怎樣才能被接受升級呢？」

當一九七零年代，中國開放以後，美國的很多公司像 Fluror Corp 都向中國大陸方面發展。那時，他們公司有很多商業項目在那裡進行，包括一億七千萬的銅礦開發計劃。當時，那家公司的副總裁的得力助手正是尹集成。在那幾年中，尹氏擔任的除了他專長的工程業務外，還作中美雙方的橋樑。因為他的關係，中方有機會保送二三十個工程師出國來美接受職業訓練。尹氏更被公司送去南美的秘魯出差，為當地人員解決技術上的難題。他為了深入工作場地，了解問題的癥結，很多次都得營宿荒山野地。

「我在美方公司學到了不少東西。我也學著應該怎樣與同事共事，交際。但是令人遺憾的，雖然我有實際能力，有學識和才能擔任工作。我更是對公司忠心耿耿。但是身為亞裔的我，要晉升到公司副總裁的機會，實在非常渺茫。我時常在懷疑，是否在美國的企業界多一層所謂「玻璃天花板」，因不同文化而隔離著我們？還是，

我根本沒有資格當公司的總裁？我要一直耐性的等，等到我退休？我在那家公司，擔任資深總工程師已有十二年了，」他深為感觸的談著。

尹氏經歷的，並非少見的獨特情形。他舉了一個例子：在洛杉磯，General Bank 總裁有位華人總裁吳澧培先生（Li Pei Wu）。該銀行在一九九八年，被全美銀行推選為最佳和最安全的銀行。在了解吳氏當時的情況後，就不難想像他和尹氏有很多相同之處。他從台灣大學畢業後，來到堪薩斯州深造並取得碩士學位。而後，進入加州大學加入商業經濟和金融，並取得學位。畢業後，他在阿拉斯加的國家銀行找到一份工作。努力工作的結果，終於將他晉升到公司副總裁的位置。他以公司高級副執行官員的身份，為公司解決了很多大小困難。尤其是在一九七零年代經濟危機中，他運用機智，努力的扭轉乾坤，順利度過難關。即使如此，建立無數業績的他，也似乎難以被「白人天下的董事會」推選為公司總裁。幸好北阿拉斯加國家銀行卻趁機聘了他為代理總裁兼最高執行長。在一年當中，他手下的六家分行，顯著的增加了盈利。

任職已久的銀行總裁宣佈辭職，準備參加公職競選。他以大力推薦吳氏接任公司總裁職位。但是，當開會決定時，在那堆積如山嘉許吳氏業績前面的董事會執行委員們，仍心存懷疑「東方人是否能在美國銀行擔任總裁職位？」吳氏在氣憤下，一怒而辭職遠走紐約任職

其他銀行。失去吳氏後，該行的股票立刻在一夜間大跌。董事會在認清事實後，別無選擇的立刻邀請他回來，執掌該銀行總裁。

他是第一位在美國銀行界擔任總裁的中國人。經過那兩次的痛苦經驗，吳氏不再有安全感。兩年後的一九八二年時，他毅然辭去北阿拉斯加國家銀行的總裁職位，接受擔任 General Bank 的總裁，負責處理大部份由台灣來的投資業務。

尹氏繼續努力的工作，同時尹春芳也不斷地在她的工作上表現良好。她不久就被調升為心理健康部門單位主管。幾年中，她也為尹家增添另外兩個女兒。全職的工作，加上家庭各項雜務，並未阻上尹氏夫婦繼續向上進取的雄心與鬥志。他們夫婦，在房地產方面試著求發展。在這方面，令人滿意的是，他們的努力也有小成就。尹氏並不因此而自滿停止更上一層樓之壯志，而同時兼營工程顧問業務，Fashion Dynamic 公司營銷等等。似乎他們能在一天二十四小時中，擠榨出來第二十五小時，以便兼顧一切。

Fashion Dynamic 公司的產品，是直接營銷制度。要多方面發展，才能建立業績。所以，他們夫婦倆還利用業餘以及周末，出城參加有關直銷的講習班等活動。尹氏在無形中發現他非常喜歡這類事業，尤其是認識新朋友方面令他發生興趣。他們的銷售業績高高在上，令人滿意。不過他們夫婦也了解，這樣的工作也不是長久之

計，也不會令人致富的。

到了一九八零年，在經濟方面，他們的確是感到不再恐慌了。他們除了各自有份穩定的工作外，也儲存了積蓄為未雨綢繆做了打算。更有那好幾份兼差，多增收入。此外，他們投資的房地產也年年增值。尹氏在經營房地產行業中，似乎也慢慢的建立出一片天地，甚有心得。他們將買進的破舊房屋，在周末時間，整修裝新，待到適當時機高價賣出。他們投資購進的房地產，作為出租的公寓大樓，由於他們都善於經營管理，因此，也為他們增加了更多收入。尹氏在不知不覺中，已經進軍在百萬富翁的行列中了。

年紀漸長，已五十多歲的尹氏，仍時時的擔心工作不安全。他不願等到有一天接到通知被遣散離職。他們夫婦，漸漸的興起了另起門戶自求創業的意念。開始各方打聽，搜求資料做市場調查。

他們調查的範圍中，包括：漢堡王（Burger King）、塔可餅店（Taco Bell）、Arby's 牛肉三明治、Sizzler 自助餐館、Denny's 家庭餐館、麥當勞（McDonald's）餐館、ARCO 加油站和中國餐館等，都是他倆考慮的商業目標。

最後調查結果，他們被那聞名全球的麥當勞速食餐館深深的吸引了。他們發現麥當勞的制度良好，經營妥善，更是符合多數人們的負擔能力，即使是經濟不景氣時期，也不會受到太多影響。因為人人都得吃飯！在匆忙競爭的今日社會，速食餐館是大家都喜歡的進食方

式。價廉、物美、老少咸宜。到處都有，環境清潔更是
符合衛生條件。

初嘗麥當勞連鎖速食店

當尹集成任職於 Fluor Corp 公司時，他時常和其他
的同事們，去麥當勞吃午餐。他那時就對這家速食餐館
發生好感。對那高水準、高效率、品質好以及服務佳的
餐館十分佩服。此外，尹黃春芳還對麥當勞的社區聯繫
網絡所作貢獻欽佩不已。

終於，在一九八四年尹氏申請並被麥當勞審核批
准，得以進入他們的培訓組織，接受嚴格的訓練。他從
打掃廁所開始，清理油膩的廚房，食物處理的安全與衛
生條件，如何管理員工，包括薪金支付，以及對顧客的
應對學問等各項知識，都得像小學生似的一步步學起。
在四個月內，他將所有必須的課程學習完畢，並得到「A」
的高等級結業。他等待著麥當勞將會賣給他餐館營業的
通知。他們早已將資本準備好做餐館開辦資金。但是，
實際的情形並非如想像那麼簡單。

麥當勞的執政單位，在審核他們送交的申請書後，
一一盤問他們的年齡，做生意方面的經驗，處理人際關
係技巧，以及文化背景等等。他們的申請書，在毫無理
由的解釋下，被打了下來。

尹氏夫婦並非新來美的新移民。他們那時住在美國

已經二十多年了。他們更在美國的大學受到高等教育。他們也分別在美國的政府機構，與大企業公司工作，並有良好的在職紀錄可查。多年智慧的投資，為他們賺得足夠的財力資金，開設麥當勞連鎖餐館。他們能說流利的英語，也熟悉美國的風俗習慣和社會制度。

盡管尹氏符合麥當勞公司所要求的所有條件，但是，不可否認的事實仍存在著，那就是主流社會人們，仍對少數民族的實力表示懷疑。少數民族必須比別人加倍努力，方搏到主流人士的信任。

意志堅強的尹氏夫婦，並未被拒絕申請受打擊而放棄一切，還是等待著適當時機，再接再厲，多方的研究下一步的策略，以求成功。

一天，尹氏接到通知，去查看一家在 Oakland 城中的麥當勞餐館。那個餐館的設備陳舊，環境髒亂，一切都不符合麥當勞的營業水平。生意每況愈下，毫無盈利可言。尹氏在觀察了一切後，深知自己的實力與不屈不撓的意志，他不惜以七十萬美元高價，忍痛買下那搖搖欲墜的生意。他毫無選擇餘地，只有下定決心，只許成功不許失敗，繼往直前。

回顧尹氏所經之路，非常坎坷又曲折。為了達到麥當勞的嚴格必備條件，尹氏夫婦是怎樣努力的工作，以達到要求的高效能水準？他們融入主流社會的經過是什麼？今天他們的成就是如何掙扎出來的呢？怎樣奮鬥出成功大道？他們的文化背景，是否為他們所經營麥當勞

餐館過程增加困擾？以及，在那種環境下，他們夫婦同時養育三個孩子的情形又是如何度過？這些問題，都是筆者幾度對尹氏夫婦專訪中，要詳細探討解答的。

在一九八四年，他們買下來那經營不善，業務一蹶不振在 Oakland 市中心第六十八街的麥當勞餐館後，為了謹慎起見，尹氏先辭去他在 Fluor 工程公司的工作，下定決心在餐飲界大展鴻圖。尹氏冒險的另外拿出一筆廿五萬元資費，將那極需整頓的餐館，內外大事裝修，換新粉飾一番。他更將那破舊的廚房設備淘汰，重新裝設新的標準用具。從此，餐廳內外煥然一新，窗明几淨，整潔舒適。

為了使顧客感到安全的用餐，他還特別雇用警衛，也讓那些閒雜份子遠離他的餐廳。他認真的與員工們共同學習，研討以求進步。他深信改進環境情況，可以間接的改善人們的觀感和態度。他保持他的處事原則，並善待員工，公平又尊敬每一個顧客。他獎賞員工們，是根據他們的認真工作成績，無關他們的文化背景。

當初，他不敢單獨站在外面，那個地區令人生懼。所以，他從不敢讓他的妻子和孩子來餐館。但是，尹氏早已立定決心，勇往直前，絕不回頭。他的執著和努力的結果，終於赤手空拳的打出一片麥當勞的天下。在一年半的短短時間裡，不但餐館的營業額直線上升，大有盈餘，並被列入麥當勞舊金山地區成長最快的第一名。尹氏有感而發的說，當他剛剛買下那個破舊的麥當勞餐

館時，有人猜測他大概只能維持三個月時間，就會關門大吉了。

　　「現在我更加相信，美國的良好制度是優勝劣敗的。只要你努力苦幹，必會生存下來，並超越一切的。你將在人際上，物質上，或者心靈方面得到多種報酬。有的也許是看不到的報酬，不過，那不是一種可以用數字來衡量的成就。遺憾的是，很多人不能看到這些，」尹氏更感慨萬千的訴說著心路歷程。

金弧門中的金色遠景

　　尹氏夫婦特殊的經歷與成就，令他們夫婦倆信心大增，很快的繼屋崙的那家麥當勞餐館，又開設了另外四家連鎖店，分佈於 Alameda 地區。那時，尹黃春芳當然必須放棄她那份社會服務員的工作，專心協力的幫助夫婿，共同創業。她的精力和時間，除了在餐館料理一切外，大部份放在社區活動，慈善機構與學校聯絡方面。他們不再對開設新餐館面臨的諸多困難和阻撓感到威脅和恐懼。在坎坷多難的經歷中，他們得到的經驗，將作為應付未來的經典。

　　尹集成是位工程師，專門解決難題。黃春芳是位社會服務督導，擅長人際關係與聯絡工作，以及社區網絡之聯誼。在麥當勞一類事業中，尹氏夫婦的的確確是最佳的夫妻伙件檔。互相輔助，合作無間。

當他們再申請開設另外的餐館時，麥當勞執行當局未給予任何阻撓和壓力。更沒再費時查詢他們的經濟狀況，文化背景，人際聯繫與溝通以及是否有經營飲食業經驗等。相反的，他們的貸款，裝修工程等申請，很快的就給予核准，促成早日開業。

　　他們辛苦的努力，贏得大家的認同與重視。他們開設的餐館營業蒸蒸日上，一再的為他們盈利及獲獎，以至佳評紛紛。

　　他們在一九八九年得到「最佳餐館經理人獎」和一九九零年的「三 A 協會優良商店獎」。同時，尹氏夫婦在屋崙地區活躍的參與青年會議，為市長推行的暑期工作訓練，以及推行馬丁路德金博士紀念日活動，以及Marcus Foster Foundation 教育計劃等項目。

　　尹氏夫婦日以繼夜的工作，他們辛苦的代價漸漸的得到回響。在七年中，他們的業務發展成功外，自然而然的終於被傳統的麥當勞大家族接受為一份子。

　　一九九一年，他們開始向灣區以外地帶拓墾。他們又繼續購買下在 Solono 縣區的另外四家餐館，發現Vacaville-Fairfield-Suisun 三角城市的環境良好，它有農村的樸實之美，視野寬闊開朗，是個非常適合教養子女的地方。他們毅然做了很大的決定，一一賣掉了在Oakland 和 Alameda 地區的五家麥當勞餐館，將整個家庭，事業同時遷移到 Solono 地帶。

尹氏在 Solono 地區重建與發展麥當勞

尹氏夫婦做事的高水準態度,永往直前的進取心,毫無疑問是他們成功的原因,但是他們夫婦那種事無巨細,大小親自動手參與的作風,更是非常難能可貴的。

雖然他們已擁有好幾家餐館了,但是隨時會看到他們夫婦在櫃檯前後,廚房裡外忙碌不堪。掃地清理,填補用具,準備漢堡麵包以及油炸薯條等。尹氏每晚一定親自協助餐館經理,處理結賬及清理環境工作。一切料理妥善後,都是清晨一點多了。但是他從未錯過參加早晨七點半在市商會的早餐會議。

他們努力的工作,辛勤的開拓,令尹氏屬下的麥當勞餐館,家家業績優異。他們認真的遵循麥當勞傳統的法規與守則,辛苦的播種,灌溉,也成功的享受那收成的喜悅。

一九九二年間的八月,尹氏應邀前往伊利諾斯州的麥當勞漢堡學院在職培訓。那是專門為麥當勞全世界,少數業主以及總經理參加所設的計劃。尹氏在受訓的二百八十人中,名列第一。

「麥當勞當局只規定一人必須參加那次的培訓,但是我還是陪同我先生去接受訓練,畢業,以求充實並加強管理知識,才讓我們做一對真正的強勢夫妻伙伴檔,」尹黃春芳補充著說。

一九九五年,尹氏夫婦在 Vacaville 的市中心 Alamo

與 Marshall 街道的十字路口，開設了第七家麥當勞餐館。這家新建的餐館，附設了不多見的兒童遊樂園地，是 Solono 縣區裡首創的第一家。黃春芳興奮的表示：「我們希望對社區有些令人新奇的貢獻。只是這個遊樂園的花費，就已經用去了約十萬元。它設有滑梯，彎曲山洞，打球地坑以及小嬰兒園地等，兒童全年都會有玩耍的地方。此外，這個餐館，裝備了麥當勞有史以來最新廚房設備及用具，我們還雇用全職與半天的員工四十八人，以提供最佳服務。」

在第七家餐館開幕不久，尹氏就再宣布將要開設第八家餐館的驚喜消息。第八家餐館的新址是在 Fairfield 市區的 West Texas 與 Beck 交叉口的新建，在 Fairfield Center 大購物中心內。這個佔地兩千八百平方呎的大型餐館，與熱鬧的購物中心來的顧客，互相呼應及方便。麥當勞提供給顧客飲食服務，而方便到商店來的人多多增加購買力。Fairfield 市經濟發展委員會主任的 Sean Quinn 先生如此表示著。

同時，尹氏還在多方與人接洽著準備另外可能開設麥當勞的三處地點，包括 Fairfield 市 Travis Blvd 與 North Texas 街口，在 Wal-Mart 平價商場中，以及另一城市 Cordelia 的市區裡。

身為麥當勞大家庭一份子的尹氏夫婦，除了必得親自在營業方面工作長時間外，更要保持並繼續推廣麥當勞傳統哲理「營業中不忘在社區裡參與活動等」。當然還

有他們自己的理想，與其他應料理事務。

　　據麥當勞的估計，大約是在每五個年輕人之中，有一個人會在麥當勞接受就業訓練的。尹氏夫婦還了解到，在麥當勞的連鎖餐館，幾乎可看到社會階層的成長經過。

　　「雖然有人只在麥當勞工作短時期，但是他們在工作中學到基本的就業知識，可以在過後的就業生涯裡時時會應用到。那些準備以麥當勞為正式職業者，麥當勞當局對業主以及經理人員都備有完整的訓練計劃。高階層經理人才的收入超過大學畢業生的薪金，」黃春芳如此解釋說：「我們不只是賣漢堡包的餐廳，而實際上麥當勞對廣大顧客，做各種社區有利的相互活動功能。所以，不論是在精神上，感情上或是實力上，我們都必須回報社區所給予的。那是一種強力的功效，」尹氏訴說著。

　　黃春芳又加以補充：「在這個行業，最重要的元素是人際關係，以及你對待人們的態度。她認為，今天他們經營的麥當勞連鎖餐館，所以都能保持高盈利，是從未忽略對人事管理方面的重要性。我們隨時加強員工的福利計劃，不只在醫藥方面，同時在獎勵和退休方面都時時調整。」他們夫婦倆對員工們的愛護是有目共睹的。他們每天都一一到各餐館實地協助，也親自照顧來餐館的顧客們。

　　他們雇用的經理人之一 Sue Drumbeller 女士說：「尹氏為員工準備了優惠的福利計劃，更為了獎勵員工而帶

領大群人馬出去旅行渡假，滑雪等優遊活動。有時，一年中會有三四次這種員工同樂活動。尹氏夫婦為人極為慷慨大方，我已經在這個大家庭工作了六年多，從開始的晚間實習經理，升任到今天的職位。」從她愉快的態度中反映出來工作環境的良好氣氛。

每當尹氏夫婦得到任何獎勵，他們永遠都與同仁共享，並將功勞歸於大家。一九九七年尹氏得到麥當勞獎後，他們給員工的通告中寫著：我們要大家知道，就是因為你們把餐館照顧的很好，我們才有時間和精力到社區裡為人們服務。你們的勤奮努力為麥當勞大家庭贏得更多的榮譽，我向大家致謝。

在速食餐業中的競爭是非常激烈的。在一九九七年紐約的一項市場調查中，顯示麥當勞的營業額從百分17.8 跌到 16.1 的數字。其他的 Burger King 以及新興的速食餐館業，使出許多新花招吸引顧客，推出漢堡包以外的食品像烤雞，Bagels 硬麵包，和披薩餅等，搶走了麥當勞許多生意。「我們面臨了競爭的威脅，大量生產等方式給予的打擊，令人難以招架。」

平價超級市場 W-Mart 等廠商，一再的削減價格以招攬生意，同時還得時時提高產品質素。這些，無疑的都對麥當勞發生直接的影響，令人感到威脅。所幸，尹氏屬下的麥當勞連鎖餐館受到影響不大。主要的是因為他們夫婦倆在當地建立的良好信譽，加上友情的精神支助，幫助他們走過很多難關。

尹氏屬下的麥當勞連鎖餐館，參加了多項新創推廣業務的方法，譬如，「Make-to-order」點菜式的速食餐點。「我們參與多項麥當勞當局推薦的計劃，最近更投下了一百萬資金，以全面改善廚房的設備。這只是尹氏管理的麥當勞連鎖店的經常改進計劃一部分而已，」尹氏解釋道。此外，尹氏獨創非傳統的新推廣方式，還有在購物中心裡增設的麥當勞餐館，包括兩家開在平價超級商店 Wal-Mart 裡面的連鎖餐館。

麥當勞在推出任何一項新產品時，都要求各地區連鎖店業主參與實行。為了配合新加上的特別活動，尹氏立刻就大批增購存貨，加雇幫手，以便應付他們屬下十多家餐館突增的顧客人數。同時，也要大做廣告，宣傳新產品以求增加營業額。他們夫婦這些努力，事實證明每次的辛苦都得到了預期的收穫。

沒有辛酸的耕耘，哪兒有豐富的收穫

看著他們領導的尹氏麥當勞連鎖餐館業績節節上升，發展擴大，的確令人驚訝不已。但不可否認的是，他們每日所面臨的衝擊與挑戰，也不是外人所能體會出來的。誤解事件與不滿意的顧客並無例外。

在買下 Solono 縣區裡的那家連鎖店不到一年時，有幾個年青黑人被經理開除。不久，有人在餐館外面持標語，抗議示威，並且向 NAACP 有色種族人權平等組織

控訴。經過 NAACP 在 Vallejo 地區主席 Frank Jackson 親自調查經過並審查後，認為尹氏並未構成種族歧視行為，因為他在屋崙那幾家連鎖店，百分之九十的員工為黑人。

尹氏表示，「我不會無故冤枉這些年輕人，大概只是管理方面需要改善罷了。」經過那次的事件後，尹氏立刻加入那為有色種族爭取人權平等的組織為終生會員，並設立獎學金。尹氏此後，活躍的參與該組織的各項活動。在一九九六年間更親自策劃 NAACP 在三個縣城（Fairfield-Vacaville-Suisun 的聯合慶祝二十周年活動）。在會中不但被讚揚為大公無私，並由分會會長 Griffin Bailey 發給獎狀。

PepBoys 汽車維護公司在 Beck 與 Texas 街道新建廣場，邀請尹氏加入此新建購物中心。當尹氏正在籌備時，該地區其他餐飲食業主發出抗議。尹氏經與都市計劃組織幾次會面商討後，取得協議，批准尹氏營業執照。在一九九七年四月一次的市政府會議討論到此事件，市長 Chuck Hammond 對 Fairfield Dailey Republic 日報記者表示：「我不能因為其他人不喜歡某某人而拒絕發給營業執照，優秀商人會成功的生存，而劣等商人是會失敗的。」

每次擴張一家新的麥當勞連鎖餐館，都會經過很多繁複手續。尤其是在組織策劃和籌備資金等方面，更是令人十分傷神。不是每一次申請擴張新餐館都能被麥當勞當局批准的。一九九三年，當尹氏夫婦申請在加州 Yolo

縣的 Winters 市的那家麥當勞餐館時，就不曾被核准發照。盡管尹氏的良好信譽，與政界關係密切並具有影響力，但是仍未被麥當勞執政當局批准。

積極參與民間，當地商界，社團以及慈善業活動

在 Vacaville-Fairfield-Suisun 三城市的社交圈內，尹氏夫婦的大名，很快的傳揚開來。從一九九一年四家麥當勞餐館業主，直線上升到一九九九年的坐擁十二家連鎖餐館，尹氏夫婦的聲望一天比一天高升。他們夫婦倆隨時以自己專長參與民間，商家，社團以及慈善活動。

一九九二年的十月，當尹氏在 Vacaville 地區開業才一周年時，當地的商會就選出尹氏為商會委員。自此，尹氏夫婦非常活躍的參與各項商會有關的籌款節目，社團活動等。商會中另一位委員 Jean Krack 說：「他們不停的施予。不只是金錢方面，他們幾乎將自己也捐獻出來了。」Vacaville 的市長 David Fleming 也說，「他們熱愛人們，善於交往，我非常敬愛他們夫婦。他們是大眾的好榜樣。他們對任何的慈善活動，都是熱心支持到底的。」

一九九六年，尹氏經 Vacaville 市商會委員選為商會會長。那第四十六屆的交接典禮是在尹氏家園別墅中舉行的。那天到達參加的來賓，創下商會從未達到的高紀錄數字。Jean Krack 女士分析著那天盛況空前的兩個原因：第一，尹氏是擁有多家麥當勞的主人，在社區裡聲

望很高。另一原因，大家都迫切的想到那別致，優美又絕無僅有的尹氏家園大開眼界。

尹氏在市商會服務的幾年中，他不但誠懇的負起領導的責任，盡心盡力的工作，他還強調著：集體努力，一起工作，是共同致勝原則。尹氏在任期中，提倡了多項以前沒有的活動，舉辦高爾夫球賽，以及萬聖節的南瓜園地活動等。所得收入，全部施惠予當地民間，和慈善機構。

Vacaville 高中學校的音樂計劃項目，經過尹氏所屬的麥當勞連鎖館的支持，也得到經濟方面補助。尹氏並認真的舉辦籌款活動，為身體殘障而設的 Eagle Lake Children 夏令營籌募基金。尹氏夫婦的成就琳瑯滿目，永遠說不完。他們對社區福利改進的貢獻，難以統計，價值無窮。

尹黃春芳親自參與的活動項目就有：倡導在當地學校間的 Interact Clubs，擔任 Fairfield-Suisun Rotary Club 扶輪社委員時，她推動當地學區利用學生的紀念冊的歷史圖片，在她的 Fairfield 麥當勞餐館中做有歷史性的展覽。那個餐館是以歷史性的圖片為裝璜的，有的遠自一九一二年。這些代表歷史的圖片，間接的教育著年青人自己學校歷史的認識。另一目的，更讓學生學到商場與學校間那密切的關聯。學區總督 Darrel Taylor 如此解釋著。

尹黃春芳又接著說：「這個主意是從我在社會服務

部門工作時學來的。社區與學校間息息相關。這些圖片
並且能把現在與從前連接起來，以便保持傳統的價值
觀。」

　　一九七七年尹黃春芳得到加州國會參議員 Maurice
Johannessen 選為第四區的最佳模範婦女。該參議員稱讚
她熱心公益從不後人，努力為社區服務。

　　一九九八年，尹氏夫婦獲得麥當勞事業的 Ronald
Award 地區獎，感謝他們在領導市場開發與社區關係方
面的貢獻。在推動此項活動中，尹氏夫婦都各展所長以
達成預期之成果。尹氏是連鎖系統的採購委員會委員，
尹黃春芳則在市場開發及業務處理顧問團中為重要一份
子。她同時是 Ronald McDonald House 委員，她的任務
主要的是，處理安排家裡不幸有患重病的兒童到加大戴
維斯所屬之醫療中心療養。

　　尹氏本人更是在社區中身兼數職，忙碌不堪。他參
與服務的項目計有：

1. 他是 Vacaville 市警察聯盟組織的十五名委員中
   的主席。他們推動及照顧大約有兩千餘兒童在
   校或課餘的安全，體育，娛樂及讀書等活動。

2. 由州議院指派的 Solano 市監獄 Citizens
   Advisory Boarrd 十五位組成輔導委員會的主
   席。

3. 一九九八年北加州麥當勞三縣市為 Lungren 助
   選加州州長籌款，共募得十萬元資金，並有千

人參與盛會。

尹氏家族與華人亞裔社團

　　尹氏夫婦生育三名女兒。大女兒 Mary 在 Solano 縣
政府任副檢察官。她於一九九一年畢業於加州爾灣大
學，取得生態兼法科學位。而後，進入南加州 Loyola Law
School 攻讀法律，於一九九四年畢業。追隨她父母的腳
步，同樣的在社區參與很多活動，並在有關亞裔的法律
組織中非常活躍。二女兒 Betty 在尹氏經營的麥當勞連
鎖事業中，擔任經理職務。最小女兒 Carol 在佛羅里達
大學就讀。

　　尹氏和岳父母的關係非常親密。他記得在大約三十
年前，剛剛結婚不久，岳父母兩位從台灣搬來與他們夫
婦同住。外婆大部時間是照顧孫女兒，岳父則一旁協助
尹氏整修買進的破舊房屋。尹氏對岳父老人家給予的有
關協助，一直念念不忘，感激至深。他說：「我六歲喪母，
父親很少在家。小時候的日子不是住在學校裡，就是在
姐姐家中渡過的。所以，對我岳父母給予的溫暖關注，
照顧意義重大，畢生難忘。所以，當我們在 Vacaville 建
造大家園房子時，特地為他們兩位老人家設計另外的單
位，盡量的能讓他們舒適的居住。同時，在設計花園時，
都處處想到他們行走的方便與安全。所以，房屋的四周
裡外，都建了特備的扶手欄杆和沒有台階的房舍。有時，

在天氣清朗的早晨，喜歡陪伴他們在湖濱散步。那個湖當中有一個小島，我們命名它為「崇明」，那是他們二老的家鄉。我岳父大人在那新建的房子裡陪我們渡過兩個寒暑，他於一九九七年辭世。」尹氏落寞的訴說著。

遠在十九世紀時期，華人們早就來到尹氏夫婦創業定居地方的 Vacaville，以農耕為生。一八五零年的人口調查中顯示，已有第一批華人開始來到 Solano 縣城。到了一八七零年代，就增長到九百二十人之多，但是，只有一名女人。記錄中指出，兩百六十一名華人，住在 Suisun 市鎮為農工，十三人為洗衣工人。一百七十一名在 Vacaville 為工人，一百八十二人居住在 Vallejo 城。其他一些華人則分別散住在 Benicia、Dixon、Rio Vista 和 Green Valley 等城鎮。

根據 Vacaville 一位史學家 Ronald Limbaugh 指出，當地以至於加州各地水果生產事業，幾乎全依靠華工的支持。一八八二年的排華法案實施後，華工來源更是大量減少。那些早期移民的後代，卻很少繼續的居住在那個地區了。到了一九五零年代時，這種情形才有改變。Vacaville 地區遷入了一些華人經營的小生意。

今天來到 Solano 縣城的新移民，大部份都不清楚華人當年在那裡的生活情形。一九八零年以前，在 Solano 的華人人數根本不多。但自從尹氏夫婦在一九九零年間選擇 Solano 地區發展他們的麥當勞事業後，華裔社區逐漸組成了不能被忽視的力量。

尹氏夫婦與當地其他華人，聯合組成第一個Solano
地區的華美聯盟協會。從那個組織下，於一九九六年，
更衍生出了 Vacaville 第一所有三十幾人參加的華人學
校。很快的，在不到兩年之間，這個由八個家庭合成的
華人團體，增長到三百名會員，華人學校中有一百名學
生。由於尹氏夫婦的倡導與極力支持，將所有的新舊移
民華人聯繫起來，組織成頗具規模的華人社團。中國新
年時間，傳統的舞獅，放鞭炮，利市紅包與「恭喜發財」
的喜氣洋洋的情形，點綴出華人數千年的固有文化特
色。當地官員，顯要們與商業代表等，紛紛踴躍參加此
項盛典。

　　一九九七年，華美協會並在尹氏家園華廈，舉辦一
場有關Solano地區華人歷史的會議。到會參加者，高達
數百人之多。學者，歷史家以及博物館負責人等，應邀
在會中做研究報導與來賓分享心得。華人的心聲與傳
統，在那次的集會中，歷史性的記載了下來。

　　尹氏時常為爭取亞裔的權益而奮鬥。一九九六年，
Tele-Communications， Inc. (TCI）決定取銷在 Vacaville
地區的KTSF， Channel 26 電視台時，尹氏立刻組成了
一個由二十五人的「Save Channel 26 Coalition」營救第
26台聯盟會，向官方領袖及電視台主管，商界代表等發
動游說爭取續播活動。那唯一以外語為主的電視台，對
很多以說英語為第二語言者的意義重大。新移民剛剛來
到陌生的國家，對英語的理解不多，如果這僅有的對外

溝通工具被奪走後，他們更難了解所處環境周圍的大小新聞，和那自己熟悉的娛樂節目。尹氏立刻採取行動，搜集了大約兩千個簽名，送交給電視台當局，請求他們根據陳訴實際案情，恢復對亞裔非常重要的二十六台。經過尹氏領導的聯盟會會員們的努力及「只許成功，不許失敗」之決心，最後，終於讓電視台當局點頭，重新核准恢復那亞裔的精神食糧第二十六號電視台。

不久，尹氏接到 Vacaville 市長 David Fleming 的親屬函件：「親愛的 C.C.（尹氏）：我非常驚奇和敬佩你迅速的行動，和執著的決心，來為亞裔爭取恢復他們喜愛的電視台。亞裔朋友們請求我親自向你致意，表達誠懇的謝意。我再次謝謝你的努力。毫無疑問的，你是我們社區的一大重要份子。」

上述各項將尹氏的輪廓清晰的刻劃了出來。毫無疑問的，他深具在亞裔社團裡的超越領袖才幹。有尹氏夫婦的努力做橋樑，才能與主流社會溝通，聯繫起來，共同為大家謀福利。他為 Solano 地區的亞裔社團，展開了受人注目的新紀元。

他們在一九九五年所建立的尹氏家園，除了是自己溫暖舒適的家外，也是時常招待員工的聚會場所。更是許多大型重要事件會議的活動場。如：一九九六年，尹氏市商會主席就職典禮，一九九七年的華人歷史會議，以及許多重要籌款，慈善晚會等，都是尹氏安排策劃在尹氏家園中完滿地促進成功。

結論

　　人人都知道經營麥當勞是一項好的投資事業，但也是競爭非常激烈的一項商業。要打入內層執業，實非易事。每年大約有兩萬件申請書，但只有百餘件被核准受訓資格，而只有一半申請人才被接受為連鎖餐館開業。平均麥當勞業主，或經理最多能擁有兩家到三家連鎖餐館。在兩萬三十多的連鎖餐館中，只有百分之六的業主是少數民族。可想而知，尹氏夫婦的成就，是多麼的非比尋常。他們除了感到自豪外，他們也感謝麥當勞當局給予的指導與完整訓練，以及有關各界的支持與協助。一九九五年，尹氏夫婦創辦了自己的麥當勞亞裔協會 Asian McDonald Corp (AMOA)。從此，亞裔同業們大家互相輔助，彼此支持。麥當勞事業中仍有很多就業機會，而且也有是對亞裔有幫助待開發的市場。在千禧年到達之時，尹氏夫婦所做的，是為亞裔與麥當勞間的聯繫築橋，但求未來子弟能因此受惠，得到更好的前途。

　　尹氏夫婦所代表的，是在加州的華裔新一代移民。他們都是有著雙語文，雙重文化，更是在美大學受教育的優良份子。他們幸運的未曾受到像早期華人移民那種不平待遇與隔離。他們有機會，選擇自己想要做的事業求發展。他們進入一般社區，商界與政界並肩平等的參與活動。美國黃金夢想，在他們夫婦身上得到證實。他們對社區的貢獻巨大，價值非凡。許多困難的路，由尹

氏夫婦走了出來。同樣地，其他人也並不是辦不到的，只要下定決心，努力而不怕打擊，勇往直前。尹氏夫婦成功的事實，不能只以財富的標準去衡量，而是應歸於他們堅定的信心，傑出的成就，以及對僑社和社區等方面獻出了積極的參與和回饋。

加州華裔的聖地：
大埠（舊金山）、
二埠（沙加緬度）和
三埠（士德頓）

馮宗祖　博士

引言

林貞（Jan Lin）的「重建華埠：種裔小天地，環球大轉變」（Reconstructing Chinatown: Ehtnic Enclave, Global Change）（1998），吳福克（Frank Ng）的「台裔美國人」（Taiwanese Americans）（1998）及方丁姆（Tim Fong）的「第一個市郊的華埠」（First Suburban Chinatown）（1994）是最近有關華人社區研究幾本值得注意的著作。方氏的書，不再以市內的

華埠,而以洛杉磯聖基博谷（San Gabriel Valley） 的市郊華人社區為研究對象。方書討論一九六五年以後華裔移民在新鄉適應、政治代表和種族關係等議題。吳書是第一本全面討論台灣移民在美國生活的專書,而林書則以紐約本地化／環球化的華埠為討論焦點。

大部份現時的研究,都以東岸例如紐約市的華埠及南加州的聖基博谷華人社區為主。此文專論華人移民／華裔美國人的不斷增長,以及他們在美國所呈現的多元面貌。因為有關華裔研究之多,並且方法各異,所以必要先簡述一下華裔的始源。

大埠（舊金山）

一些當代的華裔社區研究,認為美國一些華埠已超越舊金山華埠的規模。此文無意辯論此說法。但文獻足徵,舊金山華埠是美國第一個華埠。從一八四九年至一九六五年,舊金山港接待無數的華裔移民。例子之一,是天使島（相當於東岸的 Ellis 島）。天使島代表「移民的終站」,特別是華裔移民進入美國西岸的首站。麥禮謙等編著的「埃侖詩集」（Island Poetry and History of Chinese Immigrants on Angel Island 1910-1940）指出,從一九一零年至一九四零年,從天使島來美的移民數目約有十七萬五千人。

更重要的,舊金山華埠是發展華人其他社區的社會

典範。以後，其他近舊金山的城市例如沙加緬度和士德頓等，都是模仿舊金山華埠的社會制度。當早期華人移民進入美國的內陸之後，他們都建立以舊金山華埠為模式或大或小的華埠。即使直至今天，大部份的華人的鄉里和宗親會所總部，也是設在舊金山。甚至是較為進步的由美國土生華裔組成的同源總會，亦是在一八九五年在舊金山創辦的。同源總會現在美國多個地方設有分會，但總部仍設在舊金山。

但是，舊金山華埠過去和現在都不是一個孤島。直至七十年代，舊金山華埠仍是全美最大的華人社區，周圍有不少較小的華人聚居地。在六五年之前人們提到舊金山華埠時，通常是指包括灣區所有華埠在內而言，而以舊金山華埠為中心。在六五年之前，每個人都知道並稱舊金山華埠為「大埠」，意指第一個城市或「大的城市」。這個說法，正好表示華人對舊金山華埠地位之重視。他們稱沙加緬度為「二埠」，即第二個城市，而士德頓為「三埠」，即第三個城市。這三個城市是華裔在美國的聖地，是華裔文明的誕生地。

三埠（士德頓）

三個華埠之中，以士德頓最小。士德頓華埠的重要性，在舊金山和沙加緬度之後，排名第三。一份早期有關士德頓華埠的參考資料是「華園：士德頓的華人社區」

（Fang，1963），該文說：「早在一八二零年在士德頓仍未成為一個城市之前，已有華人在此居住⋯在一八五二年一月，一艘小蒸氣輪，載來第一批為數不少的華人。」其他有關三埠的材料，包括「三角洲的華埠：沙加緬度 —San Joaquin 三角洲的華人，1870-1960」（Chu，1970），「三埠：San Joaquin 華人傳統」（Minnick， 1988），和「驚醒一百四十年的華人社區：本地選舉之研究」（Minnick， 1994）。

二埠，沙加緬度華埠

二埠重要性僅次於舊金山華埠。一篇專論二埠的早期著作：「二埠：沙加緬度的華人社區」）（Fang，1961）指出，「對華人而言，沙加緬度是僅次於舊金山的一個重要商業中心⋯是一個最理想的居家地點⋯有一個時期居住在 Mother Lode 縣的華人，超過一萬人。」一九六一年，「約有七千華人居住在沙加緬度，其中三分一直接或間接與食品商業有關。這裡有一百五十多間雜貨店和超市，為華人擁有的，每年生意額合共超過一億五千萬元。這裡有一百四十五間華人餐館，專售中菜和美國菜。有不足三百人仍然從事洗衣行業」（Fang，1961）。

像舊金山一樣，二埠過去在其周圍也有不少較小的華人聚居地。像 Locke、Courtland 和 Walnut Grove 等農業城鎮，都屬二埠範圍。有關著作可參看：「谷地：一個

美國的華人社區」（Weiss，1974）、「洛克鎮報導：歷史概覽和號召行動」（Kagiwada，1982），和「華工田園生涯」（梁靜源，1984）。但二埠已被今天沙加緬度的華埠取代了。事實上，今天沙市存有三個華人社區：「行政的華埠」、「共存的華埠」，「和印支華埠」。

行政的華埠

什麼是行政的華埠？傳統上從三街至六街沿 I 街一帶，是沙市華人生活的中心（Fang，1961）。因為城市的建設，行政的華埠在六十年代已取代舊二埠的華埠。城市的發展將現時的二埠一分為二：部份傳統的機構，它們的總部仍設有「新的」（行政）的沙市華埠，而另外一些則搬往其他華人聚居地即共存華埠。簡言之，行政華埠代表沙市的華人，因為此華埠是中華會館、孔子廟和其他幾個傳統機構的所在地。

行政華埠位於沙市的商業區。像任何大城市的商業區一樣，要找停車位頗為困難。即使華埠是接近一條主要的高速公路，但它不像舊金山的華埠一樣，可以吸引前往商業區購物中心的遊人。另一方面，它亦沒有任何大型的亞裔超市或雜貨店，可以吸引到華人。在沒有遊客也沒有華人光顧的情況下，行政華埠就恰如城市化的洛克鎮一樣，徒具歷史意義而已。

在過去，行政華埠的主要吸引點是孔子廟。它是沙

市舉行中國傳統節日和活動的中心。除中山博物館和幾家餐館外，行政華埠將隨古舊洛克鎮的步伐走入歷史。

共存華埠

在六十年代城市發展期內，很多傳統的華人機構，都搬到距離行政華埠幾哩以外的十二街和 J 街一帶，延伸至十六街和百老匯街。林氏、李氏和其他傳統的宗親會所等，均設在十二街和 J 街地區。在十六街和百老匯另一方面，是黃氏和余氏等公所。尋找共存華埠的重要標識，是 Tower Records 和一家中式咖啡店。

我使用共存華埠的名稱，因為它與其他城市華埠不一樣，是和日本埠一起共用這個地區的。在這個共存的地區內，華人和日本人的商店、餐館及家庭經營的小生意聚集一起。與傳統華人組織一樣，日本人在這個共存的地區內亦設有一間佛廟，很多日裔的節日都在地區的「Obon」內舉行。在近十六街和百老匯街，除華人和日本餐館及商店外，並有很多其他族裔都會的商店。

行政華埠和共存華埠有很多明顯差別。與行政華埠不同，無論是華人或其他人，他們前來共存華埠購物、進餐，和社交。這些社交和文化活動，給華人帶來社區的認同感。共存華人社區提供一個經濟環境讓華人做生意，而行政華埠對商業卻無吸引力。最後，共存華埠是融和性的，其他族裔亦樂於來此。因此，這個由華人創

造服務華人的社區，配合其他可供謀生的經濟因素，使華人對此社區產生一種真正的歸屬感。行政華埠就缺少這些能培養社區歸屬感的人的及經濟的因素。

印支華埠

沙市第三個華埠亦是最新的多元華埠。很多住在沙加緬度的人，均認為這第三個華埠才是「真正的華埠」。這個華埠的社會和經濟中心地帶，位於 Stockton Blvd. 與 Elder Creek Road 交界一帶。大部份的商業都是位於 Stockton 大道一哩的一段範圍內。與其他兩個華埠不同，第三華埠包括很多小型和中型的廣場，每個廣場有不同類型的商業。

從我們實地了解所得，這裡有超過六個廣場，和眾多的華人及東南亞裔的超市。除典型的華人麵店和餐館外，這些廣場並設有書店、錄映帶店，和理髮店。這些廣場和超市都是一應俱全的，對象是合家大小，活動不僅止於購買雜貨而已。在週末，第三華埠就像舊金山和奧克蘭的華埠一樣熱鬧。

我稱這個華埠為印支華埠，因為大部份居民都是來自東南亞的國家如寮國、越南和柬埔寨。更準確一點說，印支華埠代表來自印支國家的華裔。但是，也有其他華裔在此居住，來此購物、進食，和社交。這個華埠的重要，可從超越國界的星島日報在此開設沙加緬度辦事處

中看得到。來自東南亞的華裔亦有他們自己的周報，中華論壇報，專以報導原居國和居住在美國其他地方華裔社區的消息。

　　印支華埠有多個社區機構，但最有地位和最出名的是二埠印支華裔聯誼會。聯會為社區提供多種服務，它有一座觀音廟專供善男信女拜祀，有一家華文學校是沙市最好的中文學校。很多以前的學生都表示，他們很高興曾在此校讀書，有機會參與社區眾多活動，例如作文比賽等。

結論

　　沒有人可以否認大埠、二埠和三埠是加州華人的聖地。因為一九六五年移民政策的改變，及八十年代東南亞難民潮，這三個城市均受到重大的衝擊。這三個城市的華人社區，現在都能自給自足，並且人口十分多元化，包括來自不同地方的華人。灣區華人社區現在包括來自中國、香港、台灣、越南的華人，以及土生的華裔。沙市的華裔社區亦反映灣區華人社區的同一現象。

沙加緬度的二埠印支華裔聯誼會與新華埠

馮宗祖　博士

引言

這裡所用「華裔」一詞，指在越戰期內和之後從東南亞國家逃出的難民（1963-1975：由美國國會通過的東京灣決議起，終於海軍在西貢美國領事館天台乘 CH-46 直昇機離開）。一九七五年四月三十日西貢陷共後，開始了最大批緊急移民美國的行動。從一九七五年四月至十二月，有超過十三萬越南難民進入美國。這些人中有多少是華裔並無統計。他們的數目可能太少，因而未為美國政府注意。他們通常都是併同越南人一起計算。

社會科學家將東南亞裔分為五個群體：越南裔、寮裔、柬埔寨裔、苗裔和東南亞的華裔。在這五個團體下，

又可再分為更多的小群體。南越那時有最大的華人人口，有一百四十萬人；柬埔寨，有三十一萬人；及寮國，有三萬七千人。北越有三十萬華人。一般來說大家都同意華裔來美的數目，以第二次東南亞難民潮最多，頂點是一九八零年的財政年度（即一九七九年十月一日至一九八零年九月三十日），當時有 166,700 東南亞裔難民湧入美國，其中九萬五千人來自越南。他們都是「船民」。自一九七五年離開越南的「船民」數目，直至一九七九年八月為止，華裔佔了最少百分之七十五（222,870）。

　　按他們來美的時間、家庭的社會地位、在東道主國所受的待遇而定，五個主要東南亞裔群體，在美國各自設立他們的社會組織。有關他們適應的模式，已有不少專文論及。這些研究集中於東南亞兒童在美求學的課題。但是，這些研究中，少有涉及東南亞裔社區機構對美國文化的適應，以及這些機構對教育和社會網絡的影響。

　　如要討論每個群體的社會組織，工程非常浩大。此文只集中於敘述沙加緬度的一個東南亞裔的組織：二埠印支華裔聯誼會。首先，我們將介紹一下美國的東南亞裔。然後討論一下東南亞裔社會團體的移植和結構。最後，我們將討論沙加緬度二埠印支華裔聯誼會的功能和結構。

（一）東南亞裔史簡述

東南亞國家有些華人更改姓名，原因是為謀生。Wilbur Gay Lee 的碩士論文（1960）《海外華人社區：一個比較的方法》說，「一九五六年吳庭琰發出指令，准予所有在越南出生的華裔為越南籍。而所有外國人均需登記。當登記完成後，所有外國人均給予越南的公民證書。同時南越開始了反華活動：華文學校被迫用越南語教學；中文的商店招牌需要拿下；越南出生的華裔受到壓力，需要改一個越南的名字；有十一種職業是不准外國人做的；外國人被迫在一年內將他們的商業售給越南人。」

　　美國政府在第一次難民潮時，頗為忽視了華裔難民，所以將難民分為三類：越南裔、柬埔寨裔和寮裔。後來，政府發現來自北越的苗族人，是最新來美的群體之一。美國政府當時，並未留意到他們屬另一個群體，只將他們與其他的東南亞難民合併在一起。

　　一九七九年，華裔難民開始正式受到注意。一份由眾議院擬定稱為《印支難民的生存：一九七九年八月》的政府文件，認知和識別出在東南亞難民營內，以前和現在均有華裔。在這些難民營的華裔人口數目計有：香港，12,098，印尼，4,300，及馬來西亞，23,888。一九七九年，總數為 40,286。但是，有些文件對他們的存在，並未加以關注，例如《亞太事務委員會第九十六次會議聽證，第一及第二次》就是例子之一。

　　一九八六年，統計已來美國的柬埔寨人有

138,800，寮國人有 162,000，及越南人有 506,700，合共
809,500。以八十年代末期論，每七名亞裔中有一名是東
南亞裔。到一九八七年八月，他們有 389,000 住在加州。
加州曾是，並繼續是這些亞裔難民最喜歡居住的地方。
他們都集中於四個加州的縣內：橙縣，60,000；洛杉磯
縣，93,000；三藩市縣，28,400；及聖他克拉克縣，37,600。
在沙加緬度，一九九二年的《沙加緬度縣亞太裔社區需
要評估》指出，該地最少有 22,197 的東南亞裔，包括：
越南裔，9,497；苗族，5,470；華裔，3,630；岷族，3,000；
及柬埔寨裔，600。

　　來自東南亞的華裔，來美後短短二十年的時間，發
生不少重大的改變。在九十年代，華裔的社區發展成熟。
現時有不少的華裔社區，從聖荷西的自力更生的「小西
貢」，到在東屋崙區與黑人社區共存的社區（Fong，
1992），到洛杉磯的 San Gabriel Valley 的近郊社區，以及
沙加緬度的新華埠或小西貢（Fong， 1998），到三藩市
田德隆區的印支埠等，不一而足。現在華裔已成為美國
社會有貢獻的公民，也是美國社會的一份子，在較廣大
的華裔社區中，更是如此。

（二）移植和建構東南亞裔社會團體

　　社會團體是指什麼？「社會團體」簡單的指社區組
織、協會、或其他或多或少能代表社區的聯誼會等。一

個較準確的說法，是指社區一些有影響力的機構例如中華會館、地區協會和華埠典型常見的宗親會所等（參看Lyman， 1974）。

很多社會科學家在他們的研究中，均承認東南亞裔成立的「互助社」。但這些研究中，很少討論到這些社區的社會團體。難民聚集一起，成立像互助社，參加文化活動，進行社交聯誼等，在陌生人在東道主國中，交流共同經驗和共同性，是適應新環境的重要因素。這些研究所討論東南亞裔的社會團體，都無法分辨社區機構的不同類型：它們有多少是從原居國移植過來，又有多少是在美國新生的呢？

討論一下 Min Zhou（1997）的文章《華埠的社會資本：社區機構和家庭幫助年輕一代適應環境的角色》，有助我們對此課題的認識。周文討論的是在紐約華埠成立的新的社會團體的角色，它們的作用，不一定在取代傳統社會團體，而是在「加強移民子弟的調整和創業‥」。根據她的說法，「華埠的社會團體，不論是正式或非正式的、有政府資助或植根於社區的，對適應華埠社區的社會和經濟需要，都扮演了重要的角色。」

在有關東南亞裔的論文中，Diana Bui 一九八三年的文章《印支互助社》是一篇有關東南亞裔社會團體最詳細的分析。她在文章中指出自一九七五年以來已有五百多間的互助社成立（Bui， 1983）。她並且將互助社分為八個種類，代表了這些組織的多元性：社交／聯誼類、

教育／文化類、宗教／精神類、專業政治組織類、學生組織、菁英組織、退伍軍人／婦女類，及移民安置組織類。

　　Bui 的文章富資訊性，提供有關東南亞裔社會和政治組織的概括性資料。但是，她的論點還是不夠健全，而且並非以一個特定的東南亞裔社區為對象。她所涉及的東南亞裔機構，不限於一個州而已。簡言之，她的資料缺乏深度，而且沒有論及社區的社會制度結構。另一方面，麥禮謙的《以本籍為主及／或方言為附的美國華人機構，一九四零至一九九零年代》包括來自東南亞的華裔所成立的機構。雖然麥的討論，限於來自東南亞的華裔組織，但在突出東南亞裔社會團體的多元性方面，有其貢獻。

　　考慮到 Bui 的文章發表於一九八三年，在為大眾提供有關東南亞裔社會團體資料方面，她做了很多的工作。自此之後，東南亞裔社區日見成熟和繼續成長。現在，東南亞裔社區製造和出產很多他們文化及傳統所需的產品。現時有很多東南亞裔的報章、雜誌、和錄映帶。例如,《西貢時報》就報導洛杉磯、科羅拉多、佛羅里達、聖荷西、沙加緬度、華盛頓和芝加哥的新聞;《Lang》是一份地區性的越文週刊，報導沙加緬度、史德頓和 Modesto 的新聞;而 NGUOI Viet Tu Do 是沙加緬度本地社區的月刊。

　　另一個社區機構資料的來源，是亞裔電話簿。過去

在屋崙、沙加緬度、洛杉磯和三藩市的實地工作中，每個城市的東南亞裔社區，都出版有他們自己的電話簿。有幾本電話簿，例如 Vietnamese Director/USA 1994，宣稱發行全國。沙加緬度的華裔，也出版一本電話簿，即沙加緬度中文電話簿／黃頁，1997-1998。一本典型的東南亞裔電話簿會列出該地的東南亞裔社會團體。在黃頁上，列出的團體不一定包括所有的社區組織。但是，即使是部份的名單，亦已提供一個窗戶，讓我們對難民和移民社區的內部運作，有一個認識。

在東南亞裔中，看來華裔有最多不同的社區組織，包括移植過來的、在這裡創辦的、非牟利式的，和全國性的。來自印支的華裔，最低限度移植了五個主體的地區和方言組織：潮州話、粵語、客家話、福建話和海南話（Haines， 1985）。例如，聖荷西的潮州會館，就被認為是一個移植的組織，因為在越南、寮國和柬埔寨均有潮州會館。而洛杉磯的華裔耆英會（The Elderly Chinese Association），則是一個非牟利機構的例子。

洛杉磯的寮裔華人協會（The Lao Chinese Association），被認為是一個全國性的組織，入會資格以所屬原居國為主。這些全國性的組織的發展，通常是該群體的人口太少，無法成立一個姓氏或地區性的組織。可資比較的全國性組織是新的組織。沙加緬度的二埠印支華裔聯誼會，就是一個新的組織，因為它取代了並包括來自越南、寮國和柬埔寨的聯誼會。我們需要記得，

這些組織可能有重疊，而會員均可自由擁有雙重會員籍。更重要的是，這些華裔的組織，存在於每個亞裔和東南亞裔社區，例如潮州會館，能連繫本地、全國乃至全球的潮州會館組織，為會員服務。

沙加緬度有不少華裔組織，加州首府華人俱樂部（Chinese Capital Club）及包括典型宗親會，如黃氏宗親會等。在沙加緬度這個多元的華裔社區裡面，兩個人口最多的華裔群體，是美籍華人和來自東南亞的華裔。美籍華人，包括在美出生的華裔和他們的先輩。這個群體既有可上溯至十九世紀末期的傳統結構的團體，也有由土生華裔領導的社區服務機構。另一方面，來自東南亞的華裔，被認為是這個社區的最新成員。所以，沙加緬度的華人組織，有一九六五年前自十九世紀以來已存在的組織，也有在一九八二年新成立的二埠印支華裔聯誼會。一九九七／一九九八年的沙加緬度中文黃頁電話簿，列出最少有十四間華人組織。這些組織的服務對象各異，功能各異。

（三）二埠印支華裔聯誼會的結構和功能

二埠印支華裔聯誼會於一九八二年八月，由越南、柬埔寨和寮國的難民成立。該會的第二任主席 Hao Hau 說，「聯誼會可以促進來自印支華人的團結。為了印支華人的福祉，我準備花多一點時間為他們服務，並幫助他

們解決不同的問題」（Ma， 1998）。聯誼會的主要目的，
代表了沙加緬度的華裔，及「為華人社區帶來福利」
（Ma， 1998）。

聯誼會的成立是頗為艱辛的。我們訪問了不少聯誼
會的幹事，黃先生就提到他們曾經面對的困難：「我們開
始時犯了不少錯誤。我們不知道美國的法律。當我們為
聯誼會購入一座物業時，我們不知道與建該物業應當遵
循什麼法例？在我們辦中文學校時遇到的問題則最多，」
他說。他們的會議是在會員家中或會員的商業處所舉行
的。一九九六年二埠印支華裔聯誼會的年刊，述及他們
早期的掙扎，例如租用的地方搬遷的困難。直到成立中
山華文學校後，才開始有一個永久的會址。

二埠印支華裔聯誼會的永久會址，位於新華埠或稱
小西貢的中心區，在士德頓大道和 Elder Creek Road 之
間。會址佔地五萬平方呎，有三座主要建築物，及一個
大型的停車場（Ma， 1998）。中間的建築物是觀音廟。
廟前是一個空地，可以搭建表演舞台。廟側有華文學校
教室。華文學校共有六個課室，兩個辦事處和一家書店。
廟後是另一座大的建築物，有高的天花板，很多時是用
來做禮堂，供私人的社交和文化活動用。

現時聯誼會有五百三十三名會員（一九九六年二埠
印支華裔聯誼會年刊）。每名會員有一個會員號碼。該號
碼是永久性的。身為耆英部的領導人，Von 先生提供一
個合理的解釋，「有些會員離開而再入會，再給他一個新

號碼，就會製造混亂。所以每名會員，均有他們自己永
久的號碼，不論他們是不是活躍的會員。」如夫婦二人
均是會員，他們分別有自己的號碼。因此我們可以假設
這五百三十三名會員內，會有來自同一家庭的成員。假
設有家庭成員在內，則四百或五百名會員·依然代表了
沙加緬度四至五百個家庭。

　　聯誼會包括八名董事及主管。最高層負責聯誼會三
個主要部份：中山華文學校、觀音廟，和耆英康樂組。
每個部份有其本身的經管單位，服務沙加緬度華裔社區
的需要。開始時，聯誼會大部份的財政支援，來自社區
和商界領袖。例如，一九九六年前任主席 Venh-Sau Vong
籌了四十萬元興建觀音廟（Ma， 1998）。現在，從觀音
廟所得的捐助以及其他的籌款活動，可以幫助聯誼會保
持經濟獨立。

（A）中山華文學校

　　中文學校的組織體，包括校長和資深教師。他們負
責管理中文學校。中文學校的作用，是向住在沙加緬度
的華裔年輕一代，介紹中國的文化傳統。為了關心年輕
的一代，印支聯會的高級幹事，決定為聯會設置一個永
久的會址，以便有一個地方可讓年輕一代學習中國歷史
和語言。據一名熟知聯會情況的人士透露，「有一個讓年
輕人可去的地方是好的。在這之前，我們看到很多年輕

的華裔吸煙，在電子機遊樂場留連。我們不喜歡那種作風。」

　　中山華文學校每天上課，星期日除外。基本上，華文學校分為兩部：第一部是星期一、三、五下午三時三十分至六時三十分上課；第二部星期二、四、六上課。像大部份美國的華文學校一樣，中山華文學校提供至八年級的課程。因為很多學校學生，在八年級以後就無興趣繼續。根據我們的研究，大部份人同意「從一年級至六年級，大概有二百個有興趣的學生。由六至八年級，有興趣學習中文的學生大幅度下降，八年級至高中，只有寥寥幾人而已。」學生包括在美出生的華裔和移民子弟。除教授中文外，學校並教授中國舞蹈和繪畫。有些學生，組織自己的交誼會，例如乒乓球會等。

　　根據學校的幹事張先生說，「我們這都是為孩子服務的工作。學費差不多免費。書籍是免費的。我們的目的，是教育下一代認識中國文化。我們不在營利。」和以往的學生交談，他們承認張先生的說法。如學生沒有錢購買學校的課本，學校就免費提供。學費每月是三十元，按學生的經濟情況而定。「學費是用來維持學校設施的，而不是使用支付教師的薪金，」張先生說。學校有教無類一視同仁，接受所有想學習中國文化的學生。

（Ｂ）耆英康樂部

聯會第二個單位是耆英部。有一位可予信任的會員，專責總管工作。耆英康樂對會員和大眾來說，可以有多種意義。它與美國耆英康樂組織，同樣提供一個場所，讓上了年紀的人休閒和運動。華人耆英部的另一功能，是為耆英會員提供非正式的「壽終保險」。這種非正式的「壽終保險」目的有二：（一）確保有適當的殯葬，及（二）照顧經濟有困難的家庭。此非正式的「壽終保險」必須從美國的涵面來觀察，因為在美國，政府基本上沒有予華人家庭對逝者的承諾和責任。

　　參加耆英部的資格，必須是沙加緬度的居民，年齡在六十歲以上。在享用福利方面，年齡是一個重要的因素。它按會員的年齡和會籍長久，決定他或她享用的福利。現時聯會會員年費每月三十五元，月費兩元（耆英手冊，一九九八）。當會員去世時，耆英部的會員須每人捐款十五元用作死者的殯葬費（耆英手冊，一九九八）。如耆英部的會員人數眾多，捐款所得，除支付殯葬費用外，尚有餘款，則交給死者的親人。如捐款不足，聯會則填補其餘所需。

　　當東南亞華裔難民來美時，他們面對很多新土地上的社會和文化問題。沙加緬度華裔面對的困難之一，是家中老人去世，朋友、家人和社區能提供的財力支持是有限的。更重要的是，不少華人來美，有的是合家大小前來，但亦有孤身前來的。在一個新國家裡，他們都缺少經濟資源，進行適當的殯葬。華人社區對此都有共同

經驗。所以他們設立這個「壽終保險」的政策。這種政策，更推及到更大的華人社區，包括沙加緬度的華裔印支聯會各單位。

（C）觀音廟

觀音廟於一九九六年成立，是聯會的最新措施。觀音廟內供奉很多神祇。除觀音外，尚有關公和天后。這種敬奉戰神關公和天后，適宜大部份在美信徒的崇拜。正如 Vong 所說，「當印支難民投奔怒海追尋自由時，他們向天后祈禱，希望能安全的抵達彼岸，而實際上大部份人，都能抵達他們的目的地」（Ma，一九九八）。

與耆英部的結構相似，觀音廟由專人負責照顧。觀音廟通常服務華人婦女，大門常開，供人崇拜。此外信徒亦可求籤問前程。通常人們會在農曆的初一十五前來拜神，這兩天是最忙碌的，也最熱鬧，大家亦趁機，可以會面聯誼。在這兩天，廟內供應齋菜招待來賓。

聯會三個組織中，以觀音廟收入最可觀。善男信女捐給觀音廟的捐款，必須交給聯會，維持聯會的經濟穩定。人們樂意捐助供添置香油和念經費用。簡言之，每月初一十五經常有信徒前來拜神，捐款自然不斷流入。

華文學校、觀音廟和耆英部是今天沙加緬度華人社區的三個重要份子：包括服務年輕、年老的一代，以及婦女。這三個單位亦反映了社區的人口，和適應這些人

口的需要。聯會的特點,是其融和性,和人們對該會的歸屬感。這都說明了聯會的成功、發展和穩定的原因。現任會長 Vong 說,「我們需要通力合作,那是一種責任」(Ma,一九九八)。提到印支社交團體的發展時,他說,「年輕一代只要肯參與,作出多一點貢獻,就能幫助這些團體繼續下去,穩步發展」(Ma,一九九八)。

（D）結語

　　二埠印支華裔聯誼會的成立不是獨一無二的。在美國各地,大部份華裔組織的成立情況頗為類似。按本地環境的需要而定,大部份的華裔聯誼會,都有類似的結構和功能。在一些華裔人口眾多的地方,例如洛杉磯和三藩市,很多社交機構,均反映了來自東南亞華裔人口的多元性。例如,代表東南亞五個重要華裔人口——潮州、客家、福建、海南和廣東——的機構,均已轉移以洛杉磯為根據地。

　　另一方面,一些城市地區和郊區,可能只有一個代表當地整個華裔的組織。二埠印支華裔聯誼會,就是一個好的例子。不論是只有一家組織或多家組織,華裔的社交組織均是彼此有連繫的。特別是,轉移來美的社交機構,性質上是超國度的。例如,轉移來美的潮州會館,保持與世界各地,特別是亞洲的潮州會館的連繫。換言之,潮州會館不只與本地的機構有連繫,並與全國和世

界各地的潮州會館有連繫。

　　一九九三年九月四日至六日，第七屆國際潮州會館會議在聖荷西會議中心舉行。從中文報章報道所知，約有四十一個來自世界各地的潮州會館參於盛會。其中有超過一千二百人，來自聖荷西地區。這個國際會議，由美國九個地方的潮州會館聯合主辦：紐約、北加州、南加州、俄勒崗州、美國南部、華盛頓、芝加哥、夏威夷、聖荷西。

　　就我們所知，與這些華裔組織相似的其他亞裔組織，包括華埠的其他社區團體。這些團體開始時以宗親會、地方會所的形式出現，而最高的體現形式，是中華總會館。上述兩個聯會，從功能和結構來看，有一個明顯的不同。我們無須溯源早期華人社區團體如何成立，但它們現時的功能和結構，並無印支聯會一類的包融性。以沙加緬度來說，無論內外，大家都認為這裡的華裔社區是「新華埠」。

華裔成長和發展的根源
（加州沙加緬度的
華裔社區機構）

梁靜源　教授・梁張愛齡

壹 百五十年來，沙加緬度的華裔社區已演變為一個十分多元化的社區，包括第二至第六代的土生華裔，從五十年代至九十年代有來自中國、台灣和香港的移民，和自七十年代後期從東南亞來美的華裔。

華裔社區在沙加緬度有長久的歷史。一八四八年當馬歇爾在 Coloma 發現金礦後，就出現了早期的華埠，為前來主礦區（Mother Lode）掘金的華人，供應雜貨、工具和日用品。今天舊沙加緬度部份地方，即早期華人居住的原址。新華埠在一九六九年至七二年建成，位於第四街及第五街，和 J 街及 I 街。

與早期華人有關的文物及口述歷史，可以在沙加緬度鐵路博物館、沙加緬度歷史博物館、加州博物館、Folsom 歷史博物館和中山紀念堂等地方看到。一個新設名為「早期沙加緬度華人先驅歷史」的永久性展覽，現在第六街和 I 街的聯邦法院展出。

洛克（Locke）鎮是一個早期華人居住的鄉村小鎮，位於沙加緬度三角洲。從十九世紀末期至二十世紀初期，不少華人在此參加築堤和從事農耕，現在此鎮已被定為一個國家歷史景點，每年吸引數百萬的遊人。

除影響華人和他們社區的早期立法和法律，華人社團和社區領袖的影響亦非常重大，值得留意。現時在沙加緬度有七十多個華人組織，有教會團體。有些組織並不僅限於華人，他們並接納其他族裔的成員。每年這些組織舉行數以百計的活動，代表了他們的視野、創造力、理念、傳統、藝術和習俗。這是一個充滿動力的社區，繼續為沙加緬度的多元傳統作出貢獻。華裔在沙加緬度已穩紮基礎，並在他們聚居之地，促進繁榮。以下簡介幾個對沙加緬度華人社區，對主流社會作出貢獻的主要組織，以及他們的活動和成員。

因為篇幅和此計劃的資源所限，這裡無法一一列舉其他的組織和個人，但他們對豐富沙加緬度華裔社區的貢獻，實在值得我們給予同樣的表揚和尊敬。

（一）中華會館及宗親會

中華會館是沙加緬度華人社區歷史最悠久的組織。這個機構包括八個宗親會：至德三德會所、至孝篤親會所、林家公所、李安敦宗公所、鄧高密公所、溯源會館、黃家公所和余風采堂，還有多個其他的團體，包括秉公堂、國民黨，和中山紀念堂協會。

中華會館位於 I 街和第四街，設於一座宏偉的孔廟內。這是一座多層的建築物，包括一家華文學校和一個社區中心。會館的主要入口是一座大階梯，直入一個可容一千多人的禮堂。舞台正中是一幅巨大的孔子像。大堂內有兩幅壁畫：一幅表現早期華人掘金和建築鐵路的歷史，另一幅是表揚今日華裔從事的各種專業，例如醫藥、法律、工程，甚至參政等。華文學校有一個辦事處和五個教室，可以容納三百多名學生。地庫包括一個體育館和廚房，可供舉行體育和社區活動用。

該館的一些主要功能，是維護和弘揚中國的傳統及文化。因此他們成立華文學校，提供華語課程。在農曆新年裡，上述的每個宗親會都會設置「春宴」，通常是在二月至四月的週末舉行。「春宴」一方面慶賀新年，一方面讓會所的幹事和成員，有機會和其他組織的成員聚會保持聯絡。「春宴」不只為本地華埠的餐館和雜貨店帶來生意，並且是一個加強各方政要和華人社區溝通的活動。

沙加緬度中華會館和宗親會，在美國多個城市和世界其他地方都設有分會，因而形成一個環球性的強大網結，華人無論居住在什麼地方，都有機會連繫他們的同

種與宗親。

此類組織和宗親會等，很多都設有獎學金，獎勵華文學校讀書及在公校讀書的華裔子弟。很多傑出的領袖，對他們的組織乃至整個華人社區的福祉，都做出人才與財力的貢獻。因此，此類組織都自供自給。新一代華裔未必能充份欣賞和明白他們的掙扎和努力成果，但他們還是華裔社區的重要資源。

（二）沙加緬度印支聯會

來自印支的華人，估計有一萬五千多人。他們大部份居住在南沙加緬度 Stockton Blvd. 和 Lemon Hill 一帶。一九七五年南越陷共，很多非牟利機構和政府機關，申請這些難民來美，他們都居住在這一帶。他們抵美後，立刻形成一個新的華人社區。他們大部份都講粵語，越南語及國語。

沙加緬度印支聯會，是在一九八二年成立的。那時在這一區，已有三千多華人居住。今天，他們經營超一百多種小生意。此外，還有多個大型的超市和餐館，為同鄉提供數百個就業機會。這可說是沙加緬度的第二個華埠，發展迅速。沙加緬度印支聯會位於 6117 Elder Creek Road，設有一個文化中心，一家華文學校和一座觀音廟。

因為有多種新的華人商業和擴展計劃，造成此區相

當多的新建設和復建工程，增加人們的就業機會，並改變了 Stockton 大道的面貌。沙加緬度印支聯會領導，推動不少裨益社區的計劃，並積極支持多項公民和慈善項目，實在值得稱頌。

來自印支的華人的領導方式，可從以下摘要中理解。當沙加緬度印支聯會在一九八二年成立時，聯會租用一個（三千平方呎的店址），設立華文學校。從一九八二年至八四年，每名董事承諾每月捐出五十至一百元，用於支付學校的租金和其他費用，且支援一個為老人服務的耆英自助委員會。董事和志願工作者，親自出力將租來的地方間成多個課室，並親自建造桌椅供學生使用。那時約有三百至五百的學生，在公校上課之後，且每星期一至五下午四時至六時，及週末上午前來華文學校上課。

在一九八五至八六年，每名董事捐出高達五千元的捐款，共得八萬元孳息，用於購買 6117 Elder Creek Road 的三座舊建築物，作為聯會和華文學校的永久會址和校址。耆英自助委員會買了一架小巴，接載耆英來往聯會。一九八六至八九年，因為舊建築物需要裝修，華文學校暫時停辦三年。聯會的籌款活動，從沙加緬度至舊金山至洛杉磯。在這段時期，聯會籌到十萬元的經費，修建三座建築物，並購入一座木製的活動屋，搬到校址來。華文學校於一九九一年重新開課。

耆英自助委員會有五百名會員。委員會已經無須董

事會的補助。會員費不只已足夠支持其活動所需，並且尚有餘款，供興建觀音廟和改善會址。從一九九一年至九四年，聯會改善了停車場和園景設計，並興建一個操場和設置籬笆。

自一九九五年至今，聯會擴大學校設備增加課室，新建一個浴室，一個供耆英活動的大堂，一座美麗的觀音廟，和宏偉傳統中國風格的大門。這些新建設，標誌聯會在美國立足不到三十年的成就。雖然很多董事和志願工作者不大嫻熟英語，他們對社區的領導和奉獻，並未因此而有所阻隔。

（三）沙加緬度社區服務中心（SCCSC）

沙加緬度社區服務中心，在一九七八年成立，是一個秉承中美傳統的非牟利機構。中心後來成為慈善金庫的成員。它以服務新僑、印支難民和耆英為主要目的。

中心為不諳英語，需要醫療、房屋和其他社會直接服務對象的人士予以協助，例如，提供雙語傳譯和翻譯服務，為領取福利的亞裔出力，提供就業及訓練和介紹工作的服務。它並為邊緣青少年提供諮商、輔導和社交活動。中心的經營費用，來自慈善金庫的資助、地方補助、籌款和捐款等。

所有董事、志願工和職員的努力，沙加緬度華人社區服務中心，已經成為一個成熟的團體，為沙加緬度的

華裔、亞裔和太平洋裔提供多元服務和支援。中心位於 915 T Street，承本地人士及社區各界的慷慨捐助，中心擁有自己永久的會址。中心每年舉行中秋之夜，是社區領袖、政府官員、專業人士、志願工作者和職員共聚一堂，齊心支持社區的福利活動。

（四）沙加緬度中華文化基金會

該基金會由汪冶宜先生在一九八六年創辦，他個人為基金會捐出二萬多元的孳息基金、協調人力資源，推動在沙市多家公校舉辦中國語言和文化的活動，這些公校包括 C.K. McClatchy、Mira Loma、El Camino、Luther Burbank 等。一九九六年，基金會幫助 Kennedy 高中開辦三班國語課程，到一九九八年擴增到五班之多。

基金會並提供三千元，資助一個筆友計劃，鼓勵沙市高中生和台灣及中國的學生通信交誼，促進地球不同地區的學生個人交流學習，增進了解彼此文化。此外，一名來自台灣 Shin-Hwa 中學的教師，曾在一九九七年及一九九九年，組織學生團到加州訪問各中學，作為期三週聯誼。這個訪問，極受加州中學的教師和學生歡迎，許多學校的學生，都有參加這個筆友活動。

基金會也是加州大學戴維斯分校亞美系實習計劃的協助成員。基金會捐出三千元，從一九九六年至九八年，在週末為西沙加緬度的 Iu-Mien 學生補習。基金會

吸引不少熱心支持者，擴大這些交流服務。

　　除支持教授中國語文外，基金會也是在沙加緬度市唯一主辦中華表演藝術的機構。它在一九九二年主辦「西藏的歌與舞」，一九九六年和一九九八年主辦「中華表演藝術節」。一九九七年和九八年，它重新組織其表演藝術的多元計劃。很多本地的音樂家和舞蹈家，都在藝術節的舞台上大顯身手，極受觀眾歡迎。因此，在一九九七年，多個新的表演藝術團體成立，例如天使弦樂團等。該樂團的指揮是 Ho Dong，同時兼任中文歌詠組的指揮。

　　且基金會參與多個其他機構主辦的活動，例如太平洋食品節、沙加緬度華人社區服務中心中秋之夜、社區每年野餐，和農曆新年慶會等。

（五）沙加緬度華美協會

　　該協會於一九八六年成立。它費時七個月舉行會議、討論、募集，擬訂會章和申請成立的非牟利機構。著名餐館業巨子和社區領袖鄧世發先生，發動朋友和多方支持而達成。他表示希望成立一個有力的機構，能影響對本地商業、經濟和政治的政策決策；應為華裔社區請命，鼓勵年輕一代，參與政治，確保華埠社區的心聲。他並希望機構有雄厚的財政資源，通過本地和在全國各地籌款，支持維護華裔利益。

　　鄧世發先生的夢想已經逐漸成真。過去十年，董事

會由一群年紀輕、活力充沛和果敢的專業人士組成。除
推行協會眾多內部活動外，它並且是代表華裔社區促進
民權的強力機構。協會的歷史委員會，曾主辦多個華裔
歷史的座談會，並參與多個保持本地早期華人文物的計
劃。它並為沙加緬度華人社區中心籌款。協會最近參與
沙加緬度房屋和重建局的平園廉租屋計劃，是最能表現
協會使命的眾多例子之一。

華裔在教育方面的成就研究報告

司徒永俊博士

美國華人雖然面對著種族偏見和歧視，仍然在社會上作出很多成就和貢獻。尤其在教育方面。華人及其他亞裔在學業上的努力，有正比的成功。全美十八歲至二十四歲的年青人，有百分之三十四，在社區大學或四年制大學中攻讀。而華人的比例，卻占了百分之六十六多數。這個明顯多數包括男女均衡趨勢。他們在大學錄取資格、持學率、低退學率、進取入學核心課程資格、考取博士學位等等，都顯示出華人及其它亞裔，在教育上的卓越成績（Hsia & Peng， 1998）。因此，很多華人獲得全國傑出學人計劃獎學金，以及西屋科學覓才計劃的特優獎。不過，美國華人中亦有相當多人數，沒有受過什麼高等教育。促使上述正面結果遭受淡化及忽視。

美國華人為何能取得如此令人讚歎的成就？是否
華人和其它亞裔多來自社會上層的富裕家庭，他們可以
給子女提供特別的關照和機會？事實上並沒有足夠的證
據，可以解釋這種民族上的優異性。也沒有証據可以充
分解釋他們的成就因素。我們若將那些已具有高等教育
水平的亞裔留學生，加上已是公民和永久居民在內，或
可解釋一些教育上的成就因由。但目前尚缺乏這種深度
研究方案。研究方向之一，如移民法較優惠受過教育的
人士，因而出現非本土出生的人，較美國本土出生的人，
有較高教育水平的傾向，但是土生亞裔在四年制大學的
就讀人數，仍比土生白人為高。(Sue & Okazaki, 1990)。

　　又如琳博士（Lynn 1987）曾提出一個優生學的假
設，嘗試說明不同種族成就上的差異。他提出一個進化
學上的理論，來解釋為何華人和亞裔在空間距離辨識潛
能，較其它種族的潛能為強。他的觀點，認為現代人在
十二萬年前，從非洲向北遷徙到歐洲和亞洲，而那些在
亞洲東北部定居的，遭遇到嚴寒的氣候，因正逢冰河時
期由北而降，為應付這種惡劣環境，他們要增強求生能
力，例如：造房、儲糧、備冬技術等等。琳氏認為這些
蒙古種人，比高加索人和黑人，要受到更大的物競天擇
的挑戰，經過如此一段長時間的天人比賽，他們的智商
便因此而得以增長。而且他們需要增進狩獵技巧，適應
寒冷的地域，促使他們發展了優越的視距能力，卻忽略
了語言方面的技能。畢竟腦袋的體積，不能再增大去配

合智商的全面的發展，因而大腦皮層‧就集中發展空間
距離辨識能力，而促使語言功能退居第二。

　　但琳氏的解釋在很多方面受到質疑，特別是在於他
假設多數亞洲人口，都是由東北亞遷移來的族裔這一說
法。他作此假設的目的，是要解釋不同地區的中國人，
如香港、星加坡、台灣等地的中國人，均具有同樣發達
的視距能力，原因他們同屬一個源流。然而有相當多的
證據，顯示由非洲來的移民，不只是遷徙到寒冷的北亞，
事實上他們亦同時移徙到較暖的東南亞。東南亞到處可
找到這些早期文化遺物。亦有證據顯示，日本人的源流，
也是來自世界各地，其中包括東南亞。

　　有些研究學者（Herrnstein & Murray， 1994; Lynn，
1987），相信華人和亞裔可能在遺傳上，比其它種族聰
明。這個論斷缺乏充份合理的證據。若要充份論證美國
亞裔，在遺傳上的優越性這個問題，我們必需列出他們
具有較高層次的智力和意識運作的事實。可惜很少這類
研究學會，就各種族的智商程度作出比較。某些研究學
者提出這樣的論點：美國華人包括美國的土生，在智力
測驗成績上，往往相等或超過全國平均數智商。但是有
關美國華人這部份的研究，有著方法學上的限制，以偏
概全。

　　限於美國亞裔的調查取樣不足，調查人員在研究測
試不同種族智力差異時，亦包括海外或外來的亞裔為研
究對象。由此可見，方法學上的不完善，使我們不能給

予有關中國人智力，有遺傳的優越這一說法，而下一肯定的結論。史蒂芬及其同事，精心設計了一套語言學習能力測驗，去直接比較中美學生，其結果顯示，有幾組在非主要題目上有差異（例如中國學生比美國學生在數學試題上得分較高），但是在智力上，並沒有整體的差別。因而遺傳因子優越一節，證據是不夠完整的。

總的說來，最能解釋美國華人在教育方面的成功典範，必須根據他的文化與學習方式因素。我相信文化因素在美國華人的教育成就上，扮演一個非常重要的角色。其次，由於他們所處的少數民族地位，使他們偏向于將教育作為他們向上進昇的階梯。最後，美國華人已找出各種有創見的進取方法，提高成就水平。

文化方面：

許多社會學家，把美國華人在教育方面的成功，歸究於良好的鼓勵精神，也是亞裔勤奮向上的文化價值觀——這種價值觀，強調勤勞，家庭團結，堅忍和克儉。劉氏（Liu，1986）已確認，中國文化價值觀的社會化，能增強學業表現。中國人已把那些有助於增強學業成績的行為規則社會化。例如，「敬老」、「強記」和「勤練」這些規則，有助于那種需要記憶和運算的學術課題。但是「敬老」這個觀念，或則妨礙亞裔的語言技巧和口語表達能力，因為他們自幼便被教導多聽訓少發言。再者，中國極尊崇教育，因此家長經常強調在校讀好書，接受

好教育的重要。正如劉氏所言，許多中國小孩，很快就懂得教育的重要性，而且那些能幫助他們在學業上取得好成績的行為準則，已在他們身上潛移默化。

相對功能主義

鈴木（Suzuki， 1977）在談到美國華人的成功例子時，也曾從文化的角度作演譯。他雖然認同推崇教育是中國人和其它亞裔的文化價值觀，但亦提出這樣的假設：他們之所以追求教育是鑒于他們的少數民族地位。四十年代，很多勞工團體歧視亞裔，拒絕他們參加工會。加上，二次大戰後，經濟蓬勃，科技進步；對受過教育的專業人才和白領人士的需求日增。因此，一方面勞力的職業機會受到限制；另方面，對受過高等教育的科技專業人才大受重視。在這種情形下，利用教育作為仕途便顯得越來越重要。這一因素遠遠超越亞洲文化價值觀的貢獻。基于這些見解，作者與蘇媚（Sumie & Okazaki，1990）對為何美國華人在教育上取得傑出成就這問題，提出另一套理論。我們相信，美國華人在學業上的成就，不能僅歸因於中國文化的價值觀，而是，恰如其它少數族喬一樣，他們的行為模式，包括各種成就，都是文化價值觀與身為社會少數族裔這一地位共同合力的成就。用相對功能主義的觀念來分析，我們認為美國華人在教育上的成就，是大大受到社會地位提升的機會所影響。

這影響不僅體現在教育上所作的努力，亦同樣影響非教育範圍。非教育範圍，包括各種職業活動，例如：領導才能、娛樂事業、體育和政治等等。這些方面的成就，並非與教育有直接關係。非教育範圍的上進機會越是受到限制，教育作為上進的工具越是明顯。換言之，當其它上進途徑遇到阻攔時，教育實質上就倍加成為上進的工具。在早期對柏克萊華裔學生的調查中，鄧氏（Ong，1976）從學生的意見引證及發現：接受教育的原因在于能多賺錢，求得好職業以及其它上進渠道，以便解脫受到歧視的阻力。何志文及黃氏（Hirschman and Wong，1986）提出這樣的論點：教育之所以成為亞裔提升社會地位的階梯，部份原因，是他們在其它經濟領域受到排斥。當人們感覺其它上進機會遙不可及時，教育便倍受珍視。唯有此途，可覓得良職，並得到社會的敬業。美國華人往往信仰「讀書為上策，苦讀功必成」，他們相信教育不單是成功的手段，還是通往成功至為重要的途徑。

創造性策略

縱觀美國華人的成功模式，或許還有其它解釋原因。我發現許多中國人，會用某些策略以拓展進取途徑。我和曾氏（Nolan Zane， 1985）曾試圖研究而找出美國華人，如何提高大學學習成績的方法。我們的假設，集中於那些尤其是英語能力欠佳的中國人，如何適應大學

生活要求。由於我們特別感興趣于外國出生的美籍華人的成就及其適應能力，我們將取樣分為三組。(A) 組，美國出生華裔學生；(B) 組，早期移民華裔學生（在美居留超過六年）；(C) 組，近期移民華裔學生（居住美國六年或少于六年），這些近期移民學生雖然英語水平較差，但是數學技能優越。

　　這一研究結果顯示，美國華人大學生，甚至新移民，都能獲得較高的數學分數成績。這種高成就模式，是藉由幾種策略來增強實現的。首先，這些新移民的中國學生·比土生或早期移民的學生，選讀較少學科。(把新移民中國學生的社會階層和經濟地位考慮，他們所選的課程且較輕)，因為他們的英語能力比較差，為了能有更多時間用於所選課程上，他們只選讀較少課程。其次，比較那些已接受美國文化的中國學生，新移民學生多同意這一說法，就是英語水平，會對他們選何種主修科目有所影響。自然地，這些新移民多主修數學、工程和自然科學。這些主修科目，並不會像其它人文科學和社會科學那般，需要強性向的英語背景，而數學方面則不受此障礙。那就是，新移民學生選那些可「揚長避短」的科目，作為主修。其三，據他們說，新移民學生，比美國本土學生和早期移民學生，花更多時間用功學習。由此可見，英語水平較弱的中國學生，是使用不同進取策略，來獲取較高的大學成績。

結語

　　美國華人在教育方面所取得的成就，值得我們感到非常驕傲。華人作為一個族裔，與全美國其它族裔相比較，展現了極高的教育成就，美國華人在獲取博士學位——最高學位，人數上佔相當大的比例。顯然美國華人並非是少數族裔的模範，而且他們中很多根本沒有受過任何教育。更甚的是，美國華人學生，常會埋怨來自親朋的寄望成功的壓力。若說中國人最初來美的目的是希望找到金山，那麼他們和下一代的金山夢，已通過教育而實現了。

　　美國華人為何在學業努力上取得這樣大的成就？我們認為這不可以用遺傳來解釋。沒有足夠證據，顯示美國華人超卓的智商是來自遺傳。就算有的話，亦只是傾向後天培養多於自然天生。中國文化價值觀，非常重視教育並崇尚刻苦努力的精神。如劉氏所言，這種價值觀亦重視強記、勤練和溫故知新，促使學業成績得以提高。再者，美國華人一貫以來，認為在某些職業範圍例如演藝、體育和行政管理等方面是頗難成功的事業，其原因包括英語水平不足，遭受偏見和歧視。鑒于在某些領域，缺乏晉升機會，教育就理所當然地成為美國華人出人頭地及找尋良職的最佳途徑。在解決有關身為少數族裔所存在的問題上，除了文化價值觀外，教育也是行之有效的方法。美國華人學生，為在大學取得成功，表

現出極大的適應能力，那些英語能力不足的，則索性選修較少科目，加倍努力學習，選讀那些能發揮他們的優勢的科目，來維持他們優秀成績的好效果。

華裔女作家作品的
新天地：

發掘父女的故事 [T]

何美雲　博士

‧‧‧活在我們內心的，才是重要的。心不會游離。
　　　——引自 Fae Myenne Ng 小說《Bone》
　　　　　　　內人物 Leon Leong 的話。

在六十年代，七十年代和八十年代，婦女積極參與發掘和檢討有關婦女心路歷程，特別著重母女關係的故事。但對很多亞裔的婦女作家而言，卻在發掘亞裔男性所扮演的角色，

[T] 此文改寫和節錄自我即將出版的一書《在她母親家內：亞裔母女題材作品的政治》（In Her Mother's House: The Politics of Asian American Mother-Daughter Writing）；該書屬亞太裔系列批判叢書第六種，加州 Thousand Oaks：AltaMira/Sage Press 出版，一九九九年。

特別是父親，以及他們邊緣化的家庭和社區的故事，同樣重要。Merle Woo（1981）在「給媽媽的信」中，寫出了她對母親的愛、憤怒和失望，但她將個人的感情掙扎，轉化為社會政治行動，寫出身為勞工階級移民婦女的母親，在美受盡艱辛爭取正義。與此同時，她的這些作品，也承認她父親遭受到種族主義、性別主義和階級主義的多重壓迫，以及他在家人和社區面前，受到精神和社會暴力的侮辱刻劃入微的表述。[1]很多華裔女作家像 Kathy Fong Bates、Lan Samantha Chang、Ying Chen、Sara Chin、Gish Jen、K. Kam、Maxine Hong Kingston、Sky Lee、Mei Ng、Sigrid Nunez、Kit Yuen Quan、Fae Myenne Ng、Amy Tan 和 Merle Woo 等，都通過她們的故事，反映她們並沒有忘記家庭和社區的苦痛。即使在她們毫不留情進行批判時，她們仍然在字裡行間，回到這個有愛，有痛苦和記憶的世界。這些故事中的女兒的敘述，在她們暫時和有時必須抽離自己的客觀敘述，仍然深深的繫住了家庭，繫住了社區。

　　華裔（亞裔）男性的故事，仍然是一個有待發掘的寬廣領域。雖然亞裔歷史中有些關於亞裔男性的重要故事，但這些故事都集中於勞工階級「留美」

---

[1] Ng 以「骨」一字來做小說的書名。這個字字義廣泛，象徵了很多美國移民勞工階級的經驗——深入骨髓；骨髓；骨肉相連；骨頭；全乾；骨灰；骨塵；骨粉；骨層；挑剔者；骨魂；骨園；坦白無隱；糾紛待決；刻骨銘心；爭論的焦點；骨灰瓷等。

或「單身」的階段，或集中於他們謀生的歷史
（Yanagisako, 1995）。要走出早期主要以華埠男性
社會，和娼妓史為重點的歷史，繼續敘述以後的亞
裔男女的故事，是非常重要的。[2]例如，發掘重構三
十年代到五十年代華裔男性的故事亦是非常重要
的，當時有更多移民來美，有中國婦女出現，而已
婚華裔男子亦有機會與妻子、子女與家人團聚。因
此，重構單身或已婚男子在建立新和更永久的華埠
社區時，他們所作的適應調整，亦是非常重要的。

　　八十年代末到九十年代，人們對討論「男子氣
概」（男子漢大丈夫）課題的興趣不斷增加，但這個
有關男子氣概研究的新浪潮，主要集中於白人或黑
人丈夫氣概如何形成的課題。亞裔男性的男子氣概
課題，其實亦應是一論題的重要題材。這些邊緣化
的男子氣概，可以為現時的理論，提出一個另類的
而無上限討論餘地的看法。[3]在華人生活於加州已有

---

[2] 有關發掘早期華埠男性社會的故事，可參看 Chu (1961)、Nee and
Nee (1972)、Siu (1987)、Takaki (1989)、Cheung (1998)和 Hall (1998)、
Chu (1976 和 1986)、Hirata (1979 和 1982)、Asian Women United
(1989)、Yung (1986、1990 和 1995)、S. Chan (1991a, 1991b 和 1998)、
Dong (1992)、Zhao (1996)、Okihiro (1994)一些有關美國華裔婦女歷
史的例子。

[3] 除觀察異性愛底的男子氣概之形成外，例如，仍有很多工作要做，
來探索其他基層形成的華裔（亞裔）雄性和性的特性。已有作品開
始認真的討論此課題。例如，可參看 Hwang (1988)、Leong (1996)、
Hinsch (1990)、Fung (1991)、N. Wong (1994)、Manalansan (1995)、Chua
(1998)、Eng and Hom (1998)。

一以重十年，和是反及這種歷史的轉他活中，我邊信，重十發掘男性和女性的故事，家以為我們進入緣十一世化給以庭社。

華裔女作家一區都集中寫婦女特別是母親的掙扎故事，這些母親都是家庭主婦同，樣這樣（。作家）而的，「心給媽了的人物，性信多是」家的婦女的故事，她們，對面對中寫的不出不了，，對她愛、她們感情所及社會所的多重壓力，以及她們和作憤的關係。在發掘母親的心而社會怒面時，這些作家重十失討母女望間的關係，並將這個痛苦的失討過程中，個感關情，掙扎歷史。

女兒將了轉母親世界的為政，治出了行繫和別深了轉她們父親、家庭和社區，這些了轉動不是身勞的工媽，也不是階級的移民。而是，在）而她們自己和母親的內心和記憶世界時，她們話了一美受盡的、微艱的「感情辛爭」，取《Bone》正女兒敘述憤 Leila Fu 的話會說，這些辛爭家和取於這個游家十的家庭、社會、「義和此化時活所面。。母女取十的批判性的「感情辛爭」，會這說她們對社會世界的而轉時，她們對「關情的些品」（Cheung, 1993）不性關也，並承認婦女不同的「遭和觀活。這些十出的辛爭，是」我掙扎的一到種，表離了一個不轉族、在族裔所不主壓，和不有迫面力的身種和社區話才。這男自我掙扎的敘述，前精了我們對

　　　　華人在加州一百五十年的歷史

移民社群變位、適應、抗拒和再創造動力的探索。

　　這些華裔作家，在他們的故事中，描述華裔母女間、實際和實地的每天感情輾轉時，亦嘗試反映家庭內，身為父親的男性的故事。Thomas Laqueur 說「男性的歷史因而是男性作為父親的歷史，已包含在普遍的家長制歷史內──繼承和合法後代的歷史，公共權威的歷史和其代代謰遞的歷史。因為人們認為男性屬於外面的公共世界，女性屬於家庭內的私人世界（一個十九世紀性別角色的確實觀點），人們沒有去了解，男性身為父親的家庭角色（Clark, 1996:25）。此外，雖然傳媒渲染（流行或學術性的）亞裔男女的永遠對立和爭持，很多女作家，並沒有將華裔男子或父親描寫成無情的權威大家長，在她們生活中，只是一個壓制或保守的形象。」

　　很多關於男子氣概專制和反對性的論述，均無法套用於華裔男性父親的身份上；這些男性為了家庭，被迫要和惡劣的社會、經濟和政治暴力對抗或讓步，其實是一種英勇的行為。更重要的是，此類論文，不提或否定了民主化，或即興形成的華裔男性的男子氣概，簡單重複或具體化傳統資本主義和大家長理想形象了事。而是，有些男子甘冒性別角色的風險，作出調整，俾適應兩個或多個收入的需求，從而照顧孩子和操作家務、同時維持一個關愛性的、穩定的家庭環境，並與獨立的女性相處。生

活方式和性別角色的轉變，使他們成為不同類型的男性，從某些角度來看，有可能不大像男人。但這種轉變也可以視之和定義為是英勇的，道德的行為，而不是「功能有問題」、「病態」、「無男子氣概」、「出賣尊嚴」或「模範少數」。[4]如認真的參與這種行為，其對可能重構美國社會之新社會和政治從屬的理論和連繫，看來會更有成果。

華裔（和其他亞裔）身為父親的男子（不論是否親生父親），說到底，對家庭和社區建設至為重要，特別在考慮到他們長期在法律上和歷史上，在美國無機會接觸其他女性、家庭和社區時，更是如此。「在大部份的移民團體裡，適齡工作的男子通常是比婦女、兒童或老人是移民第一人。但在華人的例子裡，因為排華正好發生在移民社區開始發展，當已來美的男子準備接他們的妻兒來美的時候，排

---

[4] 「少數模範」一詞需要重新予以觀察，正如 Sylvia Yanagisako (1995) 所建議的一樣。她認為用這個詞來說明亞裔的成功，太過簡單化和輕視。

　　此外，如我們小心細看，女子作家探討華裔家庭的故事時，並無支持家長或女兒需完全文化移入或融入白人主控的社會。她們事實上在故事中，為家庭和社區提供更靈活的空間。我想說的是有些華裔移民家長，忍受屈辱和辛勞工作，以便他們的子女在社會和經濟方面有較好的機會，以及生活有保障，不像他們一樣　生勞苦。但不是所有人在這個過程中成為少數模範（Chin 所謂的「榮譽白人」）。很多華裔家庭並無忘記他們的文化傳統，或他們生活經驗中求生、受苦、種族主義和抗拒等本質。我們需要找新的方法來談論和理論化這些項目，並寄望能進一步更急進和更公平的轉變社會——而那是很多爭取權益活動的行動者的目標。

華政策因而切斷了一個社區的自然發展（S. Chan, 1991:05）。」根據 Roger Daniels，「直至一九二零年，在移民七十年後，華裔人口中，婦女的數目不足百分十。在十九世紀末期，婦女的數目更少（1988:16）。就算在三十年代，在華埠也很少看到婦女、兒童和家庭（參看 Chu, 1961）。」嬰孩因為稀有，以致無論單身或已婚的華裔男子，均予溺愛（Takaki, 1989:254）。在一九零零年，只有百分之十一的華裔，是在美國出生的；到一九三零年，美國出生的華裔有百分之四十一，再十年後，增加至百分之五十二（同上）。所以，大部份移民的華裔——單身，或已婚有家庭妻兒在中國的——都無法在美國取得傳統的男子氣概標記：為人父親、照顧婦女和家庭，伴侶和性，入籍歸化（一九七零年的歸化法案），和擁有土地（一九一三年加州外人擁有土地法不准外人擁有土地）。

華裔（其他亞裔）男性沒有機會可以不著痕跡的適應美國白人男子氣概的形態。但我相信亞裔男性，有機會可以認真介入而不是攻擊亞裔的女性主義者，表現出更有滲透性的和轉化色彩的男子氣概。積極介入亞裔婦女的女性主義多元觀點，並與婦女合作成為她們的盟友，形成一個更急進的合作關係；考慮到亞裔男女，均受到種族主義和性別主義的壓迫，不少文化民族主義者，認為白人之種族

主義化和支配性的男子氣概，在社會和感情上，都使華裔男子的男子氣概變形，受到排擠，如果不只剝奪他們的權力，也剝奪了婦女、家庭和社區的權力。他們因而嘗試提升某些傳統的男子氣概形式為英勇的行為，或集中於無法秉承傳統的悲劇——例如，他們遺憾不夠「男子漢」，無法保護他們的女人，或不夠強力可以控制女人和兒童，從而加強亞裔男性的權力。

　　人們很多時都從母女情的角度來討論譚恩美的《喜福會》。譚自己承認因為她集中於母女的故事，所以沒有充份的講述亞裔父親或男性的故事。但是，父女的故事，仍然緊密的附繫於她的婦女故事中。喜樂會內的母親，說出她們年輕時候在中國受盡像 Wu Tsing 和 Tyan Yu（Lindo 的童子丈夫）的經驗，被男性欺壓。但雖然有這樣的不快經驗，喜樂會有三個母親，都愛上華裔的男子，並和他們結婚；這些男子，都能和聰明、實際和獨立的婦女生活。例如，An-mei Hsu 和 Lindo 在簽語餅工廠認識結為朋友。在移民婦女擴展的社交和政治圈子中，婦女找到支援、工作，和丈夫。An-mei 和她的丈夫為 Lindo 介紹一名電話技工 Tin Jong。Tin 和 Lindo 克服了他們的省籍障礙（一個講粵語一個講國語），大家用一種新的語言——英語——傳情達意。他們有一個愉快的、實際的戀愛——而不是 Waverly 所說的

笨拙故事。自信而實際的 Lindo，不再容忍別人為她安排婚事，這次要自己選擇自己的所愛，要改變她的人生命運。她告訴 Waverly 不只應以母家孫家為傲，也應以父家莊家為傲。

喜樂會的母親與她們的丈夫一起，教導子女保持文化傳統，適應英美社會文化的重要。夫婦一起旅行，打麻將，社交，及學習將他們的資源積聚一起，為未來退休作出投資。這個擴大的夫婦社交圈子，使他們能互相支援大家的子女。男子尊重妻子照顧子女的工作。易地來美之後，這些夫婦折衷了他們的工作身份，在自己的社區中，秉承早期中國的教育，大家均明白彼此的處境。大部份喜樂會的母親，都不是通過安排的婚姻，而是自己找到華裔的丈夫，她們有更和諧和順利的婚姻。此外，這些母親沒有告訴她們的女兒，不要和華裔男子結婚；而是，她們告訴她們的女兒，首先要堅強獨立，然後找真正愛她們和尊重她們的伴侶。

喜樂會中的華裔父親，在女兒眼中是有尊嚴的、受到愛戴和尊敬的。例如，June 的父親 Canning Woo，叫她的女兒在喜樂會中，替代那去世的母親的位置。June 愛她的父親，因為他關心她，也尊重他妻子掙扎的故事。Canning 在家族的檔案中保留她的記憶，以一種顛倒的祖先崇拜形式，尊重他的妻子和自己。他小心照顧她的創傷，建構一個回憶，

連繫母女一起。通過他對生命中兩個女人的照顧和尊敬，他說出 Suyuan 的故事，使 June 對母親有更進一步的了解。他告訴他妻子的故事，給他在中國的家人和他女兒知道。在講故事的時候，他並沒有略過感情上的細節——她的掙扎和內心的翻騰。他愛憐地重述她的故事，和他們共同的生活。

　　Suyuan 和 Canning 在革命戰爭年月的重慶認識。她心煩意亂有自殺的念頭，因為遺棄了一對孖生女兒，充滿罪咎感，並且有痲疾。她的當兵的丈夫死於戰爭。在動蕩不安的年月裡，Canning Woo 照顧 Suyuan 恢復健康。她和他結婚，然後到上海找尋她的孩子。經過長期在中國香港飄泊，他們最後在一九四九年來到美國。Canning Woo 一直照顧妻子和家庭，那是他認為身為男子應有的義務。故事結尾時，他陪同 June 到中國，和擴大的家庭及同母異父的女兒團聚。

　　譚恩美發現和表揚的，是父親在建設和團結家庭與社區所擔任的角色，不止於公共層面或工作地點，並且在家裡的重要性。Canning Woo 所述並不太吻合英美或亞裔文化民族主義，要求男子扮演一戰鬥者的身份。從他女兒和家庭生活中看出，與偏見形象不同，他不是漫無心肝的專制大家長，也不是打功夫的拳擊手。更不是無男子氣概或閹割了的懦弱的人。反而是，Canning Woo 樹立一個男子漢

的新模範，這個模範，是在感情上和社會上，都是肯負責任和關懷他人的典範。這是一個更民主和更有滲透性格的華裔男子漢，無須呈現或表現傳統的男子氣概形式，那種經常排拒女性化的形式，也無須要與婦女分出彼此才算得上是男子漢的形式（參看 Kimmel, 1996:318）。此外，更需要治療的不是父親的傷口，而是男性中的母親的傷口（318）。也就是，男性自我否定，或拒絕感情起伏多端的部份，那些脆弱、恐懼、低沉，需要愛、被愛、關懷、和被關懷，作為人的情境的部份。在推崇和重複限制性有所減弱的父權系統時，有些男性已「放棄了那些最需要的感情技巧，如果要使婦女達到平等的話；這些感情技巧是：關懷、感性、和情感上的回應性」（318）。Sheila Ruth 說得好，「能處理感情是有感性的人，而無法處理紀律和作出理性〔或知性〕判斷的說法是荒謬的‧‧‧它指出沒有討厭的柔情（再次，尚勇的信念，是輕蔑「柔情」的），沒有理智的缺乏，是力量的缺乏」（1990:215）。認為所有的華裔的女兒，對華裔父親或男性，只有對抗性的關係是錯誤的。

在《Bone》一書中，作者 Fae Myenne Ng 明示華裔移民工人階級的父親，在他們家裡可能是個權力象徵，但在一個尊崇白人男性和他們的家庭和社區，種族階級有別的權力中心，他們沒有特權、權

力或地位。華裔男子很多時,都被迫要找一些做「女性」的職業,一些被貶為「女人做的工作」;在主流社會和反女性的意識形態中,他們往往被視為被動、無男子氣、柔弱,和馴服。Ng 在她的書中,嘗試發現華裔父親更複雜和更有建設性的經驗,但她並沒有否定他們的性別主義作風,因為這些作風,繼續削弱了家庭可以提供和培養爭取權力的社會及政治活力。與此同時,Leila Fu 以女兒的角度,批判性別主義(以及種族主義)的作風,她也感性地評估 Leon Leong 的多重處境,在愛恨交織的交叉點和距離上,述說他的故事。她從女人的角度,恢復他作為男子和父親的角色,照顧他的感情和身體創傷,他在一個華埠家庭和社區的進退,在不同程度上,受到制度化的種族、族裔、階級、性別和性的特性不平等的影響。在該書中,作者從熟悉的家庭社會空間,以草根現實政治的形式,表述父親們的複雜故事。

社會和感情的聯繫及關係,是建設一個強大社會和政治社區的重要工作——需要一點一點的來做。政治行動不只是戰鬥,來恢復或構成優越的「社會」、「經濟」、「公共」和「政治」據點。這只是狹窄男子氣概概念(或「社會性變形理論化」)而已。這些故事的女兒們,在生命的一段期間內,通過她們的內心世界,能批判性的明白,她們母親在不同

的家庭和社會環境中，日常、實際和非常「政治」性的生活及工作處境。父親們和女兒們，則通過解決他們的難局，開始主動，不是被動的解放自己，結成親情盟友。

Raymond Williams 敏銳的觀察到人們有時囿於「舊意識」的思維和行為，分明界限地的將「感情」和「理智」分開。「可以理解的是，人們仍然囿於舊意識，視我們現在的行動——鼓吹和平、環保及女性主義——主要是「感情」性的。那些將感情誇大為「歇斯底理」的人損失最多，但即使只說「感情」亦別有含義在。其暗示或明言的相反情況，是流行系統的理智・・・在否定「感情」時——對實在的人之直接和不妥協的關懷——舊意識最能表示出其徹底失敗・・・但在人們實際生活中，被認為是「感情」的事卻有絕對和主要的意義・・・如果我們注意留心生命的整體，那麼感情和理智就不可能是相反的」（1983:266）。此外，Williams 認為，「變形的社會秩序」部份，也有它的基礎性的、感情和理智雙元理論化的結果，「既不特別合理或理智化」。「在其專門或分開的領域來說，這個說法是足夠精明的，但集合一起來說，通常是既愚蠢又混亂。它並且在其一些中心驅動力中，是一個產生劣質情緒的生動發電機，特別是侵略和貪婪。其最壞的結果是擴大戰爭和罪惡。在富裕生活和普遍情緒痛苦不大可能共

同互存時‧‧‧它已取得成功」(同上)。

　　在我們政治的，社會、感情和個人的連繫，而將行動理論化時，共同建設我們的政治未來和社區時，頗為重要；這種連繫是建設和維持一個更有愛心的世界的重要工作。戰爭作為一種後繼敘述及作為一種生活方式，並沒有說出喪失、憤怒、隔離、恐懼、混亂、悲傷、罪咎、脆弱，要求愛和關懷等，這些都是邊緣人生活，但也是重要部份。戰爭和暴力作為一種生活方式只有歪曲、壓制和破壞了可能解決此類感情和需要的社會及制度所需的建設性方案。

　　因此，很多有色人種的婦女，多時都將家和社會建構為一個孕育生存，和政治行動技能的主要空間。雖然家並非個體和精神對暴力掙扎的城堡，或沒有種族主義和性別主義的性別歧視，但人們認同「家」是培養個人和社區力量的泉源。我認為文化批評家 Bell Hooks 在「Homeplace」一文中所說極是；她說黑人婦女抗拒日常的社會經濟剝削和種族歧視主義，將家變成一個她們可以「自主，而不受制於人，可以肯定自身的精神的聖地，即使是貧窮，艱難，和匱欠，她們還可以獲取外面公眾世界予以她們的尊嚴」(Hooks, 1990:42)。支配性和反對派的論點及行為，可以消除少數民族婦女的經驗的急進意義，以及她們的生產力和繁殖力。也就是說，她

們可以將家中的工作，定義為婦女天性的、生物性的工作；他們可以稱自我犧牲和照顧孩子（不論是自己或他人的）「沒有反映選擇和意志」（同上）。「無法看到選擇，無法看到黑人婦女，有意識地而出色的，重新界定婦女的角色和「家」的概念，不會阻礙提升種族的政治承諾，和阻礙消除種族主義；而投入社區和家庭正是促進這些目標的哲學核心」（同上）。同樣地，華裔母女的故事，亦批判性的將在政治性認識身份，和集體中經常被疏視和否定的婦女有關社會據點和行為理論，推到前面。或者現在是婦女、男子、家庭和社區重新思考，使我們分別和隔離論點和行為的時候了，這些敵人，是如此接近我們的家，我們的心。

文化與民族主義者批評者，很少留意華裔女作家筆下的男性故事，不能連繫更廣泛的，或不能更順易表明個人和政治身份。他們沒有提到亞裔女性主義者的著作，與亞裔男性聯盟探索在一個種族主義、性別主義的世界中亞裔男性的英勇本質和受苦本質的傳統，這個傳統承認華裔男子對他們家庭和社區的貢獻，為尋求療傷、轉化的行為，包括個人和制度的現況、如社會改變，及公義。只提出某些男子漢的形式，或只提出可接受的種族主義化的、性別化的和性的特性化的男子氣概理論，只會削弱了這個男子和婦女的豐富經驗成果，使之變得不存

在。從他們限制性的修辭中，他們無法看到這些可能性的取捨，並拒絕接受這些男性的故事是英勇的，而只當是「柔弱的」或「女性化」的故事。正如文化批論家 Judith Newton 說，應該要做更多工作來「探討男子氣概的問題」，這些工作應連繫到「經濟和政治，家庭和個人，大眾和私人」（1994:575）。在我們進入二十一世紀之際，此類連繫，對探索婦女，男子，家庭和社區，是否可以實行史解放和道德上更負責任的行為，至為重要。

表揚艾娜‧柯琳
（ILLA COLLIN）議員

葉殷博士

沙加緬度縣議員柯琳夫人服務我們的社區已經超過二十一年（一九七九至今）。她代表第二個縣參事轄區，是沙加緬度亞太裔人口最多的一個選區。我們特意在「一百五十年華人對加州貢獻史實」的書中表揚她，因為這是個合適和合時的榮譽。我們基於她對環保問題，包括交通和空氣質素、廢水和廢物處理，以及加強多元族裔社區力量所作的重要功績。雖然，她對大沙加緬度大都會的出色而多元服務，無法在此一一列舉，表揚她的貢獻。我們謹舉兩個例子：（一）全國縣公園和康樂公務協會（NACPRO）頒贈的「傑出環保公務員獎」，表揚她過去二十年服務沙市，在公園、藝術和公共環保課題上促成的工作，使我們的社區生活質素更為健美。（二）長期擔任沙加緬度就業和訓練局的

董事，促進和推動多項社會建設計劃、啟蒙教育、社區福利和難民協助方案。她是一位具前瞻性有深度的女強人，她的功業，不限於在政治方面的貢獻，更促進社區的健康發展與成長（參看註腳部份她所獲得的眾多獎狀和榮譽）。

柯琳縣議員真是大沙加緬度華裔社區的好朋友。她對華裔和中國文化的深厚感情，可溯源於她在求學時期和華裔同學建立的摯誠友誼。這些寶貴的友誼持續至今，更增加她對華裔社區的關愛。她為華裔社區促進不少出色的民生福利。提名她登上我們的風雲人物榜，是眾望所歸，絕無異議。她的貢獻和成就，反映她建立安樂家庭和人際的價值觀，也是我們所有人應該珍惜而著重的模範。

她在懷俄明州落春市（Rock Springs）出生，在該市和俄勒崗州波特蘭市完成小學至高中學業，而後在俄勒崗大學畢業。曾在俄州波特蘭和加州畢芒市（Piedmont）擔任過小學教師。她早年從事教育工作，而從參與草根政治活動，使她對政府和文官制度的分層運作，有深度的了解。多年前她決定從政，她致力改善教育、福利、婦女、兒童和家庭融合的事業而有大成。她精力充沛，視野廣闊，富幽默感，實事求是，是一個真正的領袖人物。她深具前瞻能力，能在問題發生之前洞察先機，防範於未然。她好像一個大家都愛親近的姑姑，對人充滿關愛、摯誠、有趣。

「平權法」是柯琳縣議員信守的一項法案。她的看法，符合開國先人設定分權制度的法則。開國先人設定的政府結構，確保制衡，俾使我們有機會，重估充滿人性的良策良方。她再進一步說「平權法是一個制止我們偏頗思想和行為的方法。為了要維持公平正義，我們有需要警惕我們的動機，以及我們實施的程序。」她對一個民主進步中的政府，充滿樂觀。她認為我們會有一個無限憧憬的未來。

　　柯琳縣議員的丈夫唐·柯琳先生（Don Collin）是一名律師，在一九九八年退休之前，是加州建築業協會政治協調代表，後來並出任該會的律師。他們有三個女兒，兩個孫女和三個孫子。他們全家都住在加州沙加緬度市及縣內，分享家庭生活的樂趣。

註腳包括六個別類：

（一）參與亞裔社區事務：

● 任沙加緬度就業和訓練局董事，支持資助亞裔資源方案（Asian Resources）協助沙加緬度華人社區中心發展。
● 支持亞裔社區中心服務和成立亞裔老人院。
● 支持社會福利服務和精神健康服務，促進亞裔社區的發展工作。

- 一九八三年，通過沙加緬度縣法令，紀念日裔在二次大戰時的成就、設立一個永久的紀念碑、並補償被送入拘留營的日裔縣政府工作人員。

- 代表沙加緬度縣議會，以沙加緬度市長私人代表身份，一九八九年和一九九九年，參訪由日本松山姊妹市協會主辦的日本親善交換工作。

- 代表沙加緬度縣議會，一九九一年參加沙加緬度／濟南姊妹市協會主辦的中國濟南親善大使工作。

- 通過沙加緬度縣議案，表揚亞裔童子軍（Asian Eagle Scouts），並參予該組織各種活動。

- 熱烈支持表揚亞裔對沙加緬度貢獻的歷史，例如支持發掘文物、保持洛克市（Locke）在沙加緬度縣為一個「活的禮頌」，見證華裔移民在沙加緬度歷史上貢獻。

- 在財力上支持亞裔的活動，例如捐助 Amanda Chiang 骨髓籌款運動、和日裔公民聯盟（J.A.C.L）.基金。

- 支持並通過多個有關亞裔社區的議案，例如 VFW 中美報四十五週年紀念議案、Hiroshima Nikkeijin Kei 八十五週年紀念議案、亞裔資源方案（Asian Resources）的週年紀念決議、沙加緬度華人社區中心週年紀念議案、沙加緬度寮裔社區新年議案、和歡迎濟南市長和濟南代表團議案等。

- 大力推動和支持委任亞裔出任沙加緬度縣的各個委

華人在加州一百五十年的歷史

員會的委員職務。

● 撰寫「尋金熱潮華人的重要貢獻」一文，刊於歷史學會的文獻中。

● 寫信給戴維斯州長，支持華裔出任多個州級委任的職務。

● 任沙加緬度華人社區服務中心的榮譽顧問董事。

● 為亞裔律師公會和亞裔總商會的幹事就職宣誓。

● 寫信支持李亮疇任聯邦司法部民權副部長。

● 是亞太裔活躍領導委員會的顧問。

（二）獎項：

● 一九九五年日裔公民聯盟 Florin 分會頒與「社區之友」獎，表揚她對社區的傑出領導和服務，以及她長期以來關心日裔社區問題。

● 一九九五年日裔公民聯盟沙加緬度分會頒與社區服務獎，表揚她對日裔社區的大力支持和促進 Nikkei 社區福利的工作。

● 一九九八年亞太裔社區表揚她的傑出貢獻。表揚的機構包括：亞裔民主黨、亞太東南亞裔協會、沙加緬度華美協會、美華協會、沙加緬度中華文化中心、沙加緬度印支華人聯合會、沙加緬度濟南姊妹市協會、日裔公民聯盟、大沙加緬度韓裔社區協會、沙加緬度大台灣人協會、亞太活躍領導委員會等。

（三）其他社區服務的獎項和表揚：

● 一九八零年，養祖父母／耆英同伴：「年度社區之友獎」
● 一九八六年，精神健康協會：「總統獎」
● 一九八七年，加州公園及康樂協會：「獻身政治及傑出服務獎」
● 一九八七年，全國猶太婦女會：「漢娜所羅門社區服務獎」
● 一九八七年，Alpha Kappa Alpha：「傑出公共服務獎」
● 日裔公民聯盟：特別表揚其領導通過一九八八年公民自由法案的工作
● 一九八九年，亞裔社區中心：「傑出領袖獎」
● 沙加緬度樹木基金會：「Arbor Day 獎」
● 一九九零年，沙加緬度弱智人士協會：「Albert S. Rodda 獎」
● 一九九一年，精神健康協會：立法獎
● 全國大學運動員協會：一九九一年致力推動年輕人運動項目傑出貢獻獎
● 一九九一年及一九九二年，新聞及評論雜誌：「最佳縣議員」
● 一九九一年，猶太國家基金：「生命樹獎」
● 一九九二年，沙加緬度雜誌：「地區服務政府獎」
● 一九九二年，Southgate 公園及康樂區：以 Illa Collin

名字命名該區一個公園

● 一九九二年，慈善金庫：「傑出社區服務獎」
● 一九九三年，男青年會：「傑出政府／法律婦女獎」
● 一九九五年，沙加緬度房屋聯盟：「致力推動公民負擔房屋傑出工作獎」
● 一九九五年，全國縣公園及康樂官員協會：「傑出公務員獎」
● 一九九八年，沙加緬度弱智人士協會：「總統獎」
● 一九九九年，沙加緬度縣民主黨：「傑出公共服務獎」
● 一九九九年，精神健康協會：「立法獎」
● 一九九九年，普天同健：特別表揚獎
● 一九九九年，科連路合作計劃（Florin Road Partnership）議案：表揚她對計劃和科林路改善工程的貢獻

（四）柯琳夫人創辦以下各團體福利工作：

● 沙加緬度樹木基金會
● 美國河邊公路基金會
● 托兒議會
● 沙加緬度科學中心未來計劃委員會
● Florin Road 工程計劃

（五）Illa 代表縣議會參加以下公職工作：

華人在加州一百五十年的歷史　　　　　　　　219

- 沙加緬度就業及訓練局，一個負責管理就業計劃、啟蒙計劃、社區行動和難民援助計劃的機構
- 區管機關成立委員會，作出「兼併和合併」有關之合作計劃
- 沙加緬度大都會有線電視委員會，監管有線電視連營公司
- 沙加緬度大都會空氣質素管理委員會，致力保持空氣清新，保障公共健康和環境
- 沙加緬度公共圖書館委員會，管理沙加緬度的公共圖書館
- 沙加緬度運輸委員會，負責管理 A 提案計劃。選民通過 A 提案，於一九八九年至二零零九年，在縣內加收零點五的銷售稅。稅收所得，用於資助一個全面改善公路和運輸的計劃
- 聖喬奎因谷（San Joaquin Valley）鐵路委員會：改善行走「聖·喬奎因」鐵道走廊（San Joaquin Rail Corridor）火車乘客服務

（六）Illa 並服務以下機構

- 父親和家庭中心，董事
- Tierra de Oro 女童軍協會經理
- 沙加緬度華人社區服務中心，榮譽顧問董事

余江月桂博士致華裔美人的肺腑之言

余江月桂

以下是一九九九年五月八日在華美協會沙加緬度分會，
余江月桂博士接受頒獎後致詞原文：

今天我非常高興在此接受你們給予我的獎勵，並
與大家共享此夜晚。

接受這個獎牌，正是我從事美國的一生政治生
涯中很特別的時刻。我用去四十多年的時間在公眾服務
上。當我開始從政時，少數民族，尤其是婦女，根本是
在政界少見的。從我的漫長政治記錄中顯示，無疑的已
經被我在那玻璃天花板上劃開了封口。在此，我可自豪
的願意帶領大家，作個開路先鋒。

當我在一九九七年從駐外大使身份退休回國時，我
感到非常欣慰的是，本人已經為亞裔人士，尤其是美國

華裔人士在參政權上打開一條門路。

　　但是只兩年左右之時間發現，那被我劃開玻璃天花板上的漏封，不只是裂開而已，它竟向我們強力沖擊而來，令人不能阻擋。為了一九九六年的總統競選時的國外籌款事件，在兩年過去引起了後遺症，被對方利用媒體大事渲染，像夢魘般的跟隨我們亞裔。

　　事情發展快的令人不能相信，一下就有三個聯邦聯查單位負責處理此事件。一個是通過 FBI 組成的司法調查單位，一個是眾議院和另一個國會的組織。他們一起全力追查國外有亞裔名義助選費用是否合法。自此，亞裔的名字尤其是華裔名字都被多方的盤問和調查。調查組織對亞裔人們以電話詢問，當面質詢，出庭作證等，以至於對他們的公民身份都有懷疑。他們努力的追查那些助選費之來源，和捐獻那些款項的目的為何等等。

　　一些亞裔和華裔姓名的電話記錄，生意往來帳戶等都被調查和歸檔入案備用。

　　在一九九九年的今天，很多對美國盡忠的華裔人士，竟無端端的，在缺乏任何證據下，被誣告為中國間諜！這些事件在今日發生，令我們感到非常恥辱，而聯想到一八八零年代的聯邦和州政府，在通過排華案件時用的口號，「中國人滾出去」。這一件不幸的過去，突然又重新出現在我們眼前。我們華裔美國人忽然變成非美國人，對一向被贊為具有豐富文化背景者的我們視為罪人。簡單的說，我們是不受歡新的一群。

222　　　　　　　　　　*華人在加州一百五十年的歷史*

在今天這種低壓的政治情況下，接受你們發給我的獎狀。對華裔美人來說，是令人悲哀的時刻。不過，請大家不應就此感到失望。

讓我們大家一起努力，將亞裔和華裔人士帶入美國勢力中間管道裡。不管用何種方式，我們應公開指責美國政府以特權施予大家的威脅。讓我們一齊來選出合格而願獻身從政的亞裔人士，為我等仗義執言。支持任何族裔競選人士，只要他們挺身為我們的人權和民權奮戰。讓你們的民意代表知道，你們對當前情勢不滿。

讓美國知道，我們也都是美國人，而美國人是由各種不同形狀、尺碼與顏色所構成的。我們不應退回那種曾經貧困的社區情況，而與所有的美國共享目前豐盈更多彩的美國文化。因為，我們也是美國的一部分。

余福慶閣下的故事——
非凡的人贏得非凡的機會

葉殷　博士

壹 九九九年十一月七日，余福慶先生（Mr. Jimmy Yee）成為有史以來第一位出任沙加緬度市市長的華裔。沙市是美國最大的都會之一，成立於一八四九年，也是加州第一古城。話雖如此，它只有一百五十年的歷史，並將繼續在未來的年月，發展興盛。

　　華人走過了一百五十年，才能出任這個高職，正好配合此書「加州華人一百五十年歷史」的出版。這個非凡的機會，開始於一九九九年，現已去世的當時市長史諾先生（Mr. Joe Serna, Jr.）請余氏接受出任副市長職。一九九九年十一月七日，史先生過世，出住代市長。一九九九年十二月十四日，在沙市市議會一致投票通過下，余市議員被選為市長，真除史市長未能完成的任期。

一九九二年，余市議員第一次被選出任四年期的市議員，代表選區包括東青港（Eastern Greenhaven）、福園（Fremont Park）、小口區（Little Pocket）、楓葉公園（Maple Park）、貧橋區（Poverty Ridge）、力夢林（Richmond Grove）、南路公園（South Land Park）、南邊公園（Southside Park）、上路公園（Upper Land Park）和札別公園（Z'berg Park）的第四選區議員。一九九六年，余氏再度當選連任，然後在二千年三月七日，三度當選連任。

他樹立了一個良好的政治風範，雖然身為市長，有相當充足的資源競選連任，但他不作此圖，昇華競選的清風亮節。

他出生沙市，在本地公校讀書。一九五六年他畢業於加州大學柏克萊分校土木工程系。一九五九年他任職加州政府，直至一九六五年。

一九六六年，他創辦獨資的建築工程公司。二十五年來，他的公司成為沙加緬度地區最大的結構工程顧問公司之一。他的公司曾設計沙市多個里程碑的建築，包括沙加緬度會議中心（Sacramento Convention Center）、首都銀行（Capital Bank）、河邊廣場（Riverview Plaza）和順德總醫院大樓（Sutter General Hospital）等。

余氏是沙市樂觀俱樂部（Sacramento Optimist Club）和沙市華美聯誼協會（Chinese American Council）的活躍成員。他支持沙市的華人鼓樂隊二十多年。他曾為沙

市無數社團籌款出力。一九八九年，他組織第一個亞裔捐助骨髓協會，登記了二千五百多名捐助人。（請參看附註 Yee 議員的公績記錄）

余議員和妻子結婚已有四十六年，婚姻美滿。他們有六個孩子，都是大學畢業生，分散全國各地，各在專業的領域上有所成就。他們有十個可愛的孫兒女。

公共服務

● 沙加緬度市／市長（1999-2000）
● 沙加緬度市／副市長（1999）
● 沙加緬度市／市議員，第四區（1992-現在）
● 市長發展委員會／主席（1999）
● 沙加緬度市地區防洪局（1993-1994）
● 用水顧問委員會（1993-1994）
● 人事及公務員委員會（1997-1998）
● 美國河水資源委員會（1996-1997）
● 沙加緬度大都會電纜委員會（1994-1998）
● 沙加緬度市交通委員會（1993-現在）
● 沙加緬度－尤多（Yolo）港口委員會（1996-1998）
● 沙加緬度市縣固體水聯合委員會（1993-現在）
● 沙加緬度地區衛生局（1999-現在）
● 沙加緬度－白臘谷（Placerville）運輸走廊聯合委員會（1998-1999）

- 警察社區關係顧問委員會（1989-1992）
- 沙加緬度市銓敘委員會（1974-1977）／主席（1976）
- 沙加緬度警察風範市民監督委員會（1973）

榮譽／獎狀

- 沙加緬度華人社區服務中心／社區服務獎（1990）
- 國家工程觀察家委員會／傑出服務獎（1987）
- 加州土木工程及土地探測委員會／傑出服務獎（1984）
- 加州專業工程師協會／對工程和科學界傑出貢獻獎（1982）
- 製造工程師協會／傑出工程成就獎（1982）
- 沙加緬度谷工程委員會／年度工程師獎（1978）
- 中加州結構工程師協會／傑出結構工程師獎（1977）

專業機構會員

- 美國土木工程師協會／研究員（1954-現在）
- 中加州結構工程師協會／研究員（1959-現在）／主席（1971）／董事（1971-1975）／秘書－司庫（1974）
- 加州顧問工程師協會／會員（1965-1992）
- 加州專業工程師及土地探測師註冊委員會／州長任命（1977-1986）／主席（1981）

● 國家工程觀察家委員會／加州代表（1978-1986）

社區再投資

● 沙市樂觀俱樂部（Sacramento Optimist Club）／沙
加緬度亞裔者英關切會／沙加緬度亞裔社區療養院
／沙加緬度亞裔鼓樂隊／籌款及捐助：張小妹白血
症基金會（Amada Chlang Leukemia Fund）、朵森罪
案基金會（Sim Yee Crime Reward Fund），及歧視種
族聯合基金會（Hate Crimes Unity Fund）／沙加緬
度華人協會／亞太裔商會／亞裔和平工作者協會／
沙加緬度亞裔運動基金會

教育／註冊／服役／人事

● 土木工程學士，加州大學柏克萊分校（1956）
● 加州結構工程師 No. 1404（1966）
● 加州土木工程師 No. 12703（1961）
● 美國後備軍工程師團／上尉（1957-1965）
● 與妻子 Mary 結婚四十四年，有六名子女，十名孫
兒女

接緒─繼往開來

梁靜源教援的《從金山到千禧的風與雨》見証遺作，已成他與我們「幽明路隔」，甚堪惋惜。但是，他豐厚學識所奠定的文章基礎，表述華人對加州一百五十多年的貢獻，不允許我們終止這些重要歷史的繼續任務。因為，「花落不是無情物，化作春泥更護花」。

所以，沙加緬度中華文化基金會與加州大學戴維斯分校亞美系，以經濟與人力的全面支援，擴大篇章，促成這本文獻面世，敘述中華兒女，如何在美國加州的第二家園，流汗耕耘的點點滴滴，值得我們慎終追遠，不可對過去無知，對將來無識。

因此，本人衷心祈盼諸君子，若珍惜中華文化及傳統寶點，請繼續見証歷史，發表炎黃子孫的悲喜故事。這本《從金山到千禧的風與雨》，是加州不可忽略的歷史見証，也是美國成長的重要指標。

承史達博士主筆「序言」。這位「加州一百五十年

華人在加州一百五十年的歷史   229

歷史慶祝委員會」主委，對中華文化的智慧分析，令人十分敬佩。本人有幸為其校友，又是華裔，卻感汗顏。更有幸能借此尾聲，敬謝各有關機構及同仁，對文獻的協助。其中必須申謝的，是沙加緬度中華文化基金會、加大戴維斯亞美系、舊金山中文翻譯服務中心、太陽印刷公司，以及沙加緬度圖書館。敬佩的同仁，有美國華文世界日報的出色記者，崔以聞女士，加州戴維斯分校財務主管，張愛齡女士，她的英文造詣，本人鮮見，以及曾任銷拉努（Solano）縣圖縣館主任，林民柱先生，一位中文結構傑出的學者。最後，非常感謝梁賀山先生，這位梁靜源教授及梁張愛齡夫人的大公子，多才多藝，為這本文獻設計的中英文封面，不但包容了「龍的傳人」的龍圖，而且加添美國國旗，表述中美一家親。

　　本人謹再度祈望諸君子，認知這本文獻意向，敘述華人奮鬥的開始，一種開啟多種文化互動基礎，是促成共識的美國核心文化良性動力。借前英國首相邱吉爾爵士名言：「今日此非完結篇，亦非完結開始篇，或可能為開始指標篇。」或謂「前車之轍，後車之鑑」。

葉殷
寫於美國加州
二零零一年八月四日